D0090321

Mar 2016

THE PROFITEERS

Bechtel and the Men Who Built the World

SALLY DENTON

Simon & Schuster

New York   London   Toronto   Sydney   New Delhi

Simon & Schuster
1230 Avenue of the Americas
New York, NY 10020

First Simon & Schuster hardcover edition February 2016

SIMON & SCHUSTER and colophon are registered trademarks of
Simon & Schuster, Inc.

For information about special discounts for bulk purchases,
please contact Simon & Schuster Special Sales at
1-866-506-1949 or business@simonandschuster.com.

The Simon & Schuster Speakers Bureau can bring authors to your
live event. For more information or to book an event, contact the
Simon & Schuster Speakers Bureau at 1-866-248-3049
or visit our website at www.simonspeakers.com.

Interior design by Joy O'Meara

Manufactured in the United States of America

1   3   5   7   9   10   8   6   4   2

Library of Congress Cataloging-in-Publication Data is available.

ISBN 978-1-4767-0646-7
ISBN 978-1-4767-0648-1 (ebook)

For John L. Smith,
let me count the ways.

And for Kathy Kinsella and Ed James,
whose generosity knows no bounds.

The author wishes to thank the Black Mountain Institute
for making this book possible.

CONTENTS

Preface: Mission Accomplished   1

Prologue: The Spy with a Fan Club   13

PART ONE   **We Were Ambassadors with Bulldozers** 1872–1972

ONE   Go West!   19

TWO   Follow the Water   28

THREE Hobo Jungle   34

FOUR   That Hellhole   38

FIVE   Wartime Socialists   45

SIX   Patriot Capitalists   53

SEVEN The Largest American Colony   59

EIGHT Going Nuclear   66

NINE   McConey Island   74

TEN   Weaving Spiders   83

ELEVEN Covert Corporate Collaboration   91

TWELVE The Energy-Industrial Complex   100

PART TWO   **The Bechtel Cabinet** 1973–1988

THIRTEEN   Bechtel's Superstar   109

FOURTEEN   Cap the Knife   116

FIFTEEN   The Arab Boycott   124

SIXTEEN   The Pacific Republic   130

SEVENTEEN The Bechtel Babies   137

EIGHTEEN   The Reaganauts   145

NINETEEN   A World Awash in Plutonium   153

TWENTY   It Would Be a Terrible Mess   160

TWENTY-ONE	Ultimate Insiders	167
TWENTY-TWO	A Witch's Brew	174
TWENTY-THREE	The Territory of Lies	180
TWENTY-FOUR	A Tangled Scheme	187

PART THREE **Dividing the Spoils** 1989–2008

TWENTY-FIVE	A Deal with the Devil	197
TWENTY-SIX	The Giant Land of Bechtel	204
TWENTY-SEVEN	Some Found the Company Arrogant	211
TWENTY-EIGHT	Global Reach with a Local Touch	217
TWENTY-NINE	A License to Make Money	225
THIRTY	More Powerful Than the US Army	232
THIRTY-ONE	The Hydra-Headed American Giant	238
THIRTY-TWO	Profiting from Destruction	245

PART FOUR **From Muleskinner to Sovereign State** 2009–2015

THIRTY-THREE	A Convenient Spy	251
THIRTY-FOUR	Privatize the Apocalypse	256
THIRTY-FIVE	Nukes for Profit	262
THIRTY-SIX	The Buddhist and the Bomb	267
THIRTY-SEVEN	The Four Horsemen of the Apocalypse	274
THIRTY-EIGHT	The Captain Ahab of Nuclear Weapons	280
THIRTY-NINE	A Trial Lawyer Goes to Battle	285
FORTY	The Exxon of Space	291
FORTY-ONE	A Nasty Piece of Work	298
FORTY-TWO	The Kingdom of Bechtelistan	304

Acknowledgments 313

Notes 317

Bibliography 369

Index 409

*These capitalists generally act harmoniously
and in concert, to fleece the people.*
—ABRAHAM LINCOLN

If you can't trust a man's word, you can't trust his signature.
—WARREN A. BECHTEL

We're more about making money than making things.
—STEPHEN D. BECHTEL

There's no reason for people to hear of us. We're not selling to the public.
—STEVEN BECHTEL JR.

We will never be a conglomerate. At least not on my watch.
—RILEY P. BECHTEL

The company's goal has always been to be the best.
—BRENDAN BECHTEL

THE PROFITEERS

Mission Accomplished

APRIL 2003

American soldiers had seized Saddam Hussein's opulent Republican Palace in some of the fiercest fighting of the entire Iraq War. Iraq was smoldering in ruins, "conquered" by President George W. Bush. Its cities bombed out. Baghdad's museums and shopping centers, villas and military bases, looted, its hospitals torched. Aerial bombardment of the colossal royal palace—the official headquarters of the Iraqi presidency—was tactical as well as symbolic. Under a turquoise dome considered an architectural wonder of the world, the palace held valuable Iraqi government documents in addition to priceless art and furnishings.

Overlooking the Tigris River, the palace had been built in 1958 by the US-sponsored monarch King Faisal II, who was assassinated in a bloody coup before he could take up residence. Its capture by US-led troops, forty-five years later, was emblematic of the victorious return of American influence in the Persian empire—an oil-rich region that had eluded the West since its puppet Faisal was overthrown.

Joining American Special Forces as they sorted through the rubble of the fortress—once the sex and porn parlor of one of Saddam's two sadistic sons, Uday—was a select group of employees of the San Francisco–based construction company Bechtel. "This place is surreal," Bechtel's Thor Christiansen said of the sumptuousness of the grounds now occupied by the "Bechtelians," who were overseeing the US government's $3 billion job to rebuild war-torn Iraq.

Saddam, Uday, and his other son, Qusay, had fled during the final air strikes on the palace, but evidence of the debauchery remained, from gold-plated Russian Kalashnikovs, to mirrored beds, to photos of Uday beating naked women. Uday called one room that served as a torture chamber his Tower of Babylon. "Saddam's 'I'm-on-crack' decorating style had been left untouched," is how a State Department official described the scene. Strewn throughout the sprawling complex were pornography, designer wardrobes, fine wines, liquor, Cuban cigars, heroin, swords and submachine guns, and boxes of handguns amid piles of *Guns & Ammo* magazines. Hundreds of photos of nude *Playboy* magazine "Playmates" donned the bedroom walls, along with portraits of President Bush's twin twenty-one-year-old daughters, Jenna and Barbara, and posters of Iraqi university coeds whom Saddam's sons trolled for sexual encounters.

Outside bronze gilded gates and white marble colonnades was a network of manmade lakes and the remnants of Uday's personal zoo. Abandoned and starving lions and cheetahs paced in cages as American soldiers fed them whole live donkeys and sheep from adjacent pens. The luxurious presidential compound encompassed some 1.7 square miles of the wealthy Karada district of Baghdad. A small city, it had six-lane avenues, swimming pools, a hospital, a gymnasium, a fleet of hundreds of European sports cars, and a cloistered dormitory that housed the Hussein men's harem. Peacocks and gazelles roamed the pine and eucalyptus forest surrounding swan-laden ponds. An American diplomat found it reminiscent of "Sinatra's Vegas for all the red velvet and brass."

An ironic shrine to American culture and excess—from the stockpile of Kentucky bourbon to the Playboy Mansion–inspired pleasure palace—Saddam's headquarters was an emulation of Western greed and imperialism. Most mocking of all was that Bechtel—the privately held, secretive American corporation that epitomized the extreme and unfettered capitalism that Saddam claimed to loathe—was now rooted in the heart of his kingdom.

A month earlier, on March 19, 2003, Americans had awakened to learn that the United States had invaded Iraq. After the terrorist attacks of September 11, 2001, on the World Trade Center and the Pentagon, the Bush administration determined to wage war against Saddam, claiming he was harboring Al Qaeda terrorists and hiding weapons of mass destruction—allegations that turned out to be false. Iraqis, who would rush in to overthrow their tyrannical dictator, as Bush officials described the projected bombardment, would welcome the so-called shock and awe campaign. The thousands of American soldiers would be greeted as liberators. The assault, called Operation Iraqi Freedom, would cost $50 billion, Bush assured the public, and would end with Iraq a democratic jewel and strategic US ally in the turbulent Middle East. The "script," as a US foreign service officer on the ground later described it, "imagined Americans being greeted as liberators like in post D-day France, with cheerful natives rushing out to offer our spunky troops bottles of wine and frisky daughters."

It didn't work out that way.

"My fellow Americans: Major combat operations in Iraq have ended," Bush told the country on May 1, 2003, just forty-two days after the invasion began. The president addressed the nation from the aircraft carrier USS *Abraham Lincoln*, appearing under a dramatic banner stating "Mission Accomplished"—a premature assessment. Twelve years later—after the loss of nearly five thousand American and more than a hundred thousand Iraqi lives and with a cost of $2 trillion and rising—the US military was still mired in the country, while Al Qaeda's splinter group, the barbaric ISIS, was seizing Iraqi territory and trying to establish a caliphate.

"What *did* work out was a luxurious compound in the heart of Baghdad on the banks of the Tigris where the thousands of Americans who would remain behind could work, shop, eat, and relax in a palatial, $750 million embassy," as one account described it. The transformation of the Republican Palace into the base of the American occupation provoked the Iraqi people. "The World's Largest Public Relations Failure," a government official depicted the arrogance and insensitivity of the subjugation. "We placed our new seat of power right on top of his old one, just as the ancient Sumerians built their strongholds on top of fallen ones out in the desert." The world's largest embassy on the 104-acre campus known as the Green Zone was the size of Vatican City—the equivalent of eighty football fields, six times larger than the United Nations in New York City, and two-thirds the acreage of Washington's National Mall. As with the lights of Las Vegas, astronauts can see the vast compound from outer space.

The construction of the fortress-like embassy, with its fifteen-foot-thick walls guarded by US Marines and the private security firm Blackwater, was shrouded, as was the cost to American taxpayers that would swell to more than $1.3 billion. The identity of the companies working on the compound was largely secret. The classified undertaking was part of the sensitive transition from military to civilian control. All construction workers had to have US security clearances in order to be cleared to work on the building. A number of sources report that Bechtel was one of the contractors, though the company denies that it was.

A world unto itself, the top secret, self-sufficient project was comprised of twenty-one buildings including a central utility power plant, a domestic water and sanitary sewer system, and its own telecommunication system and defense force. Six apartment buildings housed thousands of American contractors, military personnel, diplomats, and staff from eleven government agencies, whose recreation options included tennis courts, movie theaters, swimming pools, gymnasiums, a food court, and what one resident described as "the world's worst bar scene" at a place named Baghdaddy's. All of it starkly out of context in Mesopotamia, after all, "the biblical Eden."

A "hideous modernist bunker," as a British journalist characterized it, the building "scowls at the world" and is "an insult to a city of great historic visual culture." Few of the thousands of Americans dared venture beyond the fortified "bubble," also called Emerald City, into the violence beyond its walls. More than a concrete bunker, the bastion symbolized the labyrinthine trail from 1950s CIA assassinations and coups in the region to the twenty-first-century Arab Spring. Even more shadowy than Bechtel's role in building of the super-embassy was its role nearly

half a century earlier in building the original palace for King Faisal II—
Stephen D. Bechtel's coveted ally and client in the Middle East.

———

US construction giant Bechtel National Inc. arrived in Iraq in April
2003, along with US troops, even before President Bush had declared
the war over, and with the first lucrative government contract to rebuild the country. The influx of Bechtel engineers into Baghdad came
immediately after the bombing of Saddam's palace. Bush had launched
the reconstruction of Iraq a week after the invasion, and Bechtel was
the primary recipient of hundreds of millions of dollars of government
contracts with its profits guaranteed. The company was among a handful of American firms that had made sizeable political contributions to
Bush's Republican Party before receiving a secret invitation to bid on
the lucrative postwar government reconstruction contract. The largest
nation-building program in history, it dwarfed even the post–World
War II Marshall Plan to rebuild Germany and Japan. "War began last
week. Reconstruction starts this week," the *New York Times* reported.
Even before asking the UN Security Council to authorize military action against Iraq, the Bush administration had been quietly soliciting
proposals for peacetime rebuilding. "We were the ones who famously
helped paste together feathers year after year, hoping for a duck," wrote
a former State Department official of the reconstruction undertaking.

Bechtel received the coveted contract as the principal vehicle to fix
the entire Iraqi infrastructure: the power grid, water supply, sewage
system, roads, bridges, seaport, airports, hospitals, and schools. The
government's decision to waive competitive bidding under the aegis
of "national security" provoked little attention among lawmakers or
the media in the United States, though European allies criticized as
"exceptionally maladroit" the unseemliness of inviting bids from "only
well-connected domestic companies." For Bechtel, it was business as
usual. Due to its relationship with Dick Cheney, Halliburton received
most of the "contractor" and conflict of interest attention during the
war. This, ironically, on the whole, left Bechtel overlooked by the media.

Priding itself as the company that can "build anything, any place,

any time," Bechtel grew from a scrappy Nevada road-grading operation at the dawn of the twentieth century to the world's largest construction company. Initially established in a geography inhospitable
to humans, Bechtel became the prototype for taming remote and
forbidding landscapes as exemplified by its historic signature project,
Hoover Dam. "The bigger, the tougher the job, the better we like it,"
company president Stephen Bechtel once bragged to *Fortune*.

Claiming to have worked on more than twenty-five thousand projects on all seven continents, Bechtel's far-flung enterprise has always
been obscured by its privately held structure and paternalistic family
dynasty. Bechtel claims to be able to handle any project, no matter
how challenging or how remote its location. As the leading engineering and construction firm in America, Bechtel has reaped billions in
profits, thanks to its quasi-government posture, an unprecedented revolving door between its San Francisco headquarters and Washington's inner sanctums, and a business model based on federal contracts
that are antithetical to the company's free-enterprise espousals.

Bechtel has had closer ties to the US government than any other
private corporation in modern memory. No other corporation has
been so manifestly linked to the presidency, with close relationships
to every chief of state from Dwight Eisenhower forward. For nearly
a hundred years, Bechtel has operated behind a wall of secrecy with
its continually evolving military-industrial prototype. *Newsweek* once
attributed the company's success to its "wheeling and dealing not only
in private operations but with governments themselves."

———

The Profiteers is not a business biography but an empire biography—
the story of how a dynastic line of rulers from the same American
family conducts its business. European and Asian dynasties go back
hundreds of years. In a nation as young as the United States, the Bechtel family is a rarity as one of a handful of American industrial giants
that have continued to dominate through five successive generations.

This book is a portrait of an American corporation so potent, and with such a global reach, that it has its own foreign policy that has often been at odds with US foreign policy. Bechtel is "an entity so powerful, so international in scope, that its officers . . . could move to the CIA, the Department of Defense, and the Department of State respectively as if they were merely shifting assignments at Bechtel," wrote the California historian Kevin Starr.

Its wielding of unelected power is a cautionary tale, although unheeded by a nation that in recent decades embraced private concentration over public distribution of wealth. Still, for all its outsize ambitions and profits, the family empire has been ruled by stunningly prosaic figures.

To comprehend this system of revolving-door capitalism and the part the Bechtel family has played in it, one must go back to the company's regional western beginnings. It is a classic American story of money and power, bootstraps and courage, brawn and genius.

Or at least that's the myth of the Bechtel family dynasty.

Wild West Capitalism

Like all stories of empire building, the rise of Bechtel—one of the first megacompanies born and bred in the American West—is a complex tale of technological ingenuity and corporate craving. "Wild West capitalism at its most earnest," a Nobel physicist described one of Bechtel's gigantic twentieth-century construction projects located in the Mojave Desert. In their century-long quest, five generations of Bechtel men have harnessed and distributed much of the planet's natural resources—hydroelectricity, oil, coal, water, nuclear power, natural gas, and now solar geothermal power and asteroids.

Bechtel's position as the fourth-largest private company in America in 2013—after the Cargill food-processing company, Koch Industries, and Dell computers, according to *Forbes*—must be taken at face value since its voluntarily reported revenues that year of $37.9 billion are not subject to federal Securities and Exchange [SEC] regulation. "What appears to an outsider as an almost paranoiac preoccupation with privacy is instead a strategic business policy with several motives," as one account depicted the company's historic resistance to public scrutiny. Bechtel family members and a select group of top executives and their spouses hold its stock, and guard financial as well as personal details. One of the world's wealthiest families, the Bechtels are preoccupied with security and the need for personal bodyguards. The family once petitioned a California court to have their voter registration records sealed, and family members' personal assets are held in the name of a private corporation. "In fact, if they had their way, they would be known only by their customers, a few key Cabinet members and perhaps a dozen bankers," wrote journalist Mark Dowie. Since many of the company's activities have long been concealed by a shield of privacy, journalists and historians face unusual challenges in piercing that shield.

Bechtel is part-and-parcel of what has been called the Corporate West—a community that throughout the twentieth century, and before, preached the gospel of the free market, although government stood as its primary business partner. The relationship began with the railroads, especially in California. In the twentieth century, the main pillars of the California economy followed this pattern: Agribusiness, Banking, Energy, and Transportation. Following World War II, the pattern continued with Defense construction that would ultimately spin off into the software industry centered in northern California. In many respects, Bechtel not only stood as the quintessential example of the Corporate West, but also spearheaded that path for others, where the West moved East, and then globally.

Bechtel's obscurity—the protection from public scrutiny its private corporation structure affords—allows it to operate below the radar. With no public stock, no public reports, and thus no public scrutiny of its operations or profits, the company enjoyed benefits that other public corporations in America do not share.

Bechtel Group Inc. grew after the mysterious death in 1933 of its founding patriarch, Warren A. "Dad" Bechtel. Dad, who first determined to "break" the Colorado River as if it were a wild horse, and who, with primitive mastery of the steam shovel, had built the founding fortune, left no succession plan. His three sons—Warren Jr., Stephen, and

Kenneth—vied for control of the family company. (Not unusual for the era, the only daughter, Alice Elizabeth, was not in the running, nor was her husband, Brantley M. Eubanks, even though he held an executive position with the firm.) After a string of legal machinations, the rival brothers settled on middle son "Steve," who would later become known as "Steve Sr." after the birth of his only son, Steve Jr. Senior would forge the company's deep ties to national and international politics, and establish the close relationship between Bechtel, numerous American presidents, and the intelligence community—first through the Office of Strategic Services (OSS) and then its successor, the Central Intelligence Agency (CIA).

In 1960 Steve Sr. turned over the business to Steve Jr., who doubled the size of the organization and oversaw the company's worldwide expansion that transformed it into the geopolitical powerhouse it is today. In 1990 Steve Jr. relinquished control to his son, Riley, who remains chairman of the board. In August 2014 the sixty-one-year-old Riley turned over the presidency to his son, Brendan. At the time, Riley had a net worth of $3.2 billion, putting him among the fifty wealthiest people in America and making him the 127th richest person in the world.

Specializing in what it calls "multiyear megaprojects," Bechtel received $24 billion in new contracts during 2013. Its fifty-five thousand "employees"—most of whom are subcontractors—are divided among projects in six "markets": civil infrastructure; communications; government services; mining and metals; oil, gas, and chemicals; and power. Its website lists dozens of "signature projects" that read like a roundup of nearly every high-profile undertaking throughout the world. The Channel Tunnel between London and Paris. The Dulles Corridor Metrorail Extension in Washington, DC. The Bay Area Rapid Transit (BART) system in California. The San Francisco–Oakland Bay Bridge. The Trans-Alaska Pipeline System (TAPS). Boston's Central Artery/Tunnel Project known as the "Big Dig." The construction of ninety-five airports throughout the world, including Hong Kong International, Gatwick in London, Doha in Qatar, and McCarran in Las Vegas. It has built 17,000 miles of roads, eighty ports and harbors, 6,200 miles of railway, a hundred tunnels, fifty hydroelectric plants, thirty bridges, and twenty-five entire communities, including the futuristic Saudi Arabian city of Jubail—a $20 billion project hailed as the largest project in construction history.

The company has laid tens of thousands of kilometers of pipeline, enough to circle the earth twice, including plans for the Keystone from Canada to the United States, slated to be one of the longest crude oil pipelines in the world. A leader in the liquefied natural gas market, Bechtel has built a third of the world's liquefaction capacity, not only throughout America but also in Australia, Egypt, Algeria, and Russia. The website describes the company's involvement in many of the largest and most visible projects for the US Department of Defense (DOD) and the Department of Energy (DOE). Bechtel is building the nation's massive radioactive-waste treatment plant in Hanford, Washington—a $12.2 billion contract courtesy of the DOE. Under contract with the US Navy and US Army, Bechtel has constructed more than thirty bases and airfields on numerous Pacific islands.

But the industry to which Bechtel is most closely linked is that of nuclear power and weaponry. Describing itself as a "global leader in design and construction of nuclear power plants for the past 80 years," Bechtel completed the world's first nuclear plant at Arco, Idaho, in 1951. The nation's first experimental breeder reactor—called the National Reactor Testing Station—was the beginning of the nascent electric power generation industry that a decade later would lead to a worldwide expansion of nuclear power plants. The company made history when its nuclear fission plant supplied energy to generate electricity for the first time anywhere in the world. Then, four years later, Bechtel built America's first major nuclear power plant in Dresden, Illinois. By the end of the 1960s, Bechtel had completed twenty-seven nuclear power plants in the United States, three thermonuclear plants in South Korea, and was consulting with numerous foreign governments about their nuclear programs. It then received contracts to clean up Three Mile Island in Pennsylvania and Chernobyl in the Ukraine after disastrous nuclear accidents at those facilities in 1979 and 1986, respectively.

As part of President George W. Bush's effort to privatize the country's national nuclear warhead complex, the government solicited bids in the mid-2000s to transition "to industrial standards and capitalize on private sector expertise." DOE received three bids and awarded the coveted multiyear, multibillion-dollar contract to a Bechtel-led partnership to manage the country's premier national laboratories—Los Alamos in New Mexico and Lawrence Livermore in California—in addition to other key nuclear facilities in the country.

Considered the crown jewels of what Bechtel describes as "the U.S. Nuclear Security Enterprise," Los Alamos and Livermore are legendary for developing the atomic bombs dropped on Hiroshima and Nagasaki in 1945. The University of California had managed the labs as a public service since their inception more than a half century earlier. But Bechtel was in it for the money, and the transition to a for-profit venture resulted in a tenfold increase in management fees—costs that would be paid by taxpayers. The takeover of the labs by private industry prompted Republican congressman David Hobson to complain that they had become "a playground for political patronage."

Indeed, the succeeding generations of Bechtel men have navigated—if not designed—the powerful and profitable symbiosis between government and industry. Politically reactionary, the family has long been identified with the Republican Party. Like their archconservative corporate peers, they advocate a consolidated, freewheeling capitalistic, monopolistic economy unrestrained by government oversight or taxation. In 2013 much of the budget of Grover Norquist's advocacy group, Americans for Tax Reform, came from just a few sources, including two private giants—the Bechtels and the Koch brothers. Throughout the decades of its existence, Bechtel leaders have nurtured and polished its image as "a deep-pocketed, well-wired member of the global power elite," according to one published account, "an image referred to internally as the 'mystique.' "

Despite its fiercely antiregulatory, antigovernment stance, the Bechtel family owes its entire fortune to the US government, dating back to its first Depression-era construction projects in the western United States. The company tenet of free enterprise obfuscates the fact of its dependence upon government. "Bechtel espouses the standard free-market philosophy—get out of our way and let us build—while it simultaneously cultivates and manipulates government policy at home and abroad," as one account described the company's historic private-public tango. "It uses government to secure new contracts and subsidies, to open new markets and to win protection against risks." Somehow, the irony seems lost on them, as epitomized by Steve Jr.'s rebuff of an interview request by *Newsweek*: "There's no reason for people to hear of us. We're not selling to the public."

It seemed that Steve Jr. embraced the legend of Dad Bechtel's Horatio Alger–like biography. The privately financed 1949 hagiographic tale of the so-called Bechtel achievement depicted the accomplishments of a self-made man who rose to greatness despite "frequent discouragements." It was a narrative that "showed what men could do in the free air of America after the humblest of beginnings." But this rags-to-riches arc belies the real Bechtel story: the creation of a regional corporate power in the American West subsidized by the US government. "The California settlement had tended to attract drifters of loosely entrepreneurial inclination, the hunter-gatherers of the frontier rather than its cultivators, and to reward most fully those who perceived most quickly that the richest claim of all lay not in the minefields, but in Washington," wrote Joan Didion of the money and power in her native land.

Dad Bechtel personified the caricatured mogul of the new western industrialism that blossomed during the Great Depression. Fashioning a fruitful coalition with the federal government, Bechtel and a handful of his peers shaped a resource-based empire that would dominate national affairs for decades to come. At its heart was the then largest civil contract ever let by the US government—the dam that remade the American West.

"Western builders will build the Hoover-Boulder Dam, a Western project in the West for the West," gloated the *Pacific Builder* in 1931 when a Bechtel-led California-based consortium won the historic US Bureau of Reclamation contract. Dad Bechtel's "single most remarkable achievement up to that time was the invention of a folding toothbrush that fit neatly into a vest pocket." Two years later, he would derive $2 million in profits (roughly $600 million in today's terms), and his company would suddenly be one of the preeminent engineering and construction firms in the world.

The Spy with a Fan Club

Shouting at Barack Obama, a young Israeli activist implored the president to free Jonathan Pollard—America's most controversial Jewish prisoner. It was March 2013, during Obama's first official trip to Israel, and the president was addressing a throng of students in Jerusalem when the Hebrew-speaking heckler interrupted. Pollard, who has served nearly thirty years in a federal prison in North Carolina for passing classified information to Israel during the early 1980s, has provoked sympathy, outrage, and extensive pleas for clemency. His lifetime sentence—unprecedented in its harshness, considering that he was charged neither with treason nor spying for an enemy state—has divided the Jewish community in the United States and beyond. Since Pollard's 1985 arrest, the cause célèbre has inspired every Israeli prime minister—from Yitzhak Rabin to Benjamin Netanyahu—to petition every US president—from George H. W. Bush to Barack Obama—for his release.

At the heart of what one journalist called "the endless Pollard intrigues . . . is one haunting question towering above all others: Just why has Jonathan Pollard been imprisoned so long?" His offense, spying for a friendly government, carries a median two-to-four-year penalty. In his plea agreement, Pollard admitted guilt to a single count of disclosing documents to an ally foreign government. He expressed remorse, apologized, agreed to cooperate with the US government in its damage assessment, and was promised by prosecutors he would have his sentence commuted to time already served. So in 1987 when a US District Court judge in Washington, DC, reneged on that promise—citing that Pollard's interview with a journalist violated his plea agreement—Pollard was shocked by the double-cross. The courtroom on Constitution Avenue—teeming with dozens of reporters and Pollard friends and supporters—erupted with shrieks from stunned spectators when the life sentence was announced. He had received a more severe sentence than the numerous other spies arrested in 1985 in what the Federal Bureau of Investigation (FBI) christened the "Year of the Spy" for the numerous high-publicity espionage cases of the "last gasps" of the Cold War.

The moment the sentence was pronounced, a "Free Jonathan Pollard" crusade was born. Hundreds of Jewish organizations mobilized, representing millions of members. Israel considered him a soldier for Zion, and efforts were mounted among both Israeli and American Jewish groups to seek his release. The groundswell spread through intellectual and celebrity circles, with dozens of movie stars and academics calling on US presidents to review the case. "The Spy with a Fan Club," as *Washingtonian* magazine dubbed him, Pollard was emblematic of the post–Cold War shift in American intelligence and foreign policy in the run-up to the collapse of the Soviet Union. Caught in the crossfire between the diplomats of the State Department and the chauvinists in the military, between Arabists and Zionists, neocons and pragmatists, Pollard was the poster boy for the trampling of civil liberties under the guise of national security. "Whoever has studied the Pollard case keeps wondering what the government is hiding," a venerable journalist described the " 'Catch-22' Plight" of the imprisoned spy. Decrying the "bullying tactics" of federal prosecutors, the *Wall Street Journal* opined that "Even Pollard Deserves Better Than Government Sandbagging."

Revelations in 2013 by former US National Security Agency contractor Edward Snowden that the United States had spied on at least two Israeli prime ministers brought new frostiness to Israeli-American relations—and new life to the "Free Jonathan Pollard" movement. A number of high-level US intelligence, diplomatic, and military officials joined the escalating campaign to protest the sentence and call for mercy.

Then, anti-Pollard sentiments were inflamed when, in August 2014, Snowden revealed that "Israel has been caught carrying out aggressive espionage operations against American targets for decades," an allegation denied by Israeli officials, who insisted that Jerusalem stopped spying on the United States after the conviction of Pollard in the late 1980s.

At the heart of the complex case of Jonathan Pollard is the Bechtel corporation and the netherworld of espionage and national security it inhabited. Later events would show how Bechtel's interests were served by the pro-Iraq, anti-Israeli foreign policy "tilt" of Ronald Reagan's presidential administration, and how Pollard had threatened those interests. That world would be a maze of covert intervention and shifting alliances. In the middle of this world were the Bechtel executives turned Reagan Cabinet members—Caspar Weinberger and George P. Shultz.

Weinberger especially went to great lengths to insure Pollard would never be free to tell his story—a story that would have included Bechtel's long-standing business relationships with Israel's enemies in the Middle East—especially Saddam Hussein.

PART ONE

WE WERE AMBASSADORS WITH BULLDOZERS

1872–1972

This extreme reliance of California on federal money, so seemingly at odds with the emphasis on unfettered individualism that constitutes the local core belief, was a pattern set early on.

—JOAN DIDION, *Where I Was From*

CHAPTER ONE

Go West!

A "tall, beefy man with a bull-like roar," Warren Augustine Bechtel, whose legacy would be one of the greatest engineering achievements in American history, came into the world on September 12, 1872. The fifth in a family of eight children, he was raised on a hardscrabble farm near Freeport, Illinois. His parents—Elizabeth Bentz and John Moyer Bechtel—were descendants of pioneer Pennsylvania German families. When he was twelve, his parents moved to Peabody, Kansas, where they eked out a living "at a time when he saw many men missing an arm or a leg from service in the Civil War," as one account described the setting.

It was a backbreaking childhood that he fantasized about escaping from an early age. Because he was tasked with farm chores since he was a toddler, Warren's schooling was confined to the winter months when the crops lay beneath frozen ground. Like many of his contemporaries, he hated farming as only a farmer's son can, but he disliked the classroom with equal fervor. Still, his father, who was also a grocery store proprietor, insisted that he finish high school. In 1887 the first railroad came through the area, and during the summers, Warren hired himself out to the construction crews to learn grading and machinery. He also worked for neighboring ranchers, branding cattle and driving herds. But his passion was the slide trombone, which he practiced while roaming the land. He dreamed of playing the instrument professionally.

Upon graduation at the age of nineteen, he hit the road with an ensemble of performers who called themselves the Ladies Band. He hoped music would spare him a future in farming. "Either the music of the ladies' band was very bad or the Western audiences were lacking in appreciation," the *New York Times* would later describe the venture. "The troupe came to grief in Lewiston, Ill., and the young slide-trombonist was stranded." Disheartened, he returned home to the unwelcome plow to raise corn for livestock feed. He remained there until 1897, when he became infatuated with a slender brunette named Clara Alice West. She was visiting relatives in nearby Peabody. After a fleeting courtship that alarmed her affluent Indiana parents, the two married, and Warren ventured into the cattle business. He embarked on his scheme to fatten Arizona draught steers as they awaited slaughter in the Kansas stockyards. But the bottom dropped out of both the corn and cattle markets to record lows at the end of the nineteenth century, leaving the newlyweds bankrupt. With their infant firstborn son, Warren Jr., their personal possessions, a slip grader, and two mules, they struck out for Indian Territory, where the Chicago, Rock Island and Pacific Railway Company was putting new lines westward from Chickasha in what is now Oklahoma.

Earning $2.75 per day—a good living for a man with his own mule team—Warren found the work plentiful, as rail companies were expanding westward with boomtown gusto. His nascent construction company consisted mostly of muscle and ambition. As the railways forged west, so too did the little Bechtel family, with Warren grading track beds in Indiana, Iowa, Minnesota, and Wyoming. Though a rugged and itinerant existence, the couple was optimistic, and welcomed the birth of their second son, Stephen Davison, while visiting Clara's parents in Aurora, Indiana.

When he was offered a job as gang foreman with the Southern Pacific Railroad in Reno, Nevada, during the winter of 1902–03, Warren was grateful for the opportunity. Eager for a more secure financial position, he had set his sights on the West Coast and the post–Gold Rush promise that existed in California. Warren embraced newspaperman

Horace Greeley's famous 1871 career advice to a young correspondent: "Having mastered these, gather up your family and Go West!"

"I landed in Reno with a wife and two babies, a slide trombone, and a ten-dollar bill," Warren later recalled. The railroad supervisor who had promised him the job had gone bust. Twenty-seven years old, Warren lived with his wife and small sons in a converted railroad boxcar. Discouraged, he hitched a ride on a buckboard to Wadsworth, Nevada—a remote railroad site on the banks of the Truckee River known for its wild mustang herd and native Paiute population. He found a job there as an estimator for the Southern Pacific, earning $59 a month. "He was learning all the time, but he seemed to me a natural engineer," his supervisor later recalled. An engineer who worked with him during those early days described him as "a horse-drawn fresno-scraper type of contractor"—meaning an old-fashioned laborer who had come up the hard way on the railroad construction gangs.

A series of jobs ensued from which Warren acquired technical experience in lieu of a formal education. From Wadsworth, he moved to Lovelock, Nevada, where he became a gravel pit superintendent at a quarry. He, his wife, and two young sons were a familiar sight at the primitive migrant job sites. He soon acquired the nickname "Dad," as his ubiquitous brood called him. He bounced around various posts, gaining a reputation for efficiency and, especially, for mastering the newfangled modern transportation and construction equipment— most conspicuously the giant excavating machine called the steam shovel. "Many of the old-timers were reluctant to have anything to do with the big, belching mechanized monsters," according to one account, "but Bechtel put them to immediate—and profitable—use." That specialty brought him to the attention of an inspector for a construction firm, based in Oakland, California, that had a contract to build the Richmond Belt Railroad and to extend the Santa Fe line into Oakland.

In 1904 Dad moved his family to Oakland, where a third son, Kenneth, was born. The city, named for the massive oak forest that dominated the landscape, was surrounded by redwoods, farmland,

and rural settlements. Even then a sad relative to booming, raucous San Francisco, located six miles west across the San Francisco Bay, the city's future as Northern California's busiest seaport was not yet apparent. Still, its sunny and mild Mediterranean climate lured an increasing number of immigrants from throughout the country, and its population (eighty-two thousand upon the Bechtels' arrival) would double in just six years. A few blocks away from their Linden Street home, tracks of the interurban electric line to San Francisco were being laid. Dad had the contract to fill the swamp at the head of Lake Merritt for Oakland's Lakeshore Park.

By 1906, Dad was ready to strike out on his own. At thirty-four years old, he obtained his first subcontract with the Western Pacific Railroad, building a line between Pleasanton and Sunol. This independent undertaking marked the birth of the modern Bechtel company. Dad began assembling the team of colleagues that would help him make construction history. For an extortionate fee, he rented the impressive Model 20 Marion steam shovel that had been memorably developed for the Panama Canal construction. When he purchased the imposing machine, thanks to a loan from his well-to-do father-in-law, his company was officially launched. His steam shovel was in great demand, and he undertook ever-larger railroad projects while expanding into building roads, tunnels, bridges, and dams. In large white block script, he stenciled "W. A. BECHTEL CO." onto the red cab door. It would be another sixteen years before he would formally incorporate his business. Home now to a family of five, their residential boxcar was called WaaTeeKaa for the combination of their three toddlers' baby names: "Waa-Waa" for Warren, "Tee-Tee" for Steve, and "Kaa-Kaa" for Kenneth.

"Still largely undeveloped, California was booming . . . and, with the recent addition of the steam engine, railroads couldn't lay track fast enough to link the new west to the rest of the country," a newspaper described the moment. A man of unlimited ambition, Dad expanded his vision to the western slope of the Rocky Mountains, where he came into contact with the imposing and pugnacious sheep-ranching Wat-

tis brothers of Ogden, Utah. W. H. and E. O. Wattis were the founders and chief executives of the Utah Construction Company—one of
the great railroad construction firms of the West—who were devout
members of the Church of Jesus Christ of Latter-day Saints. The sons
of a forty-niner "whose trek to California ended six hundred miles
short in . . . northern Utah . . . they were reared in the dynamic, enter-
prising environment of Brigham Young's Mormon commonwealth,"
wrote historian Joseph E. Stevens. They were notoriously reluctant
to work with non-Mormon "gentiles." But they admired Dad's abili-
ties and resourcefulness and, as W.H. reportedly put it to his brother:
"Might as well ask him in as to have him bitin' our feet."

The Wattis brothers wielded extraordinary political power in Utah.
David Eccles, patriarch of the single largest Mormon fortune, leading
tither to the church, and the father of Marriner Eccles, who would
later become chairman of the Federal Reserve Board, supplied most
of their capital. (The Eccleses' formidable Utah Corporation was an
international conglomerate of mining, shipping, and construction involved in the production of iron, coal, and uranium ore on three continents.) The Wattises gave Bechtel his most lucrative jobs to date: three
large contracts for railroad lines in Northern California and central
Utah. His work with the Northwestern Pacific Railroad required more
sophisticated construction techniques, and he became the first contractor in the country to replace the horse- and mule-drawn freight
teams with chain-driven, gasoline-powered dump trucks. At a yard
in San Leandro, he retrofitted 1912 model Packards and Alcos with
dump bodies. Referred to later as the "coming of age" period for the
Bechtel organization, the completion of the last 106-mile stretch of
the Northwestern Pacific line signaled the beginning of the company's
rise. "I never expected to have that much money in a lifetime," the un-
lettered son of a small-town grocer confided to a friend upon receiving
his nearly $500,000 payment.

Now flush, he turned his attention to family—which included
daughter Alice Elizabeth, born in 1912—purchasing a spacious Victo-
rian home and furnishing it lavishly with rare Oriental rugs that had

been exhibited at the 1915 Panama-Pacific International Exposition in San Francisco. He chose the Estudillo Avenue house in nearby San Leandro, where the children would have "more room to grow." Evocative of his farm upbringing, the house was surrounded by acres of tomatoes and elaborate flower gardens. A tennis court on the grounds affirmed the family's fresh wealth.

But just as the official history of the company smooths over the "near misses, the bad judgment calls, and the numerous failures" of Dad's early climb—as an academic critique of the corporate culture of Bechtel portrayed his dismal performance in the cattle, farming, and grading enterprises, not to mention the nomadic lifestyle to which he subjected his young family—so too are his subsequent fiascos whitewashed. "It is difficult to connect the sober-headed, hard-working straight-shooter depicted in the official history with the man whose main ambition on leaving home, for instance, was to play the slide trombone with a largely female dance band," wrote Canadian postcolonialist professor Heather Zwicker.

Despite the revisionist and mythologizing company narrative of Warren A. Bechtel's entrepreneurial individualism—the American exceptionalism that would be much ballyhooed by later generations of Bechtels—in the years following the Northwestern Pacific windfall, Dad made a string of bad calls. Smug with his newfound success, "and still fancying himself the wheeler-dealer of his youth," according to *Friends in High Places: The Bechtel Story—The Most Secret Corporation and How It Engineered the World*, by Laton McCartney, he sank tens of thousands of dollars into an unsuccessful Oregon gold mine, followed by several hundred thousand more invested in a folding toothbrush company that tanked. The salvation of his fortune and future would lie not in the up-from-the-bootstraps chronicle that would become family legend, but with the US government. With government patronage, Bechtel was able to build a network of tracks and highways throughout the land at the very moment that railroad expansion and the automobile industry were exploding.

Sales of Henry Ford's iconic black Model Ts had passed the five hundred thousand mark by 1918—giving the Ford Motor Company a veritable monopoly, as a Ford was driven by more than half the car owners in America. Dad was not alone in recognizing that all of these cars needed roads to travel on, but he was among a handful of California builders positioned to capitalize on the new construction market. The Federal Aid Road Act had been approved in 1916 to meet the overwhelming demand, resulting in the creation of the US Bureau of Public Roads. Bechtel lobbied for a role, and in 1919 received the first federal highway contract in California. He first built the Klamath River Highway near the Oregon border; the scenic byway, considered an engineering marvel at the time, jutted through volcanic rock and granite. The following year, he built another highway for the federal government in Los Angeles County that ran through the rugged San Gabriel Canyon; this one required a bluff to be blasted down with the rarely used powerful explosive, picric powder. Next was the Generals Highway in Sequoia National Park, named after the largest, most famous giant sequoia trees—General Sherman and General Grant—and famous for its steep, often-impassable switchbacks. Then came the job of making additions and improvements to the highway system in Yosemite National Park, followed by contracts in New Mexico and Arizona to double track the Santa Fe Railroad from Gallup to Chambers.

Dad, fleshy and always well groomed, gained a reputation for keeping his jobs orderly and his equipment in top condition. He espoused a "cleanliness is next to godliness" motto. He wore a trademark felt fedora and gold watch fob, and his dapper style set him apart from the workers on his many sites. Known for his hearty appetite, he hired the finest cooks and bakers he could find to accompany him to his worksites. Since his California labor force was composed mostly of what he called "eye-talians," his cooks became expert at cooking spaghetti, for which Dad acquired a penchant. A stickler for verbal agreements and handshake deals with his associates—"When you can't trust a man's word, you can't trust his signature," he would declare—he also insisted on fifty-fifty partnerships. "Dad had no patience with 51-49 arrangements," a former partner once said. "He used to say 'No man with a sense of self-respect wants to be controlled on that kind of percentage.' "

Although the business of road and railroad construction was steady and profitable, Bechtel began turning his attention to oil—the coming boom that accompanied the automobile. Predicting a surge in the development of the West's oil and gas resources to meet the energy needs of a growing industrial economy, Bechtel envisioned a network of refineries and pipelines snaking throughout the country. The vision turned out to be prescient, heralding the establishment of an alliance between the Bechtel corporation and the largest oil and gas companies in the nation and, ultimately, in the world. Situated as he was in the heart of a flourishing American West, Dad garnered more contracts than he could manage, and in 1921 he partnered with a fellow Bay Area entrepreneur named Henry J. Kaiser. An "egomaniacal small-time construction tycoon," Kaiser joined Bechtel in building major arteries that wound along the entire West Coast. The company took off in 1929 with the firm's first gas line for the Pacific Gas and Electric Company (PG&E). Building more than a thousand miles of pipeline for Standard Oil and Continental Gas, he amassed a fortune of more than $30 million by the end of the 1920s, making his company one of the largest construction firms in America.

At fifty-eight years of age, Dad was once again self-satisfied with his role as a newly minted western mogul. He gloried in the national and international influence he and his western partners exercised. He might have been content to enjoy the luxuries of his life, and the sweep of his enterprise, if not goaded into a construction challenge being called the "Eighth Wonder of the World."

When the Herbert Hoover administration announced in 1929 that it would accept bids to dam the Colorado River, Dad was leery. "It sounds a little ambitious," he remarked drily to his protégé, Kaiser, about building the world's tallest dam in a forbidding desert gorge. But when Kaiser compared the gargantuan project with the Egyptian pyramids and the Great Wall of China, promising that the Bechtel name would be etched on a bronze plaque at the dam's crest in perpetuity,

Dad was sold. That year he was the first western builder to become national president of the Associated General Contractors of America—a booster organization and powerful lobbying group—and he planned to brandish his political clout in both the state capital in Sacramento and in Washington's inner circles. His petitioning would pay off.

Meanwhile, Kaiser's company followed the same path as Bechtel, by raking in government contracts for roads, dams, public works, and later the Kaiser shipyards.

CHAPTER TWO

Follow the Water

For twelve million years, the nation's wildest river snaked and slashed to its final destination in the Gulf of California. Then, one winter day in 1935, a massive wedge of concrete successfully plugged the destructive 1,450-mile Colorado River, ending its tempestuous journey in Black Canyon on the Arizona and Nevada border. The largest public-funded project up until then, Hoover Dam ushered in what author Marc Reisner has called "the most fateful transformation that has ever been visited on any landscape, anywhere."

The Colorado is not the longest, widest, or most abundant of American rivers. It has never been a major transportation or commercial thoroughfare, as its quarter-million-square-mile drainage basin meanders through some of the most rugged and desolate land in all of North America. Instead, what has defined it throughout history is its violent, irrepressible personality. "The Colorado has always been best known for the scars it left on the landscape, among them the greatest of all natural works, the Grand Canyon, a testament to the river's primordial origin and its compulsive energy," wrote Michael Hiltzik in *Colossus: Hoover Dam and the Making of the American Century.* "No river equaled its maniacal zeal for carving away the terrain in its path and carrying it downstream, sometimes as far as a thousand miles. No river matched its schizophrenic moods, which could swing in the course of a few hours from that of a meandering country stream to an insane torrent."

But thanks to a Bechtel-led consortium of little-known western construction companies, the unruly river was finally tamed, puddling up behind the six-million-ton curved concrete arch. As tall as a sixty-story skyscraper, as wide as two football fields at its bedrock base, and embodying enough concrete for a sixteen-foot-wide highway from San Francisco to New York City, Hoover Dam was an engineering epic. The greatest dam ever built in the entire world, Hoover "unequivocally announced the untapped industrial capacity of California and the West," as California historian Kevin Starr wrote. The project made a lot of money for a lot of men, but it propelled Bechtel into a condition approaching that of a corporate nation-state.

How the formation of the famous Six Companies joint venture came about has taken on mythological proportions. Over time Bechtel emerged as the primary builder of the dam, so that today the company website highlights it as its flagship megaproject. What is undisputed about the consortium's provenance is the fact that on a February morning in 1931, a group of twelve West Coast contractors assembled at the Engineers' Club in San Francisco. "Two were aging Mormons who had graded the roadbed for the Western Pacific when it went through Utah," *Fortune* magazine reported about the meeting. "Two others mixed railroad work with general contracting. One specialized in sewers and tunnels, one was a bridge builder, one a building contractor, and one . . . a sand, gravel, and paving man." The dozen men had a conspicuous lack of formal engineering education, but an entourage of engineers, lawyers, and bankers were on hand to advise.

Although they were the most powerful contractors in the West, none had the singular capacity to scrape together the $5 million bond required by the surety companies underwriting the construction of the dam—the largest bond ever written on a single job. The men, most of whom had never met one another, "came together to do collectively what they could not do individually: to set up an organization to bid on and build the huge dam on the Colorado River," as *Fortune* described it.

There were actually eight companies represented at the meeting:

Henry J. Kaiser Co. of Oakland; W. A. Bechtel Co. of San Francisco; Morrison and Knudsen of Boise, Idaho; the Wattis brothers from Utah Construction Co. of Ogden; MacDonald & Kahn Co., Inc., of San Francisco; J. F. Shea Co. Inc. of Los Angeles; Pacific Bridge Co. of Portland, Oregon; and General Construction Co. of Seattle. But when it came time to naming their group, Kaiser insisted on calling it Six Companies, borrowing the name from the six tongs of San Francisco's Chinatown— the Chinese crime families' equivalent of the Mafia that mediated clashes between rival factions. "Hocking everything but their shirts, they could barely scrape together the few million dollars they would need to buy enough equipment to begin the job," Reisner, the renowned American environmentalist and water management expert, described the dubiousness of the venture. Each of the eight firms was required to put up $500,000 toward the bond. The $1.5 million contributed by Bechtel and Kaiser combined gave them a resounding 30 percent equity in the project. Six Companies Inc. was incorporated in Delaware, just two weeks before the bids were to be submitted.

Symbolic of all that was right and wrong with America, Boulder Dam (renamed Hoover Dam in 1947) created the water and energy infrastructure that would power the rest of the century's burgeoning development in the American West. Sunbelt metropolises never before envisioned—Los Angeles, Denver, Las Vegas, Phoenix, San Diego—would become a sudden, slightly daunting reality. The central thrust of the massive population shift from the East to the West depended upon the control of water and energy, and Bechtel would be firmly installed as a powerbroker in exploiting the western resources of water, coal, uranium, oil, and gas. Depicted throughout as a New Deal Depression-era public works project, the dam was in reality a government-funded private enterprise "put in motion by the business-oriented Hoover administration to help the landowners of the Imperial Valley of Southern California," according to *Unreal City: Las Vegas, Black Mesa, and the Fate of the West*, by Judith Nies. The journey to Hoover Dam had begun in the early 1920s, when a burgeoning California set its sights on the Colorado River as a source of both water and electricity. More than half of the entire American West's ten million population lived in California, and even though the state's tributaries contributed little to the Colorado River, the voracious developers of San Diego and Los Angeles began pushing Congress to authorize a dam that would primarily benefit California. Most of the water and nearly two-thirds of the hydroelectricity generated by the dam would go to light up Los Angeles and make California the wealthiest state in the country. Developers and political leaders in the other six riparian states were outraged by the blatant water grab—especially Colorado, Wyoming, and Utah, which collectively contributed more than 83 percent of the runoff.

On November 24, 1922, representatives of all seven states— including New Mexico, Nevada, and Arizona—had met at a dude ranch on the outskirts of Santa Fe to divvy up the river's annual estimated 17.5 million acre-feet of water. Then–US commerce secretary Herbert Hoover, longtime promoter of public-private partnerships in the name of what he called "economic modernization," brokered the contentious gathering. That night, in the Ben Hur Room of the Palace of the Governors, they finally applied their signatures to the negotiated Colorado River Compact that separated the river basin into "upper" and "lower" divisions, arbitrarily partitioned at Lees Ferry, Arizona. The compact allotted 7.5 million acre-feet to each segment, with whatever was left a sop to Mexico. The state legislatures in seven state capitals bickered, and eastern politicians on Capitol Hill railed against allocating millions for a project in the hinterland. Finally, six years later, Congress took control and authorized construction of a dam, and hydrologists and geologists for the US Interior Department stepped up their exploration for a site on the lower Colorado.

For a quarter century, Frank T. Crowe had envisioned backing up the Colorado River near the walls of Black Canyon. A legendary engineer, Crowe was often compared with George Washington Goethals, the hard-driving army officer who oversaw the building of the Panama Canal. The six-foot-three Crowe was "wild to build this dam, the biggest dam ever built by anyone anywhere," he told a magazine writer.

"I had spent my life in the river bottoms, and Boulder meant a wonderful climax—the biggest dam ever built by anyone anywhere." Born in Quebec in 1882, Crowe had studied civil engineering at the University of Maine. So eager was he to jump-start his dam-building career that he skipped his 1904 commencement and hurriedly joined the US Reclamation Service. Over the next twenty years, he built dams in Idaho, Wyoming, and Montana, all the while maneuvering to become the contractor for the world's largest dam. Cultivating contacts within both the public and private sectors, he immersed himself in the early design work. He wanted to go down in history as the greatest dam builder in the world.

By 1924, Crowe had become the general superintendent of construction for the Bureau of Reclamation. But he eagerly left the government to join Six Companies, where he would become the consortium's secret weapon. As a former government insider, the man whose motto was "Never my belly to a desk" knew the bureau's bidding process and was acquainted intimately with all 119 of the complicated specifications for the dam. He also possessed inside technological information unknown by rival bidders that could radically reduce traditional construction costs and guarantee sizeable profits to the partnership. He crafted the consortium bid to total $48,890,955—coincidentally just $24,000 more than government engineers had calculated and a whopping $10,000,000 below the highest bid. Not surprisingly, on March 4, 1931, the bureau awarded the contract to Six Companies, whose offer—as Crowe well knew—was the lowest among the three competing bids. Such preciseness of a bid had never been seen before in construction history in the American West.

Despite congressional grumbling, the government ultimately did not begrudge what were astronomical profits for the era. "When the last bills are paid and the turbines begin to turn, the Six Companies will have turned a profit estimated at $7 million and upward for all their work," *Fortune* magazine wrote. "The U.S. is willing to pay a good profit for a good dam built rapidly." At $165 million, the Boulder Canyon Project Act—signed into law by President Hoover—would be the largest congressional appropriation in American history until that time.

"In *All the President's Men*, Deep Throat tells [*Washington Post* reporter Bob] Woodward to 'follow the money,'" according to authors Peter Wiley and Robert Gottlieb. "For the Southwest, it is a question of following the water, the resources, the migratory trails. Where they lead tells us not only about the Southwest but about the future direction of the United States," the two wrote in their definitive *Empires in the Sun: The Rise of the New American West*.

CHAPTER THREE

Hobo Jungle

Built at the height of the Great Depression, under the most harrowing and inhumane conditions, by the country's hungriest men, Hoover Dam was a towering metaphor for the overwhelming challenges facing a desperate nation. Conceived by a river runner, designed by a civil engineer, facilitated by an indecisive president and hostile Congress, brutally micromanaged by an arrogant contractor, overseen by a handful of calculating corporate titans, and built by circus acrobats and Indian skywalkers, the feat was a historic convergence of implausible circumstances. A marvel of design, engineering, architecture, and construction, it stands as a stark emblem of humanity's conquest over nature, if not the subjugation of the American frontier.

The government's plan called for Six Companies to move ten million cubic yards of rock in order to build the largest hydroelectric power plant in the world, create a massive reservoir, and erect an entire town to house and provide services for thousands of workers. Many scientists believed it could not be accomplished—that the six-million-ton structure placed between two earthquake fault lines in the canyon floor and lodged between two vertical rock walls would never be stable. Naysayers feared that the weight of the lake created by the dam would provoke massive tremors and "unleash a flood of biblical proportions." One engineer recalled, "We were all scared stiff."

A week after Six Companies won the bid, Crowe took the Union Pacific Railroad to dusty Las Vegas, Nevada—a remote desert town inhabited by five thousand souls. By the time he stepped off the train, Crowe, "like a general preparing for a major battle, had planned his strategy," wrote historian Al M. Rocca in *America's Master Dam Builder: The Engineering Genius of Frank T. Crowe.* "The enemy, notorious Black Canyon, arrayed an impressive list of natural obstacles." Having been designated chief engineer on the project, he drove to the isolated dam site thirty miles to the southeast. The "road" consisted of two vanishing tracks through the sand. "When one set of tracks grew too soft to follow, cars simply moved over a few feet and forged a new trail," he described it according to dam historian Dennis McBride.

Crowe understood that the job would require an army of men and machines, and that maximizing profits would depend upon the skilled management of both. "He knew it would take the best in heavy equipment: tractors, dump trucks, shovels, jackhammers, drills, and concrete buckets," wrote Rocca, his biographer. "And what about his army? Who would serve in Frank Crowe's army?" He would be shocked to see that thousands of unemployed men had already made their way to Las Vegas from every corner of the country, hoping to be the first applicants when the hiring began.

America had hit rock bottom, the national unemployment rate soaring to 25 percent. One out of every four heads of household were out of work. Millions wandered from state to state in search of a job, and when word spread of the dam construction, they poured into Nevada in droves. Within weeks, more than ten thousand prospective workers were loitering around the train depot and the temporary Six Companies headquarters in downtown Las Vegas, resembling what one account called a "hobo jungle." They would compete for fifteen hundred jobs. "Instead of the young miners they expected to hire, the Six Companies employment office in Las Vegas faced long lines of workers of every age and background—some in three-piece suits— from all over the country," according to one report. "Many arrived with families and children and were living in tents or cars if they had them . . . The unemployed patiently waited for someone to die or be fired."

"This will be a job for machines," Crowe told the *New York Times*, emphasizing that the scale and development of modern machinery would set the project apart from anything previously constructed in America. Mack engineers built the largest truck ever—a huge 250-horsepower vehicle capable of moving 16 cubic yards of earth. General Electric constructed the most sophisticated X-ray unit of its time to photograph 24 million square inches of pipe welding. Lidgerwood Manufacturing produced steel ropes three and a half inches in diameter capable of lowering 150 tons of concrete or steel into the construction pit. The most ingenious invention of all would be a motor-driven rig set on a 10-ton chassis that supported four massive platforms carrying thirty 144-pound rock drills. Becoming the project's historic signature device, it enabled the workers to drill and place dynamite and then drive away before the explosion.

The first challenge at the dam site was the most complex and treacherous: diverting the Colorado through four tunnels, two on each bank, that would draw the river off its course and leave the original riverbed dry for construction. Workers drilled and dynamited through 3.5 million tons of volcanic rock to build the tunnels—each three-quarters of a mile long and, at 56 feet, as wide as a four-lane highway. Three feet of concrete, manufactured a mile upstream at a plant erected by Six Companies, lined each tunnel, which was capable of carrying 200,000 cubic feet of water per second. Barges transported generators, jackhammers, and air compressors to the site, access roads and railroads were built, and power lines were strung. Workers raised a 98-foot-high cofferdam on the Nevada side, 600 feet downriver from the inlet portals of the diversion tunnels.

On November 13, 1932, the entrances and exits of the two Arizona tunnels were blasted open, and, within seconds, a convoy of more than a hundred trucks began dumping loads of rock and muck into the river's path. The next morning, the river finally abandoned its long-worn course and gushed into the shiny new tunnels. Still, work continued for another year. A second 66-foot cofferdam was built downstream before the engineers turned their attention to the 700-foot concrete dam and began digging down to bedrock to lay the foundation. One and a half million cubic yards of silt and gravel were dredged and hauled away, and more than six thousand sticks of dynamite were fired before striking bedrock at 139 feet below the surface of the river. The solid-rock river bottom was pumped dry through a network of pipes in preparation for the concrete-pouring phase of the famous convex arch.

In June 1933 a giant bucket suspended from a cable spanning the gorge dumped the first load of 60 million tons of concrete that would form the dam's iconic streamlined face. The "pour" went on twenty-four hours a day, seven days a week, for nine months, with a bucketful dropping every seventy-eight seconds. Crews simultaneously built two giant spillways, four intake towers, penstocks to carry water from the intakes to the turbines, 222 miles of electricity transmission lines from the dam to Southern California, and diversion tunnels to control irrigation to California's lush Imperial Valley farms.

On January 31, 1935, a steel bulkhead gate weighing more than a thousand tons was lowered onto the canyon floor, closing off the fourth and final diversion tunnel. The Colorado River, now barred from its ancestral path, began pooling behind the futuristic monolith. Completed two and a half years ahead of schedule, using 3.25 million cubic yards of concrete, Hoover Dam glared white against the desert canyons. "The structure spanned ideology as it spanned Black Canyon," wrote historian Roger Morris, "joining public purpose and private enrichment in a marriage the West . . . took for granted."

CHAPTER FOUR

That Hellhole

Just as the construction statistics were significant and legendary, so too was the human toll. The safety violations and labor unrest that characterized Hoover Dam's construction site would become synonymous with Bechtel over the coming decades, dogging the company all the way into the next century and earning for Dad Bechtel the reputation as the "bête noir [*sic*] of American labor," wrote Laton McCartney. Corporate profits were astronomical, as Frank Crowe kept the project moving way ahead of schedule, with workers paying the price. Crowe's worksite "resembled a battlefield on the eve of the clash of armies," wrote Michael Hiltzik.

Frustrated by conflicting orders from Six Companies partners, Crowe threatened to quit at one point, prompting the bosses to form an executive committee headed by Bechtel. Installed like a pasha in a sumptuous Spanish colonial–style hacienda high above the scorching construction site, the hulking Bechtel summoned Crowe to informal "board meetings" that he held every Saturday afternoon during a pinochle game. Dad, along with son Steve—who had become vice president of Six Companies and was in charge of purchasing and expenditures. The cost of labor, materials, and equipment had plummeted as the Depression deepened, swelling the profit margin greatly. The government contract paid $8 for every cubic yard of earth excavated, while the actual cost to Six Companies was $5.50. The contract provided $850 reimbursement for each house built in Boulder

City—the government-sponsored community for dam workers and their families—but the company built them for $145. The project had proceeded so far ahead of schedule that by early 1932, Six Companies had recovered its $5 million surety bond and "pocketed an additional $1 million in contract incentives," according to one account.

More than twenty-one thousand famously taut and muscled men had worked on the dam as miners, nippers (steel cutters who ran the drills over to the miners), chuck tenders (drill placers), muckers (unskilled laborers who removed dynamite debris), shovel operators, cat skinners (bulldozer operators), electricians, and powder men (dynamite placers). High scalers performed the most audacious tasks, rappelling along the sheer cliffs, stripping them clean of any loose rocks and scree fields that often broke loose and killed workers below. The walls needed to be totally clean where the concrete dam and the canyon would meet. No cranes could adequately remove all of the debris, so the job was left to the four hundred high scalers, who quickly gained the reputation as fearless acrobatic show-offs. Held only by slender ropes, they scrambled across the towering walls like monkeys, carrying their tools and water bags. Once suspended in their swing-like seats bolted to the rock, they pulled out forty-four-pound jackhammers, drilled holes, and inserted dynamite. Former sailors, ironworkers, and circus performers, their daredevil showmanship and athletic contests irked Crowe, whose hotheaded and demanding nature left little room for humor.

Called "Hurry-up Crowe" for the breakneck speeds he demanded in order to maximize profits for Bechtel and fellow corporate bosses, he pushed his laborers hard in summer temperatures that averaged from 120 to 130 degrees on the floor of Black Canyon. As Reisner wrote, "Besides the hazards of the construction work (the falling rock, the explosives, electrocution, behemoth machines), besides the hazards of off-hours (fist fights, drunken binges, social diseases from the whores who camped about); besides all this, there was the heat." With no shade and little fresh drinking water, body temperatures rose high enough to push men into comas. In one five-day period alone, fourteen workers died from heat prostration. It was not until a visiting team of Harvard University physiologists came to the site in the summer of 1932 that dehydration was identified as a leading cause of death. The diversion tunnels often reached a smothering 140 degrees and were thick with carbon monoxide, resulting in many deaths. Six Companies deliberately misdiagnosed these deaths as pneumonia to skirt legal culpability.

Almost daily, the wives and children ensconced in nearby Boulder City heard ambulances heading to the dam site. "That siren—oh, it scared you 'cause you wondered if it might be your husband," recalled the wife of a pipe fitter whose heat stroke rendered him nearly unconscious. Six Companies did not provide first aid or medical service on the canyon floor as the human misery and death rate rose. Instead, Crowe drove his men harder, with three shifts working around the clock, seven days a week.

A particularly gruesome blasting accident underscored the lack of workplace safety, drawing the ire of Nevada state officials who cited Six Companies for illegal practices such as using gasoline-fired engines in unventilated spaces. Claiming the job site was effectively a federal reservation and not a mining operation, Bechtel and his partners contended it was "exempt from the prying attentions of state mining inspectors." The group did not carry liability insurance, and Dad Bechtel "showed up in Las Vegas with a corporate attorney bobbing in his wake," according to one account, to settle all accident claims "quickly, quietly, and privately." They would furtively settle at least fifty cases of carbon monoxide poisoning.

Still, the Big Six could not keep the horrendous working conditions secret from the outside world, and the situation drew the attention of the once formidable, now besieged, Industrial Workers of the World. Once the most powerful labor union in the American West, its membership rapidly declined during the 1920s as it became a hotbed of radicalism. Headquartered 1,700 miles away in Chicago, the Wobblies began agitating, and by August 1931, more than two-thirds of the workforce threatened to strike. Their grievances were notable for their rudimentary benefits: free ice water, helmets instead of crude baseball caps boiled in tar, payment in real money rather than the scrip negotiable only at the company store. "We feel it's a crime against humanity to ask men to work in that hell-hole of a heat at Boulder Dam for a mere pittance," the American Federation of Labor (AFL) wrote to the US secretary of labor. Workers claimed they were underpaid compared with laborers throughout the Southwest. They were charged half their wages to live in unsanitary conditions in the company town. Indeed, although the government contract estimated wages of $5.50 a day, workers were paid an average of $4. Meanwhile, racism and anti-Semitism were rife, and Asians and African Americans were barred from employment. Bechtel and his partners blamed the workers' dissatisfaction on outside Communist rabble-rousers, and the Hoover administration was obsequious toward the contractors. "They will have to work under our conditions or not at all," W. H. Wattis told the *San Francisco Examiner*. Crowe stood firm against his disgruntled men, and the strike collapsed for lack of support from either the state of Nevada or the federal government.

In the November 1932 presidential election, a whopping 78 percent of voters registered in Boulder City cast their ballots for Franklin D. Roosevelt. "In the town that was building a great monument to his name, Hoover had been trounced by a margin of more than three to one," wrote Hoover Dam historian Joseph E. Stevens. Word of FDR's victory spread like wildfire through the construction site, as workers rejoiced, shouting, "He is elected!"

Harold L. Ickes, FDR's newly appointed interior secretary, who was a progressive former newspaperman, wasted no time in challenging Six Companies' appalling labor practices. He launched a federal investigation into the workers' complaints. In response, Dad dispatched his acolyte Henry Kaiser—the consortium's de facto lobbyist—to Washington, DC, to oversee a public relations blitz and deflect Ickes's criticism. Kaiser's whirlwind speaking tour and media campaign gained national attention, as he flooded members of Congress, newspapers, and government officials with press kits and propaganda including thousands of copies of a hastily published book about the dam—what was described as a "crisis-filled narrative called *So Boulder Dam Was Built.*" Ensconced at the opulent Shoreham Hotel, Kaiser "coaxed and manipulated, grandstanding his way toward successful appropriations, contracts, and loans," wrote Wiley and Gottlieb. Undeterred by what he called "a telegraphic bombardment," Ickes ordered Six Companies to pay its workers in dollars, charged it with seventy thousand violations of the eight-hour day, and fined the group $350,000. But Kaiser's Washington glad-handing paid off, and the fine would eventually be reduced to $100,000.

"Flooded gorges and an unsavory company town led to more than a hundred dead, violent labor unrest, and bloody racial bigotry," one history drew the final conclusion. Still, Six Companies made a profit of more than $10 million, and Dad had gained a national reputation as a rough, often callous, operator.

———

"This is a good time to see what the rest of the world is doing," Dad told his partners in the summer of 1933, claiming to have been invited by Joseph Stalin's government to visit the Union of Soviet Socialist Republics (USSR). Now that he was suddenly the most famous builder in the world, the Soviets supposedly sought his expertise. Hoover Dam was not yet completed, but he felt confident he could leave the project not only in Crowe's capable hands but also in those of his three sons now installed on the job.

Given Bechtel's—and Six Companies'—rabidly antilabor, anti-Communist, anti-Socialist corporate culture, it seems implausible that Stalin would invite Dad to visit Russian technological sites. The United States had not officially recognized the Soviet Union since the US intervention against the Bolsheviks in their 1917 civil war. All that would soon change, thanks to FDR, who, in a few months, would formally acknowledge Stalin's Communist government and dispatch the first American diplomats to Moscow since the coup. Still, the United States had no certified representation in Russia during the summer of

1933, so Bechtel's mission as the first American contractor to inspect the Soviets' great dams and subways was momentous, at the least, for its lack of institutional protection.

In the midst of an infrastructure offensive, the Soviet government was rapidly building hydroelectric dams throughout the country. Dad was eager to inspect its handiwork and consult with that government's top scientists and engineers, according to the company's history. Of particular interest to him—and presumably to the US government as well—were the recently completed Dnieprostroi Dam near Kiev, the renowned Magnitogorsk dam in the Ural Mountains, and, especially, the fabled Moscow subway.

In early August 1933, accompanied by his wife and daughter, Dad set sail from New York City bound for France and then on to Austria by train. He left Clara and Alice in Vienna—apparently under instruction from Soviet authorities that he travel alone to the Russian capital. Once in Moscow, he spent three productive days and nights at the historic National Hotel near the heart of Red Square and the fortified Kremlin. He got on well with his Russian hosts, by all accounts, but on the fourth night before he was to depart for Kiev, he died suddenly in his hotel room from what the *New York Times* described as "an overdose of a medicine which he had been taking for several years on doctors' orders." Just fifteen days shy of his sixty-first birthday, the legendarily tough and robust Bechtel fell into what his family would later characterize as a diabetic coma from an insulin overdose. "Fumbling with a syringe, he injected himself with insulin, something Clara had always done," according to one account of the death. "Whether through unfamiliarity or grogginess," he gave himself too much and slipped into death on the night of August 28, 1933.

Meanwhile, his stunned widow and daughter were stranded in a foreign country a thousand miles from Moscow. The frosty American-Soviet relations made it nearly impossible for the family to retrieve Dad's body. According to the Bechtel version of events involves a well-connected Austrian count named Zucatur who had become enamored with the twenty-one-year-old Alice during her brief stay in Vienna. Zucatur had reportedly been on the verge of proposing marriage at the time of Dad's death—after just a three-day tryst, according to family lore—and although the romance fizzled, Zucatur was able to intercede to get Dad's body transported back to Oakland for burial.

Warren A. Bechtel—along with the Wattis brothers—was among the three founding fathers of Six Companies who didn't live to see the completion of the dam. For the surviving founders, the dam's dedication marked the creation of an epic international empire that would enrich them all beyond any notions. With an unprecedented building organization, an unparalleled inventory of modern technological equipment, and the crowning achievement of what was being called one of the greatest feats of mankind, the Six Companies men were unmatched in their position as the earthmovers of the world. Leading the way for the Bechtel family firm would be the middle son, Steve, who, after a brief power struggle, became president. The company's assets would soon mount into the billions, its projects emerging on every continent.

Behind it all would be the legacy of Hoover Dam. Steve would trace Bechtel's tremendous success to its roots in Nevada's Black Canyon. "Coming at the time it did, [Hoover Dam] was very important," he told an interviewer in 1984. "It put us in a very prime position . . . as being [regarded as] big-time thinkers, real thinkers."

CHAPTER FIVE

Wartime Socialists

"Warren Bechtel was a very successful businessman. But the man who really dreamed great dreams and put them into effect was Steve," said a close colleague. Destined to lead the company—as much by default as ability, given his siblings' personality disqualifications—Steve was exceedingly smart, determined, confident, and driven. In contrast, his brother Warren Jr. was "aggressive, boisterous, charming—the archetypal hail-fellow-well-met," as one account described him, who enjoyed both whisky and women to excess. Though Dad's firstborn Warren Jr. was the obvious heir apparent, as well as his father's favorite, he lacked the resolve and intensity to oversee the next phase of the Bechtel empire. Third son Kenneth's reserved temperament was also unsuited for the rugged world of construction. Although he was the most studious and contemplative of the three sons, and might have been a natural leader as a result, his disdain for his father's partners and employees was off-putting to company insiders.

The sons owned equal shares of the company—Dad had given them each 5 percent upon incorporation in 1925 of W. A. Bechtel Co.—but Steve had pushed for more, against Dad's objections. At the time of Dad's death, lawyers were preparing for a legal battle. But Warren and Ken deferred to the more tenacious Steve, and named him president of the company. "They wanted me to lead, and naturally, I was glad to do it," he told an interviewer somewhat disingenuously.

Born on September 24, 1900, to Warren and Clara, Steve was the second of their four children. He was "on the job from infancy," the *New York Times* reported, "living with his family in make-shift railway carriages on rugged construction sites as he grew up on the Pacific coast." He graduated from Oakland's Technical High School in 1916 and shipped out with the US Army's Twentieth Engineers Expeditionary Force to serve nineteen months in World War I—"burning up the French countryside as a motorcycle dispatch rider," according to a company profile. Upon his return in 1918, he enrolled at the University of California at Berkeley, intending to study engineering. But his college career was tragically cut short during his sophomore year. In the fall of 1919, the car he was driving struck three pedestrians, killing a mother and daughter and seriously wounding the survivor.

Steve was traveling to a dance at the Claremont Country Club with a carful of classmates when his speeding car hit a local dentist, H. G. Chappel, his wife, Jessie, and daughter, Elizabeth, on November 8, 1919. The car skidded 136 feet after the collision, Oakland police reported. Although Steve was arrested and charged with manslaughter, he was never prosecuted.

"The incident, which the Bechtel organization would go to great pains in later years to cover up—including, for a time, concealing the fact that Steve had even attended Berkeley—was, according to friends, a deeply scarring one for Bechtel, and accounted for much of his subsequent obsession with secrecy," wrote McCartney. Despite the seriousness of the accident, the charges were dismissed. "There was no explanation, either then or later, why Bechtel was not prosecuted."

Soon after, he dropped out of college and joined his father's business, punching rail lines and highways through the California wilderness. In 1923 he married Laura Adeline Peart—a fellow student he had met at Berkeley—and they moved across the hall from his parents in the swanky Art Deco apartment building that Dad and his partners had built near Lake Merritt in Oakland. Decades later, in 1998, *Time* magazine portrayed him as a visionary who as early as the 1920s foresaw an American expansion into energy and turned his company toward pipeline construction. By the time he was in his midtwenties, he was managing all of Dad's rapidly expanding pipelining projects, and even "went east to talk to the Continental Gas people" about bidding on a 1,500-mile gas line from Tracy, California, to Crockett, Texas, according to company reports. "As a newcomer from the Far West, he had to do some first-rate selling."

But it was his position as chief administrator of Six Companies that gave him the proficiency to transform Bechtel into the world's largest contractor. Second in rank only to the indomitable Frank Crowe, Steve gained a reputation on the job site for ruthlessness and precision. His farsightedness was opportune, informed as it was by his wartime experience in France. He was "more sophisticated and worldly than his father, who, for all his success, was, at bottom, a knockabout earthmover who threw up dams and gouged out mountains to make way for the roads and railways, never thinking much further ahead than the next job," as one account explained the difference between father and son.

"The ancient Western dream of an advanced industrial economy controlled at home and able to compete nationally is brighter now than it has ever been," historian Bernard De Voto wrote in a 1946 *Harper's* essay about the modern-day miracle of the Six Companies consortium. From Hoover Dam on through World War II, Bechtel and what *Fortune* magazine called the "lusty, uninhibited men" of Six Companies—sometimes individually, sometimes together—pursued a moneymaking, precedent-setting confederacy with the US government. By the end of the 1930s, following political turmoil in Europe, the federal government began focusing on national defense, and Six Companies would transition from earthmovers and dam builders to industrialists with billion-dollar defense contracts. Of all the Six Companies principals, Bechtel would be positioned to profit the most handsomely, landing the lucrative shipbuilding contracts that would make Steve a central figure in the American war industry. In the early 1940s, Bechtel and his associates thrust themselves into the top echelons of America's shipbuilding and steel works. Leading into World

War II, they shrewdly maneuvered into the key recipients of US military contracts.

By then, the Bechtel company had reached a turning point that propelled it into the economic stratosphere. The pivotal moment came when Steve brought a college classmate into the fold. John Alex McCone was a year behind Steve at Berkeley. The two had become friends before Bechtel dropped out of school. Born in San Francisco on January 4, 1902, McCone was the scion of a Scotch-Irish family that had been in the machinery business for generations, having started an iron foundry in Virginia City, Nevada. He graduated with an honors degree in mechanical engineering and went on to work first as a riveter in the boiler shop of an ironworks factory, and then as a surveyor and foreman with the steel erector crews of a construction gang. In 1931, ten years after the two met at Berkeley, McCone became sales manager of the Consolidated Steel Corporation in Los Angeles. At the time, Steve was in charge of purchasing for the Hoover Dam construction project, and the two reconnected when McCone visited him to try to sell steel to Six Companies. By the time the dam was completed, Consolidated had supplied Six Companies with fifty-five million tons of steel, insuring McCone's swift ascension to top executive at Consolidated Steel. The men had forged a powerful personal and professional bond. They vowed to stay in touch after the dam project, and in 1937, when Steve was eager to expand his company beyond construction, he sought McCone.

"Steve's vision was of energy—all types of it, but particularly of oil as a universal power source," a colleague described his interests. For years, he had directed Bechtel's pipeline construction throughout the West, and he began thinking about how California's oil refineries depended upon pipeline engineering firms located east of the Rocky Mountains. As a steel salesman, McCone had a powerful set of contacts in the oil industry complementary to Bechtel's own connections to Standard Oil Company of California (SOCAL) and Continental Gas dating back to the late 1920s. What Steve foresaw was a tilt westward of the nation's industrial complex, and he brainstormed with McCone on ways to capitalize on the shifting winds. "Steve and I shared a sense of imminent change," McCone recalled, "of great projects about to break at last upon the West. We were sure we could have a place in them."

They concocted a scheme that would serve as the prototype for Bechtel's famous "turnkey" contract. For a fixed fee, the company would design a project, build it, and deliver it to the owner complete at a set date, and ready to turn the key and start operating. The concept of a negotiated contract rather than a bid contract would be the company's signature for decades to come. It was an outgrowth of Steve's philosophy to free the firm from competitive bidding and to control the entire project. "The client benefits because this arrangement makes possible the close coordination of engineering, procurement, and construction with the continuity needed to deliver the most plant in the least time," Steve described it. "We like responsibility. We have organized and prepared for it, and we have scored our greatest successes when we have had control of projects in their entirety." He envisioned a "wholly self-contained economic technical organization able to handle projects of any size anywhere, from feasibility study to finished plant."

The two would also be credited with inventing the clever "cost-plus" model of a business contract in which the government guaranteed contractors all *costs* of production *plus* a built-in profit of 10 percent. They decided to partner in a firm that would not only seek government contracts but also market to private industry, offering the mushrooming oil companies an entire construction package. "Not just pipelines, but storage tanks, refineries—the works," as one account described their vertical integration model. They formed the Bechtel-McCone Corporation and opened a Los Angeles headquarters in May 1937. McCone became president, and Steve, with controlling interest, became chairman. "It was a success from the start," Steve boasted later. They soon brought in as a partner Ralph M. Parsons, a forty-year-old Chicago refinery designer and aeronautical engineer. But Parsons's tenure would be short due to a personality conflict with the irascible McCone.

Bechtel and McCone made a formidable team. Steve was a heavy-set "jaunty fellow," a workaholic and consummate salesman with male-pattern baldness and naked ambition. McCone was a tough "hard-boiled" man with a "molten temper"—a rigid Catholic convert whom muckraker I. F. Stone once accused of having holy war views. Bechtel thought McCone "the perfect material for a business partner," once describing him as "a real grind, with rare analytic ability and no-nonsense personality." Bechtel-McCone obtained immediate contracts in the fields of both petroleum and chemical processing. SOCAL hired the firm to build a refinery in Richmond, California; Hercules Powder Company contracted for an ammonia plant; Union Oil Company awarded a contract for a solvent treatment plant; and Standard Oil Company of Venezuela brought them in to build three pipelines in that country. Before Bechtel-McCone was formed, there had been only one Bechtel concern that had evolved from Dad's early contracts throughout the West. Now there were two distinctly different entities divided according to undertaking. W. A. Bechtel Co. pursued heavy construction projects, while Bechtel-McCone specialized in engineering and construction of processing plants and refineries. Steve remained at the helm of both.

Barely a year after its formation, Bechtel-McCone had more than ten thousand employees working on pipelines, chemical plants, and oil refineries throughout the West and extending into South America. But even those burgeoning start-up results were paltry compared with what was about to come. In 1939 Adolf Hitler invaded Poland, and by June 1940, Nazi Germany controlled Belgium, Norway, the Netherlands, Denmark, Luxembourg, and France and was preparing to launch an air assault on Great Britain. It didn't take any "great foresight," as the company's internal history put it, to see that America would soon be drawn into the war in Europe. "Like others, the Bechtels were alert to the implications and lost no time getting their resources ready for the country's service." Two years earlier, Bechtel and McCone had studied the shipbuilding industry, envisioning a new market that "seemed about ripe to become a big-volume business," Steve would say.

Once again, the federal government would deliver a historic, unprecedented boon to the Bechtel combine. In 1939, in preparation for war, the US Maritime Commission announced the creation of a massive shipbuilding operation and called for bids on a wartime cargo fleet. The British followed, declaring that it sought American shipyards to rebuild that country's antiquated merchant fleet. Since the eastern shipbuilders were operating at full capacity, both the British and American naval services were seeking contractors on the Pacific Coast. By summer 1940, the various Bechtel entities—a veritable syndicate of interwoven companies and subsidiaries—were building the navy's air bases in Texas and the Philippines, the army's Fort Ord and Camp Roberts in California, and its massive aircraft modification center at Birmingham, Alabama, where the B-24 and B-29 bombers were retrofitted. Before the end of 1940, Bechtel-McCone had a $210 million order for sixty freighters—a contract that would swell to $3 billion within the next three years. Thanks to government contracts, Bechtel-McCone became one of the world's largest shipbuilders of cargo vessels, tankers, and troop transports, earning McCone the moniker "the American Onassis."

At the same time, they built the top secret 1,600-mile pipeline from Canada to Alaska in the face of the most remote and rugged conditions. Under the aegis of the War Department—and in response to what Bechtel called the "Japs" threat to Alaska—the CANOL project was so clandestine that no formal contract was executed. Its budget was buried in a war appropriations bill. The four thousand workers would not learn of the location until they arrived in the unexplored Yukon wilderness, where, as the "Bard of the Yukon," poet Robert W. Service described it, "the mountains are nameless and the rivers all run God knows where." A congressional investigation led by Missouri senator Harry S. Truman found that the obfuscation on the part of Bechtel and the War Department was less about the Japanese and more about hiding the project from a longtime Bechtel critic, Secretary of the Interior Harold Ickes. By the time the pipeline was completed, two years behind schedule and just three months before the

Japanese surrender in 1945, the costs had quadrupled from $25 million to $100 million, with Bechtel and McCone profiting enormously.

Enwrapping their empire building in patriotism, Bechtel's official statements proclaimed that the company had "just begun to fight!" and was "strengthening the nation's sinews for war." With his typical cockiness—albeit with some validity—McCone told a Washington audience that without the ships produced by Bechtel-McCone, "the war would have been lost." Perhaps their nationalistic instincts were sincere—for they had "built the ships that carried the guns that had won the war," as their sponsors saw it. But their detractors, which included members of a congressional investigative committee, were equally passionate. The two men had turned an initial investment of less than $100,000 into gross revenues of hundreds of millions—bounty that many in Congress considered obscene plunder. "I daresay," testified Ralph E. Casey of the General Accounting Office (GAO) in 1947, Congress's watchdog arm, "that at no time in the history of American business, whether in wartime or peacetime, have so few men made so much money with so little risk and all at the expense of the taxpayers, not only of this generation but of generations to come." Still, despite numerous allegations of wartime profiteering lodged against Bechtel-McCone, no formal charges materialized. Since the firm was held privately—like all of the Six Companies spin-offs—it was impossible to "cast up a worthwhile profit-and-loss statement," *Fortune* reported, despite the fact that the monopoly was built entirely with public money.

CHAPTER SIX

Patriot Capitalists

"We're not worried about any postwar letdown," Ken Bechtel told a magazine at the war's end. It was a moment when wartime contractors feared the public trough would dry up. "For us, the postwar is the period when we will really come into our own." With distinctive prescience, the Bechtel enterprise turned its attention overseas to war-torn Europe and the oil-rich Middle East. Steve's vision was not unanimously endorsed within the family firm, but his brash insistence overcame the internal resistance. "Nobody around here wanted to go foreign," one of his senior executives recalled the pushback against Steve's international diversification.

Bechtel-McCone had first moved overseas with the construction of the far-flung naval bases stretching ten thousand miles from Alameda, California, through Pearl Harbor, Midway, Wake Island, Guam, and the Philippines. During the war, the firm had also built refineries in Saudi Arabia for the Arabian American Oil Co. (Aramco), as well as the entire Aramco headquarters city at Dhahran, and railroads, port facilities, and highway systems for the Saudi royal family. Called "quasi-industrialists" by *Fortune* magazine, the company's tentacles were beginning to reach around the globe. "Size can work to your advantage if you think big," Steve once told *Time* magazine. "You just recognize it and move the decimal point over."

Along the way, Steve Bechtel and John McCone had made millions of dollars personally through buying large blocks of stock in their wartime clients' companies, such as SOCAL. After the war, their interests diverged, with McCone preferring to work for the government rather than private industry. The result was the formation of a new umbrella entity that included all of McCone's and the Bechtel family's corporate interests. Steve would guide the new megacompany, now called the Bechtel Corporation, while McCone advised the Truman presidential administration on matters relating to military preparedness and the creation of the Department of Defense.

McCone's move into the highest circles of government—first in defense and atomic energy, and ultimately in intelligence as director of the CIA—marked the genesis of the infamous "revolving door" that would define the Bechtel business model for the rest of the twentieth century and beyond. For a multibillion-dollar-a-year corporation whose profits were dependent on government contracts, the value of such high-level government access would be incalculable. In 1946, with McCone ensconced in official Washington, Steve Bechtel bought a controlling interest in the firm from McCone and other Bechtel family members, signaling what the company called "the birth of the modern Bechtel Corporation." With Steve in command of all operations, "the company took off like a rocket," according to his friend and lawyer, Robert L. Bridges.

Steve formed a series of new corporate entities under his total control. He broke the family's long-standing ties with Henry Kaiser and other Six Companies executives and brought in a new team of professional managers. Like-minded in temperament and vision, Steve's men mirrored his conservative values: stalwart churchgoers, Boy Scouts loyalists, and earnest teetotalers. Native Californians who were educated primarily at Berkeley and Stanford, they were "hard-working WASP Republicans with equally hardworking WASP Republican wives," a journalist observed. The Bechtelians were a colorless, sober bunch. "They are not always the easiest people to deal with—you wouldn't want to go out for a drink with them after work," a corporate insider once told a newspaper. "But they get the job done."

The most notable exception—and most crucial addition to the

company going forward into the profitable Cold War period—was John Lowery Simpson, the uncle of Steve's wife, Laura. Erudite and worldly, the San Francisco–born Simpson traveled in the most rarified circles of national and international finance and intelligence. He had spent the years leading up to and during World War I in Europe, where he worked for Herbert Hoover's brainchild, the Commission for Relief in Belgium, which controlled the distribution of food in German-occupied territory, and had become a close personal friend of the future US president. A classic Renaissance man, Simpson embraced the adventures and opportunities presented during his seven-year tenure in Western Europe—a stint that "determined the entire future course of my life." Brilliant and curious, cultured and fluent in three languages, the 1913 Berkeley graduate recalled being "full of virtue and high purpose" upon joining Belgian Relief. "Everything followed directly or indirectly from that decision," he wrote, "interests, vocation, avocations." And, especially, the associations he made with US government and business figures that lured him into the complex realm of America's nascent intelligence apparatus.

As Steve's closest confidant and lifelong financial partner, Simpson possessed the stellar Wall Street and OSS credentials that set the stage for Bechtel's future fortune building. It was Simpson who would collaborate with influential government officials to insure the Bechtel family's trajectory in Washington for decades to come.

A voracious reader, Simpson had gone to Europe with literary ambitions, planning to pursue a career as a novelist and essayist. Based in Paris, he became an unabashed Francophile, immersing himself in the contemporary French literature of Anatole France and attending the theater, opera, and symphony. But when he was recruited by a fellow American "who had some sort of relationship with our Government although not a defined official status," as Simpson put it, his calling took a turn. He decided to become an "actor in" rather than an "interpreter of" the world scene when he was enticed into what he described as "a rather Machiavellian scheme" to alter economic patterns and international trade relations by selling relief grain to bankrupt

countries. "At this point I hope the incident is no longer classified," he
would write decades later. "It was rough play, but that is war . . . I was
picked because I was considered discreet." In his clandestine work for
the US government, Simpson thought he was "making history" and
"saving the world," while creating a great American trade organization
along the lines of the legendary nineteenth-century British firm Balfour, Guthrie and Company.

Upon his return to the United States shortly after World War I,
Simpson joined the New York office of J. Henry Schroder Banking
Corporation—an investment bank founded in Germany that had become a global financial empire. There Simpson met three men associated with the firm who would do as much to direct the hidden forces
of American government for the rest of the century as any other figures: John Foster Dulles, Allen Welsh Dulles, and William "Wild Bill"
Donovan. The Dulles brothers and Donovan—powerful lawyers for
the Schroder firm—were impressed with Simpson's keen mind and his
compatible view of world affairs. They invited him into an elite, secret
organization known as "the room," which was a cabal of three dozen
bankers, businessmen, and corporate lawyers with backgrounds in intelligence who met in a nondescript Upper East Side brownstone to
discuss geopolitical events throughout the world.

Simpson rose through the Schroder organization, becoming a director and shareholder. During World War II, he took a leave from
the firm to become the chief financial advisor for the US Army in Europe. Based in Switzerland—where Allen Dulles, as OSS station chief,
was running a shadowy network of intelligence operatives out of the
American Embassy in Bern—Simpson served as a liaison between
Schroder's clients throughout the world and the OSS. "An intelligence
agency had been created for the first time in the United States which
brought together under one roof the work of intelligence collection and
counterespionage," Allen Dulles later described the OSS, antecedent
to the CIA, "with the support of underground resistance activities,
sabotage, and almost anything else in aid of our national effort that
regular armed forces were not equipped to do." As Simpson navigated

between Schroder and the army, he passed along vital intelligence information that he gathered in his travels to both Dulles and Donovan. The latter would become known as "the father of Central Intelligence."

As the war wound down, Steve Bechtel made an overture to the well-connected "Uncle John" Simpson, asking him to join the newly incorporated Bechtel Corporation as a consultant on "major politics, finance, and foreign operations." In 1946 Simpson took Steve up on the offer, becoming chief financial officer of Bechtel. While Simpson brought a much-needed monetary expertise to the company, it was his role as a rainmaker that was his real value. Among those to whom Simpson would introduce Bechtel were the Dulles brothers. (John would become secretary of state under President Dwight D. "Ike" Eisenhower, while Allen would become the first civilian director of the CIA.)

With Simpson, the company gained entrée not only into the highest levels of the American government but also into the blue-chip world of East Coast and international finance. As an original stockholder in the prestigious Schroder firm, Simpson's associates included Avery Rockefeller and C. Douglas Dillon of Dillon, Read & Company. Through Simpson, Steve would be invited to become a director of J.P. Morgan & Company in New York. Simpson's contacts would also result in Steve's election to membership in the Washington-based Business Council—an exclusive group of major corporate executives invited to meet with the president, members of the Cabinet, and other key government officials to weigh in on matters of foreign, domestic, and economic policies.

Once Simpson joined Bechtel, the air of secrecy and furtive arrangements more evocative of a spy agency than a multinational corporation took hold. The firm's executives moved between the murky world of national intelligence and the only slightly more transparent dominion of private industry. Soon the lines became ever more opaque, and it was often difficult to determine if Bechtel Corporation was doing favors for the US government, or if it was the other way around.

"Fast friends and golfing buddies," one account described the relationship between Steve Bechtel and Allen Dulles. While "shanking
irons into the Pacific at Pebble Beach, the two men would discuss the
clandestine opportunities for a privately owned firm like Bechtel in
Dulles's shadow world." Increasingly, their conversations took on the
tones that would dominate the next decades in American politics:
"America's unadvertised geopolitical intent." Internationalist, probusi-
ness reactionaries, the two men traveled in what one author described
as "those lucrative thickets where business, politics, and diplomacy
overlap." Convinced that the national security of America depended
upon its access to oil, and containment of the Soviet Union, they
turned their attention to the Middle East, which they saw as ground
zero for future American—and Bechtel—supremacy in the world.

Encouraged by Dulles to step up its operations in Saudi Arabia—
where the company had built a refinery and pipeline in 1943—Bechtel
became entrenched in the Persian Gulf. Steve began cultivating King
Abdul Aziz ibn Saud, that country's spiritual and temporal leader,
whom he considered a "forward-looking monarch"; his son, Prince
Faisal; and "a tight circle of Saudi advisers." The relationship that
Steve built with the Saudi royal family, as well as with a family-run
empire called Bin Laden Construction, would transform Bechtel into
a "globe-girdling behemoth."

With projects that included secret defense installations, military
bunkers, airports, railways, chemical and fertilizer plants, and palaces
for potentates, Bechtel eclipsed its few rivals in the Middle East, con-
tributing to the rise of the notoriously potent oil cartel OPEC, or the
Organization of Petroleum Exporting Countries. "In the Middle East
program I cannot help but foresee tremendous possibilities pointing
towards potentially the biggest development of natural resources ever
undertaken by American interests," Steve announced to his board of
directors in 1947.

CHAPTER SEVEN

The Largest American Colony

"Bechtel Corporation, which is to the United States what the Bin Laden construction firm is to Saudi Arabia, a colossus itself and a maker of colossi . . . emerged from the building of the Hoover Dam to become a major force in reshaping the West and then the world," wrote journalist Rebecca Solnit in 2009 about the exploitation of the Colorado River. Bechtel, boasting of its benevolent efforts to "modernize this ancient region and bring prosperity to its peoples," vowed to build the first contemporary nation in the Arabian Desert. "If only the pharaohs could have hired Bechtel," a press commentator once quipped about the company's creation of modern kingdoms.

A major part of Steve's postwar restructuring of the company involved creating International Bechtel Inc.—an entity that would be the backbone of his and Simpson's vision of expansionist capitalism. From the beginning, the new division was meant to capitalize on the cultivation of Saudi leaders. Allen Dulles and the OSS were simultaneously seducing the Saudis with millions of dollars in financial inducements designed to guarantee a steady supply of oil to the United States. Geologists working for Standard Oil Company of California—the company in which Steve was invested and McCone was the second-largest stockholder—had discovered this ostensibly inexhaustible supply of fossil fuels. As a result, SOCAL received an exclusive fifty-year right to search for oil across 395,000 square miles. Bechtel prepared to transform primitive Saudi Arabia—the most oil-rich nation on earth—into "a country that could match any in the world with highways, utilities, airports, and the other manifestations of modernity."

Reminiscent of Black Canyon on the Colorado River, eastern Saudi Arabia was an inhospitable wasteland where temperatures rose to 120 degrees Fahrenheit. When Steve arrived there in July 1947, he found one of the least explored regions of the world, with no vegetation or potable water—not "even a Bedouin camp to break the monotony." Undaunted, Steve was prepared to tackle what he saw as the biggest job since Hoover Dam—the Trans-Arabian Pipeline from the Persian Gulf to the Mediterranean Sea. "This thirty-inch, four-hundred-thousand-barrel-per-day line will be the mightiest pipeline ever laid," Steve crowed to company managers, "bigger than any oil line yet completed and almost as long as the Big Inch line running from Texas to New York." Prior to this project, oil moved from the Middle East to Europe through a time-consuming, circuitous, and costly tanker route from the Gulf through the Indian Ocean and the Red Sea, and then through the unpredictable Egyptian-controlled Suez Canal. The new 1,100-mile "Tapline," as it was called, would deliver four hundred thousand barrels of oil a day from Saudi Arabia to "Europe's back door" at a fraction of the previous cost, while also creating what Bechtel proclaimed to be "the largest American colony between France and the Philippines."

Bechtel described it as "one of the most extraordinary of all engineering and construction projects ever carried out by private enterprise in a far country." It would have been a dream contract for any American company, but for Bechtel it was only the beginning, kicking off an eighty-year monopoly of the lucrative economic and industrial development of the Middle East. Apart from the oil companies, no other American company was as embedded in the region, thanks to the close personal relationships Steve established with the Arab leaders who were keen to modernize their desert kingdoms. His friendship with ibn Saud was particularly intimate, especially after Bechtel built a project dear to the king's heart: the first operating railroad in Saudi Arabia since T. E. Lawrence—Lawrence of Arabia—led his guerrillas in attacks against the Hejaz section of the Ottoman rail line during World War I.

"For all their obvious differences, the warrior king and the builder shared a pragmatic, unsentimental understanding of how the world worked," wrote Laton McCartney in his 1988 book about Bechtel. Indeed, once Steve pledged to King Saud that Bechtel would not hire Jewish elements in building the Tapline and assured him further that Bechtel didn't "possess any plant, firm, or branch in Israel," their bond was sealed. Arab outrage at US backing for a Jewish state in Palestine carried over to American companies, but Steve—one of the largest contributors to support Palestinian refugees—assuaged that indignation. Bechtel was "part of the corporate-intelligence team fighting against the Zionists," as the 1997 book *The Secret War Against the Jews* described the milieu of the time.

That Steve also promised to secure a $10 million loan to Saudi Arabia through the Export-Import Bank of the United States (Ex-Im) must have provided further enticement for ibn Saud, for he called upon Bechtel to build "everything from pipelines and gas-oil separating plants to houses and office buildings, and from power plants and transmission lines to hospitals and bowling alleys," according to the company's official historian. Soon Bechtel would build all of the sewer systems, roads, and airports in the thriving nation, and as oil profits amassed, the royal family contracted Bechtel for castles and palaces for the various crown princes.

"STEPHEN BECHTEL INFORMED ME TODAY HIS FIRM HAS ASSOCIATED ITSELF FOR EXTENSIVE OPERATIONS NOW PLANNED IN THIS COUNTRY," US ambassador J. Rives Childs cabled from Saudi Arabia to the secretary of state in Washington in February 1947. "BECHTEL STATES WORK CONTRACTED FOR WILL REQUIRE AT LEAST 2000 AMERICANS AND 10 TO 20 THOUSAND SAUDIS." Called the "Camel Legionnaires," the thousands of Bechtel laborers were soon building the new desert empire in a land where sweltering heat and a shortage of drinking water took a devastating toll on workers. The Bechtel-built work camps, called "Little

Americas," were hotbeds of brawling and drunkenness, and, as with Hoover Dam, complaints of worker abuse were settled privately by "a payment or bribe to the Arab," as the American Consulate in Dhahran wrote to the State Department.

"The king and his advisers asked their new American friends for materials and construction help," wrote Steve Coll in his book *The Bin Ladens: An Arabian Family in the American Century*, "but Aramco and the companies it had invited to Saudi Arabia, led by the Bechtel Corporation of San Francisco, were busy constructing infrastructure for the new oil economy."

Saudi Arabia was just the staging ground. From there Bechtel moved up the Persian Gulf to Kuwait, where it built the largest oil-loading jetty in the world. Representatives of the Kuwait Oil Company "came down to take a look at what we were doing in Saudi Arabia, and we went up there to check out their operations," Steve recalled in an interview. "Pretty soon they had us building refineries in Kuwait. Then their parent company, British Petroleum, which also owned Iraq Petroleum, asked us to build the pipeline from Kirkuk to the Mediterranean for Iraq Petroleum." That pipeline route crossed the Syrian Desert, through the ruins of Palmyra—a "city-state that existed as far back as the twelfth century before Christ," as the company described it, while claiming that the "gangs of Arabs with hand shovels" working on the line "may have been descendants of the very people who built roads for the ancient Romans through the same area." That line increased the world's oil supply by over three hundred thousand barrels per day.

At the time, the six-thousand-square-mile desert country of Kuwait was inhabited by Bedouins, herders, and pearl fishers who for generations had lived a precarious lifestyle given that "apart from a few brackish wells, it had no potable water," according to a contemporaneous account. All of that changed in 1947, when Kuwait's crude oil reserve was among the largest in the world. Bechtel moved into that country and replicated all that it was undertaking in Saudi Arabia, including the drilling of dozens of water wells for the commodity even more precious than oil. Making "life easier for man and beast in a harsh environment," Bechtel depicted its altruistic role in the Middle East. "As one well after another was brought in, concrete troughs were set up. The word spread among the Bedouins. Soon thousands of camels, sheep, and goats were brought to drink their fill."

From its Saudi base, Bechtel expanded operations into Yemen, Lebanon, Iraq, Libya, Palestine, Syria, and Iran. "In this business, you get to know people, sit on their boards, and one day when something comes up, they ask you to take on a project," Steve explained the company's good fortune and fortuitous connections. "One thing leads to another." Indeed. By midcentury, Bechtel was the largest engineer-constructor of oil transportation and processing facilities in the Middle East. From 1944 to 1957, Bechtel's work for Aramco alone "was of such volume and variety that any detailed description of it would become unwieldy and bewildering," according to the company's own privately published account, *Bechtel in Arab Lands*, which is dedicated "to the oil companies."

Throughout the Middle East during that thriving period, Bechtel executives also gathered intelligence information of both economic and military significance for the US government's newly created CIA. In the postwar run-up to the Cold War, American agents coveted information about the Soviets' encroaching spheres of influence. The US government reciprocated by providing Bechtel with vital, often classified, information that benefitted the company's foreign operations. Allen Dulles, along with other high-level government officials, had been pushing Arab regimes into infrastructure development as a bulwark against the Kremlin. "As oil flowed during the late 1940s, the Bechtel Corporation negotiated a cost-plus contract with the Saudi government to undertake an ambitious plan, influenced by Washington, to help lift the kingdom into the modern capitalist age," wrote Coll. The company so mirrored the CIA by participating in intelligence gathering and providing cover to CIA agents that it was widely considered a government surrogate, if not a full-fledged government enterprise by both the political leaders of the countries in which it operated, as well as by its rivals in industry.

Upon the recommendation of William Donovan, the chief of the OSS, Congress had created the CIA with the National Security Act of 1947 to confront the dangers of the new postwar world. President Truman signed the act into law, and formed what one account described as "an elite East Coast Ivy League Wall Street clique, patriotic but arrogant, and often amateurish." Soon to be at its helm was Steve Bechtel's friend and colleague Allen Dulles, known for his "weakness for old-boy grandstanding, OSS-style." At the heart of US foreign policy directing the embryonic Cold War establishment—of which creating the CIA was a cornerstone—was an intense belief in free-market mechanisms combined with an ardent anti-Communism. The godless Soviet Union was the designated superthreat, with its Moscow-sponsored proxies throughout Eastern Europe, Africa, Asia, Latin America, and the Middle East. The Dulles worldview—endorsed by Steve Bechtel and John Simpson—held that "threats to corporate interests were categorized as support for Communism." Dulles thought Soviet leaders were at the center of a global conspiracy bent on annihilating the West and capitalism, what diplomat George Kennan described as "a great political force intent on our destruction."

These Cold Warriors saw the Middle East as the epicenter for Soviet expansion into areas of vital commercial and security interest to the United States. As the Ivy League spymasters launched the covert operations that would eventually scandalize the new intelligence agency in the public's eye, the ever-patriotic Bechtel and Simpson were eager to assist. When the civilian Syrian government that was hostile to the United States and Bechtel was overthrown in 1949 and replaced by a Bechtel-friendly military dictatorship, deposed officials suspected Bechtel of providing arms and funding to the rebels. Though Bechtel denied any involvement in the coup, the US State Department credited an unnamed "multinational corporation" with assisting.

"I have talked this over with Steve," Simpson wrote to Dulles in December 1952 about the CIA's request that Bechtel determine whether the Iranians had the technical capability of building a pipeline to Russia, "and he entirely agrees with me that we should like to do anything we possibly can to be of service." Steve assigned George Colley Jr.—Bechtel's pipeline chief and senior vice president—to oversee a study of Iran's technological capability. Concluding that Iranians could indeed build a Russian pipeline, Colley's report alarmed the CIA, which, along with the oil cartel, had begun plotting against the popularly elected prime minister, Mohammad Mossadegh, who had nationalized British Petroleum the previous year in a move that unleashed "political forces he could not control." Convinced that Mossadegh was not strong enough to resist a Soviet-backed coup, the CIA hatched Operation Ajax to overthrow him. Restoring Shah Mohammad Reza Pahlavi to the Peacock Throne secured "Persia's oil petroleum for the five major U.S. oil companies," as former national security advisor Roger Morris depicted the American motives.

The 1953 CIA-supported coup installed one of the most vicious and brutal dictatorships in the region, and "Bechtel's 12-volume industrial-development plan for the country has strengthened, not loosened, the Shah's grip," investigative journalist Mark Dowie concluded twenty years later.

CHAPTER EIGHT

Going Nuclear

While Allen Dulles was masterminding the "New 'Cold War' Plan Under Secret Agents," as the *Boston Globe* headlined it, John McCone, who had become an extreme hard-line anti-Communist and major defense contractor, was moving up the ranks in Washington. In 1950 US defense secretary James Forrestal had appointed McCone undersecretary of the US Air Force, which had been formed three years earlier out of what had been a division of the US Army, and where he was in charge of procurement and where, according to an FBI report, "he favored his friends in the granting of contracts." In that capacity, he organized the top secret nuclear Strategic Air Command (SAC), "which put planes in the air twenty-four hours a day armed with nuclear bombs ready to bomb Russia if so ordered," according to one account. Throughout the 1950s, McCone played a key role in developing defense policy, urging President Truman, unsuccessfully, to build a guided missile program. He helped pen a report entitled *Survival in the Air Age* that led to a historic increase of the defense budget.

A "rightist Catholic," as one political pundit called him, McCone was fanatical about the designs of the Soviet Union, which he considered to be nothing short of global domination. The only way to combat that godless tyranny, as McCone saw it, was a massive military buildup with an intensive emphasis on creating a vast nuclear weapons stockpile. In addition to fashioning a muscular air force, complete with a robust anti-Soviet doctrine promoted by the hawks in the Truman Cabinet, he prepared the first two budgets of the newly unified National Military Establishment—a merger of the Department of War and the Department of the Navy created by the National Security Act of 1947—and worked with Forrestal in the creation of the CIA. "The strong-willed, stern-looking multimillionaire was not of the stuff to inspire love among the bureaucrats," wrote two journalists of McCone's unpleasant demeanor. A man so rigid that he flinched when addressed by his first name. "When he smiles, look out," a CIA official was once quoted as saying.

Along the way, McCone developed close personal relationships with like-minded anti-Communist crusaders—most notably, in addition to Dulles and Forrestal, the five-star general who would soon be president, Dwight Eisenhower. This powerful clique, comprised of devotees of media baron Henry Luce's pleas for internationalism as an extension of American influence throughout the world, embodied what Luce called "The American Century." Published in 1941 in his *Life* magazine, the editorial was the interventionists' call for America to forsake isolationism and assume the role of world leadership in the face of Nazi aggression and the Soviet Union's expansionist geopolitical designs. "We are the inheritors of all the great principles of Western Civilization," Luce wrote. "It now becomes our time to be the powerhouse."

McCone was a zealous promoter of this "devil theory" of the Soviet Union as an evil empire intent on America's destruction. In his fanaticism he joined an elite group of what a Luce biographer described as "men of great mental vigor who sank to narrowest parochialism in the area where the molten materials of their religion, patriotism, and politics fused into one great cold and flinty mass." McCone's unwavering support of this radical strategy against the Soviet Union manifested especially in the atomic warfare theories he embedded in the inchoate air force. Truman had responded to McCone's recommendations for an atomic buildup by tripling the capacity of the principal nuclear weapons plant at Oak Ridge, Tennessee, and constructing gaseous-diffusion facilities for uranium enrichment in Portsmouth,

Ohio, and Paducah, Kentucky. Proud of his influence at the highest levels of government, McCone was even more gratified that his long-time friend Steve Bechtel would be the chief contractor on all three projects.

While McCone's sway within the Truman administration was impressive, it was minor in comparison with the authority he would wield with Eisenhower—his golfing buddy and the commander of the North Atlantic Treaty Organization (NATO)—who had solicited, and then followed, McCone's advice about running for the White House on the Republican ticket in 1952. President Eisenhower would reward his friend with an appointment in 1957 as chairman of the Atomic Energy Commission—an agency with a $2 billion budget. With an eye once again toward helping Bechtel, McCone's tenure at the AEC expedited the transfer of the control of atomic energy from military to civilian hands, with Bechtel positioned to rake in billions along the way.

Bechtel and McCone had been involved with atomic energy long before the AEC was created, dating back to the Manhattan Project. Officially established in 1942 in response to the report from scientist Albert Einstein to FDR that Nazi Germany was building an atomic bomb, the top secret project was under the direction of J. Robert Oppenheimer at Los Alamos Scientific Laboratory in New Mexico. Bechtel-McCone was in on the ground floor of the largest, most complex scientific undertaking in the history of the world: the $2 billion Allied project, dispersed among numerous laboratories, which involved more than two hundred thousand people. Bechtel's role began with the construction of a facility at Hanford, Washington, and it would go on to obtain the first AEC contract at Los Alamos.

On August 6, 1945, under orders from Truman, a B-29 aircraft dropped the first atomic bomb in world history on the Japanese city of Hiroshima. Three days later, the United States dropped another nuclear bomb over Nagasaki, bringing a Japanese surrender and an official end to World War II. As one history described the sudden dilemma, "It was only after the bombing of Hiroshima and Nagasaki that the enlightened intelligentsia of the United States began to ask: *What*

*should the country do with the capability of destroying the human race,
and who should control the weapon?"*

As details of the mass destruction, unspeakable suffering, and
deaths of 225,000 civilians began to surface, Oppenheimer and the
other Los Alamos scientists fell into bitter disputes about the proper
course of developing and controlling this power. The United States
now had a weapon capable of ending all of civilization—of wiping
out the two billion people then living on earth. "Mr. President, I feel
I have blood on my hands," Oppenheimer told Truman—a remark
that infuriated the president, who had little patience for the nearly
three hundred scientists who were warning of the dangers of an arms
race, nuclear terrorism, and "the impossibility of any defense against
the atomic bomb in future wars." Annoyed by the scientists' apocalyptic alarms and attempts to influence government officials, Truman
sought to muzzle them. His administration labeled anyone who favored a peacetime atomic energy policy a traitor, placed Oppenheimer
under surveillance, gagged the scientists, and endorsed a Joint Chiefs
of Staff proposal for increasing the production of nuclear weapons.

World leaders sought new foreign policy approaches to nuclear energy, with the US supporting a United Nations proposal for international control directed toward peaceful purposes. But that plan was
rejected by the Soviet Union, which claimed the US had an unfair advantage since it already possessed nuclear weapons. Following the Soviets' successful detonation in 1949 of its first atomic bomb, Truman
had backtracked from the push for international control and began
advocating for a strong nuclear arsenal that showcased a "Super" thermonuclear fusion-based hydrogen bomb. On November 1, 1952, the
US tested its first H-bomb and Russia followed suit less than a year
later. The Cold War arms race had officially begun. In a United Nations speech known as "Atoms for Peace" in 1953, newly elected President Eisenhower called for the world to strive toward a reduction in
nuclear weapons and an increase in peaceful applications.

Despite Eisenhower's appeals, the nation's scientific and political
communities divided into the arms racers and the arms controllers—

what one history described as "two permanently opposed Cold War camps." Steve Bechtel and John McCone came down on the side of the arms racers. The Hungarian-born Edward Teller, the controversial physicist who had broken with his pacifist colleagues in favor of the massively destructive H-bomb, led the arms racers faction. "More horrific than the atomic (fission) bomb, the Super (fusion) bomb would surely escalate the nuclear arms race," wrote Kai Bird and Martin J. Sherwin in their definitive biography of Oppenheimer.

During the 1956 presidential election, McCone, then a trustee of the California Institute of Technology, and an avid sponsor of the H-bomb, had tried to get ten Caltech faculty scientists fired when they came out in support of a proposal to suspend the H-bomb testing. Incumbent Eisenhower's Democratic opponent, Adlai Stevenson, who had been roundly defeated by Eisenhower in the previous presidential election, had proposed a nuclear test ban treaty. An overwhelming majority of the nation's scientists had embraced Albert Einstein's criticism of the international community's failure to control nuclear weapons, as epitomized by his famous remark: "I do not know how the Third World War will be fought, but I can tell you what they will use in the fourth: rocks." When questioned during his confirmation hearings about his meddling with Caltech faculty, the stern, silver-haired McCone shared with congressmen his accusation that the professors were exaggerating the danger of radioactive fallout. "Your statement is obviously designed to create fear in the minds of the uninformed that radioactive fallout from the H-bomb tests endangers life," he wrote to the scientists. "However, as you know, the National Academy of Sciences has issued a report this year completely discounting such danger."

McCone was equally enthusiastic about handing over fissionable materials to private industry—particularly to Steve Bechtel. Described by the *Wall Street Journal* as a "conservative who believes in the capacity of private enterprise to deliver the goods," McCone was determined to give Bechtel access to the nation's most secret nuclear technology. One of the biggest boosters for the AEC funding of commercial nuclear power, as chairman he cleared the way for federal subsidies to pay private utilities for the construction of nuclear plants. Bechtel had long-standing connections with the California utilities, dating back to Hoover Dam, and he had built steam and hydroelectric plants for Pacific Gas and Electric (PG&E). But now he was impatient to extend his reach. "Going nuclear" would be the venue. "Nuclear power was a mechanism for getting Bechtel into the power plant business," said W. Kenneth Davis, head of the AEC's reactor program, whom Bechtel lured away, along with several of his top aides, in 1958 to open the company's new nuclear division. Davis thought his hiring "was a considered move." Davis ridiculed the naysayers of nuclear energy. He advocated building power plants as close as possible to consumers—such as on the outskirts of New York City—claiming that nuclear power "will not bring undue safety hazards to plant workers or public." Steve moved to preempt public opposition to nuclear energy, pouring money into a public relations campaign about its safety. A near meltdown of a Michigan nuclear reactor in 1966 inspired the sensational 1975 book *We Almost Lost Detroit*, which helped spawn the antinuclear movement. In response, Steve "helped finance the opposition to antinuclear referenda," according to later press accounts.

Disregarding Truman's warning that the development of nuclear energy was too dangerous to be driven by profit, the Eisenhower nuclear policy, guided by McCone, embraced its commercialization. Within a few short years—thanks to AEC contracts—Bechtel would be the world's largest supplier of nuclear power. Not surprisingly, the company, which had developed the boiling water nuclear reactor and built the AEC's Experimental Breeder Reactor in Arco, Idaho, would receive billions of dollars in government contracts to build the dozens of nuclear power plants being planned throughout the land. Steve Bechtel was one of a handful of people in the world who witnessed the first powering of a light bulb by nuclear fission. McCone—who had swung the Dresden, Illinois, contract to Steve as the first privately financed nuclear power plant in the US—showed up in 1960 at its dedication to praise it as "the largest, most efficient, most advanced" power plant in the world.

Meanwhile, McCone's harshest critic, nationally syndicated columnist Drew Pearson, was one of the only American journalists to challenge the revolving door between the AEC and Bechtel. McCone "ignored the legal opinion" of the AEC's general counsel that a Bechtel project was illegal, wrote Pearson in 1959, "and went ahead with the contract benefitting his former company." Pearson also criticized McCone for not selling his stock in various private Bechtel-McCone enterprises that continued to do business with the government while he was head of the AEC, describing a "pattern of business links McCone has kept with his old associates and war profiteers." Wisconsin Republican senator Alvin O'Konski went so far as to accuse McCone of being "merely on leave of absence from his position as Bechtel-McCone Corporation president." Senator Abraham Ribicoff of Connecticut was also alarmed at how many employees of the AEC were hired away by Bechtel. The AEC had created an industry "so incestuous that it was hard to tell where the public sector begins and the private one leaves off," Ribicoff complained.

Pointing out that McCone was involved with the company that operated the first atomic merchant vessel ever built—the *Savannah*—Pearson called on Congress to investigate McCone's blatant conflicts of interest. "McCone said he had done 'a great deal of soul-searching' and had concluded he could handle the AEC chairmanship without any favoritism," Pearson wrote. "However, the AEC law does not permit a man to search his soul and make the decision. The law makes the decision for him."

In the camp of what Pearson called the "big bomb" fans, McCone favored the spread of US nuclear technology to overseas allies. Pearson accused McCone of "telling the public one thing and doing another," while undercutting international disarmament discussions. During the "world's last chance to prevent the spread of nuclear weapons," Pearson wrote, McCone "has been calling on Senators behind Ike's back to oppose the State Department," which advocated keeping nuclear weapons out of the hands of other nations.

One of McCone's projects while at the AEC was his attempt to provide Bechtel with small nuclear reactors that could be used for building tunnels and extracting oil. "McCone was positively rabid about the notion," according to one account. "Think, he asked, of the things a Bechtel . . . could do with a few atomic bombs in its toolbox!" But Eisenhower quashed that scheme with a resoundingly simple, "No."

CHAPTER NINE

McConey Island

No one was more representative of the business and political culture of Bechtel in the modern era than John McCone. His grasp of the world oil economy and the cultivation of Arab states was singular. His vision of American exceptionalism, of corporate capitalism unfettered by regulations and interference, and of the symbiosis between government and private industry, would set the stage for Bechtel's operations during the second half of the twentieth century. McCone would ascend from the AEC to the CIA, where he would oversee the expansion of that agency—a reshaping of the US intelligence complex that would result in yet more staged coups and global interventions. Bechtel would benefit immensely.

In addition to directing highly profitable contracts his way, McCone enhanced Steve Bechtel's national and international influence by bringing him into Eisenhower's inner circle, where he would play a furtive, largely unseen role. During McCone's tenure at the AEC, Bechtel—who had been a significant supporter of Eisenhower's presidential campaign—was a familiar face at the White House. Eisenhower appointed him to a position on the President's Business Advisory Council, and at a confidential White House dinner held to "discuss implications of the Sino-Soviet economic offensive and what the US can do to counter it," Steve underscored to Eisenhower the national security necessity of a close relationship between government and private business, according to a confidential White House memorandum.

Eisenhower, Bechtel, and McCone golfed together at exclusive all-male clubs and exchanged admiring notes. "Steve Bechtel is the kind of American you want to have on your side," Eisenhower advised his vice president, Richard Nixon, recommending that Nixon consider Bechtel for a Cabinet appointment should he accede to the presidency. "There were many chores Steve Bechtel and his company would perform for presidents, many favors they would do—and had done—for the organs of government," wrote Laton McCartney in *Friends in High Places*, "including, though few knew it, the Central Intelligence Agency." Eisenhower brought Steve to Washington to assist Undersecretary of State C. Douglas Dillon in determining policy for the distribution of foreign aid and development loans—financial aid that would line Bechtel's coffers. It was Dillon who had arranged contracts for Bechtel with the Saudi Arabian government. In 1958 the president invited "two oil men," including Steve, to serve on a secret panel to study "Soviet economic warfare"—an invitation that Secretary of Commerce Sinclair Weeks feared would be "very bad" if any publicity exposed it. Steve was also a clandestine presidential advisor on "the intelligence structure of the government," according to a later declassified, top secret White House memorandum.

An FBI background report described McCone as one of Eisenhower's closest personal friends and an ardent believer in the president's domino theory: a notion that if one country succumbed to Communism, other countries would follow. Presidential administrations used his concept from the 1950s through the 1980s to justify American foreign policy exploits and interventions around the globe.

As a charter member of the San Francisco–based National Committee for a Free Asia—a covert action organization determined to "roll back the dark forces of Soviet imperialism," according to its 1951 originating prospectus—Steve Bechtel's anti-Communist credentials matched those of McCone. The *New York Times* would later expose the committee as a front organization for the CIA, which was but one of many deep and long-standing affiliations between Steve and the intelligence community which he proudly embraced. He also served as the CIA's liaison with the Business Council—what a renowned sociologist described as "the unofficial board of directors within the power elite." In that capacity, Steve provided regular reports to the CIA based upon intelligence information culled by him and other council members, which included top executives from the nation's largest multinational corporations.

The relationship went both ways. Among the more shadowy operatives that moved between the two entities was a sartorially elegant, British-based Standard Oil consultant named Cornelius Stribling Snodgrass, who became a key executive at Bechtel. A "dashing figure in Savile Row suits," as one account portrayed him, the West Virginia native once described his position to King Saud's finance minister, Abdul Suleiman, as "in charge of all affairs and relations between the Saudi Arab Government and International Bechtel, Inc." In that capacity, Snodgrass would brief his handlers in both the CIA and State Department on Bechtel's activities in Saudi Arabia, while also gathering information from his contacts about not only government interventions in international hotspots but also about projects being undertaken by Bechtel corporate rivals. While on the board of Bechtel, Snodgrass participated in National Security Council (NSC) and CIA meetings where top secret covert operations such as the Iranian coup were planned, and then provided Bechtel with classified intelligence that would further its business interests.

When Snodgrass officially left Bechtel in 1952, he formed a small energy consulting firm called LSG Associates that was a Washington-based CIA proprietary firm. He also founded a lobbying firm, with Bechtel as a top client. "With the assistance of Snodgrass and his similarly well-connected successors . . . Bechtel's operations increasingly mimicked those of the CIA," as one account depicted the synergy between Bechtel and national intelligence, as well as the compartmentalization common to covert operations. "The company drew up its plans and plotted its business operations with the same devotion to secrecy and clandestine intelligence-gathering as its governmental associate, much of them based on reports furnished by friends at the CIA and the Departments of State, Commerce and Defense."

The CIA reciprocated in kind by providing Steve with information about economic and political developments overseas from which Bechtel could profit. The foreign countries in which Bechtel operated—and where the company was often considered an exploiter—did not always welcome the interdependent relationship between the company and the agency. Bechtel was generally seen as the most brazen of those at the heart of what one national security advisor described as the "inequitable modernization by U.S.-purchased oligarchies." Perhaps nowhere was this clash vented so starkly as in the violent murder in Iraq of Bechtel Senior Vice President George Colley.

On Bastille Day in 1958, the Iraqi army laid siege to the royal palace in Baghdad and killed the US-sponsored ruling family. Seen as a symbol and manifestation of venal Western imperialism, Colley was seized by soldiers while breakfasting at the luxurious Baghdad Hotel, and shoved into a waiting black limousine along with several other American and Jordanian hotel guests. In a few blocks, the car was surrounded by fifty Iraqi civilians, who pulled some of the occupants out of the car and began stabbing, beating, and bludgeoning them. Colley was last seen being dragged from the vehicle, stoned, and dismembered by the mob. CIA agents on the ground—who had supported the corrupt monarchy overthrown by the revolutionaries—tried to retrieve Colley's body. In the following days, an Iraqi army search of all hospitals and morgues failed to find any trace of him. Even Allen Dulles, CIA director at the time, was powerless to help, cabling Bechtel "MY FRIENDS REPORT THAT COLLEY STILL MISSING BUT THAT SEARCH IS CONTINUING." Iraqi officials concluded he had been "buried in a common grave," along with other Americans taken that day. The swashbuckling Colley had been one of Dad Bechtel's earliest hires, for a road job in Nevada, and had long been Steve's closest personal friend. Steve was never able to talk about Colley's death without tearing up, and his deep-seated animus toward Iraq's revolutionary leaders would never subside.

The McCone connection in Washington seemingly became even more valuable to Bechtel after 1962, when President John F. Kennedy called McCone off a California golf course where he was playing with JFK's archrival Nixon, and asked him to replace Allen Dulles as director of the CIA. "The Agency and the company have rarely pursued separate interests since then," as one journalist put it. A fellow Catholic with a reputation as a "hard-nosed executive who could get things done quickly and efficiently," according to authors David Wise and Thomas B. Ross, McCone impressed JFK's brother, US Attorney General Robert Kennedy, who had been looking around for a successor to Dulles after the disastrous Bay of Pigs. The previous year, a CIA-sponsored paramilitary group launched an invasion of Cuba to overthrow Fidel Castro. The invading force was defeated within three days, prompting an infuriated and humiliated President Kennedy to blame Dulles and a bungling CIA. JFK is reported to have said he wanted to "splinter the CIA into a thousand pieces and scatter it into the winds," and sought a tough-minded reformer to rein in what he thought had become a rogue agency.

Secret CIA plots to destabilize the Cuban government and assassinate Castro had also backfired. Kennedy, a Democrat, was under intense criticism from Republican critics who accused him of being soft on Communism. "With his paper-thin mandate and a majority of only six in the Senate, he believed the problems of his administration would come primarily from the right, and felt impelled to make overtures," historian Barbara Tuchman described Kennedy's decision to hire McCone. Hoping the appointment of a right-wing zealot would fend off his enemies, he settled on McCone, whom his father, Joseph P. Kennedy Sr., had known from their wartime shipbuilding days. Joe Kennedy had the government contract for shipyards in Massachusetts. McCone was appointed "at a time when the agency was expanding its arrangements with American corporations to provide cover to CIA operatives and to share in intelligence gathering, particularly in countries like Iran, Algeria, and Libya, where Bechtel was constructing, designing, or pursuing large projects," according to a later press account.

"He shuns the press, makes no public speeches, grants no inter-views," wrote Jack Anderson about McCone. Anderson, who was Drew Pearson's associate at the Washington Merry-Go-Round column and who would become known as the father of modern investigative jour-nalism, joined Pearson in exposing the kind of cronyism he thought McCone embodied. "Even on his rare appearances before congressio-nal committees, he speaks softly and scarcely moves his lips," Ander-son described McCone. "During his first year as boss, he has drawn the cloak of invisibility ever tighter around the CIA. He would like it to vanish from the limelight altogether." A humorless man, McCone had moved to shake up the CIA, making it what Anderson called a "tauter, more efficient cold-war instrument," dubbed "McConey Is-land" by his detractors. He grasped the significance of the modern and evolving information-gathering technology. Obsessed with the National Security Agency's inability to break high-level Soviet codes, he sought to assert the CIA's leadership in this area. A "disciple of massive retaliation," Barbara Tuchman wrote of McCone, "who, in the opinion of the Neanderthal Senator Strom Thurmond, 'epitomizes what has made America great.' "

The CIA during these early Cold War years was engaged in what political scientist Andrew J. Bacevich described as an "all-out, no-holds-barred conflict" with the Soviet Kremlin, its clandestine wars "wrapped in an armor of moral certitude." Engaged in actions that under most circumstances would have been considered repugnant, if not diabolical, the agency was systematically "disseminating false information, suborning foreign officials, planning acts of sabotage, overthrowing governments, and ordering assassinations." McCone advocated overt intervention as well as more clandestine plots. While he had taken the position that an embargo against Cuba was prefera-ble to a full-scale invasion, he also felt that if a military offensive be-came necessary, that it should be done with sufficient force "to occupy the country, destroy the regime, free the people, and establish in Cuba a peaceful country."

If brought in to reform an out-of-control organization, McCone's

"Central Intrigue Agency," as Drew Pearson called it, would instead become what Kennedy's vice president, Lyndon Johnson, described as "a damned Murder Inc." If McCone's elevation to director of the CIA was meant to curb that agency's meddling in foreign intrigues, it had the opposite effect. While McCone was director, the CIA escalated its black operations, spearheading numerous covert plots around the world, including Laos, Ecuador, and Brazil. He directed the 1963 coup that brought the Ba'ath Party to power in Iraq and by decades-end gave rise to a "twenty-six-year-old Tikriti street thug named Saddam Hussein (himself a CIA-paid asset) along with lists of hundreds of left-leaning Iraqi political figures and professionals to be murdered after the coup," according to a former national security advisor. He also supplied mercenaries and arms to Joseph Mobutu, the corrupt and vicious leader of the Congo, where Bechtel and other American corporations had vast investments in copper, gold, and diamond mines.

On November 22, 1963, McCone was lunching in his private dining room at the CIA headquarters in Langley, Virginia, with his deputy director, Richard Helms, when he heard the news that President Kennedy had been shot in Texas. At the time, the CIA had gotten so out of hand that Helms wondered aloud if CIA operatives were involved in the president's assassination. "Make sure we had no one in Dallas," Helms said to an aide moments after learning of the shooting. McCone then rushed to Robert Kennedy's home in McLean, Virginia, and stayed with the president's brother for three hours while no one else was admitted to the Hickory Hill compound—not even the family priest. "McCone's agency had been trying to kill Castro, and just two months earlier Castro had threatened to retaliate if the assassination attempts continued," Anderson wrote, claiming that the two men anguished over the possibility that the assassination was blowback from the CIA attempts on Castro. When word came that the president had died, they "walked back and forth, back and forth, between the tennis court and the swimming pool," according to Kennedy aide Arthur Schlesinger. In one of the most dramatic exchanges in American history, Kennedy asked McCone: "Did you kill my brother?" Kennedy later said that he believed McCone's answer that the CIA had not been involved in the assassination. "I asked him in a way that he couldn't lie to me, and they hadn't," he told his aide Walter Sheridan.

The following day, McCone briefed President Johnson and told him that intelligence reports suggested "Castro was behind the assassination." Assassin Lee Harvey Oswald had not only visited the Soviet Embassy in Mexico City, meeting with the consul, a KGB agent named Valeriy Kostikov, who was an assassinations specialist, McCone told LBJ, but Oswald "had also gone to the Cuban consulate." A month later, McCone told Johnson aide Bill Moyers that he did not believe that Oswald had acted alone. "McCone thought there were two people involved in the shooting," Moyers related his conversation with McCone to Schlesinger.

CIA documents declassified in 2013 revealed that Castro felt he was being set up to take the blame for the crime, which would have spurred the US invasion of Cuba that hawks such as McCone and others in the administration had long advocated. In the aftermath of the assassination, Castro sent a back-channel message to Washington that he wanted to meet with investigators "to dispel the swirling allegations that Cuba was responsible." The day after the assassination, Castro publicly labeled the assassination "a Machiavellian plot against our country" to justify "immediately an aggressive policy against Cuba . . . built on the still warm blood and unburied body of their tragically assassinated President."

Indeed, according to the CIA documents, at the time of his death, Kennedy had reached out to Castro about normalizing relations between the two countries. At the moment Kennedy was shot, Castro was meeting with an emissary whom Kennedy had sent to Havana on a "mission of peace"—a prospect anathema to reactionary sectors in American government. The two men were lunching in Cuba, discussing Kennedy's offered olive branch, when Castro received a phone call reporting that Kennedy had been shot. "This is terrible," Castro told the messenger. "There goes your mission of peace. They are going to say we did it."

McCone, especially, was apoplectic at the possibility of rapprochement with Cuba, advocating the "most limited Washington discussions" on accommodation with Castro. He continued peddling the Castro connection theory long after the Warren Commission investigating Kennedy's assassination dismissed it. Johnson kept McCone on at the CIA where he was among the warmongers in the administration, becoming one of the earliest promoters of intervention in Southeast Asia. McCone had disagreed adamantly with JFK's interest in seeking conciliation with the Soviet Union, and, especially, with his decision to try to withdraw from Vietnam. He preferred LBJ's Vietnam policy, and in a memorandum to the president, he recommended the deployment of more troops to "tighten the tourniquet" on North Vietnamese Communists. Bechtel would be one of the two top contractors to build the Vietnam War infrastructure; the other was Texas-based Brown and Root, which for decades had financed LBJ's rise to power, and would later become Halliburton. "The two firms built air bases, landing fields, military compounds, roads, ports, support facilities, and energy depots throughout Southeast Asia," according to one history. A postwar audit by the Congressional Budget Office would reveal that Bechtel and Brown and Root "had billed the government for so much concrete that they could have put a concrete skin eight feet deep over the entire country of Vietnam."

In the end, McCone's legacy in both government and industry would be one of global saber rattling, covert intervention, war profiteering, and billion-dollar energy and defense contracts for his associate on the West Coast. McCone was "the greatest organizer in the United States," Steve told Jack Anderson.

CHAPTER TEN

Weaving Spiders

"In the councils of government, we must guard against the acquisition of unwarranted influence whether sought or unsought, by the military-industrial complex," President Eisenhower had warned in his 1961 farewell address to the nation. "The potential for the disastrous rise of misplaced power exists and will persist." He cautioned against the unhealthy alliance between defense contractors, the Pentagon, and their friends on Capitol Hill. "We must never let the weight of this combination endanger our liberties or democratic processes," he continued. "We should take nothing for granted. Only an alert and knowledgeable citizenry can compel the proper meshing of the huge industrial and military machinery of defense with our peaceful methods and goals so that security and liberty may prosper together."

Yet even Eisenhower could not have foreseen the near-total influence the defense industry would have over American foreign policy in the coming decades. Among the inherent ironies of Eisenhower's grim prescience is how two of his associates—John McCone and Steve Bechtel—would become iconic figures of his envisioned military-industrial complex. "Rarely does a big Pentagon construction project surface that doesn't have a role set aside especially for Bechtel," a press account said of Bechtel's twenty-first-century position as one of the country's top defense contractors.

Eisenhower had long worried about a post–World War II Japan turning toward China and Russia, sounding an alarm as early as 1954 that the shift of Indochina toward Communism would usher in such a tilt and declaring that the "possible consequences of the loss of Japan to the free world are just incalculable." Steve Bechtel, along with fellow California industrialists, was at the forefront of developing a Pacific Rim strategy that would open the resources of Southeast Asia to American capitalism. To Bechtel, the Vietnam conflict extended far beyond the battlefield—although his company was profiting from the war—into the creation of what one newspaper account described as a San Francisco–based "powerhouse gateway to hundred-million-dollar business ventures in the Pacific."

The intellectual thrust of this new Pacific Republic headquartered in the San Francisco Bay Area was the potent Bechtel-dominated think tank, the Stanford Research Institute (SRI). Initially conceived by President Hoover, SRI was created by a group of West Coast businessmen in 1946 and modeled on the Chicago-based Armour Research Foundation's stated principles of "the Co-ordination of Motives, Men, and Money in Industrial Research." Steve was a founding director of SRI—a high-technology scientific research organization that was affiliated with Stanford University. It would become the second-largest corporate-government funded policy institute in the country and the largest contract research firm in the world. "SRI's Pacific Rim strategy, however, amounted to nothing more than a sophisticated rephrasing of the domino theory," one critic charged, quoting an official SRI document that the "war in Vietnam . . . must be viewed as a struggle likely to determine the economic as well as the political future of the whole region." Steve was the most influential SRI policy maker, who "kept asking that the amount of international work be 'doubled and doubled' again . . . his perseverance was exceeded only by his insistence." SRI's close alliance with the US Defense Department would ultimately incite violent antiwar student protests in the spring of 1969, prompting Stanford University to sever its ties with the controversial facility. Privately, Steve railed against the campus demonstrators, calling them Communist rabble-rousers antithetical to his professed motto of "devotion to family, country, and company."

STAGES OF CONSTRUCTION IN THE BUILDING OF BOULDER DAM
ALL VIEWS TAKEN FROM THE SAME POINT, LOOKING UPSTREAM.

COMMENCEMENT OF CONSTRUCTION 1931

FIRST CONCRETE POURING 1933

THE DAM HALF COMPLETED 1934

BOULDER DAM TODAY 1936

This vintage postcard from 1936 shows the construction of Hoover Dam in four different stages, with all views taken from the same point looking upstream. Called the "Eighth Wonder of the World," it would be known as Bechtel's historic, signature project.

The safety violations and labor unrest that characterized Hoover Dam's construction site earned for Dad Bechtel the reputation of the "bête noire of American labor." By 1931 more than two-thirds of the work force were threatening to strike. Bechtel and his partners blamed the labor unrest on outside Communist rabble-rousers.

Warren A. "Dad" Bechtel and a few of his business partners and engineers associated with the construction of Hoover Dam. Although they were the most powerful contractors in the West, none had the singular ability to take on the nation's largest construction project. Calling themselves Six Companies, the men borrowed the name from the Six Tongs of San Francisco's Chinatown. From left to right: Bechtel, Walker R. Young, Elwood Mead, Frank Crowe, and R.F. Walter.

In November 1980, Reagan was elected president in a landslide. In what would become known as the "Reagan Revolution," the election marked a historic, conservative realignment with the American Southwest as the unmistakable new power center. The Bechtels were among the coalition of reactionary, antigovernment, rugged individualist western corporate titans that had made Reagan's political victory possible.

President Reagan with Caspar Weinberger, George Shultz, Ed Meese, and Don Regan—the White House chief of staff—in the Oval Office discussing the president's remarks on the Iran-Contra affair on November 25, 1986. Iran-Contra was a labyrinthine conspiracy to trade weapons to Iranian leaders in exchange for seven American hostages. Weinberger, a seasoned traveler through the Bechtel/government revolving door was later indicated for his role in Iran-Contra. Before he was tried, he received a pardon from president George H.W. Bush.

President Reagan leads a cabinet meeting flanked by two of his closest advisers, whom he had recruited from Bechtel—Secretary of State George Shultz and Defense Secretary Caspar Weinberger. March 13, 1987.

President Richard Nixon walking with his national security advisor, Henry Kissinger, on the White House lawn. The two were obsessed with political events in Chile, where socialist president Salvador Allende had threatened to nationalize utilities in which American corporations were heavily invested. Front and center in the machinations that led to the coup overthrowing Allende, was John McCone—former CIA director and Bechtel principal, now an ITT director.

An anti-Vietnam war protestor tied to a cross. The war spawned violent antiwar student protests throughout the country. Stephen Bechtel Sr. privately railed against the campus demonstrators as Communist rabble-rousers.

In July 1959 in Moscow, Soviet leader Nikita Khruschev and Vice President Richard Nixon engaged in a heated exchange about capitalism and communism. Tempers flared as the two men taunted each other. Dubbed the "Kitchen Debate," the tense confrontation came to epitomize the Cold War and the fervent anticommunist sentiments of the Bechtel family.

Steve Bechtel Sr. had cultivated a close relationship with the Iranian shah, Mohammad Reza Pahlavi, seen here with President Nixon at a reviewing stand in Washington, DC. A US-backed coup had deposed the democratically elected prime minister of Iran, Mohammad Mossadegh, who had nationalized that country's oil interests, and installed the pro-Western shah. The shah supported Bechtel's Iranian projects, and was considering Bechtel's proposal to build eight nuclear reactors and to invest in an Alabama nuclear plant to be built by a Bechtel consortium.

11

LEFT: Bechtel employees install a power pole in Mississippi after the Category 5 Hurricane Katrina caused severe destruction in the Gulf of Mexico in August 2005. The very day the hurricane struck, the US government's Federal Emergency Management Agency (FEMA) contracted with Bechtel to provide mobile homes for 100,000 people in the region who had been displaced by the storm.

BELOW: The legendary, nationally syndicated columnist Drew Pearson, seen here in the White House garden with President Lyndon Baines Johnson in 1964, was the harshest critic of John McCone and Bechtel. Pearson, and then his equally legendary successor, Jack Anderson, drew repeated public attention to the crony capitalism and revolving door they thought McCone and Bechtel epitomized.

12

13

Greg Mello, executive director of the Los Alamos Study Group, thought Wen Ho Lee "was an invented crisis, not an intelligence operation." As Mello saw it, the arrest of Lee as a spy set the stage for the nation's nuclear laboratory to be transferred into private hands.

14

Oakland California attorney J. Gary Gwilliam. In May 2008, just months after Bechtel took over, Lawrence Livermore National Laboratory in California laid off 430 career employees. Gwilliam took on 130 as clients in a high-profile case against the Bechtel-led lab manager, calling the privatization of the lab a "corporate takeover."

The Bechtel family donated millions to SRI and reaped enormous rewards from its applied research projects and economic analyses. "Among its many programs, SRI evaluated the US strategic force; conducted laser radar studies in the upper atmosphere; analyzed ballistic missile defenses; drew up studies for improving Air Force reconnaissance and surveillance systems and played a leading role in developing the US response to the launching of the Soviet Sputnik satellite," according to one published report. SRI conducted untold numbers of studies for Bechtel's direct financial advantage, including a probe into the development potential of a tiny fishing village in Saudi Arabia, where Bechtel would receive a contract to build a city from the ground up. That city would ultimately swell to a population of 370,000.

As the family's first billionaire, Steve had spent six months of every year roaming the world, "hobnobbing with kings, presidents and foreign business magnates, fishing for projects," *Time* magazine once reported. "In his overseas dealings, Bechtel has been like one of [Rudyard] Kipling's admired Men Who Get Things Done, forming partnerships with native firms when required and employing local help," as California writer John van der Zee explained Steve's business practices. He was so powerfully connected in the region, he once called in the British Royal Air Force "to buzz a group of bickering Arab tribesmen until they were frightened back into pipeline work."

During this period, Steve took a "more relaxed" approach to soliciting business, taking a trip around the world with no particular aim, as Bechtel Vice President Jerome Komes recalled. He "would fly to London for lunch with old friends from British Petroleum or to pay a courtesy call on the head of Imperial Chemical Industries. In Paris, [Steve's party] would discover that J. Paul Getty was staying in the same hotel, Steve would give him a call, and they would get together to talk about world business—Getty's concession in Kuwait, for example." President of Getty Oil Company, the American tycoon had amassed billions from a sixty-year oil concession he obtained from Ibn Saud in 1949 to drill in a barren tract of land between Saudi Arabia and Kuwait where no oil had previously been discovered.

Given Steve's legendary hands-on involvement, it came as a surprise when, with little fanfare, he turned over the company to his
thirty-five-year-old son, Steve Jr., on Christmas Day 1960. Steve
Sr., as the father was now called at the company to distinguish him
from his only son, remained a behind-the-scenes dynamo, with the
title of chairman. Retiring as a fit and energetic sixty-year-old—then
second only to oil-tanker tycoon Daniel Ludwig as the richest man
in America—was an unprecedented move for a proactive CEO of a
multinational corporate empire. But he thought his son ideally suited
to usher the company into its third generation of leadership. When
Steve Sr. had taken over, Bechtel had revenues of less than $20 million.
At his retirement a quarter century later, the company's reported sales
were $463 million. In the decade between 1950 and 1960 alone, rev-
enues had more than doubled. *Fortune* proclaimed his legacy as "the
boldest and maybe the biggest builder in the world," placing his name
alongside Henry Ford, John D. Rockefeller, and Andrew Carnegie in its
US Business Hall of Fame.

Steve Jr., a trained engineer with a master's in business administration from Stanford, was indoctrinated in the family business since
his childhood visits to the Hoover Dam worksite and his teen years
at the Bechtel-McCone shipyards. But his strong will, self-discipline,
and pride precluded him from assuming the position as a birthright.
He took his father's offer under advisement for a few weeks before ac-
cepting, with conditions. "If you want me to take over, I will," he told
his dad. "But I'll have to do it my way. When I take over, I'm the boss."
Steve Sr. agreed. As a welcoming gift, he asked his longtime advisor,
"Uncle John" Simpson, to articulate to Steve Jr. how the company had
been so successful and to suggest a path to continued profits.

With Simpson's report in hand, Steve Jr. "began working on a
major overhaul of the company" for a changed world and a new generation, according to the Bechtel website. "Energy use, fed by growing
economies everywhere, was on the rise, fueling strong demand for petroleum products, natural gas, and electric power. The need for production, processing, and transportation facilities was increasing. New

projects were getting bigger and more venturesome. This was also the golden age of spaceflight; anything was possible." In Texas, Bechtel built the largest petrochemical plant in the world, and in Puerto Rico, the world's largest chemical plant. In San Francisco, its Bay Area Rapid Transit (BART) system was the first totally new rapid transit system built in the United States in forty years.

Steve Jr. extended the Middle East projects, cultivating relationships with some of the world's more unsavory figures, including Mu'ammar al-Qaddafi of Libya, the Shah of Iran, and eventually Saddam Hussein of Iraq. At the height of the company's Arab exploits, Bechtel also branched out into mining in South Africa and South America, nuclear plants in Spain and India, pipelines in Canada and Alaska. For the next decades of the company, Steve Jr. also sought to dominate the resources in the American West, such as coal, uranium, oil, and gas.

Continuing his father's and grandfather's inveterate antilabor stance, Steve Jr. joined fellow business tycoons in a 1966 "hush-hush" meeting with Mexican counterparts to discuss how to fend off that country's labor demands and keep Mexico's "alleged socialist" government from interfering with their profits. "With all the secrecy of a military operation, 26 top-drawer American business executives slipped below the border" to Cuernavaca, shelling out " 'gratuities' to Mexican aviation officials to omit registration of the private planes in which most of the U.S. contingent arrived," wrote columnist Anderson. The four-day meeting at the swanky La Posada Jacarandas was so secret that the entire resort was closed to other guests. Bankrolled by the National Industrial Conference Board—an antiunion organization run by the chairman of U.S. Steel—discussion at the meeting "would have made the uninformed believe that Mexico was about to follow Cuba into the Soviet orbit."

Back in the United States, Steve Jr. was becoming a behind-the-scenes powerbroker in the rise to the US presidency of a like-minded California politician: the anti-Communist and domino-theory devotee Richard Milhous Nixon. Since his defeat in 1960 at the hands of John F. Kennedy, Nixon had been developing his theme of the importance of the Pacific Basin to the stability of the United States. Like other political leaders before and after him, and at the behest of Steve Jr., Nixon floated his concept at the Bohemian Grove—the 2,700-acre retreat located in a private redwood forest seventy-five miles north of San Francisco. "The world's most prestigious summer camp," as *Newsweek* called it, the guarded retreat is "the country's extension of San Francisco's all-male ultra-exclusive Bohemian Club."

The Grove has hosted the nation's corporate, political, and military elite every summer since 1880. Once described by President Hoover as "the greatest men's party on earth" (a non sequitur apparently lost on Hoover, who was once described as "that swinging Bohemian . . . who was running for the presidency on a 'dry' platform"), the Grove is where emerging geopolitical trends are discussed in the privacy of 127 primitive camps. The most esteemed of these camps is Mandalay—named for the Kipling poem—where Steve Jr., like his father before him and his father's partner, McCone, had been a member his entire adult life, following the patrilineal formation of the Grove. A "virtual personification of Eisenhower's military-industrial complex," author Joan Didion once pronounced Mandalay's roster of members and guests.

"Here, shielded from intrusion by a chain-link fence and the forces of the California Highway Patrol," wrote Laton McCartney, "men like Justin W. Dart, William F. Buckley, George Bush, Edgar Kaiser, Jr., and Tom Watson could walk in the woods, skinny-dip in the Russian River, toast marshmallows over a fire, dress in drag for a 'low jinks' dramatic production, and, for a few days at least, hew to The Grove's motto: 'Spiders Weave Not Here.' " Its edict, taken from Shakespeare's *A Midsummer Night's Dream*, refers to a strict directive that prohibits Bohemians from explicitly conducting business at the Grove. So much as an exchange of a calling card could get one ejected, or so the pretense goes.

"The all-maleness of the Club reaches back into a patriarchal past that saw women as inferior humans and encouraged the celebration of male superiority in private associational settings," wrote California sociologist Peter Martin Phillips. Long a political networking headquarters for Republicans, the Grove has hosted every Republican president since Calvin Coolidge and nearly every other GOP presidential hopeful, including Herbert Hoover, Dwight Eisenhower, Barry Goldwater, Nelson Rockefeller, Richard Nixon, Gerald Ford, George H. W. Bush, Ronald Reagan, and George W. Bush, along with dozens of Cabinet members, military generals, astronauts, government scientists, and White House officials. "I knew that I was in Bohemia when I saw Eisenhower and Nixon pissing on the same tree," a guest once remarked.

It was at the Grove that Herbert Hoover had announced his presidential candidacy. Where Allen Dulles, as a guest of Steve Sr., had warned of the threat of Communism. Where Eisenhower, then an army general, had presaged armed conflict in a faraway place called Korea, and where he later gave a political address that set him on the path to the presidency. So it was in keeping with a long-standing tradition that in 1967 Nixon would unveil his Pacific Rim thesis at Bohemian Grove as a precursor to a presidential run. Energized from a recent trip to Asia, he recounted finding that some of America's most stalwart anti-Communist allies were advocating a thawing of hostilities between the United States and the People's Republic of China. Using the forum as the basis for a public speech he would give a few months later, "Nixon declared that most Americans did not understand the growing importance of the Pacific basin; the vital role of Japan; and, above all, how to deal with China," according to authors Peter Wiley and Robert Gottlieb.

At the Grove summit, Nixon stayed at the Bechtels' Mandalay Lodge. It was there that one of the more legendary Grove meetings took place—decrees against deal making notwithstanding. Nixon met with a fellow guest, Ronald Reagan, California's first-term governor who was his main rival for the upcoming Republican presidential nomination. Reagan's hope of receiving the nomination in a brokered convention was known. But at the Grove that summer, over a drink and an informal chat, Reagan promised to stay out of the 1968 presidential race unless Nixon "faltered."

Nixon did not falter. He secured the nomination on the first ballot and went on to win a close contest against Democrat Hubert Humphrey, the sitting vice president. Steve Jr. had bet on the right candidate. Between Nixon's 1969 inaugural and his 1974 resignation, there followed a dizzying array of government projects directed to Bechtel— a period in which the company's gross annual revenues jumped from $750 million to nearly $2 billion. And that was only the beginning.

CHAPTER ELEVEN

Covert Corporate Collaboration

Comparisons to his father were predictable. Family successions inevitably generate anxiety and scrutiny, and the Bechtel leadership transition was no exception. Fewer than one in three companies survive through a second generation, and the odds plunge to one in ten among those that reach a third, according to *USA Today* research. "The biggest challenge is helping the younger generation take hold while helping the senior generation let go," observed a business analyst. "You can't put two fannies in a black leather chair." Employees inevitably pondered the old adage that with family businesses, the first generation starts it, the second runs it, and the third ruins it. "It's very unusual for one company to have this kind of dynastic continuity," San Francisco historian Gray Brechin told the *Los Angeles Times.* "When you start getting a lot of descendants, they always squabble."

Dubbed "Junior" by his detractors within the company, Steve Jr. was slight, humorless, and dull, in stark contrast to his blustering, larger-than-life father. But what he lacked in charm and intellect, he made up for in energy and tenacity. "He was in a terribly difficult position, taking over from the largest builder in the world, and it had to leave scars," a kindly employee told an interviewer. "Around the company, he was regarded as the not-so-smart, not-so-great, not-so-dynamic son of Steve senior. He could run a tight ship, be an excellent businessman and a good builder, but he didn't have his father's flair." His modus operandi called for team management—a method he

believed "permits common men to do uncommon things." He grasped
figures and analyzed data in ways his father had never been able to
do. "Steve Sr. was imaginative, intuitive, instinctual," said a company
executive. "He was the best salesman who ever came down the pike,
the best business development person the company ever had . . . But
he never had the patience with numbers that Steve Jr. has."

Still, he matched his father in workaholism, traveling 250,000 air
miles a year and regularly working sixteen-hour days. A plodder, he
didn't excel in high school but enjoyed math, science, mechanical engineering, and shop, and was a solid enough student in those subjects.
Competitive by nature, Steve Jr. had been a victorious sailboat racer in
high school, and he attributed his later success in life to the steadfastness of that experience, along with the way in which he personified the
Boy Scouts credo. He thought the saying "steady at the helm" from his
sailing ventures taught him to "function well under pressure," just as
the "scout oath and laws . . . helped clarify and confirm my personal
values and beliefs," he once wrote. While still in high school, Steve Jr.
worked as a sweeper at a machine shop and then as a stake puncher—
punching reference marks on survey stakes at his father's shipyard.
These experiences taught him the "value of a dollar." He had enlisted in
the Marine Corps Reserve in his senior year during World War II, and
was called to active duty upon graduation. He went to the University
of Colorado as part of officer training and later, according to his bio
on the Bechtel company website, he transferred to Purdue where he
earned his engineering degree in two and two-thirds years instead of
four. The war ended without him seeing combat. In 1945 he returned
to Oakland and married a girl he had known in high school, Elizabeth
"Betty" Hogan, who was, by one account, "everything a Bechtel wife
was expected to be: ever-supportive, low-keyed, pleasant-mannered."
Her hobby was collecting twine, according to one account.

His father put him on the board of directors of the newly incorporated Bechtel Corporation, and Steve Jr. enrolled at the Stanford Graduate School of Business. This time he compressed a two-year MBA
program into one-and-a-half calendar years, which would suggest a

steadfastness and determination to compensate for an unremarkable intellect. He found the competition "fierce" but was gratified by the pride his father took in his accomplishment. Upon receiving his graduate degree, his parents took him and Betty on a three-month cruise around the world—a belated honeymoon—visiting Bechtel projects in Asia and the Middle East. His original thoughts of pursuing a real estate career evaporated once he saw Bechtel's far-flung worldwide projects. As they were returning home, Steve Jr. learned that Bechtel had just received a contract for a new pipeline in Texas. He leaped at the chance to become a field engineer on the project, working for Perry Yates, one of his father's most trusted colleagues. Over the next decade, he moved up the ranks, soon becoming Bechtel's manager for all pipelining projects.

Like his parents, Steve Jr. and Betty lived an unpretentious existence that belied their affluence, though each had a taste for luxury. With his new title came an upswing in the family trappings. While passing the torch, his father surprised them with a generous gift—a spacious house in Piedmont, the posh community surrounded by Oakland—complete with a swimming pool, tennis court, and a dining room that could seat fifty. There Betty created a comfortable, quintessentially 1950s household of polite and mannered children, while Steve Jr. ruled the family with the same strictness that Bechtel employees had come to expect from him. His five children—daughters Shana, Lauren, and Nonie, and sons Gary and Riley—were prohibited from crying in his presence, and he seemed to be perpetually disappointed in all of them except for Shana, the conservative and conventional oldest girl. But the traditional sphere of child rearing was left to Betty, as the peripatetic young executive rushed into the world of multinational enterprise.

It was a far different company from the one his father had inherited twenty-seven years earlier upon the completion of Hoover Dam, when Bechtel was but one entity in the Six Companies consortium. By 1960, it had become a corporate leviathan with more than two thousand completed projects in forty states, thirty countries, and on six continents. New forces and challenges were at play in the world, as Steve Jr. saw it—"environmentalism, globalism, economic upheaval, and intensified international competition"—and he was determined to overcome and exploit them as necessary. In the early part of the decade, Bechtel expanded and completed numerous endeavors around the globe, from the Chocolate Bayou petrochemical plant in Texas, to the prototype Dresden-1 nuclear plant in Illinois, to a commercial atomic power station in Tarapur, India, to a controversial pipeline in Libya.

"Of all the business relationships the Bechtel Corporation entered into over the years, none was stranger—and few more lucrative—than its alliance in Libya with the international entrepreneur who shared his name with a baking soda," Laton McCartney wrote of the provocative association between Bechtel and industrialist Armand Hammer. Bechtel had been operating in Libya since 1958, when it partnered with the corrupt former prime minister, Mustafa ben Halim, in a joint venture to build a pipeline from the Sahara Desert to the Mediterranean coast for Hammer's Occidental Petroleum. "Although ben Halim was held in high disgrace by most Libyans," journalist Mark Dowie wrote, "Bechtel was advised by the CIA that he was the man it would have to work with to build the pipeline." Bechtel was one of the few companies willing to work in Libya through the volatile climate of the 1960s, at a time when newly discovered Libyan oil was crucial to the West and a revolutionary coup against the nation's corrupt rulers seemed imminent. By 1967, Bechtel was the engineering and service arm for American firms producing oil in Libya that didn't want to send their own executives into the politically explosive environment. They paid Bechtel an 18 percent handling fee to manage their affairs in the country. The Occidental pipeline project—with an estimated cost of $43 million—included a monthly retainer to ben Halim to guarantee his support. Occidental "used Bechtel to build the line and make payoffs to Libyan figures," wrote former Bechtel employee and international oil industry consultant Christopher T. Rand in his 1976 exposé, *Making Democracy Safe for Oil: Oilmen and the Islamic East.* By the time Bechtel completed the pipeline, it had raked in $147 million in profits and lost fifteen men along the way.

But it was with Nixon's 1968 election that the financial floodgates opened for Bechtel, as the company became integrally tied with the president's foreign policy and energy policy agendas. Nixon embraced Bechtel because the company could be useful to his Pacific foreign policy aims, especially in China. Nixon appointed both Steve Sr. and Steve Jr. to plum government posts that enhanced the company's financial portfolio. Steve Sr. assumed a position with the advisory committee of the US Export-Import Bank—an entity that funnels below-market, risk-free, federally guaranteed loans to American corporations to enhance their competitiveness with foreign enterprises, and that would add billions to Bechtel's assets over coming years. While Steve Sr. was on the advisory board, Ex-Im loans to Bechtel included $13.5 million for nickel production, $107 million for a nuclear plant in Brazil, $100 million for a pipeline in Egypt, and $439 million for fertilizer plants and liquefied natural gas projects in Algeria.

Nixon appointed Steve Jr. to the Treasury Department's Labor-Management Advisory Committee—a banal-sounding board that was among the most elite bodies in the new administration. "Anyone on that committee had no trouble getting his views to the President," an engineering trade publication defined its influence. The company then extended its reach into development, finance, and investment, launching Bechtel Enterprises Holdings Inc., and Steve Sr. was no less a prevailing force than his son, making deals in South Africa, Chile, Spain, Indonesia, and Canada. Soon Bechtel was the leader in efforts to mobilize international venture capital for infrastructure projects worldwide—a position that would put it on a par with nation-states in its financial influence and autonomy.

It was a precarious moment in international affairs. America was bogged down in Vietnam, and virulent anti-American sentiment was roiling. In response, President Nixon initially continued the previous administrations' use of the CIA to meddle covertly in troublesome countries, such as LBJ's (and McCone's) 1965 agency-backed coup against Indonesia's leftist president Sukarno. The longtime leader had become forcefully anti-imperialist, nationalizing US business interests and threatening Bechtel's massive industrialization projects, which included an oil pipeline through the jungles of Sumatra. General Suharto replaced him and opened the country's vast natural resources to Bechtel, which would become the state-owned oil company's chief contractor not only for all oil projects but also for its liquefied natural gas operations. With Sukarno removed, Bechtel would receive millions in contracts to build one of the world's most complicated telecommunications networks in Papua New Guinea, as well as to develop a gigantic copper mine on the Indonesian part of New Guinea. Bechtel then hired the US ambassador to Indonesia, Francis J. Galbraith, as an international consultant. "The Indonesian Affair," as two American academics described it later, was one of "spies, lies, and oil."

On September 1, 1969, Nixon's CIA supported a coup to oust the Libyan government, which it considered too cozy with Moscow, and installed a young revolutionary leader named Mu'ammar Qaddafi. The young man had promised to protect "all Western interests, including the pumping of oil." Seeing Qaddafi as a stalwart against Soviet encroachment into Arab oil fields, the United States embraced him— until, in one of the first acts of his regime, he shut down the British and American military bases. But Bechtel, which had been operating in the country for over a decade, would ramp up its construction of refineries and pipelines, and stay on, sporadically, for decades to come. (The company would still be working with Qaddafi at the time of his capture and gruesome death during an American-sponsored 2011 coup.) After the rise of Qaddafi, and his challenge to American interests, other major oil-producing countries, led by Venezuela and Saudi Arabia, began pushing for OPEC's increased power in the international oil-pricing system. Iran, Libya, and Saudi Arabia began demanding that the major American firms share control of production with state oil companies.

While oil was a main catalyst in the rising Arab nationalism, a wider sentiment of anticolonialism was also spawning revolts throughout the world—uprisings aimed at nationalizing resources that had long been enriching American conglomerates while the indigenous populations languished in poverty. This radical nationalism—"meaning independent nationalism not under U.S. control," as Professor Noam

Chomsky of the Massachusetts Institute of Technology (MIT) wrote—was sweeping across the Middle East, Asia, and Latin America.

Particularly disturbing to the Nixon administration was Chile, where socialist president Salvador Allende had threatened to nationalize International Telephone and Telegraph (ITT)—the most prominent American corporation invested in the country, with a 60 percent ownership of the Chilean telephone company that was worth $225 million to ITT. At the instigation of John McCone—former CIA director, Bechtel consultant, and member of the board of directors of ITT—the CIA orchestrated a coup. In an unprecedented "covert corporate collaboration," as a national security expert described it, McCone offered $1 million in back-channel, untraceable dollars to the CIA to depose Allende. The scheme to destabilize the Allende government, and McCone's role in it, was first exposed in a series of syndicated columns written by Jack Anderson in 1972. Appearing on *CBS Morning News*, Anderson "hammered home the 'fantastic' story of how the CIA and ITT plotted to 'interfere in the domestic affairs in Chile.' " Allende died during the September 11, 1973, coup that brought to power General Augusto Pinochet—a brutal dictator who protected ITT and other American companies, including Bechtel, and copper mining companies that were operating in the country. His military junta killed and tortured thousands of its political opponents.

McCone had personally offered the million dollars in corporate funds to CIA Director Richard Helms and National Security Advisor Henry Kissinger in a private meeting. In a subsequent Senate investigation of the CIA attempts to oust Allende, McCone admitted "that he had played the key role in bringing together CIA and ITT," as reported by Victor Marchetti and John D. Marks in their 1974 definitive work, *The CIA and the Cult of Intelligence*. The plot was undoubtedly discussed, if not hatched, at Bohemian Grove in the summers of 1971 and 1972, when all three men were lodged at Mandalay.

Called to testify, Helms denied the CIA's role in the coup; when charged later with perjury for his false testimony, he would become the first and only CIA director ever convicted of lying to Congress. Helms—dubbed "the gentlemanly planner of assassinations" by his

biographer—would ultimately blame Nixon for ordering him to instigate the military coup in Chile. "The only sin in espionage is getting
caught," Helms once said. In 1975 he admitted to Congress that he
had ordered the destruction of all CIA files related to the infamous
Project MKULTRA mind-control experiments of the CIA, in which
experiments on unwitting humans were conducted during a twenty-
year period from 1953 until 1973. Thousands of subjects at dozens
of American institutions, including colleges, universities, hospitals,
and prisons, were unknowingly dosed with the hallucinogen LSD.
The shocking testimony made Helms the target of public outrage and
earned him the moniker "the man who kept the secrets."

As for Kissinger, for four decades, he denied US involvement in the
bloody putsch. But his pivotal role in both preemptive covert planning
to block Allende's election, and then pressing Nixon to overthrow the
legitimate elected government and replace it with a US-friendly dictator, was exposed in May 2014, when thousands of pages of US State
Department documents on the coup and the subsequent repression
were declassified. "Kissinger asked that the plan be as precise as possible and include what orders would be given . . . to whom, and in what
way," as the files recorded Kissinger's explicit instructions to Helms.

"In the heady days immediately following, we took pride in having helped thwart the development of Cuban-style socialism in Chile
and having prevented the country's drift into the Soviet orbit," a former Santiago-based CIA agent wrote in *Foreign Affairs* magazine in
2014. Likewise, both Helms and Kissinger believed that the violent
US intervention in Chile was a patriotic act that furthered America's
best interests. Kissinger saw Allende's socialist democracy as a "virus"
that might "spread contagion," and thought that the way to deal with
such a threat was to "destroy the virus and to inoculate those who
might be infected, typically by imposing murderous national security
states"—as an academic described his foreign policy and national security strategy. Kissinger pontificated regularly about how Allende's
Marxist regime would contaminate Argentina, Bolivia, and Peru—
"a stretch of the geopolitical imagination reminiscent of the Southeast Asian domino theory," according to one history. Helms's hubris

was on full display during a rare public lecture at Johns Hopkins University during the volatile 1970s, when a student asked him if the CIA had interfered in Chile. "Why should you care?" Helms quipped. "Your side won."

In any event, both Helms and Kissinger would leave government and become highly paid international consultants for the Bechtel Corporation—expanding the company's revolving door into what would become Steve Jr.'s famous brand. "The revolving door spins so fast it is hard to keep up," wrote a journalist of Bechtel's vigorous mining of top-tier foreign policy and energy officials. While the links between government and the private sector had become familiar to Americans since Eisenhower's 1961 farewell speech, it would be Steve Jr. who perfected it, with Helms and Kissinger the prototypes in a long line to come.

"For a top job at Bechtel, former military personnel, ex-diplomats, and retired politicians need apply," a former Bechtel employee told the London *Independent*. Its ties with the CIA, through its networks of associates, "has earned it the nickname 'the working arm of the CIA.' " Still, as former CIA agent and author Robert Baer has written, in "Washington, to bring up the 'revolving door' between government and business is like discussing incest in the family." In the case of Bechtel, it seemed more of an *open* door than a *revolving* door—where those hired were rewarded with salaries and benefits that dwarfed even the highest-level government salaries.

For its part, Bechtel proclaimed that the implication that the company won business or a competitive advantage through political connections was false and, in any case, standard business practice. "Over the years, we have certainly built good relationships with important people," a Bechtel spokesman would write. "We network like anyone in business or the professions. Bechtel executives have been international industry leaders for decades. Industry leaders know political leaders, the people who formulate development plans, control budgets, set the rules for contractors to enter and operate in their countries, examine credentials, authorize contracts, and pay the bills for services rendered." Indeed.

CHAPTER TWELVE

The Energy-Industrial Complex

The foreign policy backlashes, including especially the disaster that Vietnam had become, led Nixon to reevaluate the customary American reaction to insurrections against political and corporate interests. Realizing that the United States could not engage in overt and covert operations in every nationalist uprising in the world, the thirty-seventh president reversed his long-promoted domino theory, returning instead to the theme he had first aired at Bohemian Grove of the United States as a Pacific economic power. Described as "the greatest departure in American foreign policy in the postwar epoch," central to this new Nixon Doctrine was a California-based Pacific Rim strategy spawned at the SRI think tank that concentrated on the opening of trade with China.

Nixon also engaged Bechtel in megadeals binding the country's enemies in oil-rich lands to his envisioned world economy. Bechtel "moved quickly in the Middle East," according to one account, "through huge construction projects to soak up the billions in American dollars that went to pay for the new OPEC prices of oil." As part of this foreign policy and economic doctrine, Nixon also sought to improve US relations with the Soviet Union, as well as to find new markets for American exports—the two goals interwoven with multibillion-dollar loans from the Ex-Im Bank. The unlikely mastermind of Nixon's grand plan to boost exports from $5 billion to $50 billion during his one and a half presidential terms was a California car salesman, GOP fund-raiser, and erstwhile citrus grower named Henry Kearns. Nixon had rewarded his longtime political patron by appointing him president of Ex-Im Bank—a powerful position for an unqualified political party functionary with no lending experience. It had been Kearns who suggested Steve Sr.'s appointment to the bank's advisory committee—with an eye toward bolstering Kearns's and the bank's credibility as they were embarking on a staggeringly large lending program. As much as any American businessman, Steve Sr. understood the intricacies and complexities of federally guaranteed loans, for they had built his, and his father's, company. Under the close tutelage of Steve Sr., who would assume a central role in directing Kearns toward worldwide projects for Bechtel to build—projects that had been researched and selected by SRI—Kearns served as the company's private banker, with seemingly unlimited access to funds.

Ex-Im dispensed hundreds of millions to Bechtel customers and projects: $13.5 million for a nickel-production facility in the Philippines; $100 million for the planned Sumed pipeline in Egypt; $157 million for fertilizer plants in Algeria; and $294 million to finance Bechtel's construction of liquefied natural gas facilities for Sonatrach—the Algerian state-owned oil company, to name a few. Among the more controversial Ex-Im/Bechtel deals was a series of proposed plants to be built in Russia by Bechtel and Armand Hammer's Occidental Petroleum—a $20 billion "twenty-year chemical fertilizer deal, promising U.S. technology for a Soviet fertilizer complex to be built by Oxy and Bechtel at Kuibyshev," according to an explanation of the plans. Heralded as the largest single transaction ever conducted between the Russian government and a private firm, the deal made Bechtel purveyor "of oilfield and fertilizer technology to [Soviet leader] Leonid Brezhnev, by Nixonian fiat," wrote a former Bechtel employee. There was also the proposed $10 billion development of natural gas fields in western Siberia for which Kearns had promised the financing for a partnership with the Soviets, Bechtel, Hammer, and El Paso Natural Gas—a deal that congressional investigators contended had been sweetened with Hammer's $100,000 campaign contribution to Nixon ($54,000 of which was illegal). "You must be out of your cotton-pickin' mind to dream up something like that," Democratic senator Henry "Scoop" Jackson told a Nixon administration official upon hearing of the Russian and Bechtel scheme, and maneuvered to block the Ex-Im loans and credits. Senators were further galvanized against Bechtel when a senior executive announced the firm's intention to go forward with the project with or without congressional approval, though Bechtel would back down.

The Soviet setback was offset for Bechtel by the shift toward international nuclear power. Lobbying fellow members of the advisory committee, Steve Sr. made the case for the Ex-Im financing of nuclear-energy-producing facilities abroad. "Any company which purchases U.S. equipment and services for a nuclear power plant should be able to obtain financing for the fuel required to operate that plant," Kearns announced. There followed a flurry of superdeals, wherein Ex-Im financed Bechtel-built nuclear plants around the globe.

The Ex-Im/Bechtel gravy train paused with Kearns's sudden resignation under a cloud of suspicion. The bank had made insider loans that enriched Kearns personally, and members of Congress were scrutinizing Kearns. Steve Sr. faced withering criticism as well. "Obviously, Bechtel's firm benefited while he [Kearns] was Ex-Im Bank president," charged Congressman Les Aspin of Wisconsin. "Bechtel's conflict of interest raises questions about the integrity of the bank's entire fiscal operation." Aspin cited the unambiguous impropriety of Ex-Im's approving $157 million for "an Algerian construction project coordinated by a San Francisco engineering firm while the firm's senior director served on the bank's advisory committee."

Ultimately, neither Kearns nor the Bechtels would be hampered by the flurry of bad publicity. Kearns would escape criminal charges when assistant U.S. attorney general Richard L. Thornburgh determined there was insufficient evidence against him. Like so many other scandal-ridden government officials of then and now, he would quietly steal away from Washington, only to turn up later as a high-priced consultant working the other side of the aisle. He would house his new consulting firm, Kearns International, in the Bechtel Corporation's San Francisco offices. His first major client was Sonatrach of Algeria, which paid him $350,000 to lobby Congress.

Meanwhile, Bechtel also won billions of dollars in government contracts for domestic projects, including the Washington, DC, Metro subway system. Questions about conflicts of interest would surface in all of these projects as well, including one blatant citation of Bechtel preparing a $418,000 research report for the government on the feasibility of a coal slurry pipeline at the same time that the company was participating in a slurry pipeline venture of its own, as the *Washington Post* reported. Still, Bechtel successfully lobbied congressional supporters to introduce legislation granting its pipelines the right of eminent domain across Wyoming's federally owned land—rights-of-way easements previously granted almost exclusively to railroad companies.

A native Californian and the first president from the West since Herbert Hoover, Nixon inherited what one account described as a "complex web of relationships between the federal government and the western corporations." These historic bonds—epitomized by generations of massive government subsidization of the western economy— would form the basis of Nixon's domestic energy policy. A centerpiece of this policy would be his commitment to develop America's public energy resources for private companies—especially the utilities and energy and construction companies of California. Nixon, who sent to Congress the first message on energy policy ever submitted by a US president, had issued a call to arms to the nation's utilities to build a thousand nuclear power plants by the year 2000. In response to the Mideast oil crisis of the early 1970s, when the Arab cartel raised prices by 100 percent, Nixon advocated for the private sector's role in developing nuclear energy—including the commercial production of enriched nuclear fuel such as plutonium. Bechtel would be at the forefront of the burgeoning new government-subsidized market, obtaining contracts to build more than half of the thirty-one nuclear plants on the drawing board.

In November 1972, the federal government gave tentative approval for a $5.7 billion nuclear fuel plant at Dothan, Alabama—the world's first privately owned nuclear facility of its kind—to a Bechtel subsidiary called Uranium Enrichment Associates (UEA) in partnership with the mega chemical company Union Carbide. The corporatization of uranium enrichment—which had been the government's sole province since the Manhattan Project—ushered in what journalist Jonathan Kwitny described as the beginning of "what may be the largest commercial undertaking in history." Despite fierce lobbying by Bechtel, Congress rejected the plan that would have broken the Atomic Energy Commission's monopoly on the enrichment of uranium, and would have given UEA a series of subsidies and guarantees to meet the needs of commercial nuclear power plants—with the US government assuming most of the risk.

At the same time, and armed once again with SRI research, Steve Jr. began an aggressive resource strategy to meet the needs of the explosive growth of the Southwest. Bechtel and a loose consortium of utilities, mining, and construction companies moved to "cover the Colorado Plateau with an elaborate complex of strip mines, power plants, and coal-gasification projects," as an environmental history of the West described it.

All in all, in coalition with the government, and especially under the aegis of Richard Nixon, Bechtel had shaped a powerful new energy-industrial complex to rival that of the military. Though no president warned the nation about it—the term had not been coined, nor had the Department of Energy been created yet—the network of contracts and money flow between the government agencies and the companies that implement the policies that drive the contracts was every bit as "disastrous [a] rise of misplaced power" as Eisenhower had envisioned.

So it was with a stunning sense of revisionist history that Steve Jr. wrote in *Dædalus*, the journal of the American Academy of Arts and Sciences, "the U.S. government has not had a major role in the success of our business." Espousing that the " 'private sector,' with free and open markets, creates the wealth of a country" and that excessive government "can easily lead too many people to believe that 'the government owes them a living,' " Steve Jr.'s philosophy stretched credulity.

Still, as was becoming a pattern, Bechtel was merely a shadow of what it was destined to become. As one of the biggest corporate beneficiaries of government financing—and by the 1970s, the largest privately held corporation in the world—Bechtel's political and economic authority rivaled that of policy makers. Working in tandem to further Nixon's foreign and domestic agendas, both Steve Sr. and Steve Jr. established close relationships with powerful Cabinet secretaries and high-level members of the administration—many of whom would join them at Mandalay Lodge, sometimes along with Nixon, where the personal bonds were tightened. (Though later, Nixon would be heard on the Watergate tapes calling Bohemian Grove "the most faggy goddamned thing you could ever imagine.")

Two Nixon men in particular captured the Bechtels' attention: Treasury Secretary George Shultz and Secretary of Health, Education, and Welfare (HEW) Caspar Weinberger. As the company had become expert at doing, it would lure both men away from government to top executive positions at corporate headquarters in San Francisco. It would be a history-changing action—for Weinberger and Shultz, for Bechtel, and for the United States.

"Hiring people in high places to deal with others in high places is nothing new for American corporations," journalist Mark Dowie wrote of the revolving door between big business and government. "But Bechtel seems to hire higher. When it needs financial connections it hires the secretary of the Treasury. When it needs nuclear technology, it hires the general manager of the Atomic Energy Commission. When it needs international clout, it hires an undersecretary of state. And when it needs expertise to run the bureaucracy it is becoming, it hires the secretary of Health, Education, and Welfare."

PART TWO

THE BECHTEL CABINET

1973–1988

*Every gun that is made, every warship launched, every rocket
fired signifies, in the final sense, a theft from those who hunger and
are not fed, those who are cold and are not clothed. This world
in arms is not spending money alone. It is spending the sweat of
its laborers, the genius of its scientists, the hopes of its children.*

—DWIGHT D. EISENHOWER

CHAPTER 13

Bechtel's Superstar

"If I could choose one American to whom I would entrust the nation's fate, it would be George Shultz," Henry Kissinger wrote in his memoirs. Steve Sr. was equally impressed upon first meeting Shultz in 1967, when the outsize economist and academic—then dean of the University of Chicago School of Business—made a presentation to the board of directors of J.P. Morgan Bank. Steve Sr. was drawn to his like-minded conservatism. He would watch Shultz's political rise over the next several years, as Shultz served in three Cabinet posts in the Nixon administration: first as secretary of labor, then as director of the Office of Management and Budget, and ultimately as Treasury secretary. Shultz gained a reputation as a workhorse, an unwavering free-trade proponent, and a loyal supporter of Nixon's détente policy toward the Soviet Union.

As OMB director, Shultz pushed for the company's privatized uranium enrichment scheme—"a Nixon-inspired boondoggle that eventually could have given Bechtel a world-wide monopoly on the sale of nuclear fuel," as a magazine reported Shultz's efforts. Even before his reelection in 1972, Nixon had announced his decision to reorganize the domestic side of federal government by appointing five "supersecretaries" who would be counselors to the president in addition to being Cabinet secretaries. Treasury Secretary Shultz became a White House appointee as well, with a staff in the White House and authority broader and deeper than that of Secretary of State. As a super-secretary, he took the lead on economic issues in the administration, outranking such high-level presidential advisors as Henry Kissinger and Bob Haldeman.

No less enthralled with Shultz than his father had been, Steve Jr. also observed Shultz closely in his dizzying rise to political power. "It was not Mr. Shultz's government contacts alone that caught Mr. Bechtel's eye," the *New York Times* reported, "but rather Mr. Shultz's familiarity with international economics, labor issues, and finance." Steve Jr. admired the economist's free-enterprise stance toward Russia, where Bechtel had ongoing and planned projects, and whose government officials Shultz had lobbied on behalf of Bechtel business interests. An outspoken advocate for opening the Soviet Union to American trade, in April 1973, as Treasury secretary, Shultz traveled to Moscow to arrange US credit for the gigantic $50 billion Yakutsk natural gas pipeline, to be built by Bechtel. "I understand through Secretary Shultz that the Nixon administration is doing all it can to encourage this development and to overcome existing obstacles," Vasiliy Garbuzov, the Soviet minister of finance, reported Shultz's visit to US Federal Reserve Chairman Arthur Burns, who followed up on Shultz's trip one month later. "But of course the president has his own problems with Congress at this moment," Garbuzov said, referring to congressional efforts led by Scoop Jackson to block the financing for the Bechtel deal. Echoing Shultz, Burns also sought to reassure the Soviets of the US intention to provide Ex-Im Bank funding for the Bechtel project. "The president is a very determined man—he does not depart from the path he has chosen," Burns told his Russian counterparts. "And it is also true that not only the president, but the government of the United States has started on a new path. The cold war is over." Nothing would have delighted both Shultz and the Bechtels more than for that to be true. But by the winter of 1973–74, Nixon was "mortally stricken by Watergate," as his onetime national security advisor wrote. Facing possible impeachment and a collapsing regime, the US-USSR détente he had envisioned would soon, like the Yakutsk pipeline, be shelved, as an emboldened Cold

War chauvinism took hold in the military, intelligence, and diplomatic realms of the US government.

Shultz's desire to abandon the hemorrhaging administration was well known within political and personal circles, prompting an unprecedented offer from Steve Jr. to entice him to Bechtel as a principal executive. In May 1974, just three months before Nixon resigned the presidency and Vice President Gerald Ford succeeded him, Shultz assumed his position at Bechtel with a $400,000 salary—six times his income with the government—and stock options that would make him a multimillionaire. For the first time, an outsider was established at the top of the company structure where three generations of Bechtel family members and trusted directors had worked their way up the corporate ladder "one painstaking rung at a time," as one account put it. But the amiable intellectual—"Buddha-like" in his gentle-giant demeanor and professorial deportment, as he was described by Bernard Gwertzman in the *New York Times*—was welcomed at his new corporate home.

Born an only child on December 13, 1920, in New York City and raised in Englewood, New Jersey, George Pratt Shultz graduated with an economics degree from Princeton University. Following a three-year stint as a combat colonel in the US Marine Corps during World War II, in 1949 he received a PhD in industrial economics from MIT, where he taught until joining the faculty at the University of Chicago Graduate School of Business in 1957.

An enduring collosus of the powerful Bechtel Group, Shultz was emblematic of modern Bechtel. Once out of government, he relished the perquisites of life with one of America's wealthiest and more swaggering companies. At fifty-four years of age, he was in his prime. Delighted to have relocated to California, George and his wife of thirty years, Helena "Obie" O'Brien, and their five children lived in casual opulence on the stunning Stanford University campus. He maintained his academic ties, joining the Stanford faculty and teaching courses in management and public policy while heading up the Mining and Metals Division of Bechtel. Shultz moved up the ranks, putting even

his most skeptical and competitive colleagues at ease with his ge-
nial, soft-spoken manner. Numerous high-level company engineers,
assigned to educate the anomalous nonengineer, found him a quick
study. Still, it would be the four members of the company's finance
committee—men who had worked so closely together for so many
years that they could "just look at each other and know what the other
guy was thinking," as one of them recalled—who would feel threatened to have a former Treasury secretary at its helm. But even this
tough foursome recognized the boon Shultz would be to the company.
Emotionally detached with a forceful self-assurance just shy of arrogance and a good-natured side, as evidenced by the Princeton tiger
tattoo on his buttocks, Shultz was difficult not to like.

His relationships in the East Coast financial world were imposing. But the synergy between him and Steve Sr. led to even more elite
financial contacts, as Steve Sr. smoothed the way for Shultz to join
several esteemed corporate boards, including General Motors; Sears,
Roebuck; Morgan Guaranty Trust Company of New York; J.P. Morgan & Company; the World Bank; the Inter-American Development
Bank; the Asian Development Bank; and Dillon, Read, the prestigious
"WASP" Wall Street brokerage house long under the guidance of JFK
Treasury secretary C. Douglas Dillon; as well as the International
Monetary Fund. Perhaps more momentous than any other association
was Shultz's inclusion in the by-invitation-only Business Roundtable—
the Business Council's lobbying arm, which has been described as "the
leading political organization of corporate America." When Shultz
joined the select group, there were approximately fifty members—
each a CEO or president of the country's largest corporations. While
the Business Council—on which Steve Sr. sat—consults with the executive branch, the Business Roundtable lobbies the legislative branch.

The Roundtable was key during this period for spearheading a
massive lobbying effort to roll back taxes, limit government intervention, weaken environmental and antitrust regulations, and thwart the
power of organized labor, as it sought to block antibusiness legislation
and consumer protection. In turn, the Council and Roundtable are

associated with other key policy-planning organizations. The two organizations are "tightly interlocked with the foreign policy apparatus of the government," as sociologist Nick Paretsky described the powerful government-business combine that interfaced with the Council on Foreign Relations (CFR) and the Trilateral Commission. The CFR, formed after World War I to support American capitalism's international interests, has long served as a major recruitment channel for the US Departments of State and Defense. Its complement, the Trilateral Commission, had been formed only recently, in 1973, to augment CFR's international efforts with a domestic agenda "for reforming the institutions of US capitalism," according to Paretsky. Bechtel was well represented on all four bodies. Shultz joined his old University of Chicago mentor, Milton Friedman, to become what former CIA agent and author Robert Baer once described as economists "who worship at the altar of deregulation."

Called "Bechtel's superstar" by the *San Francisco Examiner*, Shultz took full advantage of his formidable government connections, continuing to advise President Ford and other Cabinet members in the new administration—a quid pro quo that benefitted Bechtel's business pursuits. Shultz lobbied Ford relentlessly about privatizing uranium enrichment, and Ford followed Nixon's precedent in trying to facilitate Bechtel's commercialization of the government's top secret nuclear technology—lobbying efforts that Shultz would later downplay to Congress. Steve Jr. worried briefly that Shultz's high profile in Washington would bring unwanted public attention to the company—scrutiny focused on Bechtel's high-level ties to the agencies charged with its regulation. But Shultz was proving so gifted at cultivating powerful government allies, while also nurturing Bechtel's Middle Eastern clients and bringing a financial acumen to the boardroom, that Steve Jr. was determined to keep him. Thanks to Shultz's impeccable petitioning, President Ford accepted an invitation to address a huge Bechtel-sponsored World Energy Conference in Detroit, the thrust of which was to promote a nationwide nuclear power plant construction blitz, with Bechtel as the primary contractor.

In an extraordinary gesture, Steve Jr. invited Shultz to become a member of the family's Mandalay Lodge at the Bohemian Grove. Never before had a Bechtel employee been given membership in the exclusive family compound. The nod was unmistakable evidence of Shultz's position as heir apparent. Indeed, just one year after joining the company, in May 1975 Steve Jr. nominated Shultz to be president of the Bechtel Corporation, which the board of directors approved unanimously. Of the three companies constituting Bechtel at the time—Bechtel Corporation, Bechtel Power Corporation, and Bechtel Inc.—Bechtel Corporation was the most powerful. From the start, it was clear that Steve Jr. was readily sharing power with Shultz. But there was another figure on the scene, eager to derail and surpass the affable superstar—a feisty Cold War ideologue ready to settle a score. "An echo of long, bitter feuds within previous administrations," as Hedrick Smith described the infamous, often embarrassing, hostility between Shultz and Caspar "Cap" Weinberger. The Shultz-Weinberger clashes were "collisions at the tips of bureaucratic icebergs."

Often compared with bickering spouses who seem oblivious to how uncomfortable their constant infighting makes others feel, the two had been combatants since working together at the Office of Management and Budget in 1970. Shultz had been director and Weinberger his deputy director. "Shultz and Weinberger were long-distance runners," wrote White House correspondent Lou Cannon, "exceptionally well matched as adversaries and experienced in the competitive ways of Washington. Both were capable, intelligent, opinionated, energetic, and turf-conscious. Both had tempers that could unexpectedly erupt when they felt slighted or betrayed."

The two men could not have been more different, both temperamentally and physically. Where Shultz was pedantic and appeasing, Weinberger was excitable and unyielding. While Shultz was hulking and measured, Weinberger was angular and manic. It was "difficult to tell from Shultz's dull demeanor and careful record, not to mention a face as blank as a slot machine's, what he felt about anything," wrote Edmund Morris, biographer of Ronald Reagan. "One inserted one's coin and waited for the spools to spin." In contrast, Weinberger was a confrontational partisan who thrived on debate and agitation. Wiry and sharp-tongued, tenacious to the point of self-destruction— "arguing with him is like Chinese water torture," a coworker said once—he left a wake of depleted colleagues. Weinberger's approach, said Colin Powell, who worked for him as the senior military assistant before becoming Reagan's national security advisor, was "all sails up, full speed ahead, where is the brick wall—I wish to run into it now, sir."

That their ad hominem vitriol would play out in the Bechtel boardroom revealed as much about the company's hard-nosed corporate culture as it did about either man.

CHAPTER FOURTEEN

Cap the Knife

Cap Weinberger had shown up at corporate headquarters just six weeks after Shultz became president of Bechtel. Lured to the company by retiring general counsel Willis Slusser, the Bay Area native who had been Nixon's secretary of HEW was eager to return to California. He had stayed on for several months in the Ford administration, but after stints as OMB director, Federal Trade Commission (FTC) chairman, and HEW secretary, he was ready to return to the private sector. The $200,000-a-year salary (approximately half of what Shultz was earning) and what Weinberger described as "valuable shares of Bechtel stock" were alluring, and his wife, Jane, had long been ready to escape Washington politics. When he came on board as vice president, special counsel, and director, Weinberger's government tenure had overly prepared him for a corporate position that seemed mundane by comparison.

His zeal for cutting costs in his various government jobs had earned him the nickname "Cap the Knife"—an expertise that would serve him well in his new position. His decision to join Bechtel was no doubt part and parcel of other shrewd calculations as well. The position would put him "on the same political fast track trodden by so many who shuttled between corporate America and government postings," as one account put it. Indeed, he and his archrival Shultz would compete on this track, biding their time through the Ford lame-duck presidency followed by the unwelcome victory of Democrat Jimmy Carter in November 1976. All the while, both men honed their political skills and cultivated crucial allies in preparation for their reemergence on the national stage.

Hiring Weinberger had been Slusser's idea, not Shultz's. But when Slusser campaigned for Weinberger, coming on strong with both Steve Sr. and Steve Jr., his sway carried weight. Not only was the popular Slusser one of the most veteran and beloved of the employees, he was practically family—a loyalty the Bechtels took seriously, dating back as it did to the scandalous 1961 extramarital affair that Steve Sr.'s brother Kenneth had had with Slusser's then wife, Nancy. "The recruiting process had been flatteringly intense," Weinberger recalled. He received Steve Jr.'s job offer while driving with Slusser to attend the annual encampment at Bohemian Grove, where Weinberger was only in his second year of membership at the Isle of Aves Lodge.

It was not without hesitation that Steve Jr. hired Weinberger. On one hand, he worried about bringing in another Cabinet member so close on the heels of Shultz. But even more, he worried about how his Arab clients would respond to a Bechtel executive named "Weinberger," Cap's strident denial of his Jewish heritage notwithstanding. His father was the son of immigrant Jews, but Cap was raised in the Episcopalian tradition of his mother, and he flaunted his Christianity. "On religious matters, many people assumed that I was brought up in the Jewish faith," Weinberger explained, "but I was not, and neither was my father. Two or three generations back, in Bohemia, there had apparently been some kind of quarrel in his family over various factions in the Jewish synagogues."

He was born in 1917 in his parents' San Francisco home—"the year the United States reluctantly joined 'the war to end all wars,' " as Weinberger recalled his historic birth year that also ushered in "the world's first Communist state, the USSR." As it turned out, both World War I and Communism would shape the man he was destined to become. The younger of two sons born to Herman Weinberger and Cerise Carpenter Hampson of Boulder, Colorado, he claimed to have been naturally endowed with a "sunny, optimistic nature." His father got his law degree from the University of Colorado, and, with his violinist wife, moved to San Francisco to practice law. The boy was a sickly, shy child who suffered from frequent mastoid infections. He found solace in reading and conducting elaborate mock battles with tin soldiers. His close-knit family valued education and culture, and "Cappy," as he was called by his father after a fictional California skipper, would shorten his nickname to Cap in young adulthood. He graduated magna cum laude in 1938 from Harvard University. He got his law degree there three years later. At Harvard, "he suffered from being a public-school boy, a Westerner, and most conspicuously, the bearer of a Jewish surname," as one account described the discrimination he faced, enduring anti-Semitic slurs and threatening notes. He became known for his right-wing editorials in the *Harvard Crimson*.

Weinberger volunteered for the army in 1941 and ended the war on General Douglas MacArthur's intelligence staff. His intellectual interests drew his attention to Europe, especially Great Britain, where he watched politics and international relations with a special admiration for Winston Churchill and memorized lengthy passages from Shakespeare. Steeped in politics from an early age, one of his first memories was listening to the radio coverage of the infamous 1924 Democratic convention, which took 102 ballots to pick John Davis as its nominee. A relatively obscure conservative ex-congressman from West Virginia, Davis had lost that election to White House incumbent Calvin Coolidge. Inspired by an early campaign rally for Herbert Hoover, Weinberger became a lifelong Republican. Franklin Roosevelt's New Deal expansion of government—his "alphabet soup of programs"—solidified Weinberger's view that the "best government was the least government."

During the 1950s, he immersed himself in California politics. An early supporter of Republican congressman Richard Nixon, he was especially gratified when Nixon "defeated the radical Democrat Helen Gahagan Douglas" in the 1950 Senate race. That campaign would go down in the annals of political dirty tricks, in which Nixon had tagged Douglas "the Pink Lady" to impugn her as a Communist. She in turn would create the sobriquet "Tricky Dick"—a nickname that would haunt Nixon for decades.

Weinberger had his own lackluster political career, with three terms in the California Legislature—1952, 1954, and 1956—followed by an unsuccessful 1958 bid to become California's attorney general. In 1960 he became campaign cochairman for Nixon's presidential candidacy, pilfering Eisenhower's slogan of "Peace, Prosperity, Progress." After Nixon's narrow defeat by JFK, Weinberger continued to practice law in San Francisco and bounced around California politics, serving as state finance director appointed by Governor Reagan. After Nixon was elected president in 1968, he brought Weinberger into the administration as chairman of the FTC, and then as deputy director of OMB under Shultz. Once Shultz went to Treasury, Weinberger became head of OMB and ultimately HEW secretary, where he remained until his retirement in 1975.

"On . . . my last day in office . . . I considered this the end of my government career," Weinberger wrote later. "The main contribution I expected to make to the government from then on was to pay a large income tax." A month later, he had accepted the position with Bechtel, and he and Jane had moved into a lavish white Tudor home in Hillsborough, twenty miles south of San Francisco. The house included a ballroom, a library, and "splendid redwood trees in an old garden." In keeping with its penchant for privacy and security, Bechtel had the property surrounded with gated fencing before the Weinbergers moved in.

Steve Jr. installed Cap in a large corner office on the twenty-first floor of the twenty-three-floor Bechtel building in San Francisco's financial district, where he was in close proximity to the ever-looming Shultz. "As seemed to be the case every time we worked together . . . we often had differing viewpoints," Weinberger wrote with no hint of irony. "This was most evident when lawsuits were brought against the company, particularly large class-action suits . . . generally I would recommend that we fight rather than yield, but invariably George would want to settle."

While things had been going superbly for Shultz during his first year with the firm, Weinberger's arrival coincided with a downward spiral in Bechtel's fortunes. The company was battling numerous lawsuits on grounds of sexism and racism. A sex discrimination case brought by 6,400 female employees claimed that Bechtel functioned "like a men's club" that kept women employees—4,000 of whom were college graduates—in low-paying secretarial jobs. Meanwhile, 400 black employees who claimed they were victims of racial discrimination and harassment had filed a separate lawsuit.

As those two cases wound through the courts, Bechtel was also being pummeled by a sudden, unfamiliar, and relentless bout of bad publicity. The *Washington Star* had been running an investigative series of articles about Bechtel's business practices, its ties to government agencies, and its uncanny ability to obtain no-bid contracts. Then there was the bribery scheme involving a pipeline right-of-way in New Jersey that led to the convictions of four Bechtel employees. The indictment of six Bechtel employees at the Calvert Cliffs, Maryland, nuclear plant, charged with extorting nearly a quarter million dollars, followed. Characteristically, Shultz and Weinberger disagreed on how the company should respond to these attacks: Shultz the golden boy conciliator versus the combative, scrappy Cappy.

Even larger woes were plaguing the company in its global nuclear power monopoly. The directors of Consumers Power in Michigan were suing Bechtel over the failure of the Palisades nuclear generator. Claiming that Bechtel had failed to warn the utility "about potential operating problems" that would have prevented "errors in design and manufacture of equipment and components," the company sought $300 million in damages. A firestorm of controversy had also been set off when, during a panel discussion at a nuclear energy conference in Washington, an Atomic Energy Commission official remarked that "there is likely to be a major nuclear disaster in the world, and the prime candidate is Tarapur," referring to a Bechtel-built nuclear reactor in India. The official, Dr. Stephen Hanauer, went even further, charging Bechtel with acting irresponsibly and against the best interests of the United States by failing to deal with the breakdowns, radioactive leaks, and unexplained deaths at the plant. Hanauer claimed that an AEC colleague had visited the plant located on the Arabian Sea sixty miles north of Bombay, and had witnessed Indian laborers using primitive bamboo poles to try to disperse radioactive waste. On the heels of the Palisades and Tarapur failures, Chicago's Commonwealth Edison notified Bechtel that its Dresden-1 prototype was experiencing problems similar to those in Tarapur. The utility was estimating a cleanup cost of $30 million.

Still, Bechtel continued pushing the sale of eight nuclear reactors to the Shah of Iran, was peddling a uranium diffusion plant to Brazil, pitching a nuclear power plant to Pakistan, and negotiating with Belgium and Greece for nuclear fuel enrichment facilities. Secretary of State Henry Kissinger shilled for Bechtel, pressing the Shah to invest in the Alabama diffusion plant, assuring him that a $275 million investment with the Bechtel consortium would guarantee Iran an endless supply of fuel for the eight reactors that Bechtel would build for him. Bechtel executives also sought financing from the Shah for a uranium enrichment facility in Japan. All the while, journalistic exposés brought a barrage of unwelcome coverage to the firm and a growing public awareness of the potential for catastrophe in the nuclear industry. Because Bechtel "doesn't own the plants it builds, it doesn't have to worry about being saddled with billions of dollars' worth of obsolete and dangerous machinery," reporter Mark Dowie wrote about the company's business model. "Leaving that problem to its customers, Bechtel has quietly changed directions and set its sights where the smart new money in the energy business is: on coal."

Indeed, with nuclear power waning as a growth industry and with American utilities continuing to get 60 percent of their electricity from coal, Shultz convinced Steve Jr. to diversify away from nuclear into coal. An engineer from the firm's Scientific Development Department told a journalist that the company had a secret plan, directed by Shultz's Metals and Mining Division, to increase its investment in coal technology and cut back on nuclear. After all, Bechtel had built the new technology that would change the economics of coal: the coal-slurry pipeline. "Bechtel sometimes likes to pioneer a new construction technology and get as much profit as it can out of it while no one else is around," the engineer claimed. "Then when the competition gets stiff, as it is in nuclear power, it moves on to something else."

Taking his personal axiom to heart—"a builder is measured by the length of his shadow"—Steve Jr. endorsed Shultz's vision. "No longer would utilities have to build expensive railroads to transport coal to their new plants," author Judith Nies wrote of Bechtel's new and timely venture. Like its expansion in the nuclear industry, Bechtel sought an international coal market, especially in Russia, China, and South Korea. Shultz set his sights on Peabody Coal—a subsidiary of the Kennecott Copper Corporation, which was then America's largest coal producer, with vast coal reserves in ten states. Kennecott Copper initially refused to sell Peabody. But when the FTC found Kennecott in violation of antitrust laws and ordered the company to divest itself of Peabody, Shultz was waiting patiently. When the timing was right, he orchestrated a $1.2 billion buyout by a Bechtel consortium—a private holding company that included its rival construction firm, Fluor Corporation, along with Newmont Mining Company, the Boeing company, and others.

Another profitable divergence, comasterminded by Shultz and Steve Jr., was Jubail: the largest civil engineering project in the world, located in the eastern province of Saudi Arabia. Unveiled by Bechtel in 1976, the $40 billion, nearly forty-year undertaking, would turn a provincial fishing village into a modern metropolis. Complete with four airport terminals, three runways of seventeen thousand feet, the world's largest desalination and power plant, a golf course, a dozen shopping centers, a military base, a hospital and clinics, a mosque that would accommodate 8,000 people, factories, highways, oil refineries, and a sex-segregated swimming marina, its tiny population eventually swelled to over 370,000, according to the company website. "What you *really* need is a new city," Steve Jr. had told King Faisal, planting the seed that led to the gigantic undertaking that would amount to $200 million in Bechtel profits every year for four decades, and would be the home of Saudi Arabia's petrochemical industry.

Bringing Parker T. "Pete" Hart into the fold was a fortuitous addition to the corporate family as it negotiated with Saudi Arabia over the Jubail development—what Steve Jr. had taken to calling the company's first "gigaproject." Hart, a former assistant secretary of state, had been ambassador to Saudi Arabia, North Yemen, Kuwait, and Turkey. A huge expatriate labor force, more than 50,000 workers—transported by Bechtel from the Philippines, India, Taiwan, Korea, Algeria, and Indonesia, and often segregated by nationality—would move billions of cubic yards of earth, producing what one account described as "a myriad of closely held secrets developed, traded or brought to the company in the brains and files of more than 1,000 scientists raided from competitors and foreign countries." At one point, Steve Sr. alerted the State Department that he intended to bring a foreign Muslim workforce into Jubail—specifically, Filipinos from Mindanao—according to a recently declassified State Department cable.

The Saudi port at Jubail would be the prototype for Bechtel's next iteration—first the building of entire cities, then the industrial development of entire nations. It was Shultz who devised this new strategy, drawing on his analysis of international economics and capitalizing on the close friendships with Middle Eastern officials he developed while in the Nixon Cabinet. "In all the expansive sweep of civil engineering from the pyramids of the Nile to the construction of the Suez Canal, nothing so huge or costly as Jubail has been attempted," *Time* magazine championed the venture.

Despite the financial bonanzas that Peabody Coal and Jubail were for Bechtel, the company's problems and negative publicity only intensified. As it was, not surprisingly, the prickly Weinberger would find himself at the center of the storm—and would soon be seeking an out.

CHAPTER FIFTEEN

The Arab Boycott

Steve Sr. had created close business relations with the petroleum industry as far back as the 1930s through his association with SOCAL, including a decades-long association and friendship with the Saudi royal family. That long relationship with Saudi Arabia, as well as Bechtel's ties with the leaders of Libya, Iraq, and Iran—Qaddafi, Hussein, and the Shah, respectively—had long sparked distrust among Israeli leaders.

Despite working with all of Israel's neighbors on hundreds of projects in the region, Bechtel built nothing in Israel. The company had long been dogged by allegations of systemic, companywide anti-Semitism, due in part to its unwavering support of the anti-Jewish Arab boycott prohibiting trade with Israel. At a time when oil companies fostered a growing suspicion of Israel in response to its declaration of an independent state and its 1948 war with the Arabs, Steve Sr.'s remarks often included blatant anti-Jewish sentiment. He routinely referred to Jewish associates as "He's a Jewish fellow, you know," as if the distinction indicated a stereotyped trait. A former personnel manager once even claimed that the company "ran deep with Aryan blood." Bechtel's anti-Israel wariness was further galvanized by its early experience in Palestine. Steve Sr. blamed Israeli Zionists for forcing the company to abandon a major pipeline project in Haifa that had resulted in the loss of millions of dollars in investment and profits.

Steve Sr. had also once promised Saudi leaders not to hire Jewish elements—either Jewish-owned subcontractors or Jewish workers—in building the Saudi Arabian pipeline and the king's railroad, and regularly assured other Arab clients, including the Egyptians, that Bechtel was not, and would not, operate in Israel. Careful not to offend King Faisal, "who repeatedly harangued Steve senior about the alleged perfidy of 'Zionists,'" as Laton McCartney described it, Steve rejected all business opportunities that arose in Israel.

The boycott, which the Arab League established in 1945, was meant to isolate Israel and to thwart the rise of its military and economic power. Steve Sr.'s good friend Faisal was aggrieved "by the loss of old Jerusalem to the Jews," according to a history of the era. "As guardian of Islam's Holy Places, he felt a personal responsibility to recapture what had been lost, and his hatred of Israel went deeper than the antipathy and wounded pride common to all Arabs."

For nearly thirty years, complying with the boycott presented no problem for Bechtel. The boycott prohibited Arabs from trading with Israel directly, from dealing with firms that traded with Israel, and from conducting any business with firms that had Jewish ownership. The League kept a blacklist of more than fifteen hundred firms—mostly American—which the Arab nations shunned. Because Bechtel was one of the few American companies to side with the League against Israel, its political and economic clout in the region rose. Bechtel's anti-Israel stance went unchecked until the Arab League ratcheted up the stakes in the mid-1970s. It expanded the terms of the boycott, which drew the ire of the Anti-Defamation League (ADL) in the United States and spurred pressure on Congress and the White House.

In response, President Ford asked the Justice Department to conduct an investigation into the alleged conspiracy to restrain trade, and his tough-minded prosecutor, Edward Levi, seized the opportunity to take on Bechtel. A son and grandson of rabbis, Levi was the first Jewish US attorney general. Not only was he aware of Bechtel's anti-Israel bias, but also he had some historic animus with Shultz, dating back to 1968, when he was president of the University of Chicago and Shultz was the dean of the business school. The two men had clashed over the handling of Vietnam War protestors on campus, with Shultz taking a less tolerant stance than Levi toward the demonstrators.

While Levi couldn't prosecute the Arabs, he determined that Bechtel's compliance with the boycott was a violation of the Sherman Antitrust Act. Although there were nearly a dozen American firms adhering to the boycott, Levi targeted Bechtel because of its high-profile image, with two former Cabinet members as executives, combined with additional complaints from the ADL about ongoing discrimination against Jewish employees, both in the United States and abroad. Ford administration officials pressured Levi and his assistants intensely not to file charges against Bechtel, although Ford personally maintained a hands-off approach—fearing a backlash from Justice lawyers, who were already suffering a morale crisis following the Watergate scandal. The Jewish community was also monitoring the case, especially coming as it did during the presidential election season. But Ford's proxies, Treasury Secretary William Simon and Secretary of State Kissinger, bombarded Levi—Simon with public opprobrium and Kissinger with private cajoling. "It will do grave damage to our foreign policy," Kissinger said to Levi in a phone call on January 6, 1976, trying to dissuade him from pressing charges against Bechtel. "It comes with bad grace from the US, which is conducting boycotts itself."

The next day, Kissinger called the president and warned him, "The Jews would oppose you in an election unless it looks like you will win," adding that the "Jews are trying to so embroil us with the Arabs that we are paralyzed . . . all [Bechtel] is doing is obeying the law of the country." Ford replied, "It amazes me that such a tiny people can raise so much havoc here."

The *Washington Post*, in a lead editorial, took up Kissinger's and Bechtel's cause, reporting that the State Department had tried to block the suit for fear it would alienate Saudi Arabia, interrupt American oil supplies, and cost American companies billions of dollars throughout the Arab world. A Bechtel spokesman told the newspaper that its

Arab business was conducted "in areas and in ways compatible with US foreign policy goals." Both Simon and Kissinger would later serve as Bechtel consultants.

Despite the intensive petitioning by Simon and Kissinger, the Justice Department filed suit against the company on January 16, 1976, charging that Bechtel and four of its divisions or subsidiaries had refused to subcontract work in the Middle East to American companies blacklisted by the Arab League as part of their economic boycott of Israel. While Shultz distantly defended Bechtel's role with the League, Weinberger bore the brunt of the criticism. As general counsel, he had approved the company's compliance with the boycott. Unwilling or unable to restrain his pro-Arab partiality, he advocated a bellicose confrontation with the Justice Department.

The bad publicity in the middle and late 1970s was taking its toll, threatening to bring unwanted attention to the massive Jubail project, which was just getting under way, as well as expose Bechtel's escalating Iranian nuclear operations under the direction of its new consultant, former CIA head Richard Helms. A close look at Bechtel would also have bared the company's relationship with Prince Mohammad Bin Fahd. In line to become king, Fahd and fellow members of the royal family were demanding exorbitant "commissions" from Bechtel in exchange for letting it do business in Saudi Arabia. At the time, Bechtel was competing for contracts to build a second industrial city at Yanbu, with a price tag of $1 billion, as well as a $3.4 billion international airport in Riyadh. But Mohammad was muscling Bechtel financial executives, demanding a 10 percent fee from the projects. When Steve Jr. and Shultz agreed to let the University of California–educated prince become a shareholder in Saudi Arabian Bechtel Company, some company executives—including Weinberger—feared that the formal association with the playboy could cause embarrassment for the firm. (Bechtel would ultimately obtain the contracts for both Yanbu and the Riyadh International Airport.)

At the same time, Bechtel executives were conspicuously promoting the sale of sixty F-15 warplanes to Saudi Arabia. The intensive

lobbying of Congress by Bechtel, along with Saudi leaders and the educated and sophisticated Saudi lobbyists, sparked the attention of both
the Israeli and American press. "The Saudis have thrown some of their
most personable and articulate representatives, guided by ring-wise
American political and public relations advisors, into this lobbying
struggle," the *Washington Post* reported Bechtel's involvement in the
incendiary debate.

With its international activities expanding, drawing more and
more media attention as the company hired Helms and other former high-level foreign policy officials, rumors of Bechtel's ties to the
Central Intelligence Agency were ubiquitous. While whispers of such
connections might have enhanced the company's prestige twenty
years earlier, by the late 1970s the CIA had been the subject of intense
investigation on Capitol Hill, resulting in legislative reform (including a presidential ban of CIA assassinations of foreign leaders) and
widespread exposure about illegal covert operations and allegations
that the agency was in the service of multinational monopolies. In the
post-Watergate congressional investigations of the CIA, to be linked
to the agency was poison for an American company. "Despite its
[Bechtel's] prominent employees, the company shuns publicity," wrote
a *Times* reporter. "Nonetheless it has come forward to deny occasional
reports of inappropriate cooperation between its international employees and the Central Intelligence Agency."

The most explosive of the federal probes were the 1975–76 Church
Committee hearings. Named for the investigative committee chaired
by Senator Frank Church that uncovered the CIA abuses, the Senate
Select Committee to Study Governmental Operations with Respect
to Intelligence Activities had published fourteen reports labeled "the
family jewels." While some of the files had been splashed on the front
page of the *New York Times* in an explosive article written by Seymour
Hersh, nearly all of the several thousand pages of documents from the
investigation were classified and hidden from public view for the next
thirty-five years.

Meanwhile, Weinberger had become such a lightning rod in the

Arab boycott controversy that the Bechtels and Shultz decided to bring in outside counsel, soliciting the help of one of Washington's powerful law firms, Hogan and Hartson. Bechtel did not deny that it had complied with the boycott but argued that doing so did not violate federal law, and claimed that the company had been singled out.

Sharp disagreements permeated the discussions within Bechtel's executive suite about how the company should handle the lawsuit. Steve Jr. and Steve Sr., who would have normally favored stonewalling the media, were persuaded by Shultz to be more cooperative. "With the benefit of hindsight, I recognize that my 'penchant for privacy' as an individual, along with the privately owned status of our company, made us targets," Steve Jr. would reflect later. "Being more open and accessible earlier in our history might have alleviated some adverse publicity that we experienced." In any case, to stave off the scrutiny that was anathema to the Bechtel family, Steve Sr., Steve Jr., and Shultz decided to settle the antitrust case out of court, agreeing to a consent decree stating that it would not participate in an Arab boycott. Later, Bechtel would try to change its position, arguing that it did not have to abide by the decree, and appealed the case to the US Supreme Court. The court refused to review the appeal.

CHAPTER SIXTEEN

The Pacific Republic

Sidelined, undermined, and overshadowed by Shultz at Bechtel, Weinberger stepped up his plotting for a return to government. His hopes for a Cabinet appointment in Ford's second term had been dashed when the little-known former governor of Georgia, Jimmy Carter, narrowly defeated Ford in 1976. By the late 1970s, Weinberger had chosen Ronald Reagan as his most likely avenue back to Washington. He had known Reagan since 1958 and became California's finance director during Reagan's gubernatorial administration. The two were on friendly terms, both were staunch Cold Warriors, and Weinberger felt sure that if he got on board at the outset, Reagan would reward him with a Cabinet appointment—preferably the State Department.

Weinberger's enthusiasm for Reagan was not shared initially at Bechtel corporate headquarters. Steve Jr. had already given millions in campaign contributions to Reagan's leading challenger, former Treasury secretary and Texas governor John Connally. Bechtel's lobbyist, Charls Walker, was Connally's chief economic advisor. "Reputed to be the most powerful business lobbyist in Washington," and credited as being the "grandfather of corporate coalition-building," according to sociologist Nick Paretsky, Walker had served in the Treasury Department under the Republican administrations of both Eisenhower and Nixon. Walker, along with Connally, had spearheaded the formation of the Business Roundtable and was its chief tax lobbyist. He was also cofounder, with George Shultz and John McCone, of the Committee on the Present Danger, the influential militaristic lobbying group push-ing for a reinvigorated military buildup to fight Soviet expansionism.

In their support of Connally, the Bechtels had joined the nation's corporate elite backing the wheeler-dealer. The flamboyant Texan would later become known mostly for having been wounded as a passenger in the car with John F. Kennedy when the president was assassinated in 1963. "What John Connally stands for . . . is a glorification of strong centralized government working in partnership with large powerful corporations," a Republican critic described the candidate who had raised more money than any other. Connally was so passionate about government and private partnerships that he once proposed to Nixon "we create a United States oil company. Buy half the reserves of Aramco in Saudi Arabia. Then when [the US] took over, Aramco could say, 'Don't talk to me, talk to Uncle Sam.'" The economic theories of the brash and arrogant Connally were described by a Texas magazine as "aimed mainly at befriending the top economic layer—sort of a warmed-over Trickle-Down theory with the government holding the spout."

While the Bechtels found a natural affinity for Connally's do-mestic agenda, they had an even stronger passion for his Middle East position—for which he had been dubbed the "candidate of the oil in-terests." In a contentious speech at the National Press Club in Wash-ington on October 13, 1979, Connally called for Israel's withdrawal to its pre-1967 borders, to abandon the West Bank, the Gaza Strip, and relinquish its exclusivity in Jerusalem. The speech brought indigna-tion from fellow Republican leaders and rival presidential candidates. Kansas senator Robert Dole said it "smacks of trading Israeli secu-rity for our oil savings," calling it "more like an energy program than a peace plan." Senator Howard Baker, Republican of Tennessee, said that Connally's proposal "represents a fundamental shift from a po-litical and moral base to an economic base," adding that America's oil supply "is not a bargaining chip for Mideast peace negotiations." Israel's supporters were outraged, charging Connally with "rehashing the stale arguments of the Arab potentates and dictators."

For their part, the Bechtels were so enamored with Connally's foreign policy vision that Shultz recruited Connally's speechwriter, Samuel Hoskinson, as Bechtel's manager for international corporate strategy. A former CIA analyst, Hoskinson had served as a Middle Eastern specialist on the National Security Council in the Nixon, Ford, and Carter administrations, working, respectively, for Kissinger, Brent Scowcroft, and Zbigniew Brzezinski. As it turned out, neither the American media nor the public was as taken with Connally as corporate America was. He won only one delegate vote at the 1980 Republican National Convention—for which he spent $11 million.

Once Reagan was the presumptive candidate, the Bechtels and Shultz got behind their fellow Californian and did everything within their power to insure his victory. Whatever reservations that they had about him—revolving mostly around his "supply-side" economic views—were mitigated partly when the former California governor appointed William Casey manager of his presidential campaign. Shultz and Casey had been close friends since the Nixon administration, when Casey was first chairman of the Securities and Exchange Commission (SEC) and then undersecretary of state for economic affairs. The relationship continued after Shultz joined Bechtel, and Casey became head of the Ex-Im Bank under Ford, while also serving on the president's select Foreign Intelligence Advisory Board.

Having been chief of secret intelligence in Europe for the OSS during World War II, the native New Yorker had returned to Manhattan, where he became a multimillionaire Wall Street lawyer. Casey made his first fortune by providing legal and economic intelligence information to corporate clients, and then became a venture capitalist before taking the SEC appointment in 1971. His intelligence background, his anti-Communist stridency, his stalwart Catholicism—all attributes reminiscent of McCone—influenced both Steve Sr. and Steve Jr., who recognized him as a fellow patriot capitalist.

Tensions between the supply-siders and the traditionalists had become "acute," as Reagan biographer Lou Cannon described the battle of the economists. At the moment, the nation was reeling from high unemployment, high interest rates, and runaway inflation. Casey worried that Reagan's vague understanding of the issues endangered his candidacy, and thought the support of Shultz and the Bechtels would be a decisive factor. Six years earlier, then-Governor Reagan had invited Shultz to lunch in Sacramento to pick his brain about "how the federal government worked, how the budget worked, what the process was, and what the problems were," as Shultz later recalled of the meeting. While many economists of the era were contemptuous about Reagan's intellect, Shultz thought him earnest in his desire to become informed. Then, in the spring of 1980, Casey summoned Shultz from the Bechtel boardroom to a meeting with Reagan in Los Angeles.

Shultz was only slightly more impressed than he had been at their earlier meeting in the state capital, but again he came away feeling optimistic about the candidate's seriousness and thought him educable. Casey seized the moment, inviting Shultz to chair a coordinating committee to advise Reagan on economic affairs. Weinberger and Walker were also on the committee.

By late spring, it seemed possible that Reagan could defeat Carter. After a failed mission to rescue fifty-two American hostages being held by Iranian revolutionaries at the US Embassy in Tehran since the previous November, Carter's ratings plummeted. Operation Eagle Claw, as it was known, was a humiliating disaster that resulted in the deaths of eight US servicemen. From that point forward, the Bechtels, Shultz, and Weinberger all played key roles in Reagan's campaign strategy, even as both Shultz and Weinberger angled for the same Cabinet post: secretary of state. While Shultz had powerful behind-the-scenes lobbyists pushing for him, including former Federal Reserve chairman Burns and former defense secretary Melvin Laird, Weinberger's long-standing friendship and devotion to Reagan trumped Shultz's grasping. Steve Jr. lamented the possibility that Reagan would lure Shultz back to Washington, and he and his father hoped the president elect would tap Weinberger instead. They had no intention of firing Weinberger, an act that would only bring more unwanted attention to the company. But he had never fit in with the corporate culture and had few allies within the firm. "Cap's being at Bechtel was like a heart transplant that just didn't take," Bechtel treasurer Raynal Mayman told an interviewer. "The system rejected him."

Shultz, on the other hand, had been an extraordinary addition to Bechtel, ushering in major changes that insured the company's success for years to come. During the previous three decades, there had been a bipartisan consensus that "Republicans as well as Democrats favored stronger regulation of business and industry to protect consumers and workers from the excesses of American capitalism," as one account of the era put it. Consequently, by 1980, the company was reporting a decline in fortunes, characteristically blaming an overreaching government. "The lack of a US energy plan, a slowdown in the demand for electricity, and increased financial restraints led to an epidemic of project cancellations and delays," according to official Bechtel publications. Increased government regulation, tougher environmental policies, and changing economic conditions both nationally and internationally demanded that the company shift direction. In response, Shultz effectively overhauled the company, reorganizing it toward a holding company structure for Bechtel Corporation's three principal operating divisions, all managed by Shultz: the Bechtel Power Corporation, a construction company that was the nation's largest builder of nuclear plants; Bechtel Petroleum Inc., which built refineries and other oil and gas industry facilities; and Bechtel Civil and Mineral, a builder of mass transit systems and other major infrastructures.

The Bechtel Corporation changed its name to the Bechtel Group, and Shultz assumed a formal role in developing megaprojects in newly industrialized countries. Under his guidance, the company evolved from a direct construction company into project management, engineering, and construction management, which, by 1980, accounted for two-thirds of its revenues. With Shultz's leadership, Bechtel also diversified into financing and operational services—most notably acquiring an 80 percent interest in the prestigious Dillon, Read & Company investment firm. "We found ourselves with new owners whose operations were an integral part of the military and intelligence communities and who had demonstrated a rapacious thirst for drinking from the federal money spigot," a Dillon, Read employee wrote later. "Unusual things started to happen that were very 'un-Dillon-Ready-like,' as the new management recommended expanding into merchant banking and participating in the leveraged buy-outs sweeping Wall Street at the time. Through Sequoia Ventures, the quasi-independent financial investment company owned mostly by the Bechtel family," the firm held Dillon, Read, the family's shares in Bechtel, and other parts of the organization's assets. Shultz invested company profits, as well as his and the family's personal wealth, in real estate and oil and gas leases—"little acorns," he called them. "We can afford as a private company to make investments we can be patient with," Shultz described his investment strategy to *Forbes*. Sequoia also offered a venue for Bechtel to marshal international venture capital for massive infrastructure projects worldwide.

Shultz—a former Labor Department secretary—had another, "less often mentioned," reason for creating a holding company: Bechtel had acquired a famously nonunion firm, Becon Construction of Houston. "Through the holding company, Becon can be kept well apart from the rest of the organization, which is covered by extensive union agreements," as the *Economist* reported.

Shultz had also assumed responsibility for Bechtel's unapproachable public affairs division, and he was credited for bringing the first semblance of transparency the firm had ever practiced. Under his direction, the company issued its first annual report, which included billings and current projects, and provided employees with a booklet on how the $7.6-billion-a-year organization was doing. "The booklet is long on generalisations, short on figures and the financial nuts and bolts," the *Economist* described it. "An inquiry about profits to an otherwise charming Bechtel boss produces a sharp reminder to mind your manners. Such things remain the concern of the Bechtel family (who still own the vast majority of the stock) and a handful of top officers." So essential had Shultz become to Bechtel that both Steve Sr. and Steve Jr. were overcome with concern that Reagan would appoint him secretary of state—a role that Shultz coveted.

In November 1980 Reagan defeated Carter in a landslide: 489 to
49 electoral votes. In what would become known as the "Reagan Revolution," the election marked a historic conservative realignment,
with the American Southwest the unmistakable new power center.
The capital of this new economic and geopolitical region was California, christened the "Pacific Republic" by its then governor, Jerry
Brown, with San Francisco the designated corporate headquarters.
The Bechtels and other uberwealthy California businessmen who had
made Reagan's political victory possible—the coalition of reactionary,
antigovernment, rugged-individualist western corporate titans—were
now established as the New Right elite. "Ronald Reagan represented
the triumph of the corporate West," as one history of the region put
it—an empire that Bechtel had essentially ruled for fifty years. "The
West was Reagan country, the media proclaimed, a solid base from
which he pursued his long quest for the presidency," wrote Peter Wiley
and Robert Gottlieb in their *Empires in the Sun.* "He was the candidate
of the corporate boardroom, the hero of the Moral Majority, the *gau-
leiter* of the white middle class, the polished figurehead who preached
the religion of free enterprise."

In the aftermath of the election, speculation was rife that Reagan
was going to name Shultz secretary of state. "Republican presidents
have a smaller pool of talent from which to choose their teams than
do Democrats," the *Economist* proclaimed, "and Mr. Reagan's advisers
were noticeably short of experience of Washington." The notable ex-
ceptions, of course, were Shultz and Weinberger, and, given the dire
straits of the economy, Shultz seemed an obvious front-runner. His
depth and breadth of experience in economic affairs were formidable.
He had been Reagan's chief economic advisor during the campaign
and had served in three Cabinet posts dating back to 1969. But Weinberger was working at cross-purposes to make sure his nemesis would
not outshine him again, as Shultz had done both within the Nixon
administration and at Bechtel.

CHAPTER SEVENTEEN

The Bechtel Babies

Early in the interregnum between election and inauguration, Wein-berger accepted Reagan's offer to become secretary of defense—the largest department in the federal government, with over a million civilian employees. If disappointed that he wasn't chosen for State, Weinberger was gratified to become the president's chief military advisor at a time when the two men were unified in their zeal on national and international security issues. "When Reagan named his old buddy Weinberger to manage the largest peacetime military buildup in the republic's history, the right went into a frenzy," according to one account. Cap the Knife was known as "the hard-eyed budget director who prided himself on cutting" expenditures. But a closer look would have revealed his long-standing fanaticism about protecting the military budget coupled with paranoia about the Soviets' arms buildup. "He is one of the few genuine anti-Communist Cold Warriors in Washington," said Admiral Gene La Rocque. "He believes this [Cold War] stuff, and now he's in a position to do something about it."

Weinberger moved to head off any overtures Reagan might have been contemplating toward Shultz, planting the seed that it would be destructive to appoint two Bechtel executives to the nation's foremost national security positions. He also passed along false information that Shultz had assured the Bechtels he had no intention of leaving the company for a Cabinet position. Some close to Reagan, such as his deputy chief of staff, Michael Deaver, thought that Reagan intended to appoint Shultz to State all along and had been disappointed to learn, incorrectly, that Shultz was not interested.

Shultz was equally deflated and confused when, on Thanksgiving Day 1980, he received a phone call at his California home from the president elect. Expecting the appointment he so desired, Shultz was dispirited when Reagan said he "had heard" that Shultz was "very happy with his Bechtel job," but hoped he would be able to help out in the administration in a part-time capacity if asked. Stunned, Shultz knew that the phone call was a polite way of telling him the post would go to someone else. He turned his attention back to Bechtel, which increased his salary to $600,000 and gave him more shares of the company stock. By the time Reagan came into office in 1981, Bechtel was "not really one company," as a team of investigative journalists concluded after a three-year investigation. "It is many companies incorporated in different states of the U.S., and even in other countries, notably Panama. However, they are all controlled by one organization called the Bechtel Group of Companies, which has its own separate board of directors chaired by Stephen D. Bechtel, Jr. Various members of the Bechtel Group board are also 'executive sponsors' of operational functions in the other Bechtel corporations." Shultz was both vice chairman of the Bechtel Group board and executive sponsor of the internal auditing division of Bechtel. In 1981 Bechtel employed 120,000 engineers, managers, and laborers at 111 major projects throughout the world, and would report $11.4 billion in earnings for that year. While Shultz was extolled and credited with the company's great success, Weinberger disappeared from the Bechtel corporate façade.

On an unseasonably warm Washington, DC, day in January 1981, while Ronald Reagan was being inaugurated as the fortieth president of the United States, the hostages held for 444 days were released. "Literally at the moment that Jimmy Carter handed over the reins of government," as an author described it, the hostage taking by Iranian militants that had terrorized the American psyche for the previous fourteen months came to an end. The Iran hostage crisis had plagued, and then emasculated, the Carter administration, and had been the key campaign issue in the 1980 presidential race.

In an oblique reference to Carter's ineffectual weakness, Reagan waxed symbolic on the theme of military might and preparedness. His newly appointed secretary of defense, Weinberger, would manifest that theme as he presided over a colossal expansion of defense spending, all the while trumpeting Reagan's good-and-evil view of the world. "In an administration that constantly harped on the need for more and better weapons," wrote a historian, Weinberger was "the chief harper." Nowhere would Weinberger's imprimatur be plainer than the reversal of Middle East policy he brought to the Pentagon—a "pro-Arab disposition" that, if not born in the boardroom of Bechtel, was certainly nurtured there.

As Bechtel's general counsel, Weinberger had negotiated numerous contracts with Israel's enemies throughout the Arab world, including Libya, Iraq, Syria, Egypt, Saudi Arabia, and Lebanon. So it was with apprehension that Israel greeted Weinberger's appointment. Whether rooted in anti-Semitism or political ideology, Weinberger's disdain for Israel was plain. He "seemed to go out of his way to oppose Israel on any issue and to blame the Israelis for every problem in the Middle East," wrote Marine Lieutenant Colonel Oliver North. "Caspar Weinberger has reversed American policy in the Middle East," Senator Joe Biden observed after Weinberger had been in the Reagan administration only one year. Even his deputy defense secretary, Lawrence Korb, thought "Weinberger had almost a visceral dislike of Israel's impact on our policy."

Indeed, Weinberger's "predilection to support Saudi Arabia to the extent that it's in Bechtel's interest" raised concerns on the US Senate Foreign Relations Committee. "Weinberger believes that what's good for Bechtel is good for the US," a senior staff member of the committee told the *Los Angeles Herald Examiner.* "Weinberger's anti-Israel tilt was an underlying current in almost every Mideast issue," according to a journalist. "Some people explained it by pointing to his years with the Bechtel Corporation. Others believed it was more complicated and had to do with his sensitivity about his own Jewish ancestry."

In keeping with his confrontational personality, Weinberger clashed repeatedly over Israel with Alexander M. Haig Jr.—the former general and Nixon chief of staff who became Reagan's secretary of state. The dispute between Weinberger and Haig reached a climax in early 1982 when, in the midst of delicate Middle East peace talks, Weinberger traveled to Saudi Arabia, Oman, and Jordan, omitting Israel from the itinerary. Despite efforts to downplay the conflict between the two Cabinet secretaries, it erupted into public view when remarks attributed to Weinberger while on his air force plane indicated that the United States was going to "redirect" policy away from Israel and toward the Arabs. That, coupled with his public announcement that he supported selling F-16 fighters and mobile antiaircraft missiles to Jordan, brought a public protest from Israel. The *New York Times* declared the dispute momentous because the administration's two top national security officials "seem to have differing assessments of the importance of Israel to the United States."

Israeli prime minister Menachem Begin, a close ally of Haig's and to whom Haig made assurances of America's support for Israel, accused Weinberger "of being hostile to his country," according to the *New York Times*. Weinberger was outspoken in his belief that the United States had "neglected its ties to friendly Arab countries because of being hostage to Israeli policy." Writing in the *New Republic*, Morton Kondracke called Weinberger part of the "Bechtel oil group," which is "further to the Arabist side than the traditional State Department Arabists." Even Jeane Kirkpatrick, the US ambassador to the United Nations, with her own hard-core anti-Communist bona fides, accused him of slavish groveling to the Arab world. "Cap, you talk about [Palestinian leader] Yāsir 'Arafāt as if he's some kind of agrarian reformer. 'Arafāt is a Soviet-backed international terrorist. You have lost your sense of perspective," Kirkpatrick once told him.

Weinberger pushed Congress to approve the sale of $8.5 billion worth of AWACS (Airborne Warning and Control System) reconnaissance planes to Saudi Arabia. Shultz, as head of Bechtel's government-relations department, organized a Bechtel-led coalition of American corporations doing business in Saudi Arabia in a massive lobbying campaign in support of the sale. The effort appalled and alarmed Israel, which saw Bechtel's unmistakable hand behind the machinations. Bechtel, which had $40 billion in contracts in Saudi Arabia, hired a Washington lobbyist to write a letter to every member of Congress stating, "The AWACS deal is vital to the national interest as well as to the stability of the Persian Gulf." Despite Haig's passionate refutation, the Senate voted to authorize the sale. As Haig saw it, Weinberger's enmity toward Israel, and toward him, was undermining his efforts to negotiate an agreement between Israel and Egypt on Palestinian self-rule.

Weinberger's long-standing antagonism toward Israel had been further galvanized when, the previous summer, Israel carried out a surprise air strike destroying a nuclear reactor under construction in Iraq. With sixteen US-made bombers, the Israeli air force flew the longest mission in its history to destroy the Osirak facility that Iraq's president, Saddam Hussein, claimed was intended for peaceful scientific research. Israel charged that it was designed to make nuclear weapons.

Weinberger was especially infuriated that the reactor was attacked at a moment when the Reagan administration was secretively engaged in an effort to turn Saddam into a centerpiece of American foreign policy in the Middle East. "This was a policy in which . . . Weinberger had a personal stake," wrote a senior staff member for the Senate Intelligence Committee. "The policy was building up Iraq, a policy to which Weinberger and much of the rest of the US government sacrificed real American interests during the 1980s." Thanks to the lobbying by what critics called "the Bechtel Babies"—thirteen powerful Washington lobbyists now maneuvered on behalf of Bechtel—in 1982 the Reagan administration took Iraq off its list of countries that sponsored terrorism. By this time, Iraq was mired in a long war that it had waged since 1980 against Iran. The United States could transfer weapons and other high-tech material to Iraq denied to countries on the list. The Reagan administration wasted no time authorizing "the sale to Iraq of numerous items that had both military and civilian applications," the *Washington Post* reported, "including poisonous chemicals and deadly biological viruses, such as anthrax and bubonic plague."

When Reagan's new "activist CIA director," William Casey, refused to show Israel the American spy satellite photographs of the bombed Osirak reactor and Baghdad's air defenses, "the Israelis began to understand that the Reagan administration had a two-tier policy." Few American companies were more vested in Iraq at the time than Bechtel, which was beginning secret and sensitive negotiations with Saddam to build a colossal crude oil pipeline that would double Iraq's oil exports and bring hundreds of millions of dollars in profits to Bechtel.

Meanwhile, Weinberger's strife with Haig quickened, and in another behind-the-scenes twist from "the boys from Bechtel," Shultz intervened to hasten Haig's demise. Communicating through back channels at both the White House and the State Department, Shultz recommended the appointment of Philip C. Habib, a Bechtel consultant, to replace Haig as a special presidential envoy to Israel and Lebanon. A Lebanese American, Habib had been a career diplomat since the 1950s, and, at the time of his retirement, had held the number three job at the State Department. A celebrated Middle East expert, he was distrusted by the Israelis. Shultz lobbied on Habib's behalf with William P. Clark, the president's close friend and national security advisor. Shultz saw Haig's pro-Israel policy as detrimental to Bechtel's, and America's, interests in the region. Shultz had lured Habib out of retirement, giving him a cushy contract with Bechtel. He thought that Habib, whom he described as a "tough-talking, explosive-tempered, arm-waving Brooklyn kid," could help end the Lebanese civil war that was escalating the conflict between Syria and Israel.

His displacement by Habib was a terminal setback for Haig, who submitted his resignation to Reagan on June 25, 1982. That same day, Clark called Shultz, who was in a Bechtel meeting in London, and said in confidence: "There may be a change in secretary of state. Would you be interested, George? I hope you are."

"Yes," Shultz replied, "but I have to wait for Steve Bechtel to come out of Alaska from a fishing trip and talk to him about it."

"George, you have thirty-six hours," said Clark.

"Do you mind if I run it by my wife?" Shultz asked.

A half hour later, Shultz received a call from Reagan, telling him that Haig had resigned and that he wanted to name Shultz as his successor. The president requested an immediate answer. "It's not a good idea to leave a post like this vacant," Reagan said, making clear he hoped to make the announcement at the same time that Haig's resignation became public. Shultz talked it over with his wife and accepted the position within thirty minutes. He then attempted unsuccessfully to reach Steve Jr. in Alaska. As it turned out, a shaken and allegedly displeased Bechtel first heard the news on the radio. Steve Jr. cut short his vacation and hurried back to San Francisco.

"I was shocked," Steve Jr. told *Newsweek* later. "I just didn't think it would happen. But," he added, "I knew George well enough that I felt that if the president really wanted him, put the arm on him, George would go."

Shortly after Shultz's appointment, President Nixon called Clark with a forewarning about Shultz. "Bill, I want you to tell President Reagan one problem with your new secretary of state . . . My experience was, and I'm sure you're going to experience the same thing, a wonderful ability to, when things look iffy or are going wrong, he'll contend he never heard about the issue and was never briefed and was not a part." Clark recalled later that he never told the president of Nixon's warning and wished that he had. But that would be years in the future, near the end of Reagan's second term.

It had been Weinberger's irascibility that led to his rival Shultz coming on board as secretary of state. The tempestuous blustering that was undermining US foreign policy—the Weinberger-Haig feud that Nixon described as "sniping or guerrilla warfare"—would be replaced by an older, deeper antipathy. Shultz, as it turned out, whether by chance or design, had landed his dream job. The rancor between him and Weinberger would play out once again, but this time on an even larger stage of history—and with Bechtel never far from the drama. "Reagan seems to have had no inkling of the long rivalry between Shultz and Weinberger before they actually began arguing in front of him during cabinet meetings," wrote a Reagan biographer. "As it turned out, the conflict between Shultz and Weinberger proved more enduring and certainly as damaging as Haig's frequent skirmishes with Weinberger."

CHAPTER EIGHTEEN

The Reaganauts

"There are too many people from Bechtel in this administration." Republican senator Larry Pressler drew the conclusion felt by many of his colleagues on Capitol Hill.

Secretary of State designate George Shultz had been calming but vague during his 1982 nomination hearings before the Senate Foreign Relations Committee, "providing artful nonanswers to the senators' fuzzy questions on every aspect of foreign policy," as one observer saw it. Then the characteristically unflappable Shultz lost his temper when grilled about the giant and secretive multinational corporation that he had served as president—"a company with a long history of feeding at the public trough and with involvements in the Arab world," wrote Peter Wiley and Robert Gottlieb.

"I . . . took some jabs that caused the temperature to rise a bit," Shultz described his mood during the two days of often contentious hearings. He suspected he would be in for some tough questions related to his eight years with Bechtel and had hired the high-powered establishment lawyer Lloyd Cutler to help prepare him. A Democrat who had been White House counsel to Carter, Cutler advised Shultz to resign from all his business organizations, to put his financial holdings—now in the millions, thanks to Bechtel—in a blind trust, to disassociate from Bechtel, and to set up a recusal process within the State Department regarding all matters relating to Bechtel. It was all well and good in theory, but senator after senator honed in on

Bechtel's business ties to the Arab world. "A hot issue was my Bechtel association and a presumed pro-Arab tilt," Shultz wrote later. The supposed bias was underscored by a remark Shultz had made to a reporter in 1980 while Reagan was campaigning as a resolute friend of Israel. "If I have any differences with Reagan, it's about Middle Eastern policy," as set forth in a speech Reagan had made before the Jewish community service organization B'nai B'rith. Pressler of South Dakota was unrelenting, pressing him for details about his role in Bechtel's intensive lobbying campaign for the AWACS. "We did not go around twisting arms," a defensive Shultz replied, denying that Bechtel had "an organized, systematic campaign of any sort"—an assertion that belied the sophisticated letter-writing operation undertaken by Bechtel lobbyists.

As committee members cross-examined Shultz about the role Bechtel played in the Middle East, the bantering became testy. Shultz could barely contain his contempt for Congress. California senator Alan Cranston interrogated Shultz about his personal feelings regarding Bechtel's adherence to the Arab boycott, implying unethical, if not illegal, behavior on the part of the company.

The tough questions did not end with the Middle East. As one of the largest builders of nuclear power plants around the world, Bechtel was singled out by antinuclear activists for its global proliferation without regard for American national interests. In a feisty exchange, Cranston accused Bechtel of secretly offering to sell Brazil " 'the entire gamut' of nuclear enrichment and fuel-processing technology" at the moment that President Ford and Secretary of State Kissinger were trying to convince West Germany not to traffic sensitive nuclear technology to that Latin American country. Not only did Cranston see Bechtel's role as undermining US efforts to "curb the spread of nuclear bomb making," but he also accused Bechtel of making its own foreign policy that undercut the US government and "weakened our diplomatic efforts." Bechtel had close ties with the Brazilian government, for which it had built the largest-capacity long-distance iron-ore slurry pipeline in the world.

Cranston's insinuations maddened Shultz, provoking him to interrupt the senator. "Cranston took me on, attacked my association with Bechtel, and implied that Bechtel was in some way reprehensible and unprincipled," Shultz recalled of the interchange that left him feeling like he had to "stand up" for himself. Shultz popped off that he resented Cranston's "smear against Bechtel," and as Cranston continued, Shultz cut the senator short. "Well, now, wait a minute. You had your say. Let me have my say." He went on to describe Bechtel as a "marvelous company, an honorable company, a law-abiding company that does credit to our country here and all over the world," a company that would never, "ever . . . undercut the policies of the United States."

During the hearings, a Connecticut rabbi fasted outside the Senate Office Building to protest Shultz's appointment, and though Shultz was confirmed in a 97–0 Senate vote, speculation about Bechtel remained a subject of concern to several senators. Howard Metzenbaum (D-OH) expressed alarm about the "pervasive" connection among Shultz, Bechtel, and the Arab world. Just days after the confirmation hearings, the *Washington Post* reported that Habib—the presidential envoy trying to negotiate a settlement in Lebanon—was also on Bechtel's payroll as a consultant. Senators felt that Shultz should have disclosed the Habib-Bechtel relationship, and should have admitted that he had hired Habib to work for Bechtel and then insinuated him into the White House, circumventing Secretary of State Haig. The revelation outraged Senator Pressler. He accused Habib of conflict of interest and called for his immediate resignation. Appearing on the Sunday-morning television talk shows, Pressler described it as a "very, very serious matter." The senator argued Habib should resign because he was a paid consultant to a company "that actively lobbies for pro-Arab causes" and as such could not be trusted as an unbiased negotiator and ambassador. Pressler felt personally "betrayed" by Shultz and incensed that Shultz had been dishonest with the committee.

The Associated Press was simultaneously reporting that CIA Director William Casey and a number of other officials in the Reagan administration also had connections with Bechtel, bringing media attention to the revolving door between government and Bechtel for the first time since Drew Pearson wrote his exposés of Bechtel-McCone in the 1950s. (Bechtel denied later that Casey was "an employee or consultant to Bechtel—contrary to irresponsible claims," and issued a formal warning to journalists to "beware" of reporting it as fact.) Newspaper editorials echoed Pressler's objections, and a Florida congressional candidate used the issue during his campaign, proclaiming, "Bechtel is controlling our Middle East policy."

Habib did not resign and reportedly "gave the stink little thought," wrote John Boykin in *Cursed Is the Peacemaker*. He would claim later that he had an "understanding with George [Shultz]" that his job was not to lobby Congress or to solicit business abroad for Bechtel, but only to advise Bechtel "about the facts of life in various countries." The administration expressed full confidence in Habib. A White House spokesman said any "implication of any conflict is absurd." The controversy soon died down. For his part, Habib found sardonic humor in the suggestion that his Bechtel connection would make him more pro-Arab than his "having Lebanese blood in his veins."

Still, not even the company's most cynical critics could have predicted how Bechtel's political influence in Washington would set the stage for privatizing foreign policy and transforming the Middle East, a development that tilted foreign relations more toward the benefit of private interests than those of the US and the general welfare of its public. After the media coverage of Shultz's confirmation hearings, Americans were becoming familiar with the Bechtel name for the first time. "The essential point . . . is not that Bechtel is anti-Israel or pro-Arab," journalist William Greider concluded. "It is that Bechtel is for doing business. Anywhere, anytime. Just as it wants to open a world market for plutonium, Bechtel wants to build whatever it chooses, regardless of foreign policy interests."

For his part, Steve Jr. expressed disappointment at losing his two top executives, complaining to a reporter that the government would now go to such lengths to avoid any hint of conflicts of interest that his company was sure to suffer. He claimed to be bothered by the negative media attention brought to Bechtel as a result of its revolving door with Washington. The "insinuations about our supposed influence with the government" especially irked him. "It's unfortunate that we don't have all the power it's alleged we have. If we did, we could help fix some of the problems that exist around the country." At the forefront of Steve Sr.'s complaints about the direction the country was heading was the "rising tide of overregulation" of industry by government.

Yet Bechtel's ties to the government increased during the Reagan presidency, enhancing hugely the company's revenues. Exploiting a vast and profitable new industry, Bechtel's numerous lobbyists were pressing Congress to fund multibillion-dollar cleanup efforts at radioactive and hazardous waste sites from the old Manhattan Project. The new industry had been spawned by the partial meltdown of the reactor core at Three Mile Island in Pennsylvania on March 28, 1979. It was the worst accident in nuclear power plant history, and posed a great danger to the nearby population, as radioactive materials were released from the core into the reactor building and beyond. *The China Syndrome*, a box-office hit about a fictionalized accident at a nuclear power plant, had been released just twelve days before Three Mile Island occurred, so public awareness was at a heightened state.

The thriller, starring Jane Fonda, was a dramatic portrait of what global disaster a nuclear meltdown would cause. Fonda used the film and the Three Mile Island accident as a launching pad for her antinuclear activism. To counter the actress and an escalating antinuclear movement at a moment when the public was calling for government to implement tighter regulation of the industry, the nuclear lobby dispatched Edward Teller. The tireless father of the hydrogen bomb—called "one of the most hawkish physicists ever to serve the US government"—Teller began a massive promotion about the safety of nuclear power. "The antinuclear propaganda we are hearing puts democracy to a severe test," Teller prophesied. "Unless the political trend toward energy development in this country changes rapidly, there will not be a United States of America in the twenty-first century."

Three Mile Island signaled a personal call of duty for Steve Jr., even though Bechtel had not designed or built the reactor. He "became obsessed with proving that nuclear power really was safe and with keeping the industry viable," according to a senior Bechtel executive. "He was absolutely determined that Bechtel should devote its full resources to keeping atomic energy alive." He and thirteen of the country's leading utilities formed a lobbying group—the United States Committee for Energy Awareness—to repair what they saw as the character assassination of the nuclear industry, and to press Congress to renew its commitment. The organization's founders pledged $100,000 each from their companies to launch what would mushroom into a $30 million advertising and lobbying campaign. The committee developed a sophisticated strategy that included placing supposedly independent energy experts on radio and television talk shows and submitting letters to the editors and Op-Eds to dozens of newspapers throughout the country—all designed to establish the credibility of the group "as more than a propaganda organization," wrote Howard Kurtz in the *Washington Post*. "What its slick, low-key television ads failed to mention is that the group gets more than half its funding from 50 utilities, some of which have billed their unsuspecting customers for the media blitz."

As the world's largest builder of nuclear reactors, Bechtel was poised to profit from the next phases of nuclear energy: decontamination, remediation, and storage of nuclear waste. The legacy of decades of Cold War bomb making left dozens of sites from the old Manhattan Project that posed health and environmental risks. Even before Shultz joined the administration, Bechtel had obtained a $320 million contract from the US Department of Energy to clean up thirty-two radioactive sites.

Energy had been the core of Jimmy Carter's domestic agenda, and DOE his "pride and joy." The newly created Cabinet-level department was designed to regulate nuclear energy, material, waste, and weapons, while also stimulating alternative energy and efficiency as part of a doctrine for America to become less dependent on Middle Eastern oil. Steve Jr., like Reagan, was convinced that the only energy problem in America was government interference. Free enterprise could do a better job of energy production than government, Reagan declared. On the campaign trail, Reagan vowed to eliminate the DOE, citing it as the quintessential example of ineptitude and waste. "If the Reagan administration has its way, DOE will soon be dispersed to the bureaucratic winds," one account described Reagan's opinion of the giant bureaucracy of twenty thousand employees and a $10.5 billion budget. Once president, though, he changed his mind. Following the election, when Reagan's advisors took a closer look at the department, "the story goes that they were surprised to find that the Department of Energy actually designed and built the nation's nuclear weapons." Reagan had a new affinity for the department he had considered dismantling, and the DOE mushroomed under his watch, becoming a revenue stream for Bechtel of unprecedented scale. Ironically, despite Bechtel's virulent assaults on the agency, it would become the company's financial propeller into the next century, with Bechtel securing its place as DOE's prime contractor for the next thirty-five years.

When Reagan took office, the American economy had slipped into the most severe recession since World War II, with the rest of the world soon following. Steve Jr., seeing "few megaprojects in the offing" as a result of the downturn, decided to expand operations even further onto the international stage. The nuclear power market, which had been Bechtel's biggest moneymaker, had taken a nosedive, with no new nuclear power plants ordered since the mid-1970s, and with a robust nuclear-freeze movement gaining ground. The last nuclear power plant in the United States had been licensed in 1976. "For one thing, it took a long time to build nuclear plants, and the cost estimates at the beginning were not the same as the actual costs at the end of a completed installation," Judith Nies explained the changing face of nuclear energy even before the Three Mile Island meltdown. Not only was nuclear electricity more expensive than projected, but the public was becoming alarmed about the dangers of the reactors.

In the first year of the Reagan administration, Bechtel scored additional multibillion-dollar DOE contracts. "We have to approach projects as a multinational organization with a multinational staff and multinational sources," Steve Jr. told employees, explaining that Bechtel was establishing what it called "bailout teams—flying squads of engineers, scientists, and other specialists who could be rapidly deployed to emergency situations to assess what needed to be done and to do it." The company's decontamination business expanded after it was awarded $1.5 billion to clean up Three Mile Island. It was but the first of many contracts that Bechtel won from the federal Formerly Utilized Sites Remedial Action Program (FUSRAP) to reduce radioactivity and treat hazardous waste at the nuclear sites, established in 1974 by the US Army Corps of Engineers. Bechtel's thirty-year, $2.5 billion contract was particularly ironic, given John McCone's misleading denials that radioactivity endangered life. "Winning FUSRAP put us in the vanguard of the nuclear cleanup business," said Craig Weaver, a Bechtel executive. "It gave us the technical know-how we needed to perform this work successfully, and led to the establishment of our office in Oak Ridge, Tennessee, near our DOE customer." DOE was no longer Bechtel's nemesis that threatened its extinction, but was now its coveted "customer" that would insure its survival.

As part of the FUSRAP golden goose, Bechtel also received contracts during that first year of the Reagan administration to oversee the cleanup of uranium mining operations in the American West, to design and build the Waste Isolation Pilot Plant in New Mexico, and to engineer a government uranium enrichment facility in Ohio. Even that was but a glimpse into the future steady stream of profits that DOE would provide Bechtel over the coming decades. When yet a third Bechtel executive joined the Reagan administration as DOE's number two official, the company's good fortune soared, proving Steve Jr.'s pessimistic forecast to be unfounded.

CHAPTER NINETEEN

A World Awash in Plutonium

For more than twenty years, W. Kenneth Davis had headed Bechtel's nuclear division, having been hired away from his government job as head of the Atomic Energy Commission in 1958. So when the US market for building nuclear power plants tanked in the 1970s, Davis was the innovator at Bechtel who had anticipated the collapse and guided Steve Jr. and Shultz into the international nuclear marketplace. By the early 1980s, two presidents—Ford and Carter—were "sufficiently alarmed by the potential of a world awash in plutonium that they tried to slow down Bechtel," according to a 1982 press account. Congress had even enacted nonproliferation legislation intended to curb Bechtel's and other American nuclear manufacturers' global ambitions. But all that changed with the "Bechtel Cabinet," as journalist and author William Greider dubbed it, which mixed "their private interests with their public obligations."

While still at Bechtel, Davis had drafted the Reagan transition report on nonproliferation policy. Under the guise of nonproliferation, that policy rolled back the law and allowed Bechtel to pursue overseas nuclear customers. Like Davis, Shultz had been an outspoken opponent of the Carter administration's nuclear nonproliferation policy, claiming that it gave foreign competitors, especially France and West Germany, an advantage in the world market. That position was at odds with Shultz's creation thirty years later of an elite nuclear deterrence group, officially christened the "Four Horsemen of the

Non-Apocalypse," and with the grandiose vision of ending nuclear weapons "as a threat to the world." But that side of Shultz would be decades in the future. For now, Davis and Shultz advocated sharing uranium enrichment and reprocessing with all nations that have "a legitimate need." Davis's report included a recommendation that the nuclear export decisions that had been regulated by the US Nuclear Regulatory Commission (NRC) be shifted to Shultz's State Department. The administration wasted no time, and Bechtel expanded its nuclear facilities around the world.

No other individual did as much to shape the nuclear power industry as Davis, who had been there at the creation of the atomic age. An MIT-educated engineer, Davis had operated in the nuclear arena since the late 1940s, working on breeder reactors and helping design the federal nuclear laboratory at Livermore, California. He, like his colleague McCone at the AEC, zealously advocated a partnership between government and industry to build nuclear power plants across the country, if not the world. Called "65-degree Davis" by his friends because he once skied a slope that steep, the avid hiker and outdoor enthusiast did more to promote nuclear power than anyone in America.

Throughout all of nuclear power's setbacks during the 1970s, Davis had been its indefatigable champion—a believer long after most of his scientific colleagues had become apprehensive about the risks associated with the industry. He downplayed the perils of weapons proliferation as trivial and thought nuclear power was the most revolutionary energy source in the history of mankind. He dismissed the supposed dangers of radiation as a bogeyman confected by antinuke extremists, and was a fanatic believer that nuclear power was the only high-density, low-carbon energy source that could meet the needs of the world. Once, in a chance encounter with antinuclear physicist Amory Lovins, Davis was so venomous toward him that Lovins felt he had been greeted as if he were "the Antichrist."

Like his fellow Bechtel partners Shultz and Weinberger, Davis had also become a wealthy man working for the company. His financial disclosures upon joining DOE in 1981 revealed that he was receiving more than $500,000 annually in Bechtel salary, bonuses, and stock benefits. He also had assets worth at least $4.5 million, including $750,000 worth of Bechtel stock alone, as well as substantial shares of SOCAL, Occidental Petroleum, and Pacific Gas and Electric. Many congressional staffers were alarmed by Davis's appointment as assistant secretary of energy, believing that the Department of Energy had brought him in to represent Bechtel's interest in energy policy. Those qualms were rattled further when the DOE sought a waiver that would allow Davis to participate in decisions and bids involving Bechtel—a brazen request met with vigorous opposition by some members of a House oversight committee.

Davis, as deputy to Secretary of Energy James Edwards, was widely seen in Washington as the department's real muscle. An alter ego to the unsophisticated figurehead Edwards, Davis was the DOE representative at the White House and in Congress. He backed Reagan's vision of energy policy, which included removing federal energy price controls and massive subsidies for nuclear and synthetic fuels, while gutting any emphasis on solar energy, alternative resources, and conservation. Like Davis and Steve Bechtel Jr., he saw environmentalists as diabolical subversives. Although Edwards was in line with the administration goals, he was nonetheless a Washington neophyte whose inarticulate bumbling undermined his authority with the White House, which bypassed him to deal directly with Davis. It was an "open secret" that Davis ran the department. The offices of the inspector general, general counsel, and directors for international, congressional, and public affairs all reported to him. From the start, there was widespread speculation that Edwards wouldn't last long in the Cabinet. Indeed, just a year into the administration, he decided to resign and told Davis he planned to recommend him as his successor. On June 25, 1982, while on vacation at Lake Tahoe, Davis heard on the radio that Shultz had replaced Haig as secretary of state. He knew that had sealed his fate, certain that Reagan would not risk the scrutiny that three Cabinet members from Bechtel would produce.

While the Department of Energy is a benign-sounding name con-
noting the ethereal realms of the sun, wind, and water, the agency is
far more about nuclear weapons and national security than it is about
natural resources. "When the average person, or the average scholar,
or even the average presidential adviser ponders international relations, national security, and the Cold War, thoughts do not necessarily
turn to the Department of Energy. The Central Intelligence Agency
and the Departments of State and Defense come readily to mind," the
official DOE historian once said. But DOE "shaped the way the Cold
War developed and played out and kept the Cold War from developing into a full-fledged 'hot' war." The department and its predecessor
agencies designed and built the nation's nuclear arsenal, and its leaders
participated at the highest levels of domestic and foreign policy relating to those weapons.

DOE's primary budget goes to designing, building, and managing
the country's nuclear weapons and the infrastructure necessary to
support them. Herbert S. Marks, general counsel of the AEC under
President Truman, observed after a visit to the Los Alamos National
Laboratory that the nation's atomic program "was a separate state,
with its own airplanes and its own factories and its thousands of secrets. It had a peculiar sovereignty, one that could bring about the
end, peacefully or violently, of all other sovereignties." In the thirty
years subsequent to Marks's observation, the nation's nuclear weapons complex, with Davis effectively at the helm, was on the verge of
metamorphosing into a huge agency with hundreds of thousands of
government employees and private contractors overseeing dozens
of weapons labs, radioactive-waste sites, and a massive stockpile of
bombs and nuclear warheads.

The underpinnings of one of the largest industrial projects in the
world, the DOE's nuclear weapons program includes the nuclear fuel
cycle for both bombs and commercial nuclear energy. The first step
in the cycle is the mining and milling of uranium ore that is then
shipped to the DOE facilities for enrichment to either reactor- or
weapons-grade level. The weapons-grade uranium is then fashioned

into an arsenal for numerous delivery systems. Enriched uranium is the key component for both civil and military nuclear power—power plants require 5 percent, bombs require 20 percent—and Bechtel is the leading company in mining uranium.

One of the most "closed" and secretive of government organizations, the DOE administers more classified operations than any other agency, including the CIA, and is second only to Defense for maintaining the largest body of secret documents. The DOE's national laboratory system, a collection of seventeen government-owned facilities spread around the country, was born to build the atomic bomb. The weapons complex includes the three laboratories: Los Alamos and Sandia in New Mexico, and Lawrence Livermore in California, as well as numerous production plants and other top secret facilities.

The organization of the labs' model—government owned and contractor operated (GOCO)—was originally selected by the AEC to avoid either an entirely government-controlled lab system or an entirely private-sector-based structure. While the government funded the labs and dictated the missions, private contractor-managed teams carried out the operations. The GOCO model had been lucrative throughout the postwar decades for Bechtel, which received the first AEC contract at the ultrasecret Los Alamos site—the flagship of the country's nuclear enterprise. "Bechtel was the poster child for the GOCO mechanism dating back to the Manhattan Project," said a former DOE general counsel. Following the massive expansion of DOE during the era of the Bechtel Cabinet, the company would be awash in government money.

Shortly after coming on board at DOE, Davis led a delegation to Mexico that resulted in a contract for Bechtel to build one of the first of twenty nuclear plants that country planned. Within a few months, the Ex-Im Bank chairman, John L. Moore, offered Taiwan generous financing for the construction of two nuclear plants to be built by Bechtel. (The next year, Moore joined Bechtel as vice president for financial development in its Far East operations.) Following Davis's

recommendation, Reagan directed the NRC to "take steps to facilitate the licensing of [thirty-five nuclear] plants under construction,"
fifteen of which were Bechtel projects. Bechtel received another windfall when the administration lifted restrictions against the sale of nuclear fuel to South Africa and Brazil, even though neither country had
signed the Nuclear Nonproliferation Treaty that went into effect in
1970. South Africa and Brazil were two of seven non-nuclear states
that were close to being capable of the technology necessary to build
a nuclear weapon.

There were even more advantages that came Bechtel's way through
the accommodating administration. While Shultz assured Congress
that he would recuse himself from matters related to Bechtel, he visited China—"a market Bechtel had unsuccessfully been trying to crack
for years," according to Laton McCartney—to make a deal for nuclear
power plant construction. The secretary of state offered to provide
US technology in exchange for China's allowing American firms to
participate in the construction of $20 billion of planned projects. A
Shultz-promoted nuclear cooperation agreement enabling US firms
to sell nuclear technology to China passed Congress two years later,
and Bechtel would boast of becoming the first US company granted a
construction license in China.

A powerbroker behind the rise of Ronald Reagan, Steve Jr. had
meticulously overseen the expansion of the revolving door between
his company and government that would be so integral to Bechtel's
continued ascent, though he would downplay those connections.
He often pointed to the decline of the engineering and construction
market during the Reagan years to deflect from the boon that Bechtel received in the expanding markets, from nuclear cleanup to coal,
chemicals, and, especially, liquefied natural gas (LNG). "Employing
former government officials added an outside perspective to the leadership and management expertise of our senior management team,"
he wrote. "They were not hired to represent Bechtel with the U.S. government; in fact, by virtue of their previous work for the government,
they brought added attention and scrutiny. However, on the whole,

the positive benefits outweighed the negatives. Their judgments and capabilities were valuable additions to our business." The great good fortune for Bechtel that the early Reagan years brought seemed to embody Steve Jr.'s personal maxim: "It's more effective to do a man a favor than to ask him for one."

CHAPTER TWENTY

It Would Be a Terrible Mess

Cap Weinberger, meanwhile, would also do his part as secretary of defense to insure Bechtel's inside position in Washington's halls of power. While busy presiding over the largest department in the federal government—in the world's largest office building, the Pentagon—Weinberger oversaw a million civilian employees and a $218 billion budget. As the president's chief advisor on military matters, Weinberger had reached the pinnacle of power he had long sought, at the head of the army, navy, marine corps, and air force.

A supporter of a strong defense budget and obsessed with what he perceived as America's weakened standing in the world, Cap proceeded to usher in the largest military buildup in peacetime history. He had traveled throughout the Middle East as a Bechtel executive, and had come to believe that America was losing the support and respect of its allies because of Carter's erratic policies. He thought that the Soviet Union had made larger strides in defense capability than it actually had, and believed, wrongly as it turned out, that the USSR had a gigantic military advantage over the United States. He publicly expressed his shock at having learned through daily Pentagon briefings of the "size of the Soviet buildup and the rapidity with which it had taken place—in all areas, land, sea, and air."

Among his first moves in the Reagan administration was to recommend increasing the defense budget by $32 billion, including a push for new and expensive weapons systems such as the B-1 bomber, the Pershing II nuclear missile, and the Trident submarine. "To para-phrase Will Rogers, I think this administration has never seen a weapons system it didn't like," Les Aspin, the chairman of the House Armed Services Committee, told a reporter. The crux of Weinberger's agenda was a strong military buildup, the protection of American al-lies, and a rejection of Nixon-era détente. Weinberger was also the embodiment of privatization: replacing government departments and programs with for-profit, private companies. He had long advocated a Defense Department procurement policy that would generate higher profits for defense contractors—Bechtel included—and insure long-term and no-bid contracts to encourage private companies to engage in the military marketplace.

"The government has a long history of overpaying for weapons, of-fering interest-free loans, waiving federal taxes, bailing out flounder-ing defense contractors, and even paying generous termination fees to unsuccessful vendors," according to one account of the military-industrial symbiosis. But in the name of national security and anti-Communism, Weinberger elevated the practice to historic heights. It all amounted to a "government-subsidized industry, doing business over a safety net," wrote journalist Dan Briody. The onetime budget-cutting zealot nicknamed Cap the Knife was now a budget-escalating zealot newly nicknamed Cap the Shovel.

Weinberger's $1.6 trillion five-year "rearmament plan" was in preparation for a winnable nuclear war—a complete reversal from all foreign policy objectives since the Manhattan Project. He also called for the production of a stockpile of chemical weapons, again revers-ing American policy against chemical warfare that had been in effect since 1969. "Our long-term goal is to be able to meet the demands of a worldwide war, including concurrent reinforcement of Europe, de-ployment to Southwest Asia, and support in other potential areas of conflict," Weinberger said. The secretary of defense sought to redirect government funds "from virtually every domestic program to the mil-itary," according to one account.

While criticism of Weinberger's plans came from political fronts, that the four top national security officials were Californians—Reagan, Shultz, Weinberger, and William P. Clark—lent an air of solidarity to the administration's military goals. One of Reagan's closest and most trusted personal friends and confidants, the Stetson-wearing Clark was a rancher and devout Catholic with hard-line positions on military spending. Credited with convincing Reagan that the Soviets could be crushed by an aggressive arms race, Clark would recruit another reactionary Californian as Reagan's chief policy advisor. Edwin Meese III would hold Cabinet rank within the administration, and at times would so overshadow his boss that he once felt obliged to reassure the press that Reagan "is really running things."

Even though Reagan's economic advisors sniped at Cap's gargantuan rearmament and its effect on the deficit—one calling the department a "swamp" of waste and inefficiency and the General Accounting Office estimating that DOD's mismanagement was costing taxpayers $10 billion a year—the defense secretary dug in deeper. Both he and Bechtel were most fanatical about the five-part $222 billion strategic program to improve the nation's nuclear war–fighting capability and, especially, the deployment of the controversial MX missile system. Based upon a proposal drawn up by a presidential commission composed of Bechtel consultants, including the two former CIA directors, McCone and Helms, the US Air Force plan involved shuffling a hundred intercontinental ballistic MX missiles (ICBMs) between shelters in Nevada and Utah. Bechtel's Washington representatives had been lobbying for the MX—a missile that could travel 15,000 miles per hour, carrying 300-kiloton nuclear warheads up to 6,800 miles away and capable of a first strike against the Soviet Union. Bechtel expected to receive the DOD contract to build the system's massive infrastructure as well as provide the necessary enriched uranium for the warheads.

Many members of Congress and most of the nation's leading physicists were alarmed at Weinberger's messianic allusions to the possibility of fighting and *winning* a nuclear war—a complete and utter shift in American foreign policy from the avoidance of nuclear war to preparation for it. For the first time ever, the United States would be committed to the idea that a global nuclear war could be won—a concept that reversed the long-standing precept that nuclear war meant mutual suicide. "Reagan and Weinberger are only advancing the mystique about nuclear weapons and depriving the U.S. of money and resources for conventional weapons. And that, of course, reduces our options," said Stan Norris, a senior analyst for the Center for Defense Information, an independent nonprofit, nonpartisan think tank founded by retired military officers to analyze and influence defense policy. "If you have five weapons, four of which are nuclear, what kind of options does that leave?"

Gerard C. Smith, director of the US Arms Control and Disarmament Agency under Nixon, also saw Weinberger's rearming of America as distressingly dangerous. "The only purposes which these new weapons can serve are apparently to bolster our self-confidence and to make it more feasible to fight a protracted nuclear war," Smith told Congress. "It is difficult to see what contribution this expansion of nuclear bombs and warheads will make to our security." Reagan had been in office less than a year when he approved Weinberger's secret plan for preparing the United States to prevail in a protracted nuclear war with the Soviet Union. Guided by the elite Committee on the Present Danger—the potent Washington-based lobby cofounded by Shultz and McCone—the conservative agenda was a geopolitical, pro-defense spending view that had been mounting since World War II.

Throughout the 1970s, Bechtel supported the foreign policy think tanks, such as the Hoover Institution and the Heritage Foundation, that were attacking détente and the idea of a peaceful coexistence with the Soviet Union by mutually assured destruction. The "Cold War cabal of unreconstructed hawks and neohawks who had never been at ease with the arms control efforts of the Nixon, Ford, and Carter administrations suddenly came into its own," with Weinberger its instrument, wrote Robert Scheer in *With Enough Shovels*. He embodied the group's ideology and rejection of the possibility of peaceful coexistence with the Soviet Union. These "threat inflators," as one account described them, "dourly predict every success for the forces of evil" to drag the world back into the dangerous Cold War era—and a multibillion-dollar arms race. "My idea of American policy . . . is simple," President Reagan once told his aides when asked his view on the Soviet Union. "We win, and they lose." Still, while Reagan championed abolishing nuclear weapons his cabinet and business advisors who crafted policy worked at cross purposes.

For his part, the Episcopalian Weinberger saw the US-Soviet dynamic in biblical terms. "I have read the book of Revelation, and, yes, I believe the world is going to end—by an act of God, I hope—but every day, I think time is running out," he replied in the summer of 1982 to a question posed by a Harvard student about his apocalyptic vision. "I worry that we will not have enough time to get strong enough to prevent nuclear war. I think of World War II and how long it took to prepare for it, to convince people that rearmament for war was needed. I fear we will not be ready. I think time is running out . . . but I have faith."

With the committee's philosophy dominant in the Reagan administration—and with a president who had long shared its "rightist suspicions of détente"—the nuclear brinksmanship was acute. "It would be a terrible mess, but it wouldn't be unmanageable," Reagan's head of the Federal Emergency Management Agency (FEMA), Louis Onorato Giuffrida, told ABC News about how America could survive a nuclear war with the Soviet Union. "I think they would eventually, yeah. As I say, the ants eventually build another anthill." The brilliant Cornell University astronomer Carl Sagan entered what he saw as a grotesquely anti-intellectual debate on a subject that was undebatable. He penned a three-page hypothesis of the Doomsday Machine— as a 1967 *Star Trek* episode called it—that would result. Sagan's 1983 article, "The Nuclear Winter," a stark and terrifying warning, was published in *Parade* magazine, the Sunday newspaper supplement that reached an estimated 20 million readers. Using a model of a five-thousand-megaton nuclear exchange, Sagan wrote that land temperatures would drop to minus 25 degrees Celsius and stay below freezing for months, creating a climate catastrophe. "This would kill food crops and livestock, and lead to mass starvation among survivors who hadn't already perished in the blast," a later account described Sagan's predictions.

This extreme shift in American foreign policy shocked the Israelis, who were seething from Bechtel's pro-Arab influence in the Reagan administration. The "pro–Saudi Arabian group is in full control," the top Middle East intelligence expert for the US Air Force warned Israel in a public statement following Haig's resignation. Calling Shultz, Weinberger, and Habib "the boys from Bechtel," Dr. Joseph Churba said, "As long as policy making is in their hands, U.S. power and diplomacy will be irrelevant in the region." The renowned arms control specialist claimed that American foreign policy was now driven by "commercialism" and "economic greed" rather than by the best security interest of the United States.

At the same time, Weinberger became embroiled in a scandal revolving around an arms request from Saudi Arabia for a squadron of twenty F-15 jet fighter bombers, further upsetting the Israelis. When a Lebanese magazine published a transcript in the summer of 1983 showing that Weinberger was attempting to keep the arms sale secret from the president, Congress, and the media, the brazenness of his scheming stunned Israeli officials. In a Paris meeting with two Saudi defense ministers, Weinberger told them that the arms request should be concealed from the president because "the administration is suffering from leakage of information." According to the transcript, Weinberger's relationship with the Saudi officials dated back to his days at Bechtel, which led to a uniquely candid conversation. "I would like to confirm . . . that President Reagan does not know of your request," Weinberger told them. "If we were to inform President Reagan of your request, it would be leaked to Congress and the press, and a problem would be created, hampering delivery of new weapons to Saudi Arabia." In addition to the bombers, Weinberger also offered to deliver a new M-1 tank for a "tryout," boasting that this "model is not even in the hands of the American Army."

Weinberger's clandestine arms dealing sparked outrage in the United States and Israel, prompting New York City mayor Ed Koch to demand an explanation from the defense secretary. Koch said he was "appalled" that Weinberger was denying the president "access to information relating to our nuclear secrets and other vital information because of a lack of trust in his integrity in keeping government secrets." In an angry exchange of letters published in the *New York Times*, Koch accused Weinberger of "hostility to the State of Israel" and asked him if there is "a secret supergovernment in which the President is not a participant?" In response, Weinberger claimed the transcript was a "fabrication" and refused to answer Koch's questions, citing administration policy "not to reveal details of classified diplomatic exchanges." Still, Weinberger's stonewalling did little to calm Israel's nerves. Just a few months later, Israel's interests were once again undermined when George Shultz's State Deparrtment dispatched a presidential envoy to Iraq, one of Israel's foremost regional enemies, to lobby on behalf of a massive Bechtel project.

Ultimate Insiders

Brash and striving, wealthy and connected, Donald H. Rumsfeld would be the latest incarnation of the well-oiled revolving door, moving seamlessly among the worlds of government, business, politics, and intelligence. As a "young pup," he had worshipped at the "feet" of economist Milton Friedman and the "cluster of geniuses" that surrounded him. By that winter of 1983, Rumsfeld had risen to power from well-heeled beginnings in a Chicago suburb, of solid German stock and with a Princeton education, a stint as a navy pilot, and four terms in Congress beginning when he was just thirty years old. Short and sturdy, he had elbowed his way into the highest corridors of power, becoming Nixon's ambassador to NATO and Ford's secretary of defense, where he indulged a "preference for uniformed right-wing tyrants" throughout the world, according to former national security advisor Roger Morris. He had then parlayed those government sinecures into a multimillion-dollar corporate career as head of a worldwide pharmaceutical empire. When Shultz tapped him to do Bechtel's bidding in Iraq, Rumsfeld was installed in the private sector as president, chairman, and CEO of the Illinois-based G. D. Searle & Company, the manufacturer of oral contraceptives, the artificial sweetener Aspartame, and nuclear medicine imaging equipment.

In 1983 Iraq and Iran were still embroiled in a brutal armed conflict that had begun three years earlier when Iraq invaded Iran in a ground assault. The two countries had a long history of border disputes, but the current war was fueled by Iran's Islamic revolution that had spurred the ousting of the Shah—a proxy for US interests in the Middle East—and his replacement by the anti-American radical cleric Ayatollah Ruholla Khomeini. The vicious war, in which Saddam Hussein was using chemical weapons against Khomeini in violation of international law, had jeopardized the flow of oil out of the region. "After the Iranian revolution, Bechtel had been booted from Iran by the Ayatollah," as one account described the geopolitical conflict of the region. "To counter this ungracious exile, Bechtel warmed once again to its old friends in Iraq."

Reportedly sent to the Middle East in December 1983 in response to the recent terrorist bombing of an American military facility in Lebanon, Rumsfeld's top secret detour to visit Saddam in Iraq would remain classified for the next twenty years. He was the highest-ranking US official to visit Iraq since 1967, when Iraq and other Arab nations severed ties with the United States over American support of Israel in its successful Six-Day War against Egypt, Jordan, and Syria. The third Middle East envoy in three years—succeeding Bechtel consultant Habib—Rumsfeld, as an "unpaid government employee," told a skeptical press that he "simply wanted to be helpful." Despite Shultz's receiving intelligence reports of "almost daily use of CW [chemical weapons]" by Iraq, he gave Rumsfeld the authority to convey to the "Butcher of Baghdad" US willingness to help his regime and restore full diplomatic relations. "We believed the Iraqis were using mustard gas all through the war, but that was not as sinister as nerve gas," an ex-army intelligence officer told the British newspaper the *Guardian*. "They started using tabun"—a nerve gas. Still, Reagan signed a secret order instructing the administration to do "whatever was necessary and legal" to prevent Iraq from losing the war even though Israel maintained a vital interest in preventing its belligerent enemy Iraq from defeating Iran.

Shultz beckoned his old buddy Donald Rumsfeld for a sensitive and covert State Department assignment. While the ostensible goal of Rumsfeld's visit to Baghdad was to improve relations with Iraq, the primary impetus was to entice Saddam to allow Bechtel to build an oil pipeline across Iraq, from Kirkuk to the port of Aqaba on the Red Sea—in a clandestine mission that would remain secret for years. Bechtel's $2 billion project had the full support of the US government, and Rumsfeld's ninety-minute meeting in Saddam's palace was focused on convincing the Iraqi dictator to allow an American company access to Iraq's gigantic oil fields—the second-largest reserve in the world. "Acting as a special White House 'peace envoy,' allegedly to discuss with Hussein and then–foreign minister Tariq Aziz the bloody war between Iran and Iraq, Rumsfeld turns out . . . to have been talking not about that war, but about Bechtel's proposed Aqaba pipeline," according to an account of a State Department memo declassified in 2003.

Wearing military fatigues and with a pistol on his hip, Hussein expressed his concerns to Rumsfeld about the proximity of the pipeline to Israel, and the possibility that Israel would bomb it as it had Iraq's nuclear reactor. "I said I could understand that there would need to be some sort of arrangement that would give those involved confidence that it would not be easily vulnerable," Rumsfeld wrote in the memo.

In fact, it was "the revolving door between Bechtel and the Reagan administration that drove US-Iraq interactions," a report based on declassified government documents and internal Bechtel memoranda concluded twenty years later. That Institute for Policy Studies (IPS) report, titled *Crude Vision: How Oil Interests Obscured U.S. Government Focus on Chemical Weapons Use by Saddam Hussein*, exposed how the Bechtel-influenced Reagan administration "shaped and implemented a strategy that has everything to do with securing Iraqi oil exports" . . . and "bent many rules to convince Saddam Hussein to open up a pipeline." Jim Vallette, one of the authors, called it a "sordid tale" in which the highest levels of the US government "focused on getting a pipeline built from Iraq to Jordan on behalf of the extremely well-connected corporation Bechtel." At the same time, "Hussein's troops were dropping thousands of chemical bombs on the Iranians in the midst of the Iran-Iraq war." But Rumsfeld—called "a bagman for Bechtel" by Vallette and a "ruthless little bastard" by Nixon—made no

mention of Iraq's use of chemical warfare, instead impressing upon
Saddam the US desire to help Iraq increase its oil exports.

"As Saddam was gassing the Kurds, Rumsfeld, acting as a special
envoy for Reagan, turned up on the dictator's doorstep," reported the
Village Voice. He met with Hussein and "went on to talk glowingly
about great opportunities for the future"—and Bechtel's proposed
pipeline, wrote an investigative television producer. Rumsfeld did not
chastise Hussein for his illegal use of chemical weapons or for his pursuit of a nuclear bomb. "He was there to beg the dictator's indulgence
on behalf of Bechtel's dream pipeline to Aqaba."

Shultz's department orchestrated the initial discussions with Iraq,
inviting Bechtel executive Parker Hart to Washington to meet with
the State Department's policy planning council. Hart told his Bechtel
colleagues that the meeting took place "at State's invitation" to discuss
Bechtel's pursuit of the pipeline project. "Out of public view, State Department officials pushed the pipeline project on behalf of their boss's
former company, Bechtel," according to the report.

Behind the scenes, Shultz's closest advisors "composed Donald
Rumsfeld's pipeline pitch to Saddam." Shultz would maintain that he
was shielded from the pipeline negotiations, writing in his memoir
that all reports on the project "were withheld from me at the time, as
it appeared that the Bechtel Corporation might have a role in such a
project, and I had totally removed myself from knowledge of any matter that involved Bechtel." The same cannot be said of the department
he headed. A secret State Department cable entitled "Briefing Notes
for Rumsfeld Visit to Baghdad" reveals that Shultz's State Department
essentially provided assurance that US financing of the Aqaba pipeline was a fait accompli. "The problem now is for Iraq, Jordan, and the
company [Bechtel] to settle the technical issues so that the company
can make a formal presentation [to Ex-Im Bank]," it reported. The
cable also makes reference to Saddam's "support and sanctuary for the
Abu Nidhal [*sic*] terrorists" and his use of chemical weapons. Nidal
founded the Palestinian terrorist group Fatah and was responsible for
a string of terrorist acts, including atrocities in Europe. Still, Shultz di-

rected Rumsfeld to convince the Iraqis that "U.S. interests in improving U.S.-Iraq ties 'remain undiminished' despite [those] revelations."

Shultz "may not have directly promoted the Aqaba pipeline, but his
pursuit of diplomatic relations with Saddam Hussein clearly paved the
way for Bechtel to do business in Iraq," as one account described his
role. For its part, Bechtel published a denial of Shultz's participation in
the pipeline on its company website. Dated April 29, 2003: "Contrary
to mistaken critics, he played no role as secretary of state in promoting
a Bechtel pipeline project in the 1980s." Bechtel wrote further: "Aim-
ing to safeguard U.S. economic security, the administration backed
several alternative pipelines, not just the Aqaba proposal. Secretary
of State George Shultz, former president of Bechtel, properly recused
himself from the matter and at no time promoted the Aqaba pipeline,
contrary to recent reports based on a demonstrably mistaken reading
of the documentary record."

Intended to carry a million barrels per day of Iraqi oil exports,
the Bechtel pipeline financing would include $500 million of US-
taxpayer-backed loan guarantees. Weinberger and others in the Reagan
White House lobbied the Export-Import Bank to finance the pipeline.
"Stocked as it was with Bechtel loyalists," as one reporter described
it, "the Ex-Im Bank didn't need much prodding from above," but the
State Department's intervention on behalf of Saddam and Bechtel "put
the project on the fast track." Even Vice President George H. W. Bush
interceded personally, calling a former Yale University classmate—
Ex-Im Bank chairman William Draper III—to tell him it was impera-
tive that Ex-Im finance the Bechtel-built pipeline.

Meanwhile, Bechtel applied for $85 million in political risk insur-
ance from the Overseas Private Investment Corporation (OPIC)—
what Republican senator Wayne Allard called contemptuously "an
insurance company run by the U.S. federal government for corporations who want to invest in risky political situations"—and Reagan's
National Security Council pressured OPIC to back Bechtel's pipeline with guarantees. "Bechtel, U.S. government officials, and their
well-connected agents shuttled between Washington, Jerusalem,

Baghdad, and Amman for dozens of meetings aimed at cementing the pipeline deal," according to one account.

"I cannot emphasize enough the need for maximum Bechtel management effort at all levels of the U.S. government and industry to support this project," a Bechtel executive pressed his colleagues in an internal company memo when it appeared that Rumsfeld's diplomacy efforts were bearing fruit. "It has significant political overtones. The time may be ripe for this project to move promptly, with very significant rewards to Bechtel for having made it possible." Bechtel had ramped up its pressure on Saddam, recruiting two more high-level US intelligence officials: former CIA director James Schlesinger and former national security advisor William Clark.

Corporate and government documents that were later released revealed "the ways in which oil interests . . . became entwined with 'national security' objectives under Reagan." Reagan and Bechtel officials "worked hand-in-glove to gain access to Iraq's massive oil reserves, even in the face of conclusive evidence that Saddam's forces were unleashing weapons of mass destruction." Thanks to the symbiotic relationship between Bechtel and the government, the "company was virtually an unofficial expediter of U.S. policy, so close to Washington's thinking were its executives," wrote Alan Friedman, the global correspondent for the *International Herald Tribune*.

For his part, Rumsfeld justified the machinations and took credit for the reestablishment of US-Iraq diplomatic relations that occurred shortly after his Baghdad meetings. "Whatever misgivings we had about reaching out to Saddam Hussein, the alternative of Iranian hegemony in the Middle East was decidedly worse." The success of his efforts was seemingly confirmed when, less than a month after Rumsfeld's second trip to Baghdad, Reagan issued a top secret national security directive ordering Shultz, Weinberger, and Casey to "prepare a plan of action designed to avert an Iraqi collapse." If still overtly "neutral" in the Iran-Iraq war, US foreign policy had officially, covertly, shifted. "I hope they kill each other," Kissinger quipped. "Too bad they both can't lose."

Rumsfeld's role as Bechtel's chief lobbyist in Iraq was secret for twenty years, until the *Washington Post* published declassified government documents detailing his mission. The 2002 revelations were met with extensive criticism. Rumsfeld dismissed the condemnation as absurd. "My meeting with Saddam . . . has been the subject of gossip, rumors, and crackpot conspiracy theories for more than a quarter century," he wrote in his memoir. "Supposedly I had been sent to see Saddam by President Reagan either to negotiate a secret oil deal, to help arm Iraq, or to make Iraq an American client state. The truth is that our encounter was more straightforward and less dramatic." Although Rumsfeld would claim that he cautioned the Iraqi leader against using chemical weapons, there was "no mention of such a warning in the state department notes of the meeting," according to the *Guardian*.

Rumsfeld's ambassador-at-large petitioning on behalf of Bechtel's pipeline would not be the end of the Aqaba pipeline intrigues, which would ultimately become the focus of an independent counsel's bribery investigation. But many more maneuverings would occur first. "No one seemed concerned about weaving these obvious conflicts of interest into the peace process in the most volatile region of the world," a *New York Times* columnist would observe about what he described as the "ultimate insiders."

A Witch's Brew

"Jews were overly sensitive about gas due to their experiences during World War II," Jonathan "Jay" Pollard's superior officer laughed when Pollard asked why the Defense Department was withholding intelligence information from Israel about Saddam Hussein's development of a nerve gas factory. The remark spurred the US Navy analyst to action. "To Pollard, that comment was akin to stabbing his heart with a dagger," wrote an author who followed the Pollard spy case. "The US Navy, like many other naval establishments around the world, was the last refuge of the patrician bigot," Pollard would write.

Pollard's "short but intensive espionage career," as the CIA described it, began officially in late June 1984. Over the next eighteen months, he passed classified material to Israel concerning military developments in several Arab countries. Israel was facing a "technological Pearl Harbor," his handler told him, as it was being surrounded by enemy states armed with chemical, biological, conventional, and nuclear weapons. Among the first documents that Pollard provided Israel were "the details of Iraq's chemical warfare factories," according to Wolf Blitzer who, as a reporter with the *Jerusalem Post*, conducted an exclusive interview with Pollard.

The spy who would become Weinberger's antagonist thought that the defense secretary suffered from an "Amalek complex," in which, because of his Jewish ancestry, he has a "pathological need for self-denial" leading to a hatred of Jews and Israel. Whatever the provenance of Weinberger's fervent and unabashed hostility toward the Jewish state, it was that enmity that incited Pollard, a devout Jew, to become a spy for Israel. Ever mindful of his Jewish roots, Pollard was alarmed when Weinberger initiated a tacit intelligence embargo against Israel after Israel bombed Iraq's nuclear facility in June 1981, in the world's first air strike against a nuclear reactor.

The CIA, under the direction of William Casey—who was the first CIA director to attend White House meetings as a full Cabinet member—had overseen the covert transfer to Iraq of US-manufactured weapons in violation of international conventions (and despite Iraq's official status as a terrorist state). Like Casey, Weinberger, as Pollard saw it, was obsessed with redirecting "the focus of American strategic concern and commitment away from Israel and toward Saudi Arabia and the various Persian Gulf sheikdoms." While Shultz and Weinberger led the secret foreign policy shift toward Iraq, the bloody war escalated, with Israel watching America's changing foreign policy with trepidation.

When, in November 1983, a classified presidential directive removed Iraq from its list of countries that sponsored terrorism, private American suppliers began exporting what one account described as "a witch's brew of biological and chemical materials to Iraq"—all licensed by the Reagan administration's Commerce Department. "It wasn't just a tilt toward Iraq," ABC News reporter Ted Koppel observed, "it was an opening of the floodgates."

Pollard saw this new foreign policy as a betrayal of Israel by the United States. In his position as a naval intelligence specialist with a "higher-than-secret clearance, he was aware of information collected by various United States intelligence branches that he believed was critical to Israel's survival," a family member wrote later. But the most shocking and terrifying information of all—the intelligence that clinched his decision to offer Israel his services as a spy—was the evidence that Bechtel was in the planning stages to build a giant petrochemicals complex in Iraq called PC2. Located about forty-four miles south of Baghdad, near the natural gas feeder lines running from the southern oil fields, the project was estimated to cost over $2 billion and "was to be the pride of the Iraqi military establishment," wrote Alan Friedman. However, it had been delayed because of the Iran-Iraq war. "Western intelligence agents knew although PC2 would manufacture normal petrochemicals, upon completion, like many of Saddam's disguised operations, it would be dual-use. This meant it would be able to generate chemical compounds needed to make mustard gas and nerve gas as well."

A distinguished chemical weapons expert, Dr. W. Seth Carus, told the *Financial Times* of London that the PC2 Iraqi project was intended for both civilian and military purposes. Weinberger, in his capacity as general counsel for Bechtel, was aware of the PC2 project. "We were hired by the government of Iraq to be the project manager for an ethylene plant," a Bechtel senior vice president would later tell the British newspaper. The Bechtel spokesman denied that Hussein intended to make ethylene oxide—not only a precursor chemical for mustard gas but also a major ingredient in what a Senate investigative committee described as "fuel air explosive bombs." The official said that Bechtel received "direct encouragement" for the PC2 project from the US Department of Commerce.

"I watched the threats to Israel's existence grow and gradually came to the conclusion that I had to do something," Pollard later wrote. "The Iraqis were secretly manufacturing nerve gas specifically to use against Israeli urban areas." Once convinced that the United States was arming Hussein with chemical and biological weapons that could ultimately be used against Israel, Pollard felt he had no choice but to act. "As Diaspora Jews, our families instilled in us the vital importance of preserving human life through the deterrence of war," wrote Pollard's wife, Anne. "It was when Jay learned that a new generation of ultra sophisticated military equipment was being quietly positioned into the arsenals of our most despised enemies that he realized he could not stand idly by and witness the potential destruction of our racial homeland."

———

Born to Morris and Mildred Klein Pollard on August 7, 1954, the youngest of three children, Jay spent his childhood in Galveston, Texas, and his adolescence in South Bend, Indiana. His father, a world-renowned microbiologist and professor at the University of Notre Dame known for his research on prostate cancer, instilled a deep love for America in his family. "My parents never ceased in their efforts to portray this land [USA] . . . as a Godsend for Jews," Jay recalled. His parents were also ardent Zionists. "The first flag I could recognize in my early youth was that of Israel, and for years our family took quiet pride in my late uncle's decision to provide the fledgling Israeli Army in 1948 with military boots and medical supplies 'liberated' from the American Hospital in Paris, which he commanded at the time."

Pollard admitted later that "he had begun dreaming about future emigration to Israel at age 12 when that country won a dramatic victory in the six-day war of June 1967," the CIA reported. The Holocaust haunted the close-knit Pollard family, which lost seventy-five of their Lithuanian relatives in the Nazi death camps. Pollard "had traveled with his father to those then-silent camps and vowed he would never stand idly by if such threats were to surface again," his father-in-law wrote. He visited the German concentration camp at Dachau and was affected deeply by the experience, which kindled an abiding loyalty to Israel and the Jewish people. Pollard had a "growing determination to assist Israel," as the CIA put it.

Pollard had begun working in 1979 as an intelligence research specialist for the Naval Ocean Surveillance Information Center (NOSIC), where he "managed to gain the respect of most of his superiors" and achieved a series of rapid promotions. He was described as a "temperamental genius and a gifted person," his work as a Middle East warship analyst was deemed "outstanding," and he seemed to be flourishing in his position. All of that changed in 1981 when Ronald Reagan became president, and Pollard was assigned to one of the US intelligence teams supporting Weinberger's so-called Interagency Contingency Operations Plan—a plan created in 1982 with three levels of US response to an anticipated Israeli invasion of Lebanon, including a limited military action. Pollard thought the plan "looked like a blueprint for an undeclared war against Israel," according to one account.

"It was widely known that Weinberger favored an 'evenhanded' arms sales policy in the Middle East," Pollard told Wolf Blitzer, "and [Attorney General Edwin] Meese never hid his desire to have Israel placed on the 'Criteria Country List,' which would have categorized her with such pariah states as Libya, Cuba, and North Korea."

June 1984 is when Colonel Aviem "Avi" Sella—an Israeli hero who was the fighter pilot that led the bombing raid on the Osirak reactor—initially recruited Pollard at a synagogue in the Washington suburbs. Sella, a former officer in the Israeli intelligence agency, Mossad, had legendarily led the team that captured the fugitive Nazi official Adolf Eichmann in Argentina in 1960. Soon, over cocktails at the bar in the Washington Hilton Hotel, the two men spoke in Hebrew. Pollard told Sella of his willingness to provide intelligence information to Israel. Sella accepted his offer, while emphasizing that Israel did not seek any information on US military capabilities. Rather, the Jewish state sought to obtain as much classified documentation as possible on Saudi Arabia, as well as on Soviet air-defense systems. Sella wanted photographs of the bomb-damaged reactor, which the CIA's Casey had refused to share with Israel.

Sella established a secure procedure for their future clandestine meetings, involving several pay telephones within a few blocks of Pollard's northwest Washington residence. He also taught the nascent spy to use a code containing Hebrew letters and numbers. A few days later, Sella drove Pollard to a remote outdoor location near the historic Dumbarton Oaks estate in Georgetown. Pollard brought with him a briefcase containing a massive, three-volume intelligence analysis of Saudi Arabian military forces and the much-coveted satellite imagery of the Osirak bombing taken only hours after the Israeli strike.

In November 1984 Pollard traveled to Paris to receive formal instruction from the Israelis. He was given a fake passport and the number of a Swiss bank account that had been opened for him under the alias Danny Cohen. He was told the Israelis would deposit $30,000 every year for the expected ten years of his espionage work. He was introduced to Rafael Eitan, the counterterrorism advisor to Prime

Minister Yitzhak Shamir, who headed Lekem—an intelligence agency run out of the Defense Ministry. Eitan, as the senior Israeli in charge of Pollard's spying operation, directed him "to provide Israel with the best available U.S. intelligence on Israel's Arab adversaries and the military support they receive from the Soviet Union."

The Israelis told him of their "collection requirements, in descending order of priority: Arab (and Pakistani) nuclear intelligence; Arab exotic weaponry, such as chemical and biological weapons; Soviet aircraft; Soviet air defenses; Soviet air-to-air missiles and air-to-surface missiles; and Arab order-of-battle, deployments, readiness." Eitan also asked Pollard to provide any "dirt" on Israeli political figures and to identify any Israeli officials who might be spying on Israel for the United States.

The Territory of Lies

Every other Friday, Pollard delivered briefcases full of classified intelligence information to a Washington, DC, apartment rented by a secretary who worked for the Israeli Embassy. He later described the Israelis' needs as insatiable, and claimed he was assured that the items he provided were "known and appreciated by 'the highest levels of the Israeli government.' " As "the urgency of their requests took on an almost infectious quality, my whole life seemed to be driven by a fear of overlooking something that might ultimately prove catastrophic," he told a reporter during a jailhouse interview. "Literally everything I showed them set off alarm bells, particularly those things pertaining to nuclear and chemical warfare advances in the Arab world."

Evidence of the Iraqi chemical warfare production facilities and the US transfer of weapons to Saddam Hussein—who had vowed to annihilate Israel—"shocked the hell out of them," according to Pollard. "Everything I seemed to show them was like adding stones on top of a man desperately trying to remain afloat in shark-infested waters, and as each new revelation confronted them with seemingly insurmountable problems, another one arose to replace it. At times, it seemed as if I were becoming the traditional messenger of bad tidings, sowing the intelligence equivalents of the proverbial dragon's teeth."

Pollard and his handlers were especially anxious about the construction by Bechtel of the dual-use PC2 facility in Iraq that required waivers from the US Departments of Defense and State—agencies headed, respectively, by the former Bechtel executives Weinberger and Shultz. Pollard had firsthand knowledge that Saddam Hussein was building one of the world's largest chemical warfare complexes. "What was I supposed to do?" he responded to an interviewer. He gave Israel satellite pictures of these factories, "together with U.S. intelligence assessments of what these factories were doing," said a staff member from the Senate Intelligence Committee. At the same time, the Reagan administration was assuring the Israelis that there was no evidence that Iraq was building a poison-gas complex. Many of the US spy photos he supplied to Israel "were of a number of Iraqi chemical weapons manufacturing plants which the Reagan administration did not want to admit existed," according to the *Wall Street Journal.*

Over the course of his short-lived spy career, Pollard reportedly provided Israel with an unknown number of classified documents. Pollard became so passionate about the urgency of the cause that he increased his document retrieval, letting down his guard and drawing attention from coworkers. At one point, he filled five suitcases with secret documents and spent four hours brazenly carrying them from his office to the car, with a NOSIC security guard helping him with the door. "Jay laughed about how easily he had sneaked the material past the lax security," CBS war correspondent Kurt Lohbeck wrote. Eventually, though, an Anti-Terrorist Alert Center (ATAC) officer reported Pollard's suspicious behavior, and the FBI opened a criminal investigation.

On November 21, 1985, Pollard sensed that his capture was imminent. Since his Israeli handlers had assured him repeatedly that they would protect him if his spy services were detected, he drove his green Ford Mustang to the Israeli Embassy in Washington to seek asylum. "Wiping away beaded perspiration from his forehead, and speaking at a fast pace, Jonathan spilled out his plight in both English and Hebrew," telling the guards he was a spy who sought the "Law of Return," which automatically grants Israeli citizenship to Jews. But as an undercover FBI surveillance team watched from outside the gates, embassy guards refused to let him enter. A guard yelled, "You must leave!" and shoved him toward his parked car off the premises—where diplomatic sanctuary did not extend. Pollard was in his car only a few minutes before US federal agents ordered him to "get out" and arrested him. Later revelations would show that Pollard's own handlers, including Eitan, had abandoned him in order to avoid "headlines" that would create problems for the Israelis, as Eitan admitted nearly thirty years later. In fact, it was Eitan himself who, in an encoded phone call with the Israeli Embassy, ordered him thrown out of the compound.

A lover of spy novels, Pollard "told his parents that if they wanted to understand his mission, they should watch the Robert Redford thriller *Three Days of the Condor.*" As part of his guilty plea and relinquishment of his right to a fair trial—and in exchange for a guarantee that the prosecution would not seek a life sentence—Pollard agreed to cooperate with government investigators. His testimony was deemed accurate and was corroborated by polygraphs. But when it came time for sentencing, Prosecutor Joseph DiGenova gave Weinberger the opportunity to "deliver the knockout punch." In a forty-six-page classified ex parte memorandum that Weinberger submitted to the sentencing judge, he wrote that it was difficult "to conceive of a greater harm to national security" than that caused by Pollard. He compared the case to the infamous 1950s spy case in which American Jewish citizens Julius and Ethel Rosenberg were executed for passing information to the Soviet Union, and implored the court to impose "severe punishment" that reflected the "magnitude of the treason committed"—despite the fact that Pollard was never charged with treason.

Shultz did his part as well to insure that Pollard would face a long prison term. "As secretary of state, Shultz handled some of the earliest high-level contacts with the Israelis when the case first broke," reported Gil Hoffman in the *Jerusalem Post.* "According to the . . . Eban Report by the Knesset committee that investigated the Pollard affair, Shultz requested and secured from then prime minister Shimon Peres a commitment to return the documents that Pollard had provided to Israel. These documents were then used by the Americans to indict Pollard, and served as the only evidence against him."

In a federal plea deal, Pollard had been promised to have his sentence commuted to time already served in exchange for cooperating with the US government. So the life sentence that he received a year and a half after his arrest shocked him, his family, and his dozens of supporters. On a cold and overcast day, in the crowded Washington, DC, courtroom, Pollard embraced his wife so tightly and for so long that they had to be separated by federal marshals. Guards removed the portly thirty-two-year-old Texas native, who had once been "a slender child with an inquisitive mind"—a "mama's boy" who had graduated from Stanford University with a degree in political science and was then rejected for a fellowship with the CIA because he admitted using marijuana. Pollard began his life sentence in a ward for the criminally insane—a freezing cell without a mattress, where he heard inhuman screams that "sounded like something straight out of Dante's *Inferno*"—and then, for the next five years, spent twenty-three hours a day in solitary confinement. He would spend subsequent decades at the Federal Correctional Institutions in Marion, Illinois, and, ultimately, at Butner, North Carolina. "I would rather spend the rest of my life in jail than mourn for thousands of Israelis who died as a result of my cowardice," Pollard described his devotion to the cause.

What became known as the Pollard affair—the epithet meant to be analogous with the historic Dreyfus affair, in which a French officer of Jewish descent was wrongly convicted of treason—inevitably divided the American Jewish community between those who felt America came first and those who saw their primary allegiance to Israel. The chasm prompted what one writer called "Jews judging Jews." Pollard, as one Israeli put it, was the "American counterpart of Émile Zola . . . who shouted the famous words, '*J'accuse*.' "

Apparently feeling that even a life sentence without the possibility of parole was too lenient for Pollard, Weinberger told the Israeli ambassador to the United States that the spy "should have been shot." His memo sabotaged Pollard's plea bargain agreement with the government, prompting widespread speculation in both the United States and Israel about Weinberger's motives. Pollard's side felt the animus seemed too deep-seated and hardened to be attributed solely to Weinberger's alleged anti-Semitism, believing that he was protecting exposure of both Bechtel's corporate interests in the Arab world as well as Reagan's erratic Middle East foreign policy.

The Weinberger memo was not shared with Pollard's attorneys, and would remain sealed and classified over the next twenty-eight years under the auspices of national security. Pollard family members long contended that Weinberger was outraged that Pollard had told the Israelis about Bechtel's PC2 plant in Iraq, which, if generally known, would have caused embarrassment not only to Bechtel and Weinberger but also to the Reagan administration, which was arming Iraq while publicly claiming neutrality. The pictures and intelligence assessments about the Bechtel PC2 plant in Iraq "contradicted what the US government was officially telling Israel. So the Israelis were coming to America, and in official meetings were calling people like Weinberger liars, which, of course, these officials did not appreciate," according to a Senate staffer.

Such revelations might have been motivation enough for Weinberger's obsession with the case. But Bechtel's PC2 plant was only one of many secrets in the convoluted crossroads where Pollard, Weinberger, Bechtel, and Israel intersected during what the CIA called that "Year of the Spy." While working for Israel, Pollard had stumbled into the middle of Reagan's global covert wars being waged from the office of Vice President Bush. While Pollard was sleuthing in Bush's covert world, the vice president was joining Weinberger, Shultz, Henry Kissinger, and John McCone at Bohemian Grove as guests of the Bechtels.

Pollard's job with the Naval Intelligence Anti-Terrorism Unit was to monitor the maritime movements of suspected arms shipments to terrorists. It was in that capacity that in the summer of 1984 he had detected an unusual series of vessels traveling back and forth from Greece to Yemen, where the Palestine Liberation Organization (PLO) had a base. Pollard tipped off the Israelis, who tipped off the Greeks, who then apprehended a ship loaded with arms for the PLO. Those arms, according to the Pollard camp, were to be exchanged for American hostages being held in Lebanon by Islamic terrorists.

Pollard had accidentally "busted the most secret White House operation of modern times," as one account put it. "Neither Pollard nor the government of Israel was aware that they had smashed George Bush's first shipment of arms to Iran." If the 1984 Yemen-bound ship detected by Pollard was indeed part of what would become known as the Iran-Contra arms-for-hostages scheme, as the Pollard defenders claim, the beginning date of that illegal covert operation was a full year earlier than has been fixed by congressional investigators. Although Pollard didn't yet know it, he had inadvertently detected, and might have exposed, what would become one of the most sensational foreign policy scandals of the twentieth century.

"Joseph DiGenova—the U.S. attorney who promised he would not seek life imprisonment for Pollard—has invoked the old canard of dual loyalty by Jews who support Israel," wrote Alan M. Dershowitz, the controversial Harvard law professor who became one of Pollard's most steadfast allies. "He has argued that a Jew who spies for Israel should receive a higher sentence than a non-Jew who spied for the former Soviet Union . . . This sort of soft-core anti-Semitism has resulted in the double standard being applied to Jews and non-Jews who work for American intelligence agencies."

"The Hunting Horse," as high-level Israeli officials reverentially called their valuable agent-in-place who had burrowed deep within the US intelligence apparatus, seemed destined to die in his North Carolina prison cell.

Despite his best efforts to silence Pollard, Weinberger would not escape his own entanglement in the Iran-Contra conspiracy, for which he would ultimately face criminal charges. "History proved that in the midst of condemning Pollard's conduct, the secretary of defense was illegally participating in a scheme to sell arms to Iran and divert the profits to rebels fighting a civil war in Nicaragua," as one account described the hypocrisy. "While Weinberger crucified Pollard for breaking the law, he was doing so as well."

On the day in March 1987 that Pollard was sentenced to life, Reagan gave a speech denying that any of his presidential advisors, including Weinberger, had secretly and illegally covered up the Iran-Contra affair. "With my eyes shut and not fully aware of the consequences, I entered the territory of lies without a passport for return," Pollard later wrote.

A Tangled Scheme

Called "the most dangerous breach of presidential authority since Watergate," Iran-Contra was a labyrinthine conspiracy to trade weapons for seven American hostages kidnapped by Hezbollah, a fundamentalist Shiite Muslim group sympathetic to Iran, and being held in Lebanon. Despite his public vow not to negotiate with terrorists, Reagan initiated covert action to deal with them in exchange for the release of the seven hostages. The convoluted scenario called for selling arms to Iran—a country that George Shultz had officially designated as a sponsor of international terrorism in January 1983—to be used in its ongoing war with Iraq, which the United States was also secretly arming in violation of both the US arms embargo and stated policy. As the plot was conceived, the Iranian leaders would then pressure the terrorist kidnappers to release the hostages.

"At the time," according to Independent Counsel Judge Lawrence E. Walsh, who investigated the case for eight years, "the United States was vigorously urging its allies to present a united front in refusing to traffic with terrorists and hostage takers and to refrain from shipping arms to either Iraq or Iran."

As part of the bizarre plot, the proceeds from these illegal arms sales would be deposited in Swiss bank accounts and then diverted to Nicaragua to fund the paramilitary activities of the Contras—Reagan's treasured "freedom fighters" who were a right-wing guerrilla insurgency group seeking to overthrow the social democratic government of that country. "One of the most complicated and intrigue-filled scandals in recent decades," the *Washington Post* described the "grand scheme that violated American law and policy all around: arms sales to Iran were prohibited; the US government had long forbidden ransom of any sort for hostages; and it was illegal to fund the contras above the limits set by Congress."

To circumvent the ban on providing arms to Iran—and to dodge congressional oversight—the White House had enlisted Israel to act as a conduit for the weapons. The plan called for Israel to ship missiles to Iran from its own stockpile with its arsenal then to be replenished by the United States through Weinberger's Department of Defense. At the same moment that America was arming Iran via Israel, top secret intrigues involving Bechtel, Israel, and Iraq were also under way— what *BusinessWeek* described as "a tangled scheme" surrounding the Bechtel pipeline project. In a continuing irony of strange bedfellows during that heightened season of espionage, covert arms trafficking, and foreign policy dissembling, Bechtel executives were pressing officials at the highest levels of the Israeli government to promise that Israel would not bomb the proposed Bechtel-built pipeline in Iraq.

What grew into an international scandal had begun after Rumsfeld convinced Saddam Hussein to let Bechtel build the pipeline from Iraq's Kirkuk oil fields to Aqaba on the Red Sea. But the Iraqi dictator was demanding that Bechtel and the Ex-Im Bank assume the responsibility for hundreds of millions of dollars in construction loans in the event that Israel destroyed the pipeline. "Saddam may have been born in a hut and he may show a peculiar fascination with romance novels, but he was more than an intellectual match for the plodding Rumsfeld," wrote investigative journalist Jeffrey St. Clair. Hussein was reluctant to hand over $2 billion to Bechtel for a pipeline that ran so close to Israel.

Saddam was "offended" by Rumsfeld's offer for the US government to intervene with Israel to seek assurances regarding the security of the Bechtel pipeline. The "underlying hostility between Baghdad and Tel Aviv was so acute that US efforts came close to backfiring," as a national security expert described the sensitivity of the subject. George Shultz's State Department, working out of public view to get the pipeline built and to restore full diplomatic relations with Iraq, was alarmed at "the depth of Iraqi feeling about Israel." That left the thorny dilemma of how Bechtel, long distrusted and despised by Israel, could entice it to pledge nonaggression. Given Bechtel's historic schism with Israel, the proposition was dicey.

The company sought a middleman and initiated a "global lobbying blitz," as *BusinessWeek* described its efforts. "That's where the intrigue began." The man whom Bechtel hired as its go-between—joining Schlesinger and Clark—was a shady Swiss billionaire banker and oilman named Baruch "Bruce" Rappaport, a close personal friend and golfing partner of CIA head Casey as well as a longtime intimate of Israel's prime minister, Shimon Peres. The Israeli-born Rappaport "surfaced in several of the most significant political events of the Reagan White House years, including the war between Iraq and Iran," according to two renowned criminologists. "In a project where the lines between corporation and government were often obscure, Clark obliterated them," wrote an analyst of the John le Carré–like drama. While on Bechtel's payroll, via Rappaport, Clark misleadingly presented himself to the Iraqis as a government official.

Rappaport succeeded in brokering a deal. Israel agreed to protect the pipeline if Bechtel would sell it oil at reduced rates for ten years—"a reduction worth $650 million to $700 million," the *New York Times* reported. Rappaport also promised Israel that Bechtel would provide $70 million to go into the political coffers of Peres, then-leader of Israel's Labor Party. "I am following with great interest the projected pipeline from Iraq to Jordan as a possible additive to introduce economic consideration to this troubled land," Peres wrote to Meese on September 19, 1985. "Apparently an Israeli guarantee may help to pave the way to the construction of this p/l [pipeline]. I would go a long way to help it out. But then discretion is demanded on our part. I shall be in the USA in the middle of October, and I intend to talk it over with George Shultz, for whom I have the highest regard." Bechtel would later deny having authorized Rappaport's offer to Peres.

Because such a payment to Peres would have violated the 1977 Foreign Corrupt Practices Act that prohibits US citizens, companies, or their agents from paying "anything of value" to foreign officials, governments, or political parties for help in obtaining business, reports of the deal prompted a federal criminal investigation. James C. McKay, an independent prosecutor, was appointed to investigate alleged financial improprieties of Meese, who, while attorney general, was also acting as a negotiator with Rappaport to establish a US-backed insurance fund to guarantee the security of the pipeline. At the same time, Independent Counsel Walsh was scrutinizing Meese's involvement in Iran-Contra. Shultz detached himself from Meese as the investigation intensified, later describing perhaps the "most derided high official of the Reagan administration . . . a kind of unfathomable St. Patrick, talking the snakes out of their holes; what he would do with those snakes afterward, I was never sure."

George Lardner of the *Washington Post* wrote: "The twists and turns of the pipeline project . . . suggest how easy it can be for private entrepreneurs to get the support of US officials by waving the banner of national security over questionable transactions." During the pipeline machinations—what was later called scornfully "a protection racket" by advisors to the National Security Council—the White House bypassed usual foreign policy channels to pursue a construction project that furthered the corporate interests of Bechtel over the national security interests of the United States. In the process, the Reagan administration had set loose an unaccountable operation that was opaque to government oversight. The episode underscored the "use of under-the-table favors that have produced political or financial benefits for private citizens by skirting procedures designed to make policy on the basis of national interest, not personal gain," as the *Los Angeles Times* described it. "The principal players in the pipeline deal—Iraq, Jordan, Rappaport, the giant construction firm Bechtel Group Inc., and a parade of bankers—had the money and expertise to stretch a steel pipe 590 miles across a desert in the middle of a potential Mideast war zone." Rappaport ultimately admitted that he personally stood to make a staggering $200 million a year from the oil sales to Israel—what he called a "quid pro quo for a written security agreement" from Israel.

As the Iran-Contra affair and the Iraqi pipeline deal converged, the scandals' respective independent counsels—Walsh and McKay— began sharing information in search of links between the two cases that involved several of the same figures. "What is clear is that . . . private citizens used their friendship with government officials to make money, and international policy was affected by business interests," the Fort Lauderdale *Sun-Sentinel* concluded. Judge Walsh and a team of lawyers reviewed hundreds of thousands of documents, which led to the indictment of several of the administration's highest-level national security officials, including Weinberger, in the Iran-Contra conspiracy.

Meanwhile, McKay granted Rappaport immunity from prosecution in exchange for his cooperation with the Aqaba pipeline investigation and subpoenaed hundreds of Bechtel documents. "That unwelcome attention has the engineering and construction giant squirming," reported the *New York Times*. "But its real difficulty these days continues to be the problem that got it involved in the Iraqi project to begin with—a dearth of large construction projects in the Middle East and elsewhere that had traditionally been Bechtel's main source of income." Saudi Arabia had also stopped construction of a $1 billion refinery Bechtel was building at Port Qasim, as conflicts in the region and oil company manipulation led to dwindling oil revenues.

Meese resigned under a cloud of suspicion, for among other things, his unseemly role as intermediary between Bechtel and various collaborators in the scheme, "becoming an object of media ridicule and late-night jokes, depicting the pudgy prosecutor of public morality as the James Watt of the Justice Department." Prior to his resignation, several top Justice officials quit in protest of Meese's improper acts as the country's top law enforcement officer. But the government's bribery probe came to a halt when, after four expensive years of Bechtel's strategizing, Saddam refused to trust the Israelis' promises and began equivocating on the pipeline.

"Though the pipeline might have had an important geopolitical context," according to an examination of the case, "just about everyone else saw it as a private financial package that contained some fairly shady elements." Despite the close ties between Rappaport, Meese, and high-level Bechtel executives—including Steve Jr. and his son and heir apparent, Riley—the company avoided charges, if not unwanted publicity. In 1988 the *New York Times* reported that Bechtel had not been accused of "any illegality in connection with the scuttled Iraqi pipeline project but is being scrutinized by the special prosecutor investigation of Attorney General Edwin Meese 3d." Bechtel executives "tried to distance themselves from any potential illegalities," according to the news report.

A company spokesman denied that Bechtel was aware of any effort to pay off Israeli officials. Steve Jr. also sought to separate the company from its close associate and go-between Rappaport, who, "though rich and successful," was thought by many who worked with him "to be a somewhat loathsome financial criminal, protected by the intelligence services of the United States and Israel." For his part, Peres—"choking with rage"—denied that he or his party received bribes. "Israel agreed not to harm the pipeline . . . so there was no need to bribe anyone," he told a radio interviewer in Jerusalem.

Such global exploits by Bechtel had been pro forma for decades, if shrouded from unsolicited inspection. But the symbiosis between Bechtel and Reagan's regime went beyond run-of-the-mill conflict of interest. So too did Bechtel's long-standing relationship with Iraq. For years Bechtel "had been bending over backward to please his [Saddam Hussein's] every whim," according to an account of the company's interactions with Iraq dating back nearly fifty years to when Bechtel executive George Colley was fatally bludgeoned and dismembered by an anti-American Iraqi mob. Undeterred by Colley's murder, Bechtel had expanded its presence in the country and assisted Saddam's corrupt regime in numerous projects. Bechtel was among what a *60 Minutes* producer, Barry Lando, described as "American and foreign businessmen, leaders of agribusiness, oil tycoons, and arms merchants from across the globe who profited handsomely from doing business with Saddam Hussein while closing their eyes to what he was up to—or, in some cases, despite knowing full well."

Bechtel's unmitigated decades-long wooing of Saddam would continue, including the relentless pursuit of the massive petrochemical plant to be built near Baghdad. The $2 billion project involved construction of a plant capable of producing 450,000 tons per year of ethylene and 67,000 tons per year of ethylene oxide. According to secret State Department cables that were later declassified, Bechtel was awarded the contract for the project. When the US Senate passed a genocide bill invoking economic sanctions against Iraq for its use of chemical weapons—a bill that prohibited American firms from selling the restricted technology—Bechtel assured Saddam it would find a way around the prohibition. In what one cable described as a "lengthy diatribe" about the US sanctions, Saddam's nephew and son-in-law, Husayn Kamil, "fulminated" to Bechtel representatives that the Senate action was "part of a Zionist conspiracy to embarrass and undermine Iraq." For one and a half hours, Kamil "vented his spleen," according to Bechtel executives at the meeting.

The Bechtel agents assured Kamil, who was also Iraq's weapons procurement commander and who directed Iraq's ballistic missile and chemical weapons programs, that if the act was signed into law, Bechtel would "turn to non-U.S. suppliers of technology and continue to do business in Iraq." Stunningly, the company's declared intention to move ahead with the project "regardless of the provisions" of the Senate act calling for strict economic sanctions against Iraq elicited no comment from US Ambassador April Glaspie, who related details of the meeting in a classified cable from the embassy in Baghdad to the State Department in Washington.

The sanctions against Iraq were not enacted, thanks to vehement lobbying by Shultz and other members of the Reagan administration. Further, Shultz's State Department refused to impose controls on the export of biological toxins to Iraq. Bechtel continued its dealings with Saddam, remaining optimistic about the pipeline long after the dictator had backed away from it.

PART THREE

DIVIDING THE SPOILS

1989–2008

War began last week. Reconstruction starts this week.

—*NEW YORK TIMES*

A Deal with the Devil

Riley P. Bechtel, "by all accounts the ablest" of Steve Jr.'s children, acquired his corporate skills as the thirty-two-year-old intermediary in the gripping maneuvers among the Bechtel Group, Saddam Hussein, and Bruce Rappaport. If his role as fourth-generation company leader was ever in doubt, the skills he exhibited as managing director of Bechtel Ltd. in London during the seminal Reagan era solidified his position. Even though the pipeline deal had collapsed, Bechtel remained in Saddam's good graces, and Iraq had contracted with Bechtel's London office, headed by Riley, to build the PC2 chemical plant. "The U.S. embassy in Baghdad was pleased for Bechtel, as was the Department of Commerce in Washington, which encouraged Bechtel to go ahead," according to a history of the US covert arming of Iraq. Bechtel, also pleased, "thought nothing of the request from Baghdad that they accept payment through letters of credit" from a tiny Atlanta, Georgia, branch of the Rome-based Banca Nazionale del Lavoro (BNL), Italy's largest state-controlled bank. The US Department of Agriculture's Commodity Credit Corporation (CCC)—a fund designed to create export markets for US farmers—was using BNL to funnel money to Saddam to avoid congressional scrutiny.

Western intelligence agents later confirmed that much of the $3 billion that went from BNL to Iraq was used to finance that country's development of unconventional weapons systems, including the Condor II ballistic missile, as well as nuclear, chemical, and biological

projects. When details of BNL payments to Bechtel's subsidiary in the
United Kingdom came to light, Tom Flynn, a senior vice president at
Bechtel, told the *Financial Times* of London that "the company never
knew there was anything suspect" about the BNL funds. Flynn said
Bechtel was encouraged directly by the Department of Commerce
to build the plant, which he denied would be used to make chemical
weapons.

For more than a decade, Iraq was "able to acquire sophisticated
U.S. technology, intelligence material, ingredients for chemical weapons, indeed, entire weapon-producing plants, with the knowledge,
acquiescence and sometimes even the assistance of the U.S. government," according to a long-running series of investigative reports on
ABC News. As secretary of defense, Weinberger had been in the thick
of weapons transfers to Iraq, even though, as former NSC official
Howard Teicher put it, "There was no way that any casual observer
who took any interest in Iraqi matters and the Arab-Israel situation,
the Middle East situation, could but conclude that Iraq was an enemy
of the United States." Teicher had heard reports from both the Defense
and State Departments about transfers to Iraq taking place illegally
through Jordan—transfers that both Weinberger and Shultz denied.

Government financing for the Bechtel-built plant capable of manufacturing chemical weapons, along with numerous other sensitive Iraqi
projects, would become a scandal of such magnitude that it earned
itself a moniker. Iraqgate left behind a trail of murky US government–
backed financing through Italian and American banks, dummy corporations, criminal allegations, and an international cast of conspirators.
Before it was over, a full-scale congressional investigation would expose the presidential administrations of both Reagan and his successor, George H. W. Bush, for their double-dealing policy of collaborating
with foreign arms merchants in arming the loathsome Saddam while
condemning such efforts publicly. The probe would find that BNL had
funneled billions of dollars, some in US credits, to build Saddam's formidable arsenal. Called "the mother of all foreign policy blunders" by
Texas congressman Henry Gonzalez, in Iraqgate, US taxpayers turned

a "run-of-the-mill dictator" into a Frankenstein monster. The BNL shell game was a case study of how the "executive branch, working with private business" ran an off-the-books foreign policy, according to one study that described it as a "deal with the devil."

Such blurred lines between Bechtel and the US government raised few eyebrows in Congress, with only a handful of legislators questioning whether Bechtel was the corporate arm of America or if America was the government affairs arm of Bechtel. "When it comes to governmental relations, Bechtel goes both ways: it penetrates the government and the government penetrates it," according to one account. This is not simply a question of conflict of interest, or the "fevered imaginings of a conspiracy," journalist William Greider wrote, but about men "mixing their private interests with their public obligations . . . These men do not need telex messages from the Bechtel headquarters to tell them what to think about America and the world. They already think it." They already think alike because they have all "slid back and forth through the door marked private money." George H. W. Bush's presidential victory in 1988—the campaign's treasure chest swelled with money from Bechtel executives and employees—insured the company's seamless interdependence and continuing influence with the government.

Saddam's production of ethylene oxide—a chemical converted easily to thiodiglycol, which is used to make mustard gas—and the US government's support of it, would spark outrage among his enemies in the Middle East. Shultz, having completed his term as secretary of state, had returned to California and reassumed his position on the Bechtel board of directors. Concerned about the looming BNL scandal, and later claiming to have been alarmed at how easily Saddam could convert the plant to a factory for weapons of mass destruction, he reportedly recommended that Bechtel withdraw from the project. His advice was ignored for several months, he said, until he became more forceful. At a board meeting in the spring of 1990, Shultz told his fellow board members that "something is going to go very wrong in Iraq and blow up, and if Bechtel is in it, it will get blown up too."

Riley Bechtel, who had become the new president and CEO in 1989 when his father, Steve Jr., stepped down, listened to Shultz and decided to withdraw the company from the PC2 plant, although Bechtel workers would still be on the site a year later.

Bechtel auspiciously abandoned the project just as the BNL investigation burst onto front pages throughout the world. Congressional and media investigations exposed how billions of dollars of off-the-books loans and credits financed Iraq's "world gray market in arms, and its plans to build viable nuclear, chemical, and biological weapons programs," according to the National Security Archive—an independent, nongovernmental research institute located at George Washington University.

For years, both the Reagan and Bush administrations were willing to ignore Saddam's brutality and use of chemical weapons while continuing to assist his regime. In just the five years from 1985 through 1989, the US government approved 771 licenses for exports of biological agents, high-tech equipment, and military items valued at $1.5 billion. "The United States spent virtually an entire decade making sure that Saddam Hussein had almost whatever he wanted," Connecticut congressman Sam Gejdenson told a House Foreign Affairs subcommittee. In fact, as late as January 1990, President Bush overrode congressional objections and authorized a new Ex-Im line of credit worth nearly $200 million for Iraq. In July 1990, less than a month before Iraq invaded its neighbor Kuwait, setting in motion the events that would soon lead to the first Gulf War, Bush lobbied against a congressional amendment that would have restricted agricultural credits to Iraq.

All of that would change, as the well-placed Shultz predicted it would. Whether driving or following American foreign policy, Bechtel joined the US government to become united in a hard-line stance against the tyrant, whom President Bush took to calling "Hitler revisited," when Saddam decided to reject the Aqaba pipeline. Iraq's refusal to approve the lucrative Bechtel pipeline signaled a drastic and irreversible schism in US-Iraqi relations. "Many trace the breakdown in negotiations over the pipeline as the beginning of the end of U.S. relations with Iraq," wrote investigative journalist Antonia Juhasz.

The investigation of BNL officials and the collapse of the US-supported backdoor financing of Iraq's military arsenal led a desperate Saddam to invade Kuwait on August 2, 1990. "American officials tolerated Hussein's despotism because they viewed his regime as a secular bulwark against the Islamic fundamentalist revolution spawned by the Iranian revolution," wrote journalist Jim Crogan. "That is, until Iraq invaded oil-rich Kuwait in 1990."

The abrupt foreign policy tilt from Iraq would have ramifications for Bechtel, which would lose billions in long-anticipated profits from the now lifeless pipeline and PC2 projects. The promoters of the Bechtel pipeline, including Shultz, Weinberger, Meese, and Rumsfeld, who had courted and supported Saddam—all the while overlooking the dictator's murderousness and brutality in pursuit of the vast oil resources he controlled—now urged President Bush to attack him.

One of Iraq's first acts within days of invading Kuwait was taking 109 Bechtel employees in Iraq hostage, many of them construction workers on the PC2 plant and on oil refineries and rigs in the Persian Gulf. Rounded up from five different hotels and other locations, the employees were housed around Baghdad. Untold numbers of employees and their family members sought refuge in their respective embassies, while still more found sanctuary in the nearby lavish estate of Ambassador Glaspie. The Bechtel hostages lived "in ways far removed from privations of hostage life elsewhere," the New York Times reported. At the British Embassy, sixty-five of them lived in "tents on a corner of the broad lawn that stretches in front of Britain's Ottoman-era chancery. On weekends, the men play cricket on the lawn. With the pillared porticoes of the embassy as a backdrop, the setting seems like something out of Rudyard Kipling or Somerset Maugham stories." Across the city, in the diplomatic quarter of Masbah, another twenty-three employees lived in a diplomatic residence guarded by an Iraqi soldier. "Within, in gardens graced by willowy palm trees and a pool, the Americans pass their days reading, watching videos, and talking."

Bechtel's official account of the hostage taking was vague regarding details but boasted of Riley's masterful negotiation for his employees' rescue. "Riley Bechtel essentially camped out in his office for the duration. He had little choice but to keep a low profile and quietly organize activities to help the Bechtel employees held hostage." Somehow, "every Bechtel person was safely out of Iraq" before Bush launched Operation Desert Storm on January 17, 1991. While US and allied forces were conducting a series of assaults throughout Iraq and Kuwait, and while Bush was pressing the Iraqi people to overthrow Saddam, Bechtel officials were meeting "quietly with Kuwaiti officials in London to lay plans for the restoration of their economic engine," as company reports portrayed its lobbying effort to rebuild Kuwait. "As the Desert Storm offensive took shape in nearby Saudi Arabia," Bechtel's three-person advance team prepared to land in Kuwait within hours after the swift forty-two day war ended in March.

Not surprisingly, the well-placed, well-connected Bechtel obtained the coveted contract for that war-torn country's reconstruction. "The destruction that confronted them was beyond imagination," Bechtel spokesmen reported. "Before retreating, Iraqi troops had methodically devastated Kuwait's prized oil fields—750 wells were damaged, and 650 of those blazed ferociously. An estimated 70 million barrels of thick crude spewed onto the desert floor, forming lethal lakes." Bechtel pocketed $2.5 billion for putting out the fires before obtaining the reconstruction contracts. The company restored the same Kuwaiti oil refineries that it had built nearly fifty years earlier, and also rebuilt the country's upstream oil and gas installations—doing so in record time and at great physical risk to Bechtel employees. After an antitank device wounded six workers and blew up part of a building, a Bechtel executive "walked across the zone to convince workers it was safe," according to a *Los Angeles Times* report. "The wells were extinguished months, if not years, earlier than forecast, at a savings to the Kuwaitis of more than $1 billion—and considerable profit to Bechtel."

Riley had proven his corporate mettle. When he succeeded his father, Bechtel was facing a slump, having lost the giant Aqaba and PC2 projects and moving into a worldwide construction downturn. The Kuwaiti reconstruction program would signal the next phase of the company in a new world of globalization and privatization brought on by the 1991 fall of the Soviet Union. It would be the thirty-nine-year-old Riley, already one of the richest men in the world, who would lead the company toward its highest pinnacle of money and power yet: nation building around the globe.

The Giant Land of Bechtel

"The white hope, the brains of the family," as he was once described, Riley had been elected president of Bechtel just two weeks after his grandfather Steve Sr. died at the age of eighty-eight. In keeping with company policy, Steve Jr. had retired at sixty-five but stayed on as chairman emeritus, as his father had before him. Steve Jr. had passed over his oldest son, Gary, to groom young Riley to take over the company. While Gary had worked several years for the family firm, he and his father were estranged because Gary had divorced his wife—the Bechtels disdained broken families—and Gary left Bechtel to work for its largely nonunion subsidiary, Becon Construction.

Like the generations before him, Steve Jr. overlooked his daughters as candidates for succession. Oldest daughter Shana's husband, Clint Johnstone, joined the company and ascended the corporate ladder. Lauren, who had rebelled against her parents' bourgeois values during the tempestuous 1960s, alienated them further when she became engaged to Alan Dachs—a liberal New Yorker with degrees from Wesleyan University and New York University. "Not only was he an outspoken left-wing activist," according to one account, "he also was Jewish." Steve Jr. threatened to disinherit her if she went through with the marriage, but following the mediation efforts of her adoring grandfather Steve Sr., Laurie and Alan were accepted into the patriarchal fold. Smart and ambitious, with a masters in business administration from NYU, Alan became an executive in the firm, and Lauren, who graduated from Stanford with a degree in psychology, would go on to work for the family foundation. Nonie, the youngest daughter, graduated from Berkeley and married Sheldon Ramsay, the blue-blooded son of an affluent California family.

From the start, though, it was Riley, born in 1952, whose mind and assertive personality caught the attention of his father, grandfather, and other Bechtel managers. Riley studied psychology and political science as an undergraduate. After receiving his law degree from Stanford, he gained a little experience working for Bechtel's longtime outside counsel, the prestigious national law firm of Thelen, Marrin, Johnson & Bridges. But with less than two years of seasoning, in 1981 he decided that practicing law was not for him, and he came on board at Bechtel, where he focused initially on learning the nuances of the LNG industry. Riley's early assignments included a stint as an area superintendent at the Pertamina LNG plant that Bechtel was building in Indonesia, followed by a 1983 move to New Zealand to oversee a synthetic-fuels plant. There, at just age thirty-one, Riley was already what he described as "number three dog on the site." His boss, a longtime Bechtel project manager, was not pleased. His rapid-fire rise continued, with a promotion to the top position at Bechtel Ltd. in London.

Bechtel's London office was the hotbed of the company's vast Middle East dealings—including the negotiations with Iraq, but increasingly focused as well on Qatar, the site of the largest natural gas reserve in the world. Riley secured a deal with the sheikdom of Qatar for a massive LNG development contract. A natural gas that has been compressed by refrigeration to a temperature of minus 161 degrees Celsius, the liquid occupies six hundred times less space than natural gas in its gaseous state, making it easier to transport. Sealing up Qatar positioned Bechtel to become the worldwide leader in construction of liquefaction facilities, and Riley's reputation inflated from son-of-the-boss to boss in his own right. Now he was seen as the legitimate heir to the legacy of his great-grandfather, Warren "Dad" Bechtel.

To face what Riley saw as the demands of the new global economy, with the Bechtel footprint spreading ever farther around the world, he organized a senior team he dubbed "One Bechtel" to coordinate the company's various sectors and markets. Worried that the company could be spread too thin in an increasingly competitive marketplace, with hundreds of projects under way in dozens of countries on six continents, Riley revisited the Bechtel mission: the commitment to the "closed-cycle process," as first pronounced by his grandfather. "An emphasis on reexamining and sharpening Bechtel's continuous improvement methodology," a public description opaquely and inarticulately expressed the company's vision for the 1990s.

The company flourished during the Bush Sr. presidential administration, beginning with the $2.3 billion Kuwait reconstruction project. Massive government contracts flowed, from construction of what the company described as "the world's most sophisticated launch facility" for NASA's Mars Observer probe at Cape Canaveral to a solar energy prototype in the Mojave Desert to a hazardous-waste cleanup job for the US Navy.

In a 1991 joint venture with Parsons Brinckerhoff, a hundred-year-old multinational engineering design firm, Bechtel received a massive federally funded transportation development project in Boston. The consortium would receive more than $16 billion to build the Central Artery/Tunnel Project designed to streamline traffic on one of the most congested highways in the United States. The "Big Dig," as it came to be known, called for replacing an overhead highway with seven and a half miles of underground tunnels and bridges. It would be the largest public works project in American history, and before it was over, would become the subject of a criminal fraud investigation by the US attorney in Boston for delays, leaks, and the tragic death of a young mother whose car was struck by falling concrete slabs. Other Massachusetts lawmakers also probed the mismanaged undertaking, with allegations from the state inspector general that "Bechtel engineers for years covered up $4 billion in costs by low-balling their projections," and accusations that the company was in collusion with top officials at the State Turnpike Authority. "There is no way that a bridge and a couple of tunnels is worth $14.6 billion, in my opinion and the opinion of most taxpayers," a state senator said in a national radio interview. "This is a pretty small job for us," a Bechtel engineer remarked in contrast.

The Big Dig would take twenty years and become the most expensive urban highway redevelopment in US history. "If total expenditures are adjusted for inflation, it cost more than the Panama Canal," according to author Judith Nies. Originally budgeted at $2.8 billion when the congressional bill passed, its final cost in 2009 would be $16 billion. Massachusetts congressman Barney Frank captured the attitude of many Bostonians when he quipped, "Rather than depress the expressway, wouldn't it be cheaper to raise the city?" Public sentiment became increasingly critical of Bechtel, as Boston was "having the equivalent of open-heart surgery—streets torn up everywhere and huge holes all over the city."

The *Boston Globe* undertook an explosive, yearlong probe scrutinizing Bechtel's role in the Big Dig. "With a cadre of lobbyists and lawyers on Beacon Hill and Capitol Hill, Bechtel has cemented bonds with policy makers to protect its profits, renew its contracts, and deflect questions about the quality of its management," the paper reported, going on to reveal that Gary Bechtel, Riley's older brother, served as the liaison between the company and Massachusetts public officials, and that George Shultz's oldest daughter, Margaret, managed human resources for the project.

Strikingly, "as the costs of the Big Dig were clicking up in hundred-million-dollar increments like a taxi meter out of control," wrote Nies, the responsible officeholders were rewarded with plum US government appointments rather than censure, in what Nies described as "a remarkable run of Massachusetts politicians' adventures in international affairs." The city's mayor, Raymond Flynn, received an appointment as ambassador to the Vatican. The state's Republican governor, Boston Brahmin William Weld—who didn't consider it a conflict of interest that his chief campaign fund-raiser was a Bechtel lobbyist—resigned to become ambassador to Mexico as a Clinton appointee. Beleaguered taxpayers embraced Weld's successor, the moderate Republican Mitt

Romney, when he announced that he was removing Bechtel as project manager amid the swirling allegations of malfeasance. But following a closed-door meeting with Riley, who flew in on his private jet for a conference with the governor, Romney changed his mind about replacing Bechtel. (A decade later, the Bechtels would be major donors to Romney's presidential campaign.)

The "Big Dig chain of command is shaped more like an hourglass," reported Boston's *Phoenix* newspaper. "Filling the bottom are a host of design and construction companies entangled in joint ventures with one another, and unions representing laborers across those ventures. At the top are a seemingly endless number of governmental bodies with oversight authority over the project but little direct control. And clogging up the middle is a solidified GLOB—the Giant Land of Bechtel."

For most companies, even other global behemoths, a project as large, complicated, and controversial as the Big Dig would have absorbed the lion's share of corporate energy and resources. But for Bechtel, it was just one of dozens of megaprojects happening simultaneously by the late 1990s—many dogged by the same complaints of cost overruns. Bechtel had landed a gargantuan $20 billion Hong Kong deal that called for the construction of bridges, tunnels, railroads, and an airport. The largest civil infrastructure program in the world, it was built on a man-made 3,100-acre island connected with what would be the world's largest suspension bridge and a planned community for twenty thousand residents. The company had also been tapped to complete the facilities in Barcelona for the 1992 Summer Olympics; a metro subway system in Athens, Greece; a 430-kilometer Greater Beijing Regional Expressway; and it began a decadelong relationship with a Motorola facility in Tianjin, China, to design and build a factory that produced pagers, semiconductors, and cellular telephones.

Riley took stock of the geopolitical situation in search of new markets. Just as his father and grandfather had often moved the company forward in lockstep with the foreign policy of the US government, or at least with factions within the government, so too did Riley navigate the global environment. "Steve Sr. had so many times cast his eye around the globe to see what was needed and then shaped the job accordingly," as company marketing literature put it. A corporate insider explained, "If we don't have a client, we find one. If there's no project, we assemble one. If there's no money, we get some." Riley would personify this mantra. Like his father and grandfather, Riley saw government regulation as tyranny and was alarmed at global rebellions demanding liberation, especially for minorities.

Bechtel prided itself on building the infrastructure for the free world—a free world that now included the resource-rich republics of the former Soviet Union as well as the burgeoning Association of Southeast Asian Nations (ASEAN). The collapse of Communism led to a global shift toward privatization, as countries released telephone, utility, and natural resources from nationalized state control. When the Soviet Union crumbled with world-shattering speed, democratic revolutions swept across the globe. "Ethnic, religious, and territorial conflicts, long subdued by the Cold War, erupted one after another. The world was remade, tossed, liberated—and reopened for international business," as journalist Steve Coll put it.

With an eye toward gaining a commercial foothold in these emerging nations, Riley was especially drawn to the powerful "tigers" of ASEAN: Indonesia, Malaysia, the Philippines, Singapore, Thailand, Vietnam, and the rest. These countries' governing elites were concentrating on nation building and economic growth. China too was attracting foreign manufacturing and investment in infrastructure and tourism, and Bechtel already had an advantage in that country, thanks to the diplomatic gestures by Bechtel consultant Henry Kissinger, and then by former Bechtel president George Shultz. At the same time, the company expanded its emphasis into one that it described as "human needs, such as agriculture, water, and housing," and away from the major industrial undertakings that had defined Bechtel throughout its history.

Just as Steve Sr. had modernized the empires in the ancient region of the Arab world—making Saudi Arabia "the largest American colony between France and the Philippines"—so too would Riley set his goals on modernizing and colonizing in far-flung lands. Many of these newly unstable countries had been off-limits to American political influence and economic trade throughout the Cold War. Now they beckoned, and Riley was eager to answer the call. Welcoming Bechtel had "become a signal of a foreign country's willingness to cooperate with the United States, and even to support Washington's interests abroad," according to an account in *Foreign Policy* magazine. "There is a sense that, if you work with Bechtel, people in Washington will smile and think more positively about your country as a partner," said Matthew Bryza, a US foreign service officer and later ambassador to Azerbaijan. "Working with Bechtel validates you as a country connected to the world where the big players operate." It never hurt that a stunning number of Bechtel executives and employees had top secret national security clearances—providing implicit government "cover" for their activities abroad.

Some Found the Company Arrogant

The four years of Bush 41's presidency that ended in 1993 had proven fruitful for Bechtel and set the stage for even more government contracts to come. In Riley's first two years at the helm, the company reported revenues of $7.8 billion, an eight-year high. New work booked rose from $5.4 billion to $9.4 billion—a whopping $4 billion increase. Still, Bechtel remained a private company with no public stockholders, no filings with the SEC, and no government-scrutinized annual reports. So, as always, any financial information released by the company was unverifiable. But judging from its protracted list of projects between 1990 and 1992, the company was growing at a frenzied pace. By now, an untold number of former legislators, legislative aides, and other onetime government officials were under contract as Bechtel lobbyists, consultants, or employees.

During the Bush tenure, Bechtel had partnered with the Turkish giant Enka—one of the largest companies in the world—to design and build part of the $1.4 billion Trans-Turkish Motorway linking Europe and Asia. Bechtel and Enka teamed up as well to develop the Tengiz and Korolev oil fields in Kazakhstan. In addition to the mega–airport project in Hong Kong, Bechtel was also building seven new airports "from Dubai to Dallas," as it touted on the company website. At Daya Bay, Bechtel helped build the first commercial nuclear power plant in China, and it was the first American company ever granted a construction license in both Japan and South Korea.

Still, during the Bush era's bounty, Riley's management team also recognized the need to evolve into a more efficient enterprise. With Bechtel projects literally all over the map, the company's interests had diversified and were no longer confined to the flagship endeavors related to fossil fuels and nuclear energy that had distinguished it for more than a half century. Tasking his "One Bechtel" crew to identify the company's "core competencies" and then create a strategy to exploit them, Riley was determined not to let Bechtel spin out of control. "The engineering and construction business will always be our primary purpose," he told an interviewer. "Most conglomerates ultimately falter for lack of a central purpose or core business . . . To me, designing and building projects is, and always will be, the spine of our business. We will never be a conglomerate. At least not on my watch." But a quintessential conglomerate is what Bechtel had become, and Riley's vow to narrow the focus of an already global phenomenon would prove empty.

He formed teams throughout the company, led by " 'homegrown' continuous improvement coaches"—presumably veteran Bechtel employees—to "formalize and clarify" the company's new strategy of "eliminating corporate waste." Proud of its Kuwaiti reconstruction project in the aftermath of the Gulf War, Bechtel executives felt the company had shown the world that it could respond faster than any other engineer-constructor to international hotspots. "The company now needed to improve its ability to decide much earlier how, when, and where to place its bets," according to the company website.

Riley inherited a corporate organization structured by his father in the 1960s based on what they called a "matrix fashion with an industry axis and, secondarily, a geographic axis." In this model, the "business lines" controlled the allocation of company resources, and bore full accountability for profit and loss. A risk-averse man of limited imagination, Steve Jr. insisted that the managers at corporate headquarters keep detailed records so that the chain of command and pattern of decision making were clear. Riley wanted a more flexible, less centralized management structure—described as a more balanced matrix in which the global business lines and regional offices would share decision-making authority. "Regions," modeled on Bechtel's European, African, Middle Eastern, and Southwest Asian operations, were given responsibility for profit and loss from the moment the work was awarded through its completion. Project managers began reporting to the regional leadership rather than to central headquarters back in San Francisco. By 1992, the new regions included the Americas and Asia Pacific, which were divided further into subregions. "The center of Bechtel's decision making was now physically closer to the company's customers," according to corporate literature. *Forbes* magazine described the difference between father and son this way: while Steve Jr. ran the company in "more of a militarylike, command-and-control fashion Riley Bechtel has spent his tenure pushing power out to the field and abandoning the prior emphasis on industry groups in favor of more of a regional approach to management."

It had also become clear to Riley and his fellow executives that "the perception of Bechtel in many parts of the world was changing—and not always for the better." The various scandals and negative publicity had taken their toll, and as closer public scrutiny of worldwide privatization occurred, Bechtel went on the defensive. "Bechtel, some thought, was a fair-weather player, maintaining a market presence only when opportunity abounded and pulling out during lulls," company spokesmen explained. But the ubiquitous skepticism was fueled by Bechtel's secrecy, if not paranoia. "Bechtel didn't sufficiently understand many local markets and important relationships. Bechtel wasn't maximizing the use of local resources to the benefit of its customers and itself. And some found the company arrogant." In addition to refining its business "matrix," the company set out to reform its image as well. But it couldn't shed the ghosts of the scandals that had haunted it in recent years: the Aqaba pipeline, Iran-Contra, Iraqgate, the Big Dig. The hits kept coming.

As the Bush administration was coming to a close, a federal grand jury indicted Cap Weinberger in the summer of 1992 on five counts of perjury and obstruction of justice for his role in Iran-Contra. He had resigned as secretary of defense in 1987, the year after the scandal had broken, and returned to private life—not to Bechtel this time but to become publisher of *Forbes* magazine. "The year 1992 was, in every way, a nightmare year for me," he wrote. "I suppose I had been in some danger of succumbing to the Greek condition of hubris during the nearly five years that had passed since I had left the Defense Department. If so, 1992 was to dispel any pride I might have retained."

Accused of participating in the transfer of HAWK and TOW missiles to Iran, and of lying to Congress, Weinberger claimed to be "a pawn in a clearly political game," calling independent counsel Lawrence E. Walsh a "vindictive wretch." The special prosecutor responded that the case had nothing to do with policy or politics, but was about lying. "Weinberger gave a little glimpse of the knife he has always carried with him during his long career," wrote syndicated columnist Mary McGrory, referring to his nickname, "Cap the Knife." She described his attack on Walsh as "breathtaking and poisonous . . . Weinberger's way with those who oppose him is viperish."

Bechtel whitewashed its long association with Weinberger, removing him from corporate propaganda. He faced a possible five-year sentence and a $250,000 fine on each of the counts. But, like most of his codefendants in the Reagan administration, he was spared the ignominy of a trial when Bush gave him a presidential pardon on Christmas Eve 1992, just weeks before leaving office. Walsh was stunned. "When confronted with scandals in their cabinets, Presidents Ulysses S. Grant, Warren G. Harding, and Calvin Coolidge had eschewed pardons," he wrote. "I did not think that George Bush, who seemed to pride himself on his character, would be the first president to use his pardon powers in a cover-up."

Riley and Steve Jr. were initially disappointed in Bush's loss to Democrat Bill Clinton in the 1992 presidential election, concerned that their long-standing alignment with the GOP might jeopardize their influence in Washington. But they need not have worried. By then, after more than a decade of Reagan and Bush rolling back the New Deal, sabotaging Nixon's détente strides, and dismantling Carter's domestic and foreign policies, the country had evolved into a bipartisan business venture. "Regulators and the regulated had fallen into a slothful embrace," wrote Steve Coll, "reflecting a national political atmosphere that emphasized the benefits of light government oversight."

As it was, Bechtel fared as well under Clinton as it had under Bush, continuing to prosper as one of the country's major defense and energy contractors, and with several senior Bechtel managers assuming positions in the administration. Bechtel, like the oil companies, "enjoyed access to the administration that was comparable to the halcyon years of the Reagan presidency," according to Coll. Its influence at the highest levels of government continued. During Clinton's eight-year administration, Bechtel would not miss a beat in receiving favored government contracts, gaining a foothold into several burgeoning new markets brought on by the end of the Cold War. The demilitarization of chemical and nuclear weapons in Russia was a particular boon. Russia had the most nuclear weapons and the largest stockpile in the world.

Company press releases described its patriotic efforts to "help preserve the peace by decommissioning relics of the Cold War," including abandoned or obsolete nuclear weapons factories in the United States and Russia. The company's close relationships and connections to that country dated back decades to Steve Sr. and Armand Hammer, placing Bechtel in a singular position to develop a comprehensive chemical and nuclear weapons destruction strategy. As part of the Cooperative Threat Reduction (CTR) program—a State Department program aimed at nuclear nonproliferation and antiterrorism based on an intitiative sponsored by Sens. Sam Nunn (D-GA) and Richard Lugar (R-IN)—Bechtel obtained a multibillion-dollar Defense Department contract to dismantle and secure Russia's nuclear warheads at a moment when its plutonium stores were virtually unguarded.

Opportunities created by Clinton's interventionist foreign policy in the Balkans resulted in gigantic nation-building projects in that region. Bechtel and the Clinton administration grew so chummy that a Bechtel executive accompanied Secretary of Commerce Ronald H. Brown on an OPIC trade mission to Croatia intended to benefit Bechtel. Their ill-fated air force jet crashed in Dubrovnik on April 3, 1996, killing everyone on board, including Bechtel's Stuart Tholan. Tholan, who had been with Bechtel for thirty-three years, oversaw operations in Europe, Africa, the Middle East, and Southwest Asia from his London base. Brown had been Clinton's most aggressive advocate for US businesses abroad; at the time of his death, the onetime chairman of the Democratic National Committee was under criminal investigation by an independent counsel for his role in a pay-to-play scandal in which he allegedly sold seats on OPIC junkets—such as his last trip to the Balkans—to corporate heavyweights.

Two years after the air crash, Bechtel signed a $600 million fixed-price contract with the Republic of Croatia to build a seventy-four-mile motorway "as part of an ambitious government plan to link Croatia to the pan-European transportation corridors" for the purpose of bringing tourism and commercial opportunities to the region. The four-lane motorway would run from the capital city of Zagreb to the Slovenian border, and then on to the Croatian border with Bosnia. It was financed largely by US export credits, including loans from the Ex-Im Bank. Again, Bechtel partnered with Enka, as was becoming routine. Other Bechtel-led consortiums during this era included a $760 million contract with the government of Ukraine to rebuild a concrete shelter covering the reactor of the Chernobyl nuclear power plant that had been damaged in a catastrophic 1986 explosion—the worst nuclear disaster in history.

"In a world increasingly long on infrastructure needs and short on private capital and government funding, Bechtel's financial leverage and entrepreneurial touch" proved to be "powerful competitive tools," as the company saw it. Bechtel had long been in the business of arranging project financing for its customers. Through its Bechtel Financing Services Inc., formed in 1969, the company assembled international export credits, through Ex-Im and other government entities, and bundled them with commercial bank loans. But by the end of the 1990s, as privatization was sweeping the world, Riley wanted the company to expand beyond developing projects into acquiring equity positions in them—forming partnerships with its customers. "Don't just build things. Own them and run them too," was Riley's new concept.

CHAPTER TWENTY-EIGHT

Global Reach with a Local Touch

"Leading the Way to Change" is how Bechtel publicly defined the period between 1990 and 1998 in its eight-part ongoing narrative titled "Building a Century," which would be published in glossy brochures and posted on the company website. Bechtel celebrated 1998 as its hundredth anniversary—designating 1898 as the company's founding year, since that was when seventeen-year-old "Dad" Bechtel got his first job on a railroad construction crew.

As the company prepared to move into the next century, Riley determined to reinvent its mission yet again. At the millennium, he reversed his earlier credo that under his watch the company would never be a conglomerate and that "the engineering and construction business will always be our primary purpose." His new vision entailed a broad span of diversification to rival that of any other conglomerate in the world, evolving from engineering and construction into mobile telecommunications, water delivery, disaster relief, urban planning, nuclear waste, management of government facilities, homeland security, nuclear submarines, aircraft carriers, counterterrorism technology, environmental remediation, data collection, aerospace, megaproject financing, telecom start-ups, e-commerce, and more. This global power grab was of massive proportions unlike anything seen in world history. Characteristically, Bechtel put a benevolent spin on the unprecedented grasp, even giving it the altruistic-sounding motto of "Global Reach with a Local Touch."

Bechtel Enterprises, the newest iteration of Bechtel Financing Services and Bechtel Enterprises Holdings, Inc., would be Riley's rocket into the twenty-first century. BEn, as it was called at corporate headquarters, created a number of joint ventures, which gave it a competitive edge in the industry and produced lucrative investment opportunities for Bechtel and its partners. The prototype for these "world-class ownership teams," as the company described them, was in the power sector, where BEn partnered with California's Pacific Gas and Electric Company (PG&E), forming the largest privatized electric power plant in the country. Passage of the US Energy Policy Act of 1992—thanks in no small part to the vigorous Bechtel lobbying—had made it possible to build and finance independent power plants. "USGen took off," the company reported, referring to the BEn and PG&E joint venture, US Generating Company, spawning InterGen, another Bechtel partnership with PG&E to develop, own, and operate electrical generating facilities outside North America, where many nations were privatizing and deregulating utilities. As power privatization expanded globally, Bechtel extended its utility partnerships into the United Kingdom, the Philippines, Mexico, and Colombia.

In short order, InterGen had contracted to build twenty plants, at a cost of $10 billion and strewn across the planet, with the capacity to power sixteen million homes. Banks "were eager for a piece of the brave new deregulating power business," as *Business 2.0* described the boom of privatized energy, "and were happy to lend the company 100 percent of the funds." Stunningly, many lenders agreed to bankroll the risky ventures without even examining Bechtel's "zealously guarded financial data," agreeing to use the unbuilt plants themselves as collateral. The few bankers who insisted on access to Bechtel's internal financial documents were subjected to strict confidences, allowed only to view the records in a secure room at corporate headquarters, chaperoned by a Bechtel employee. The banker was not allowed to bring any items into the room—not even a purse or a briefcase—and was prohibited from taking notes or making photocopies. Bechtel "does not release the details of its financings, investments, financial statements, or share price," a company spokesman responded to a media inquiry about its extreme secrecy. Bechtel executives attributed its success with the lenders to what was referred to internally as the company mystique. "The family reputation is very strong," said a former insider. "Some banks understand that, and some don't. We worked with the ones that did."

From the beginning, Riley's brainchild, BEn, set itself apart from the more staid Bechtel Group of his father's generation. "Staffed by MBA hotshots rather than engineers, it occupied offices in a separate building," according to one published account. "With its black marble floors and sweeping view of San Francisco Bay . . . it seemed worlds removed from the no-frills cubicle farms inhabited by Bechtel engineers at headquarters." Almost immediately, BEn became a leading influence on the company, with longtime executive Cordell Hull (a distant relative of FDR's secretary of state) luring outside backers to "invest in privatization projects wherever Bechtel can find them—or stir them up," according to one account.

By the year 2000, the forty-eight-year-old Riley's radical transformation of the family company from an engineering and construction giant into a conglomerate "renowned for its financial designs," as *Forbes* described it, was making senior managers and hundreds of employees nervous. The close-knit "family" of high-level engineers and executives viewed Riley's diversification frenzy with alarm, as their personal financial worth was tied up in the company's stock. While BEn had a $16 billion portfolio of electric and industrial plants, its affiliate, the Fremont Group, was "a money manager with $10 billion under its wing," according to *Forbes*—"a lot of it Bechtel family money but also a fair amount from the public." In keeping with Steve Sr.'s "no widows or orphans" motto, only those active in the business could own stock, and upon death or retirement, the stock was required to be sold back to the corporation or fellow stockholders.

A $10 million investment in the Fremont Group from Saudi Arabia's bin Laden family would soon become an embarrassment for the firm when Jane Mayer of the *New Yorker* reported it. Rick Kopf, the general counsel of the Fremont Group, declined to discuss the origin or nature of the relationship between the bin Laden and Bechtel families, both of which made fortunes in huge construction projects in the Arab world. "Ownership is private and is not disclosed," Kopf told the *New Yorker*, while also confirming that Fremont's majority ownership was held by the Bechtel family. Meanwhile, yet another subsidiary, Fremont Properties, owned more than four million square feet of commercial real estate; and Sequoia Ventures, which had divested itself of Dillon, Read & Company (acquired under George Shultz's leadership), had also branched away from the careful, conservative reign of Steve Jr.

"It's a long way in a short time for [Riley] Bechtel, who took over from his father . . . shortly before Saddam Hussein raided Kuwait," *Forbes* reported. Pushing far beyond his father's more conventional moves and into the ownership of industrial plants, Riley was putting capital at great risk. Bechtel's InterGen had become the second-largest nonutility developer of electric powerhouses, behind only Taiwan's Formosa Group.

"Enough of this waiting around. Let's go kill something." One account drew the analogy between BEn and the famous cartoon depicting two vultures talking to each other. Riley and his tiny, elite clique of trusted advisors dismissed the internal naysayers, boasting of their accomplishments. "It's been so successful, our biggest challenge is finding enough capital to do all the projects on our plate," the group's president and Riley's closest, most trusted confidant, Vincent Paul Unruh, told an interviewer. An accountant and longtime personal friend of the CEO, Unruh ran BEn.

A proposed deal to extend Portland, Oregon's, light-rail system from the city to the airport offered a glimpse into how the twenty-first-century Bechtel projects—as designed and executed by Riley and Unruh—were structured. Bechtel would contribute $30 million toward the $125 million public project and, in exchange for its investment, would obtain the construction contract. In addition, the city would give Bechtel an eighty-five-year lease on an adjoining 120-acre commercial site, where it would build infrastructure support for the rail—with government financing.

"If you're really in the game, you've got to understand what's happening in governments and markets and see a deal before they put it out to bid," an immodest Riley told an interviewer. "If the first time I hear about a big project is when the proposal is on the Street, then I don't have a good win plan."

The ambitious, bespectacled Unruh was as insatiable as his boss. While the power plant projects were taking off, he and Riley were simultaneously seeking ventures in yet more new directions. In what would later be described as Bechtel's "dot-com-era folly," they ramped up investments in telecom and Internet start-ups that were all the rage in nearby Silicon Valley. Unruh poured more than $60 million into a dozen dot-coms, and another $140 million into telecoms. Neither Riley nor Unruh saw the coming collapse of the dot-com bubble, and in early 2000 the two men were still swaggering about their prescience. At a corporate retreat that year, Unruh appeared as chief booster for BEn, proclaiming to employees that it was his and Riley's strategic investment apparatus, not the outdated engineering and construction paradigm of the old Bechtel, that was the future direction of the company. "He was seen as the Einstein of the place," as *Business 2.0* reported the enthusiastic ovation he received from the audience. All that would soon crash.

Within months, "Einstein" was on the verge of defeat, as his dot-coms started tumbling like dominos. "Red flags were popping up everywhere," according to one account, and several executives sensed that BEn was headed for disaster. "Telecoms and dot-coms were blowing up left and right." But that didn't stop Riley from promoting Unruh to vice chairman of the company. The two men continued to assure their managers and partners that all was sound. "Someone wasn't telling the partners and the board the whole story," according to a company engineer and high-ranking partner who resigned in disgust at not only the downward spiral but also the blatant dissembling.

At the same time, Bechtel was mired in a hotbed of criticism for its

$1.6 billion cost overruns on the Big Dig in Boston. But even that was overshadowed by the volatile anti-Bechtel revolution in South America that was turning violent and spawning international scorn for the company. "As vexing as the Big Dig's issues have been, the stakes for Bechtel have been even higher elsewhere," reported the *Boston Globe*, as the company became one of the most controversial and reviled water-privatization companies in the world. The World Bank had threatened to withhold debt relief from Bolivia unless the government sold the public water system to the private sector and passed on the costs to consumers in that country's third-largest city of Cochabamba. A Bechtel-led coalition, as the only bidder in the process, was granted a forty-year lease through a subsidiary called International Water (Aguas del Tunari) formed for that single purpose. Within weeks, the company had raised water prices by 300 percent for some of the city's poorest inhabitants. Families who lived on less than $60 per month were suddenly being charged $15 a month for tap water. Impoverished residents took to the streets, rioting in protest against Bechtel.

The residents of Cochabamba staged a strike that paralyzed the city. The Bolivian government called out soldiers to quell the unrest, but the anti-Bechtel revolt only intensified. When a seventeen-year-old boy was shot in the face and killed, and more than a hundred others were wounded in the melee, Bechtel executives first hid in a five-star hotel in the Bolivian Andes and then "fled the nation," as the *Boston Globe* reported it, "leaving investments worth at least $25 million." Bechtel pursued the Bolivian government, filing a legal demand for its losses in a "World Bank–controlled private arbitration." While a Bechtel spokesman said the company intended to recover its "expropriated assets," critics charged that Bechtel's investment was nowhere near $25 million and that the company was seeking remuneration for anticipated profits that were thwarted. "The fact that a World Bank court is preparing to hear this case behind closed doors, without any public scrutiny or participation, is a clear example of how global economic rules are being rigged to benefit large corporations at the expense of everyone else," said a leader of one of three hundred citizen groups that petitioned the secret trade court to make the documents and testimony in the case available for public inspection.

"For Bechtel Enterprises . . . $25 million is about what the company takes in before lunch on an average workday," wrote the executive director of a corporate watchdog organization. "For the people of Bolivia, $25 million is what it costs to hire 3,000 rural doctors or 12,000 schoolteachers for a year, or to hook up 125,000 families to public water supplies."

International citizens advocacy groups rallied around what they saw as the opening salvo of the coming "water wars," focusing on Bechtel as the embodiment of exploitation of debt-ridden countries that were privatizing their water systems. With the onset of the water privatization bonanza, Bechtel moved quickly, becoming one of the top ten water-privatization companies in the world. Within a few short years, it was involved in more than two hundred water and wastewater treatment plants that provided facilities to more than thirty million people throughout the world. Its twenty-five-year lease agreements in the Philippines were the largest in the world, but that "marriage between the major global corporations and the elite families of the Filipino oligarchy has not brought clean water to the millions of needy families in Manila," as one account described the Metropolitan Waterworks and Sewerage System.

"In Bolivia, Bechtel demonstrated that it has no moral compass whatsoever other than seeking profit off the poorest people in the world," an activist told the Boston newspaper. For its part, Bechtel blamed the Bolivian government. Spokesman Jeff Berger said it was the government that "controls water rates, structured the deal with Bechtel, and fired the shots into the crowd."

The company sought to deflect the criticism aimed at Riley, who, while maintaining the famous Bechtel secrecy, had become a lightning rod. As the patriarch of the dynasty and the billionaire heir to the family fortune, detractors were portraying him as the poster child for global economic injustice. At a moment when corporate greed and revolving-door cronyism were greeted with suspicion and contempt,

Riley flaunted his membership in the exclusive Bohemian Club and boasted of his affiliation with the ubercapitalist Trilateral Commission. He boosted the company's lobbying presence in Washington, along with a ramped-up public relations department at the corporate headquarters in San Francisco. But extensive, irreversible damage had been done to Bechtel's image.

A License to Make Money

The global wave of privatization rose throughout the 1990s, peaking in 1997 with privatization-derived revenues hitting a record $160 billion. The wave was also turning toward Asia, where a financial crisis was deepening. The "economic equivalent of extreme makeovers," as one account put it, was occurring in Thailand, Indonesia, South Korea, and the Philippines. Called "the world's biggest going-out-of-business sale" by the *New York Times*, multinational firms replaced Asian companies in record numbers, and, characteristically, Bechtel was among the first in line. By the year 2000, Bechtel had scored the contracts to privatize the water and sewage systems in eastern Manila and to build an oil refinery in Sulawesi, Indonesia.

In keeping with the family tradition, in 2001 Riley lured a heavy-hitting government official to join the BEn team. Nicholas F. Brady, a former US senator from New Jersey, a former US Treasury secretary under Presidents Reagan and George H. W. Bush, and a former chairman of Dillon, Read, entered into a joint venture with BEn to invest in the Latin American technology markets in Brazil, Mexico, and Argentina. But even that high-level connection couldn't stanch the bleeding at InterGen, where ambitious plans for an initial public offering had vaporized with a plummeting stock market, and where an estimated $700 million in debt for the numerous power plants it was building would come due the moment the plants were fired up. That debt load far exceeded the company's net worth of only $350 million, and some of the power plants were "worth a fraction of what they cost to build," according to one account. "In late 2001, the glutted power market collapsed with breathtaking speed, stranding producers that lacked customers," wrote Bay Area business reporters Ralph King and Charlie McCoy. Electricity rates tanked at the same moment that the relaxation of environmental laws under the newly inaugurated Republican president George W. Bush "gave coal-fired plants new life." Several of the plants were also behind schedule, which staved off some loan repayments. Even some lenders were sympathetic about Bechtel's downward spiral. "We knew Bechtel was going to feel significant pain if it ever had to fund all those loans," one of the bankers told an interviewer.

When the US energy conglomerate Enron filed for bankruptcy in December 2001 amid criminal charges in a financial scandal of unrivaled magnitude, Bechtel took yet another hit. The company had partnered with Enron to build the Dabhol power plant in India—financed by US government loan guarantees through Ex-Im Bank and OPIC after the World Bank refused to fund it—which was the largest single foreign investment in that country and the largest private power project in the world. The controversial plant had been the scene of numerous public demonstrations in which protestors charged the company with severe human rights violations.

All of that came on the heels of the dot-com crash, which resulted in Bechtel writing off $200 million in bad investments, wiping out a third of the company's net worth. "One of the most tightly controlled and conservatively managed companies in the world, Bechtel fell head over heels for the same new-economy sirens that created Enron and the dot-com debacle," wrote King and McCoy. Still, Riley seemed oblivious to the disastrous turn of events and continued the full support of his protégé Unruh. But by late 2002, Riley could no longer disguise or hide the precariousness of the situation, and in November the company cut the value of its stock by a quarter—setting off alarms among some fifty management partners who owned 60 percent of the company's shares. While Riley controlled the company on behalf of

his extended family, which owned the remaining 40 percent, his decisions were scrutinized and criticized by family members and employees as well. Several senior managers, along with at least one veteran
partner, suggested that Riley resign as CEO but remain as chairman
of the board. Riley stayed on, but his vice chairman, Unruh, resigned
after holding his position for less than a year.

Because of the obsessive secrecy of the firm, combined with the
complicated ownership structure and arbitrary stock value, the gamut
of the financial debacle could only be presumed. "If this were a public
company, I probably would've been fired," Riley told his partners. The
company's top engineers were outraged at Riley's massive blunder, the
full details of which were revealed in an audit by a new chief financial officer brought in by the board to look at BEn. "No one on the
engineering side would have ever let that stuff get that out of whack—
never," a top engineer and high-ranking partner said after resigning in
disgust. "In fact, there was a fear by all of us that we didn't want to be
an Enron. We kept saying, 'Get out! Get out!' "

Described as a "fiendishly hardworking, constantly traveling bunch,"
most of the Bechtel partners had been with the company for decades.
"Their big reward, often tens of millions of dollars, comes when they
retire and cash in their shares at a price set by the company. They also
collect annual payouts of profit, just like at a law firm. In good years,
partners take home a small fortune. In tough times, they don't."

Seventy-seven-year-old Steve Jr., who as emeritus had largely disappeared into a pheasant-hunting retirement, resurfaced. The sudden
presence of the beloved patriarch was both comforting and disquiet-
ing. "The old boy is asking a lot more questions these days," a longtime employee remarked. By the time 2003 rolled around, Riley had
no choice but to inform family members and their top managers that
the company had suffered devastating losses on BEn's assets. He proposed a total restructuring that included cutting overhead by nearly
20 percent—a drastic slash that, according to one account, meant reducing the 1,100-member staff at the San Francisco headquarters to
50. He also notified this elite group within the firm that its regular

dividends would be suspended, as well as the right to cash in Bechtel shares. But most alarming was the suggestion that top managers might be asked to invest $50 million to salvage the drowning empire.

Throughout 2003, hundreds of employees were laid off or quit, as the company went into a protective mode and created a blackout designed to deflect both internal and external scrutiny. "Seemingly innocent disclosures can have consequences," Adrian Zaccaria, Bechtel's chief operating officer (COO), warned high-level partners. "Every time we slip . . . we increase our exposure, and a simple cocktail party discussion can have implications for us all . . . I am not worried about being able to explain or calm our key banks and customers. But I am concerned that our newer and smaller stakeholders will demand more from us."

Then came the Iraq War, saving Bechtel from its financial tailspin, reversing a three-year slide, and setting the stage for a decadelong comeback. The so-called Boys from Bechtel would be the architects of a government strategy that would lead to military action against Saddam Hussein in Iraq. The company would reap the spoils of that war.

Within a week of the September 11, 2001, attacks on New York City's World Trade Center and on the Pentagon by hijacked planes (one of which crashed in Pennsylvania but was presumed to be heading toward Washington, DC), President George W. Bush had focused his foreign policy on taking down Iraq. Given the lack of evidence linking Hussein to the terrorist attack, the war policy was controversial in the United States and abroad, and so much of its execution occurred outside of public view. In the eighteen-month run-up to the war against Iraq, there were "twin themes that drove the Bush administration," Russ Hoyle wrote in his book *Going to War*. "The first was the presumption that Saddam possessed weapons of mass destruction. . . . The second—which perhaps began as little more than a presidential suspicion, or fig leaf for regime change—was that Saddam Hussein had somehow been involved with al-Qaeda in mounting the terror attacks on the United States."

Bechtel and the US government, both of which had been encouraging Saddam for the previous decade, had evolved from entrenched collaborators to strident adversaries. Coming full circle, it would be a core group of veteran Bechtel executives who would rally the cry for the United States to invade Iraq and topple their former cash cow Hussein. "The same men who courted Saddam in the 1980s while he gassed Iranians . . . helped plan and implement the invasion and assumption of control of Baghdad, ostensibly because Saddam harbored weapons of mass destruction," a report from the Institute for Policy Studies concluded. The Bechtel family, corporation, and foundation had long supported right-wing front groups and think tanks—such as the Heritage Foundation and American Enterprise Institute—that generated the prodefense, proprivatization, and anti-government-regulation agenda traceable back to the Reagan era.

Retired four-star general John J. "Jack" Sheehan, who managed Bechtel's petroleum and chemical operations, was a former NATO supreme allied commander who sat on the Defense Policy Board: a secretive, federally appointed prowar group of civilians that advised Secretary of Defense Donald Rumsfeld—who himself once lobbied on behalf of a Bechtel pipeline in Iraq—on its members' business interests. Bush 43 had also appointed Riley Bechtel to serve on his Export Council, which advises the president on international trade matters. The former head of Bechtel's energy division, Ross J. Connelly, was appointed vice president of OPIC—the entity that provides financial guarantees for American companies doing business abroad. Bechtel senior vice president Daniel Chao also joined the Bush team, serving on the advisory board of Ex-Im.

Not surprisingly, former Bechtel president Shultz joined the ranks of the arch interventionists, chairing the Committee for the Liberation of Iraq: a pressure group formed to mobilize public support for the war and the overthrow of Hussein. Shultz was also a patron of the neocon think tank the American Enterprise Institute. "I would be surprised if Saddam Hussein's fingerprints were not in some ways on this," Shultz said, referring to 9/11. The man whose State Department underlings negotiated with the dictator on behalf of Bechtel's pipeline while Hussein was using chemical weapons on his own citizens suddenly thought an "Iraq ruled by Saddam Hussein is basically a Kmart for terrorist weapons." Shultz's hawkish committee was "committed to moving beyond the political liberation of the oil-rich country to the conveniently profitable 'reconstruction of its economy,'" according to columnist Bob Herbert of the *New York Times*.

Weinberger also rallied with his fellow neoconservatives in stumping for war. "People will say there will be chaos," he told Congress in support of the US invasion of Iraq. "I disagree, but I must confess frankly that even chaos would be better than Saddam." This from the man who, as general counsel, had facilitated multibillion-dollar construction contracts between Bechtel and Saddam. "The more we gave Saddam, the more dangerous he got, and ultimately we had to go to war to destroy what we sold him," wrote a nuclear proliferation expert. The Mafia has a term for that: "create to alleviate."

The saber rattling by Bechtel principals gave the company what Herbert described as "a license to make money"—putting "Bechtel in the driver's seat for the long-term reconstruction of the country." Penning an op-ed article for the *Washington Post* in 2002, Shultz headlined that "The Danger Is Immediate: Saddam Hussein Must Be Removed." He went on to write that a "strong foundation exists for immediate military action against Hussein and for a multilateral effort to rebuild Iraq after he is gone." Advocating a preemptive attack against Iraq, Shultz drew the analogy that "if there is a rattlesnake in the yard, you don't wait for it to strike before you take action in self-defense." Shultz neglected to disclose to his readers that he was a member of the board of directors of Bechtel, which was positioned to make billions of dollars in postwar reconstruction contracts. "Since his role was at arm's length from the administration, he was able to whip up hysteria about the imminent danger posed by Saddam, entirely free from any burden of proof or fact," wrote Naomi Klein, author of *Shock Doctrine: The Rise of Disaster Capitalism*.

Nor were the riches now flowing limited to Iraq. Bechtel landed the contract to "remove the remains of the twin towers" after the terrorist attack on the World Trade Center. But the fact that Bechtel was also considered for the billion-dollar ground zero cleanup barely made the headlines.

CHAPTER THIRTY

More Powerful Than the US Army

"Every so often Bechtel emerges a little into the limelight, blinks, and then retreats," a writer for the *Economist* observed about the world's largest construction firm. One of the country's richest privately held companies, among the top US defense and energy contractors, and one of the most mysterious and politically connected businesses in the developed world, Bechtel had managed for its nearly eighty-year history to keep a low profile. But when, after the 2003 American-led invasion of Iraq, the George W. Bush administration gave Bechtel the first massive Iraqi reconstruction "mother contract," worth more than $1 billion, the company could no longer avoid the spotlight. Many news reports accused Bush of favoritism, pointing to Bechtel's close ties to Republicans. Some critics charged that Bechtel's win as the lead company in the restoration of Iraq hinged on its agreement to hire only subcontractors from countries that had supported the war. This directive was in keeping with President Bush's famous "You're either with us or against us" challenge to America's allies to join in a "coalition of the willing" against Iraq—or what a satirist called the coalition "of the billing."

The selection process also drew the ire of congressional Democratics who called for an investigation of the contracting process. "The rush to secure contracts to rebuild Iraq and the awarding of the first wave of deals is causing as much debate as the decision to wage war," reported the *Financial Times* of London. The US Agency for International Development (USAID) had sent a secret, detailed request for proposals to seven of the country's most politically connected multinational corporations, including Bechtel, inviting them to bid on contracts worth hundreds of millions of dollars that would be paid by the government and include a 10 percent guaranteed cost-plus profit. Of the seven invitees, only two—Bechtel and Kellogg Brown & Root (KBR)—were somehow deemed "competitive." Although those contracts were rebid in open competitions, Bechtel and KBR had an obvious inside advantage.

The structure of the cost-plus contracts provided "incentive for corporations to bloat expenditures," as one report described them. Under the aegis of national security, USAID waived competitive bidding, in what resembled a twenty-first-century gold rush. "It's a relatively small club that has both guided US military, energy, and Middle Eastern policies over the past three decades and then run the corporations that benefit from those policies," wrote Dan Baum of the *New York Times* about Bechtel and the other select companies solicited by the government. "And it's a club that had a long history with Saddam Hussein."

Critics questioned whether the federal government got the best free-market deal by limiting the bidding to a handful of American companies. The nonpartisan Washington-based Project on Government Oversight (POGO) expressed concern "that the government seems to be handpicking their buddies for these contracts." Of course, Bechtel had a four-decades-long work history of lucrative USAID contracts, building hydroelectric, power, and telecommunications projects throughout the Middle East, Central and Eastern Europe, Asia, and Africa.

Andrew Natsios, administrator of USAID, had also been the project supervisor for Bechtel's Big Dig project in Boston at a time when criminal action against the company was being considered. He bristled under critical questioning by *ABC News* reporter Ted Koppel. "I ran the Big Dig after the scandals took place," he told Koppel, who asked pointedly, "It is charged that they [Bechtel] had excessive charges of over a billion dollars here. Doesn't that give you some pause in going to Bechtel?" Bechtel was "in charge of the biggest infrastructure project in the history of America, and they screwed it up," Danielle Bryan of POGO told the *Los Angeles Times*.

Natsios defended the Bechtel Iraqi contract, claiming the company had the highest score and lowest bid—a claim that could not be veri- fied independently, given the classified nature of the process. "Only a handful of companies in the whole world have the capacity to spend that much money responsibly," Natsios contended. "So we went to the largest and best construction and engineering companies in the world." He claimed that the fact that Bechtel already had a thousand employees in the Middle East further justified the decision. Natsios repeatedly assured Koppel that the cost to the American people for rebuilding Iraq would be no more than $1.7 billion—a cost that would swell to over $2 trillion before it was over.

As for criticisms from lawmakers, Natsios derided them as un- informed. "I think some senators and congressmen, because they're under severe stress, have not maybe gone into the details of this," he said dismissively, "but their staffs have been briefed." Congress was offended not only by the mystery that surrounded the bidding but also was embarrassed to have learned about the Bechtel contract by read- ing about it in the newspaper after secret documents were leaked to the *Wall Street Journal*.

"Perhaps Bechtel's institutional knowledge was a plus," wrote Los Angeles journalist Jim Crogan, "given its status as a major player in Hussein's Iraq—during the time when doing business with Hussein was endorsed by U.S. policy. At the very least, Bechtel's ties to the old regime are not being held against it." For its part, Bechtel admit- ted having "legitimate commercial and industrial contracts" with Iraq before the war, but denied having helped Saddam's military buildup. Despite its denials, Bechtel was listed by the UN as one of two dozen US corporations that supplied Iraq with "conventional weapons, mil- itary logistics, supplies at the Iraqi Ministry of Defense, and building of military plants."

What was shocking, as one California journalist saw it, was "the relative routineness of the transaction." Upon becoming the lead contractor for the US government, Bechtel quickly dispatched a 146-member team to Iraq. Hussein's formerly opulent Republican Palace—"once party central for son Uday"—became home "to a squadron of Bechtel engineers camped out Beverly Hillbillies–style," who were accompanied by armed guards from a British security firm. Retired lieutenant general Jay Garner was appointed commander of the reconstruction effort, reporting directly to the Centcom commander, US general Tommy Franks. "Rumsfeld has sat in Abu Ghurayb Palace in Baghdad as viceroy Jay Garner receives Bechtel," a Democratic congresswoman complained, calling the Iraqi reconstruction "old men's oil wars" and an "oil bonanza even Hitler coveted." The Abu Ghurayb presidential grounds that had housed Saddam's notorious torture and execution chambers became a US military prison, where American soldiers brutalized Iraqi captives. Photographs and videos taken by soldiers of the abuses at Abu Ghurayb conducted by American GIs were broadcast on CBS's *60 Minutes II* and exposed in an explosive series written by Seymour Hersh for the *New Yorker*.

The administration essentially hired Bechtel as its contracting arm to build bridges, roads, power plants, water treatment projects, hospitals, and schools, as well as repairing airports and irrigation structures. "A motley assortment of retired Republican operatives, US businessmen, and Iraqi exiles with dubious histories and doubtful motives were the first recipients of the largesse," wrote journalist and author T. Christian Miller. News that Bechtel had received a secret invitation to bid on the lucrative contracts drew public outrage at the privatization of nation building. "We should have a separation between the state and corporations. Instead, they're acting more like partners," said a research director for a nonpartisan Washington-based think tank. "The U.S. comes in and destroys [Iraq's] infrastructure and then pays Bechtel to rebuild it," a protestor told the *San Francisco Chronicle*, prompting a response from Bechtel's head of operations in southern Iraq. "I mean, Bechtel isn't a charitable organization," said Dennis Dugas, "but we're not an exploiter. Somebody's going to build it, and Bechtel's well qualified to do it."

"Within hours of the United States military's invasion of Iraq, San

Franciscans of a certain political bent went on the offensive against one of the city's home-grown businesses: the Bechtel Group Inc.," wrote Lisa Davis in *SF Weekly*. Protestors decrying "the corporate invasion of Iraq" descended on Bechtel's headquarters at Beale and Market Streets. More than fifty were arrested when they tried unsuccessfully to shut down the building. As a precaution, the company left crowd control barriers erected in front of the building for weeks after the protestors dispersed. "Also vocal have been antiglobalization groups that accuse Bechtel of destructive environmental practices, human-rights abuses, and war profiteering," reported *USA Today*. At a Bechtel conference in London, protestors heckled the company's suppliers with chants of "Vulture! Vulture!"

The demonstrations had little impact beyond a brief and mostly localized flurry of negative publicity, with Bechtel spokesman Jonathan Marshall calling them nothing more than an inconvenience. Bechtel vice president Jim Illich tried to convince reporters that the company was sorely misunderstood. "We are a tiny, tiny part of a highly fragmented industry," he told a journalist. "This business is as tough as a night in jail." Postings on the company's website chastised journalists who criticized or scrutinized the postwar contracts. "Executives forcefully reject descriptions of Bechtel as a sort of malign behemoth," the *Los Angeles Times* reported. "Everyone says Iraq is a gravy train," a company principal complained to a reporter, asserting that the truth was more complicated. "Even for Bechtel, nothing is a sure thing."

What *was* a sure thing was that Bechtel's privatized occupation of Iraq turned the company around, bringing profits not seen since the 1960s and its construction of American military bases for the war in Vietnam. By the end of 2003, Bechtel claimed to have earned a record $16.3 billion—though there are no public filings, since, as usual, the privately held status of the company precluded outside verification of its revenue. Some construction industry rivals complained that Bechtel used its private standing to hide from public scrutiny. Bechtel's envious publicly traded competitors saw a devastating revenue drop during the same period that Bechtel was blossoming. "If a project goes financially wrong, then Bechtel can keep this to itself," a competitor told the *Independent* of London. "No current or future client ever need know if there have been problems. Couple this with its formidable network of contacts at the very top of the political tree, and it isn't hard to see why Bechtel was the first company the US government turned to for the rebuilding of Iraq."

Private active ownership "eliminates the substantial distraction and costs of dealing with the Securities and Exchange Commission, the stock exchanges, security analysts, and dissident, uninformed shareholders," Steve Jr. once wrote. "This arrangement also provides for much quicker and more thoughtful shareholder actions as they are needed." That didn't stop the firm from crowing. Its annual report acknowledged the gratifying income stream from the Iraqi construction and the windfall revenues that far surpassed those of its publicly traded competitors. "More powerful than the U.S. Army," as one account described it, Bechtel's prosperity flourished as the nation's wartime spending sent America spiraling into a historic recession. All the while, it "maintained a cloak of secrecy rivaled only by modern-day monarchies," *Time* reported.

As a high-profile and outspoken advocate for war against Iraq in 2003—a very public figure in a very private company—George Shultz sought to downplay the relaxed attitude toward Iraqi chemical weapon usage that he'd held twenty years earlier while serving as secretary of state. Just as he engaged in a moderating narrative about his complicity in coddling the "Butcher of Baghdad," Shultz defended Bechtel against charges that it was a war profiteering colossus, portraying the company instead as a benign and patriotic workhorse. Asked if he thought it a conflict of interest to campaign for war while sitting on the corporate board of the company that would benefit most from the war, Shultz demurred.

"I don't know that Bechtel would particularly benefit from it," he said with stark naïveté, if not insincerity. "But if there's work that's needed to be done, Bechtel is the type of company that could do it. But nobody looks at it as something you benefit from."

The Hydra-Headed American Giant

"Bechtel arrived in Iraq quietly," wrote Dahr Jamail, among the relatively few unembedded journalists to report from occupied Iraq during the war and its aftermath. "Before Iraqi military resistance around Baghdad melted away in the face of the U.S. military onslaught, before a single armored vehicle rolled across the Iraq-Kuwait border, while the Pentagon polished war plans, and while America was engaged in an ostensible national debate on the very question of bringing war to Iraq, the Bechtel Corporation of San Francisco was already poised to take a leading role in the reconstruction of a presumptive postwar Iraq."

On April 17, 2003, USAID, under the direction of Andrew Natsios, awarded Bechtel an eighteen-month contract worth up to $680 million. Less than six months later, the agency raised the contract's ceiling to $1.03 billion for the massive reconstruction project. L. Paul "Jerry" Bremer III, a dapper patrician, and onetime manager of Henry Kissinger's international consulting business, assumed the position of top administrator of the Coalition Provisional Authority (CPA). An "amateurish and vainglorious viceroy," as *New York Times* columnist Maureen Dowd portrayed him, Bremer oversaw the US body that managed the projects by American contractors and administered postwar Iraq. One journalist described the CPA as a "policy engine for a wholesale privatization of Iraq's state-owned entities."

The terms of the USAID contract called for Bechtel to repair the water infrastructure in ten urban areas within the first month and to restore the potable water supply in forty-five urban centers throughout Iraq within a year. "Bechtel has positioned itself very well to transition its operations into a full-blown privatization of water services," according to one report. "The company's contract could easily be extended from the reconstruction of water and wastewater systems to include the 'distribution of water,' just as Halliburton's was for oil." A former CIA senior political analyst writing in the *New York Times* warned that America could alter the destiny of the Middle East for decades, "not solely by controlling Iraq's oil, but by controlling its water."

Bechtel's representatives in Iraq were giddy at the company's good fortune in helping to create a new nation-state. Iraq "has two rivers, it's fertile, it's sitting on an ocean of oil," an ebullient Cliff Mumm, the head of Bechtel's Iraq operation, said in pointing out the strategic value of the country. "Iraq ought to be a major player in the world. And we want to be working for them long term." Installed at the contemporary Kuwait Sheraton, some fifty Bechtel engineers and managers, dressed in Bechtel-logoed golf shirts and no-press khakis, summoned dozens of British and American businessmen seeking the coveted subcontracts doled out by Bechtel. Experts estimated that 70 percent of the billions of Iraqi contract money would be paid out to subcontractors selected by Bechtel. The "hydra-headed American giant," as the *New York Times* described Bechtel, was the unmistakable keeper of the "golden keys."

In a Hyatt hotel ballroom in Jordan, Bechtel executives made a presentation to a thousand aspiring subcontractors. Appealing to what one member of the audience described as "every businessman's fantasy: rebuilding a country," a Bechtel representative defined the American role in Iraq as "institutional strengthening," "self-sufficiency," and "getting the government in shape."

Bremer, as the civil administrator of Iraq, oversaw what has been described as slush funds comparable to those used to buy local support during the Vietnam War. He distributed some $20 billion of the Iraqis' money in the first year of occupation alone. Bremer's CPA was a disastrous enterprise staffed with neocon ideologues and "God-invoking Bushies." Later critics, including its own inspector general, accused CPA under Bremer's direction of condoning wide-scale corruption in the contracting process. "The Iraqi public has not been getting value for money, while myriad contractors, bureaucrats, and politicians—American and Iraqi—have been getting stonkingly rich, a situation that the CPA fostered," wrote journalist and filmmaker Ed Harriman. An extensive investigation conducted by the British *Sunday Herald* described Garner as the overseer of a team of "military hardmen, diplomats, and Republican party place-men who will help the United States create 'Free Iraq'—aided by exiles who are returning to get their share of the spoils." This "new Gilded Age of Iraq Contractors," as American journalist and blogger Tom Engelhardt put it, led to "an unbelievable amount of money sloshing around Washington and Baghdad, some of which is unaccounted for, and a percentage of which is going into Republican and Bush reelection coffers."

A later audit of the CPA by the Office of the Special Inspector General for Iraq Reconstruction (SIGIR) would single out Bechtel, which had been contracted "on an urgent basis" to build two new generating stations near Baghdad with enough power to supply 1.5 million homes. But when Bechtel and the CPA discovered there was "insufficient fuel and no fuel delivery system of any kind in the Baghdad area," they changed tack, focusing instead on collecting and transporting natural gas from the Mansuria gas fields sixty-five miles away, where there was no infrastructure in place to deliver it from the oil fields to the two $25 million gas turbine generators they had bought. Costs soared from $78 million to $381 million before CPA canceled the Bechtel project. Still, that was only one of the CPA boondoggles that favored Bechtel. In addition to the reconstruction contract, Bechtel received billions more for what was called "task and delivery orders," which fell below the procurement radar screen, as the GAO reported, and were not open for bidding or available to Congress or the public.

When the SIGIR later began reporting to Congress its forensic audits of the major reconstruction contracts awarded to American firms in Iraq, the first of its investigations focused on Bechtel. The oversight agency found that Bechtel had completed less than half of $2 billion worth of engineering, procurement, and construction contracts. Of Bechtel's twenty-four sewage, water treatment, and electricity projects, only eleven, according to SIGIR, had "clearly met their original objectives." That did not hamper Bechtel from submitting its invoices—charging American taxpayers more than 40 percent of the contract value as "support costs" and claiming $250 million in "a large miscellaneous category" under the heading "Other." Nor did it stop USAID from paying the invoices, totaling $1.3 billion, within ten days. "Pity the poor Iraqis, who have seen a king's ransom shoveled into Bechtel's coffers in the name of 'reconstruction' of their basic utilities," concluded one reporter. Among the jobs that Bechtel did not complete was a landfill in Baghdad, for which the company was paid $3.7 million, as well as a $24.4 million water treatment plant in Sadr City. Government auditors also found that much of the funds had been diverted, legally, toward Bechtel's corporate infrastructure, to purchase "battalions of earth-moving equipment."

Before the 1991 Gulf War, Iraq had one of the best health care services in the Middle East. But two decades of war and a decade of sanctions reduced it to rubble. A Bechtel-built maternal and children's hospital in Basra—First Lady Laura Bush's and National Security Adviser Condoleezza Rice's favorite project—was to be the crowning symbol of American altruism. Despite scrutiny by congressional Democrats who questioned the need for a new, state-of-the-art pediatric hospital when existing hospitals throughout the country were in dire straits, USAID awarded Bechtel the $81 million contract. But two years later, after spending $150 million and estimating that another $98 million was needed, Bechtel was ordered to halt construction following SIGIR's damning report on the project. Auditors concluded that "USAID had cooked the books and that the State Department had withheld details of delays and increased costs in its reports to Congress." All had been done without competition or oversight. Bechtel was stung by the criticism, posting on its website a point-by-point refutation of the accusations against it, citing innuendo and the "undeserved reputation as a secretive company that succeeds through powerful friends in high places."

Bechtel blamed its failures on the insecurity and violence in the country. "Had Iraq been a calmer place while we were there, amazing things could have been done," said Bechtel's Mumm. The spokesman seemed to have remarkably little understanding of the alienating effect the US subjugation had on the Iraqi people. While Bechtel and the Bush administration had hoped to turn Iraq into a "corporate-friendly Middle East Mecca," according to one account, it was not working out that way. In fact, an American columnist concluded, the invasion triggered the rise of Al Qaeda in Iraq, which "drew from an insurgency of Sunni soldiers angry about being thrown out of work" by Paul Bremer. The Iraqis knew that Bechtel and other American companies were receiving billions of dollars for reconstruction, that "Iraqi companies had been rejected, and that the country was still without basic services. The result was increasing hostility, acts of sabotage targeted directly at foreign contractors and their work, and a rising insurgency." Bechtel had warned its potential subcontractors that only the toughest should apply. "If you're going to Iraq, it tells subs, you're hiring your own security, providing your own Kevlar vests and communications gear, lining up your own workers' comp, Medivac, and property insurance," *USA Today* reported. Terry Farley, a legendary Bechtel executive who embodied the company's "hero culture in action for his role with Bechtel in dousing the 650 burning oil wells in Kuwait, had become famous for his pep talks nicknamed "Eat Dirt and Die for Bechtel."

Deep inside the Green Zone, Bechtel's camp was set in a former garden along the Tigris River. "Resembling over-wide house trailers, the prefabricated units are roomy and nicely cool," the *Los Angeles Times* described the encampment. "Their wood paneling evokes suburban family 'rec' rooms from the early 1970s. There's a special trailer with a pool table and exercise machines, and an admonition taped to the wall: 'Drinking will occur only at the end of the day.'"

Less than three years after receiving its first contract—and after losing fifty-two workers and having another forty-nine wounded as Iraq dissolved into sectarian violence—Bechtel bailed from the country. "Bechtel—which charged into Iraq with American 'can-do' fervor," as the *San Francisco Chronicle* put it, "found it tough to keep its engineers and workers alive, much less make progress in piecing Iraq back together." Bechtel had hired a team of elite Gurkha guards from Nepal, as well as British ex-soldiers bearing MP5 machine guns to protect its employees. But Mumm, who directed the company's projects from a Baghdad trailer, faced volatile conditions, as his employees and subcontractors were maimed and killed, some kidnapped, others marched out of their offices and shot, and dozens of project supervisors fled to avoid assassination. It was the greatest loss of life Bechtel suffered during any job in its nearly century-long history, the company claimed. "The pretexts given by Bechtel to the Iraqi government to justify its failure . . . are untrue and unacceptable, especially the ones regarding the rise in security expenses," said a high-level Iraqi leader. Western engineers were rarely at the site, he claimed, where Bechtel's "complex chain" of Jordanian subcontractors oversaw the work being done by Iraqis. Bechtel had reneged on its promise to hire primarily Iraqi subcontractors, incurring the wrath of a disenfranchised native labor force.

The children's hospital was under especially vicious and unrelenting attack. The hospital's site security manager was murdered. Another manager resigned amid death threats, and a senior Bechtel engineer quit after his daughter was kidnapped. Twelve employees of a subcontractor working on the hospital's electricity and plumbing were killed in their offices. But abandoning the project was "tricky politically," as an international newspaper described it, "because of the high-profile support of Laura Bush and Rice." In its 2010 report, SIGIR drew the final imprecation, calling the Iraq reconstruction a "legacy of waste." The $171 million hospital in Basra had swelled to a final cost of $5 billion, and even though Laura Bush had officially "opened" it in 2004, by the decade's end, it had never seen a patient.

Still, all was not hopeless for Bechtel in its retreat from Iraq. The company's support of the Bush-created Middle East Free Trade Area (MEFTA)—a vehicle for trade agreements with the countries that had joined the administration's so-called coalition of the willing—insured Bechtel's continuing commercial primacy in the region.

"It is a simple fact of life these days that, owing to a deliberate decision to downsize government, Washington can operate only by paying private companies to perform a wide range of functions," wrote Donald L. Barlett and James B. Steele, an investigative reporter team. Most of this work is done outside the public eye and with little government oversight or scrutiny. "The unhappy business practices of the past few years in Iraq—cost overruns, incompetence, and corruption on a pharaonic scale—have made the American public keenly aware of the activities of mega-contractors such as Halliburton and Bechtel."

Although the privatized war-zone reconstruction was an ultimate letdown for the company, a "parallel disaster economy" was commencing, and Bechtel—with its battalions of bulldozers—was ready to capitalize. First stop: Hurricane Katrina. "The world is a messy place, and someone has to clean it up," Rice remarked unguardedly at a private Georgetown dinner.

Might as well be Bechtel.

Left to right: John McCone, Allen Dulles, and President John F. Kennedy after Kennedy's announcement that McCone would replace Dulles as director of the Central Intelligence Agency. Kennedy blamed Dulles for bungling the attempted overthrow of Cuba's Fidel Castro in the ill-fated Bay of Pigs invasion.

On November 21, 1985, Jonathan Pollard drove to the Israeli Embassy in Washington, DC, to seek asylum, since his Israeli handlers had assured him that they would protect him if his spy services were detected. Instead, embassy guards refused to let him enter, and an undercover FBI surveillance team placed him under arrest.

American soldiers seized Saddam Hussein's opulent Republican Palace in Baghdad during some of the fiercest fighting of the entire Iraq War. Under a turquoise dome considered an architectural wonder of the world, the palace would become the American Embassy on a 104-acre campus known as the Green Zone.

A defiant and downcast Saddam Hussein appeared before an Iraqi court in the summer of 2004. The former dictator faced seven charges of crimes against humanity that included the use of chemical weapons in the Iran-Iraq war. The mustard gas used against the Kurds was manufactured at a pesticide plant north of Baghdad. He would be found guilty, sentenced to death, and hanged two years later.

The Bohemian Grove is a 2,700-acre retreat located in a private redwood forest, seventy-five miles north of San Francisco. Once described by President Herbert Hoover as "the greatest men's party on earth," the all-male Grove has hosted the nation's corporate, political, and military elite every summer since 1880 in the privacy of 127 primitive camps. The most esteemed of these camps is Mandalay, where five generations of Bechtel men have been members for their entire adult life.

Bechtel sought to build a $2 billion oil pipeline from Kirkuk, Iraq, to the port of Aqaba on the Red Sea in Jordan—a clandestine mission that would remain secret for years. This Aqaba castle was built in the 14th century and made famous to a modern audience by the film *Lawrence of Arabia* set against the backdrop of the decline of the Ottoman Empire.

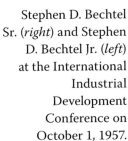

Stephen D. Bechtel Sr. (*right*) and Stephen D. Bechtel Jr. (*left*) at the International Industrial Development Conference on October 1, 1957.

Riley P. Bechtel, chairman and chief executive officer of Bechtel Group, Inc., until 2015, listens to a question during a news conference at the opening of the Business Council in Boca Raton, Florida, on February 19, 2003.

ABOVE: Jeff Grubler as Saddam Hussein is watched over by Jason Hammer (*left*) and Allen Schlossman, who were portraying CIA agents during the Stop the Corporate Invasion of Iraq protest in front of Bechtel corporate headquarters, February 24, 2004, in San Francisco. Activists sought to bring attention to what they saw as profiteering in Iraq by Bechtel and Halliburton, companies with close ties to the George W. Bush administration.

LEFT: An Israeli right-wing demonstrator holds a picture of Jonathan Pollard, a Jewish American who was jailed for life in 1987 on charges of spying on the United States, during a demonstration in Jerusalem on May 12, 2008. Pollard is a convicted Israeli spy and a former US naval civilian intelligence analyst. The Israeli government has made numerous requests for Pollard's release, all of them declined by US authorities until he was finally paroled in November 2015.

Donald Rumsfeld (*left*) and Iraq president Saddam Hussein shake hands on December 20, 1983, in Baghdad, Iraq. Rumsfeld's top-secret visit to Saddam to press for a Bechtel-built oil pipeline would remain classified for the next twenty years. Acting as a special White House envoy for former president Ronald Reagan, Rumsfeld was dispatched on the mission by George Shultz's State Department to ask the Iraqi dictator to allow Bechtel access to Iraq's gigantic oil fields—the second largest reserve in the world.

The Bechtel corporate headquarters at the corner of Beale and Mission Streets in San Francisco has long been a commanding presence. Seen here in the summer of 2015.

In large white block script, Warren "Dad" Bechtel painted "W.A. BECH-TEL CO." onto the residential boxcar that held his family. He named their makeshift home WaaTeeKaa for the combination of their three toddlers' baby names—"Waa-Waa" for Warren, "Tee-Tee" for Steve, and "Kaa-Kaa" for Kenneth. This miniature replica of the train car is seen here at the entrance to the WaaTeeKaa Bechtel History Museum at the company's San Francisco headquarters.

Profiting from Destruction

In keeping with Bechtel's sometimes being "there too early, but rarely too late," as a journalist once described the company's ubiquitousness, it would now be in on the ground floor of the burgeoning market of "disaster capitalism." The last public policy recommendation of neo-con mentor Milton Friedman—the "grand guru of the movement for unfettered capitalism and the man credited with writing the rulebook for the contemporary, hypermobile global economy"—was to turn the tragic 2005 New Orleans hurricane into a financial bonanza for a handful of corporations. One of the deadliest hurricanes in American history, Katrina was the catastrophe that "Uncle Miltie," as his power-ful followers called the famous ninety-three-year-old economist, had been seeking for decades.

In one of her groundbreaking and controversial books, *The Shock Doctrine: The Rise of Disaster Capitalism*, Naomi Klein described the free-market global economic strategy that the Friedmanites had been perfecting since the 1970s: "waiting for a major crisis, then selling off pieces of the state to private players while citizens were still reeling from the shock, then quickly making the 'reforms' permanent."

Katrina formed in the Gulf of Mexico in August 2005, causing se-vere destruction in the Bahamas and along the Gulf Coast. When the Category Five hurricane dissipated, more than 1,800 were left dead—with the majority of those fatalities occurring in New Orleans, where the levee system failed and caused catastrophic flooding. While the entire nation mourned the tragedy, the Friedmanites—including Riley Bechtel—were embracing the opportunities created by the disaster. "Within weeks, the Gulf Coast became a domestic laboratory for the same kind of government-run-by-contractors that had been pioneered in Iraq," according to one account. The very day the hurricane struck, the US government's Federal Emergency Management Agency (FEMA) contracted with Bechtel to provide mobile homes for a hundred thousand people in the Gulf region who had been displaced by the storm. Bechtel's immediate no-bid contract—one of $62 billion of "indefinite delivery–indefinite quantity contracts" doled out to the same handful of American companies rebuilding Iraq—was a boon. Only days after the storm, it was as if "Baghdad's Green Zone had lifted off from its perch on the Tigris and landed on the bayou," wrote Klein.

FEMA was under attack at the time for failing to respond quickly to the devastation in the Gulf. Described by a *Washington Post* reporter as a "hollowed out" agency being run by Bush political appointees with no disaster-management experience, FEMA became the poster child for the outsourcing of government that had begun escalating during the Clinton administration. Many of FEMA's top civil servants—including two former FEMA directors from the Clinton and Bush administrations—had left the agency to consult with the private contractors who were "rushing to cash in on the unprecedented sums to be spent on Hurricane Katrina relief and reconstruction," as journalist John Broder reported. "They are throwing money out, they are shoveling it out the door," a former president of the American League of Lobbyists told the *New York Times*. "I'm sure every lobbyist's phone in Washington is ringing off the hook from his clients. Sixty-two billion dollars is a lot of money—and it's only a down payment." Indeed, the government was spending relief money at a rate of more than $500 million a day.

Bechtel had dispatched more than a hundred employees to Mississippi, where it was reportedly "working under an informal agreement with no set payment terms, scope of work, or designated total value." The company announced it was seeking subcontractors to provide water treatment, sewage, and electricity, "as well as mess halls, showers, even helicopters to move supplies." A Bechtel spokesman dismissed criticism of the company's coziness with the Bush administration. "Political contributions are not a factor," Bechtel's Howard Menaker told the press. "It is the fact that we could get the job done."

For his part, Riley Bechtel joined the Business Roundtable—where he was cochairman of the Roundtable's Gulf Coast Workforce Development Initiative—in launching a rollout of a recruitment effort to train up to twenty thousand new construction workers in the Gulf Coast region. "This landmark public-private partnership—involving businesses, the federal government, states, and other organizations—will train the workers that will be needed to rebuild the area," he proclaimed. The Roundtable, which had grown to include 160 CEOs of the nation's leading companies, was spearheading the reconstruction effort. "This partnership between government and business will be a powerful catalyst for recovery in the Gulf region, retention and development of the local population, and a model for future disaster recovery," Bechtel said.

A later review by the Defense Contract Audit Agency—"the first line of defense for the public in policing billions of dollars" in government contracts, as DCAA has been described—questioned Bechtel's estimates for Katrina work and accused the company of systematically stonewalling auditors. The charges led Congressman Henry A. Waxman to accuse Bechtel of trying to double-bill the government, and prompted Waxman to join Minority Leader Nancy Pelosi in calling for reforms to protect federal taxpayers from waste, fraud, and abuse. "We cannot allow greed, mismanagement, and cronyism to squander billions of taxpayer dollars, as has happened too often over the last five years," the two California Democratic representatives declared in introducing the Hurricane Katrina Accountability and Clean Contracting Act. The Bush administration's Office of Management and Budget rejected those calls for reform. Still, DCAA auditors not only accused Bechtel of denying government access to company documents but also charged DCAA higher-ups of inappropriate intimacy with Bechtel officials by condoning the company's foot-dragging. Bechtel is "the slowest responding [contractor] that I've been at," a DCAA employee emailed a colleague. "You would be unnerved to know that some of my data request [*sic*] here have been outstanding for more than six months!"

Auditor Acacia Rodriguez resorted to a twenty-four-page Power-Point briefing to describe to her superiors how she and her coworkers struggled with Bechtel's " 'chronic failure' to provide requested financial records required to prove tax dollars were being spent properly." Her bosses remained unmoved, even after a special congressional investigation determined that the emergency no-bid contract that FEMA awarded to Bechtel was among a group of so-called Technical Assistance Contracts that "ballooned from approximately $400 million to about $3.4 billion." But Congress's allegations against Bechtel, along with the company's colossal failures in both Iraq and the Gulf Coast, did nothing to hinder its continued feeding at the public trough. Rather than learn from Bechtel's many mistakes in both instances, the Bush administration determined to reward the company—this time on a large scale. Even as the Special Inspector General was auditing Bechtel's poor performance in Iraq and DCAA and congressional investigators were lambasting Bechtel's "mismanagement" and "wasteful spending" on the Katrina site, Bechtel received the biggest contract of all: managing the nation's nuclear energy and weapons complex.

PART FOUR

FROM MULESKINNER TO SOVEREIGN STATE

2009–2015

When the modern corporation acquires power over markets, power in the community, power over the state, power over belief, it is a political instrument, different in form and degree but not in kind from the state itself.

—JOHN KENNETH GALBRAITH

A Convenient Spy

The same neocons who "egged on the hapless endeavor in Iraq," as scholar Hugh Gusterson described them, led the propaganda assault on Los Alamos that broke up the long-standing and largely successful "triangular relationship between DOE, the weapons labs, and the University of California" that led to the lab's privatization. The nonprofit University of California had managed Los Alamos National Laboratory in the high desert of northern New Mexico since the World War II–era Manhattan Project. At the behest of J. Robert Oppenheimer, the brilliant Berkeley physics professor considered the father of the atomic bomb, who was eager to keep civilians rather than the military in control of the top secret bomb-building program, the University of California agreed to administer the lab for the US government.

Inspired by wartime patriotism and with scant knowledge of the secret research, the university gained little from the deal. A "paltry management fee and much grief from pacifist students and faculty members" marked the arrangement from the start, the *New York Times* reported. Then, in 1952, the University of California established the University of California Radiation Laboratory at Livermore in Berkeley to compete with the atomic bomb builders at Los Alamos, championing a rival H-bomb conceived by the Hungarian physicist—and Oppenheimer's future nemesis—Edward Teller. Soon after cofounder Ernest Lawrence died in 1958, it was renamed the Lawrence Radiation Laboratory, and then, in 1971, it was changed again to Lawrence Livermore Laboratory.

Even after the Cold War ended, the US government paid the University of California to keep the weapons labs operating, with the university "plowing much of the $8 million-per-lab management fee back into the labs themselves," as Gusterson, who calls himself "the Margaret Mead of the weapons labs," described the arrangement. The open-faced and enigmatic British anthropologist, who has studied nuclear weapons scientists for thirty years, traces the Cold Warriors' takeover of the weapons labs to a trumped-up spy case against a Chinese American scientist.

On March 6, 1999, the *New York Times* published a sensational front-page story titled "China Stole Nuclear Secrets for Bombs, US Aides Say." Two days after the story, Secretary of Energy Bill Richardson leaked to the press the identity of Dr. Wen Ho Lee—a nuclear physicist at Los Alamos—and terminated Lee's employment there. A media frenzy ensued. For the next six months, television news crews camped outside the Lees' modest ranch-style home, "hoping for a glimpse of the quiet man accused of being the new Julius Rosenberg," wrote Gusterson. "Convoys of FBI agents trailed Lee and his wife whenever they went to the store for milk."

When Lee had moved with his family to Los Alamos twenty years earlier, he was among the first dozen Chinese Americans—mostly Taiwanese—ever granted security clearances at the weapons lab. For decades, the US government had refused to hire anyone with relatives behind the Iron Curtain or in China. With the end of the Cold War, though, that stance had changed, as the lab's mission theoretically expanded into unclassified projects with peacetime endeavors. In the nine months between the time that Lee was outed and his arrest, the government portrayed him as a dangerous spy who had threatened US national security.

Soft-spoken and diminutive, Lee was arrested on December 10, 1999, on fifty-nine charges of mishandling classified information—thirty-nine of which carried life sentences under federal sentencing laws. The case against Lee stunned the community of Los Alamos, which was inundated with rumors and innuendo about the phantom spy ring passing nuclear secrets to China, all masterminded by the well-liked and hapless Lee. "FBI agents descended on Los Alamos, administering polygraphs to weapons scientists, commandeering their offices, and, in some cases, dragging them from their beds in the middle of the night and driving them two hours to Albuquerque for interrogations," according to one account.

Held in solitary confinement for 278 days with handcuffs attached to a metal belt, shackled at the ankles, and allowed only one hour of exercise per week—cruel and unusual punishment for which the presiding federal judge would later apologize profusely—Lee's case incited public demonstrations and outrage in the Chinese American community and beyond. In the end, the case would disintegrate due both to lack of evidence and flagrant racial profiling—but not before it provided a boon for Bechtel by publicly demonstrating that dangerous security lapses plagued Los Alamos. While FBI Director Louis Freeh stoked the media hysteria about Chinese espionage, the public perception of the nation's nuclear weapons laboratories as a hotbed of spies and infiltrators took hold. Vice presidential hopeful Bill Richardson overzealously sought to use the case to establish his political bona fides as a protector of national security. Senior lab officials testified at a bail hearing that the information in Lee's possession would change the entire global strategic balance if passed to US enemies.

Agitated Washington politicians responded to the frenzy, with a Republican-controlled Congress creating the National Nuclear Security Administration (NNSA)—the quasi-autonomous agency established within DOE to oversee the nation's nuclear weapons and naval reactor program—and putting US Air Force four-star general Eugene A. Habiger in charge of security at both Los Alamos and the Lawrence Livermore National Laboratory. As far back as 1946, scientists had banded together to warn President Harry Truman about the danger of allowing military control over atomic energy. Now, nearly sixty years after atomic bombs were dropped on Japan—a period during which civilian control of the nation's weapons complex had been guarded furiously—powerful military forces were pushing to transfer the entire nuclear enterprise into their jurisdiction. "Reporters and congressmen were so caught up in the fever pitch of a spy hunt—a nuclear spy, no less—that no one stopped to examine the basis for the original suspicions," according to a later account of the panic.

After 278 days in jail without facing trial, Lee took the government's plea offer to drop fifty-eight of the fifty-nine counts against him. He admitted to one felony count of mishandling classified information for removing computer disks from the lab that contained copies of top secret nuclear codes. (The disks were found behind a copy machine at the lab just days after being reported missing. No evidence ever surfaced that the codes had been given to anyone else at the lab, much less to a foreign country.) At the plea sentencing hearing, US Judge James Parker—a Ronald Reagan appointee—released Lee on time served and in an emotionally charged statement told Lee: "I am truly sorry that I was led by our executive branch of government to order your detention last December." Parker went on to blame the executive branch, including President Bill Clinton, Vice President Al Gore, and Energy Secretary Richardson, for instigating a case that he portrayed as an embarrassment to all Americans. "As a member of the third branch of the United States government, the Judiciary, the United States Courts, I sincerely apologize to you, Dr. Lee, for the unfair manner you were held in custody."

The exonerated Lee and a throng of his supporters accused Richardson of racial profiling. Dubbed the "convenient spy" by authors Dan Stober and Ian Hoffman, Lee, according to them, was the victim of mendacious scheming that went beyond racial profiling. "Wen Ho Lee was an invented crisis, not an intelligence operation," said Greg Mello, executive director of the Los Alamos Study Group, the long-standing New Mexico watchdog organization that monitors nuclear safety and security at the lab. "It was a crisis designed to portray the University of California as a bad manager so the labs would go into private hands."

Even Siegfried Hecker, a nuclear scientist and former longtime director of Los Alamos, was appalled by the case. Despite the fact that Lee had indeed betrayed the trust of the weapons world by not adequately protecting the security of computer disks, he did not deserve the ignominy he received, as Hecker saw it. "The way he was hung in public and the way he was jailed was really un-American," Hecker said. Stober and Hoffman, who examined the Lee case and the politics of nuclear espionage at the beginning of the twenty-first century, agreed: "Regardless of Lee's motives, the Wen Ho Lee affair was an ugly chapter in US history. It was a time when democratic ideals were forgotten in the name of national security, when ideology and ambition overpowered objectivity, and when partisan warfare trumped statesmanship."

When it was all over, the Lee case was used to justify the privatization of the labs. Bechtel, not surprisingly, won the contract, having been handpicked by a high-level DOE official, Tom D'Agostino. After claiming to review recommendations from a board of experts, D'Agostino announced he was "quite confident" with the choice of Bechtel. It would be the first time that a corporation would manage the nuclear laboratory, marking a distinct transformation from its long-standing traditional academic atmosphere to a profit-driven post–Cold War reemphasis on nuclear arms. Under the management of the University of California, Los Alamos had operated as a relatively straightforward research facility—what one journalist described as a "fortified, forested mile-high plateau where 14,000 people work in a scientific wonderland, a place that cherishes its mystique as much as its culture of atomic secrecy." The university behaved more like an absentee landlord—financial incentivation had never before been a factor—as private industry coveted a piece of a burgeoning commercial opportunity languishing behind a storied ivory tower.

"The greatest irony is that US leaders turned over management of the nuclear weapons complex to the private sector at the very moment that there should have been an open debate about the public purposes of the laboratories and facilities," wrote Kennette Benedict, the publisher of the *Bulletin of the Atomic Scientists*. Mello concurred. "The Cold War is back," he pronounced.

Privatize the Apocalypse

President George W. Bush's administration—in its passion to turn over key government functions to private industry, and as part of the post-9/11 agenda to privatize national security—decided to corporatize the nation's nuclear warhead complex, with Bechtel at the helm. The DOE solicited bids from contractors interested in operating not only the two flagship weapons labs but also the nation's entire nuclear enterprise, including the Savannah River National Laboratory in South Carolina; the Hanford Site on the Columbia River in Washington; the Y-12 National Security Complex in Oak Ridge, Tennessee; the Pantex Plant in Amarillo, Texas; and the Nevada Test Site north of Las Vegas. In 2007 the NNSA awarded a Bechtel-led consortium a multiyear, multibillion-dollar contract to oversee the country's top secret nuclear laboratories and plants. The country's National Laboratory System, a collection of seventeen labs, was the flagship of the United States's nuclear weaponry research and development apparatus that was the primary deterrent to the Soviet Union.

Redubbed the US Nuclear Security Enterprise (NSE) by Bechtel corporate headquarters, the moniker replaced the traditional term of "nuclear weapons labs." At a moment when there was resounding political pressure for closure of the labs because of their obsolescence, the new phrase implied an urgent mission. For a decade, there had been calls for a post–Cold War downsizing of the nation's nuclear weapons complex, and an international groundswell for nuclear nonproliferation was under way. Government inspectors, DOE and DOD officials, and nuclear experts agreed that both national labs were twice as big as they should be. The dismantling of the Berlin Wall, the fall of the Soviet Union, and international calls for nuclear disarmament "sent Los Alamos and the whole U.S. nuclear complex into existential crisis," as one journalist put it. "What do we do now that nuclear weapons have no obvious role in a world of, at best, medium-sized military enemies?" wrote activist Frida Berrigan of what she described as "the urge to privatize the apocalypse."

The nuclear establishment was "deeply wounded at the end of the Cold War," said Mello. "One-third of the weapons designers had retired by 1995, and the labs' budgets were in free fall. There was a severe crisis in morale and mission. Bechtel and private industry had long wanted to get their hands on the best-funded nuclear labs in the world, and finally they did."

Under intensive lobbying by Bechtel and the nuclear industry, the Bush administration developed a solution in response to complaints from Congress that the weapons labs lacked a clear mission. A Nuclear Posture Review released by the DOD asserted the new direction of America's nuclear arsenal: "The need is clear for a revitalized nuclear weapons complex that will be able, if directed, to design, develop, manufacture, and certify new warheads in response to new national requirements; and maintain readiness to resume underground testing if required."

Congress responded by privatizing the labs, and the weapons complex became among the largest outsourcing to the private sector of the government's national security budget. DOE's $12.6 billion annual budget for fiscal year 2016 represented a 10 percent hike in appropriations for NNSA. "Washington should oversee the labs, not micromanage them," became the rallying cry for those eager to profit from the transfer of "scientific discovery into the market" for commercial application—a position detailed in a contemporary Bechtel-sponsored policy white paper advocating expanded private sector access to the labs' research. "A recipe for the enrichment of private entities with no accountability to the taxpayer," Mello described the so-called government-owned, contractor-operated (GOCO) model of transforming government research into commercial products. Renowned physicist and independent consultant Robert Civiak concurred, defining the "corporatization" of the laboratories as "self-serving ideas" and "warmed-over proposals to operate the labs more like the private sector," and calling the GOCO model "an anachronism of the Cold War."

The end of the Cold War shifted how the nation maintained its nuclear arsenal, and Bechtel prepared for that transition. America was back in the bomb-making business, but this time with Bechtel, not the government, running the enterprise. "After initial US and Russian moves to reduce arsenals, dismantle weapons, secure fissile material, and downblend enriched uranium for civilian use, the heroic steps initiated by Soviet leader Mikhail Gorbachev to end the Cold War have been followed with only timid efforts to rethink the purpose of nuclear weapons in US national security policy," wrote Kennette Benedict.

Bechtel promised to improve efficiency and security at both labs, and formed two for-profit limited liability corporations. LANS, LLC, would operate the Los Alamos National Security lab—the massive, secret site in northern New Mexico—while LLNS, LLC, would manage its sister site, Lawrence Livermore National Security, in Berkeley, California. Partnering with Bechtel in both LANS and LLNS were Washington Group International (WGI), BWX Technologies (BWXT), and the University of California, with Bechtel the consortium's unmistakable leader. "Bechtel leveraged what the University of California did well—science—with the company's expertise in management," said Todd Jacobson of the *Bulletin of Atomic Scientists*.

In exchange for the multimillions in management fees, Bechtel promised DOE it would improve efficiency and security, transition the labs to industrial standards, capitalize on private sector expertise, and increase contractor accountability. But it wouldn't work out that way. "Everybody thought that with privatization, we could save money and get more transparency," said Peter Stockton, a senior investigator at the nonprofit Project on Government Oversight, who has studied the national laboratories since the 1970s. "It's done pretty much the opposite."

In its drive to maximize profits, Bechtel would be widely criticized by numerous government, congressional, and watchdog investigations for its cost overruns, unfair employment practices, security violations, pattern of retaliation against whistleblowers, and massive reductions in its workforce through voluntary and involuntary layoffs. For instance, it promised to reduce Livermore "support costs" by 20 percent, equaling $150 million over the first three years of the contract. Instead, the $150 million cost reduction offset the increased costs of $130 million to $150 million to manage the labs, with a tenfold increase in management fees, which increased by $40 million annually. "Bechtel gets nuclear lab, taxpayers foot the bill," wrote an employment lawyer in response to the lab's restructuring.

Hundreds of career employees were fired in the labs' transition from public to private—"massive layoffs executed with the finesse of Donald Trump," as one account described them. Bechtel's elimination of the jobs—and high salaries—of older physicists generated more income for the LLCs, while also resulting in what industry observers described as a "brain drain" of the country's best nuclear scientists. Union members and scientists argued that the profit motive driving the brain drain was not only bad public policy but also set a dangerous precedent that endangered the safety of the American public.

A National Academy of Sciences investigation of the impact of privatizing the labs found that peer-reviewed articles—articles written by experts and reviewed by other experts in the same field as an indicator of accurate scholarship—dropped almost by half. The National Research Council reported that the privatized management had a negative influence on scientific experimentation and that a venerable tacit code had been violated. "There was a social contract," as a California journalist covering Livermore put it. " 'You will never get rich in science, but we treat you as adults, respect you for your commitment, and in turn you can pursue science and have fun.' " Activist Frida Berrigan agreed, writing that nuclear laboratories "are no longer to be intellectual institutions devoted to science but part of a corporate-business model where research, design, and ultimately the weapons themselves will become products to be marketed. The new dress code will be suits and ties, not lab coats and safety glasses."

The demoralized and disaffected scientists who managed to keep their jobs lived in fear of financial retaliation or termination if they raised concerns regarding lab practices, according to union representatives. Whistleblowers were once highly valued as the gatekeepers to security—with onetime secretary of energy Hazel O'Leary going so far as to declare "zero tolerance" for retaliation against them, citing that "these facilities are dangerous . . . I need whistleblowers." But the Bechtel-led management cracked down on whistleblowers. The George W. Bush–era DOE began "using taxpayer dollars to pay litigation costs and settlements for contractors who fight retaliation claims through years of hearings and appeals, a practice that costs the public tens of millions of dollars annually," according to one account. The suppression of scientists sent a clear message to workers tempted to expose safety and environmental dangers: "Keep your mouth shut."

By 2007, the DOE had become the most privatized federal department, with 94 percent of its budget going to contractors—and with Bechtel the agency's top contractor. Of its two hundred thousand employees, fewer than fifteen thousand were government employees—the rest were private subcontractors. The NNSA was even more privatized. The separately organized agency within DOE outsourced a whopping 96 percent of its budget to private entities, with Bechtel topping that list as well. "In wars in Iraq and Afghanistan, Americans have gotten used to the idea of private firms supplying logistical support and even private security services to military troops," as a nuclear expert put it. "But placing nuclear weapons design and maintenance—the US nuclear deterrent—in the hands of private business takes the outsourcing of government services to a new extreme."

As "powerful as one of its nuclear reactors," wrote David Streitfeld of the *Los Angeles Times*, Bechtel had returned full circle to the industry to which it had been most entwined historically: nuclear energy and weaponry. Having built the world's first nuclear plant in 1951, and dozens more throughout the country and the world, Bechtel's nuclear business had been thwarted since 1978 when the US government stopped issuing licenses—a year before the Three Mile Island accident. Now, after nearly thirty years of lobbying, Bechtel's efforts paid off. In the year 2007 alone, the Nuclear Energy Institute (NEI)—the lobbying group that sets policy in the industry, and of which Bechtel had been an active member since its inception in 1994—spent $1.3 billion petitioning the federal government.

Of the more than one hundred lobbyists hired by Bechtel and the nation's other top nuclear contractors, the majority were former members of Congress, former congressional staff, and former DOD and DOE officials. Senior government officials on Bechtel's payroll between 1997 and 2004 included former secretary of agriculture Daniel R. Glickman, former New York Republican congressman Bill Paxon, former IRS commissioner Donald A. Alexander, and more. In addition to privatizing the labs, the Bush administration prepared to build as many as twenty-nine nuclear facilities throughout the nation, with Bechtel the leading American company to benefit from the $90 billion worth of planned projects, even though "none of the thirty-one nations that produce nuclear power has found a safe, permanent way to store the toxic byproducts of spent fuel, including plutonium," as environmental scientist Ian Hore-Lacy of the World Nuclear Association told a reporter.

DOE had mutated into a colossal agency that contracted out nearly all of its operations, with little oversight or regulation of its contractors, and with more classified programs than any other agency dealing with national security, intelligence, and the nuclear weapons complex. A lion's share of its multibillion-dollar annual budget was now going to one behemoth, privately held, family-owned, multinational corporation that itself rivaled many government agencies in size, scope, and power. Most of the contracts that Bechtel received were overseen by a handful of congressional committees that routinely approved the appropriations without raising questions. The few legislators who sat on those committees received significant political contributions from Bechtel and were constantly lobbied by highly paid influence peddlers from the six Washington, DC–based lobbying firms employed by the company.

Nukes for Profit

"Private interests have no business with nuclear weapons," former secretary of state George Shultz testified before Congress during his 1982 nomination hearings. Like much of Shultz's dissembling—or expedient mind changing—twenty-five years later, his newfound advocacy for the labs' shift from nonprofit to for-profit was an about-face. But few in Congress or the media questioned this reversal on a policy certain to enhance Shultz's Bechtel stock portfolio.

If Bechtel's fortunes had wavered in the decade leading up to the Iraq War, if its symbiotic relationship with the American government had ever been tenuous, the two were now entangled in the US Nuclear Security Enterprise. First with Iraq, and then with Katrina, Bechtel had raked in record revenues in the years after 2007. Riley and his father, Steve Jr., shared the rank of the world's 292nd richest billionaires, each with a net worth of $2.5 billion. But those revenues, the largest in the company's history, would not compare with Bechtel's future income from controlling the nation's nuclear empire. With the labs run at a profit, and with the cost-plus, risk-free business model invented by Steve Sr. and John McCone in the late 1930s to build pipelines in the Middle East, Bechtel's 30 percent guaranteed management fee and indemnification from liability would give it a monopoly on the country's nuclear stockpile.

"From Los Alamos to Kwajalein [the Bechtel-built Ronald Reagan Ballistic Missile Test Site in the Marshall Islands] to Iraq, war, preparing for war, and profiting from war's devastation are all profit centers for Bechtel," concluded an investigation by the Western States Legal Foundation—a thirty-year-old organization that provides legal assistance to nonviolent environmental activists. Operational costs at the labs soared in the aftermath of the Bechtel takeover, with American taxpayers shelling out $40 million more per year for Livermore alone. Fees paid to LANS and LLNS to administer Los Alamos and Livermore jumped by 850 percent and 600 percent, respectively. Executive salaries also swelled, with the Los Alamos director's salary shooting from $348,000 to $1.1 million—more than double that of the US president.

All the while, the private partnership led by Bechtel continued to receive taxpayer dollars of more than $1 billion annually. Through the first seven years of its creation—2000 to 2007—NNSA's budget jumped to one and a half times what the nuclear weapons budget had been at the height of the Cold War. Calling it "the ultimate white-collar welfare," Republican Congressman David Hobson of Ohio derided the agency. Even a former general counsel of NNSA publicly stated, "Profits and nuclear weapons don't mix," and Tyler Przybylek, acting head of NNSA, would describe the "creeping privatization" as "unwise." The labs were now run by outsiders from private industry who reflected a different ethos than that of the traditional scientists.

Nowhere was Bechtel's corporate culture and leadership style more starkly exhibited than in the very first week of its management of Livermore. A senior Livermore employee described Bechtel's management style of LLNS as a combination of "the worst aspects of the Department of Motor Vehicles and Goldman Sachs." In May 2008, just months after Bechtel took over, LLNS laid off 430 career employees, whose average age was well over forty, and most of whom had been employed by Livermore for two decades or more. In thirty years, there had not been a single layoff at Livermore. "Bechtel and its partners immediately began planning to get rid of employees in order to secure their profit margin," according to a renowned wrongful termination and employment discrimination attorney, who would eventually litigate against LLNS. "Almost before they even took over, they began implementing the planned layoff," said J. Gary Gwilliam, an attorney in Oakland. "In the classic slash-and-burn fashion of corporate take-overs, Bechtel came in to trim the sails and cut the gray hair," said one fired employee.

The key "hatchet man," as Gwilliam described the Bechtel executive vice president who, in the corporate downsizing manner of actor George Clooney in the film *Up in the Air*, oversaw the swift and un-sympathetic firings, was Frank Russo. The architect of the layoff, Russo was one of forty employees who came from Bechtel corporate head-quarters to work for the lab. Russo had begun his career twenty-five years earlier, working for Bechtel's domestic and international nuclear projects. With the official title of assistant director for operations and business, Russo directed armed guards to escort the career employees off the grounds as he gutted the workforce.

Russo and his Bechtel colleague Steven B. Liedle referred to them-selves as the "kitchen cabinet," and claimed to be under orders from DOE to reduce the workforce because of a budget crisis—a claim chal-lenged by Gwilliam, who would eventually amass more than three hundred thousand documents and depose more than fifty witnesses. Bechtel, "through their limited liability corporation, really mistreated many employees and frankly lied to Congress about the reason they had to lay off long-term loyal workers," Gwilliam said. An independent con-sultant hired by Gwilliam who reviewed DOE documents related to the lab takeover determined that the budget crisis was invented, and that LLNS "intentionally overstated its budget problems," and had sufficient funds to avoid any involuntary layoffs but were motivated by profit. "At OMB [Office of Management and Budget] we called this tactic 'Wash-ington Monumenting' their budget problems," said Dr. Robert Civiak, a former OMB examiner, "an analogy to Interior Department threats to close the Washington Monument when their budget is tight." Civiak claimed further that LLNS used the "phony budget shortfall as an ex-cuse to lay off hundreds of workers for reasons not related to the budget."

Marian Barraza, one of the most senior workers at the lab, began her career in 1969 as a seventeen-year-old high school graduate. She felt like a criminal the day she was ushered off campus. Bechtel corporate agents gave her a few minutes to pack the belongings from her office before marching her out under the watchful eyes of security guards. "The sheriff was there," she recalled of the humiliating moment, "and the undercover security agents were carrying guns." After thirty-eight years of loyal service, she cried alone in the parking lot.

All former University of California employees of the lab were suddenly on the payroll of the Bechtel-led LLC. The associate director of human resources for the lab described it as the "corporate takeover" of the weapons laboratory. The National Ignition Facility (NIF), which was the crown jewel of Livermore, was the single largest project in the NNSA budget. As the largest laser-based fusion research device in the country, NIF was the most potentially profitable lab program. Because of its high value, NIF was excluded from the layoffs, and the LLNS corporate consortium focused its considerable energy and resources into developing nuclear fusion for civilian use. "LLNS put everything into NIF," said Gusterson, "starting at $1.2 billion and mushrooming up to $4 billion." The *New York Times* described NIF's "stadium-sized laboratory that contains 192 lasers trained on a target the size of a BB. The goal is to generate temperatures of more than 100 million degrees to fuse hydrogen atoms and release nuclear energy." A spokesman for the National Resources Defense Council estimated that NIF was the most expensive experimental facility ever built in US history.

Inspired by the idea that NIF would revolutionize nuclear power, Bechtel was staking its future on that laser program, constantly upping its budget estimates to Congress. Seduced by LLNS's promise that "an era of carbon-free power could dawn," key congressional figures embraced the "revolution," according to the *Times*, and readily approved escalating appropriations. Lab director George Miller met with congressional oversight committees and DOE officials several times a month. At one point, under questioning by legislators dubious about the privatized entity, he attempted to assuage their concerns by describing LLNS as more an arm of the government than a private contractor. Rather than submit bids to the US government, "[w]e are assigned missions," Miller once testified. "We are assigned work by the federal government. And for a substantial fraction of the funding of the laboratory . . . they say what the government wants done, and we tell them, 'This is what it will cost.' "

Miller focused his attention on four committees: the two defense-authorizing committees in the Senate and the House, and the two Energy and Water committees in both bodies. "So those four committees plus parallel committees for the Department of Homeland Security," he said. NIF, housed in a ten-story building the size of three football fields, is described by LLNS as the cornerstone of NNSA's stockpile steward-ship program. The government claims that its temperatures of 100 million degrees allow it to create the same states of high-energy-density matter that exist in stars and planets. Among its chief missions, according to NNSA, the fusion device would provide a clean source of energy security for America—hence its national security component.

Critics saw the LLNS budget to NIF as a slush fund for a government research program geared to benefit private industry, especially Bechtel. But the crucial factor of ignition eluded the project, rendering the "giant array of lasers designed to fuse hydrogen atoms" effectively impotent. Cynical scientists mocked LLNS as an acronym for Lasers, Lasers, Nothing but laserS, seeing NIF as a boondoggle more beneficial to Bechtel's bottom line than to America's energy or national security needs.

Still, that was only Livermore. A thousand miles away, under the blue skies of the "Land of Enchantment," Los Alamos National Laboratory was undergoing its own transformation from pointy-headed paradise to neocon corporatism. "People don't know what Los Alamos was like in the 1970s, when the humanist spirit was strong, if not dominant," said energy and climate activist Greg Mello. "Little did we know that the world and that tradition was so fragile." Mello described the Los Alamos of nearly fifty years earlier as a "far more intelligent, demanding, and conscientious environment than Los Alamos is today, with human values at the core—endangered values, to be sure, but those values were active."

The Buddhist and the Bomb

"None of my friends, or I, when we grew up, thought we were likely to avoid nuclear war long enough to have a normal life span," said Greg Mello, a trained engineer who has devoted his lifetime to abolishing nuclear weapons. "Basically, by 1970, it was clear to me from the science and from what I saw around me in Southern California every day that the world was facing an environmental apocalypse." While president of the student engineering society at Harvey Mudd—the prestigious college of science, math, and engineering located in Claremont, California—Mello came of age at the height of the Vietnam War. The native Californian steeped himself in the works of progressive historians and sociologists, scientists and philosophers, Beat poets and literary figures, essayists and educators, radical priests and counterculture peace activists. "Nixon wanted me in Vietnam. But I was reading Lewis Mumford, Ivan Illich, Gary Snyder, and the Berrigans." From those thinkers, Mello formed his self-described "strong sense of social responsibility."

Upon graduating with distinction in 1971, Mello watched as peers went to work for the weapons laboratories. "I was disgusted by what I saw in the engineering world, disgusted by the Vietnam War and the global environmental catastrophe unfolding." He had studied and worked with some of the most creative and influential minds in America's budding green movement. As he grew disenchanted with engineering, Mello turned his attention to environmental policy and found a mentor in Paul Shepard—the ecologist famous for his collection of essays, *The Subversive Science.* He was inspired as well by the chair of the Political Science Department at neighboring Pitzer College, John Rodman, for whom Mello served as a teaching assistant. Determined not to use his engineering degree to aid and abet the war, Mello leaped at the opportunity Rodman presented him to run an external studies program for research projects located in Santa Fe, New Mexico. A renowned environmental ethicist and ecology scholar, Rodman ran in a rarefied circle that included John Gofman, the brilliant Lawrence Livermore scientist and UC Berkeley professor of molecular and cell biology. Gofman had just founded the Committee for Nuclear Responsibility. One of the earliest antinuclear whistleblowers, he had raised some of the most salient questions about the safety of nuclear power, and Mello absorbed what these erudite guides imparted to him.

By the time the tall, sincere young Mello turned up in Santa Fe, his life mission seemed preordained. During the two years of working for an umbrella organization of all the newly created environmental groups in the state of New Mexico—spawning what he called "apprentice activists"—the twenty-one-year-old Mello came to idolize Rodman. "He was just a teacher," he recalled years later, "but where are such teachers now? He was everything I expected at the time, with the vast expectations of youth, and I was not disappointed. He was all I thought he should be, I having no idea at all how mediocre the world actually was." Naïve and idealistic, Mello had a passionate belief that he could effect positive and momentous change. He moved to Cambridge, Massachusetts, in 1973 to attend graduate school at Harvard. Receiving his master's degree in Regional Planning, he declined an offer to teach at the university—"I didn't fit the Harvard mold," he observed—and turned his attention to mathematical modeling and econometrics. He thought Harvard's Planning Program was churning out the kind of "economic hit men" characterized decades later by insider author John Perkins.

The more disaffected he became with the direction the country was going—"the Cold War permeated everything," he said—the less Mello wanted to pursue his doctorate. He became increasingly committed to Zen Buddhism and decided ultimately to focus his energy on his religious practices. By the mid 1970s, he was living at the Zen Center in Rochester, New York. "Essentially a monk," is his description of his six-year residence in Rochester. Mello returned to Santa Fe in 1981, where he built the Mountain Cloud Zen Center and became involved in interfaith social work and peace activism.

After volunteering for several years with an organization concerned about radiation exposure from Los Alamos—since 1944, the lab had discarded more than seventeen million cubic feet of radioactive waste—he cofounded the Los Alamos Study Group (LASG) to expand his work from nuclear safety to nuclear disarmament. "I realized that the Cold War and the arms industry represented a menace to our civilization, and I recognized that it was important to speak up before the moment had passed," Mello said. He credited two of his Zen teachers—Philip Kapleau and Robert Aitken—as the strongest influences in his decision to zero in on disarmament as a lifetime undertaking.

An outgrowth of the People for Peace movement—and in response to the 1991 Gulf War—LASG grew from an informal association of peace activists, ministers, and political progressives to a formalized organization providing technical consultation to a coalition of over a hundred loosely allied citizen nuclear groups in New Mexico, California, and Washington, DC. "Our idea was that with the fall of the Berlin Wall and the closure of the Rocky Flats nuclear weapons production facility [following a raid by the FBI for environmental crimes], we could have citizen-influenced change in Los Alamos. I felt that the institutional configurations of the Cold War of my entire life could finally become unstuck."

By 1997, LASG had become a nonprofit entity funded by small local foundation grants and private donors, with Mello its full-time executive director and primary financial contributor. Under his direction, LASG filed and prevailed in litigation, lobbied Congress on nuclear weapons policy, including energy and climate issues, generated thousands of news articles, and halted two major nuclear projects at Los Alamos. Mello and his wife and fellow activist, Trish Williams-Mello—the former operations director of Serious Texans Against Nuclear Dumping (STAND) of Amarillo, Texas—"have made standing up to the nuclear industry a way of life," as an Albuquerque newspaper described them. LASG filed two lawsuits under the National Environmental Policy Act, and in 2012 blocked a planned $4.6 billion plutonium warhead plant at LANL. The couple is passionate about thwarting the nuclear warhead complex Mello called "a gigantic self-licking ice-cream cone for contractors." He has been successful in garnering respect on all sides of the aisle by creating what Charles Perkovich, the president of the Federation of American Scientists, described as a "strange bedfellows" coalition. By making disarmament a budgetary issue, he persuaded congressional Republicans that the weapons lab was largely an obsolete and overstuffed boondoggle. University of Chicago anthropology professor Joseph Masco was equally impressed with Mello's methodology. "Greg has always been one of the few people who has consistently tried to put nuclear policy in the broader context of what kind of a civilization America is becoming," Masco told a reporter.

For more than a decade, Mello had found himself up against a formidable nuclear weapons laboratory at Los Alamos. But once the Bechtel-led LANS, LLC, took over management, Mello faced not just one lab but also the nation's entire nuclear weapons complex managed by the same team. "Few realized that the nuclear weapons business had become ninety-seven percent privatized, with Bechtel controlling the monopoly," Mello told an interviewer. "Just as the country was swinging so hard to the right, Los Alamos and Livermore were becoming more and more corporate, more secret, and more openly partisan to a new Cold War mentality. It's become a tapestry of lies and irresponsibility."

Immediately after what one of Bechtel's own executives described as the corporate takeover of the labs, Mello saw the manifestation of the quintessential Bechtel culture. "Los Alamos lost all of its public character and became a classic private corporation," he observed. Many of the longtime scientists were uncomfortable with the new corporate management and dominant profit motive, and quit or retired early. "A new mentality took hold," Mello said, "with the corporate idea that 'we work for our company, not for the taxpayer,' " as he described the pervasive attitude. "There were now private incentives all based around how well corporate goals could be met."

Still, Mello remained optimistic about an emergence of "an antinuclear complex that could challenge the nuclear complex," the *Santa Fe New Mexican* reported. Encouraged by LASG's successes—in the courts and with public opinion—Mello was gratified by the attention Americans were paying to what he saw as the bigger picture. Finally, the big environmental issues such as climate change were on the table, and the social and environmental effects of nuclear weapons came to the forefront. In the past, the antinuclear weapons movement was focused on pollution, peace, and safety—the humanitarian impact of nuclear weapons possession. "Now we have the threatened extinction of the biosphere," he said. "The peace dividend is now the climate dividend. The species and the planet are at stake."

Mello was encouraged by government oversight and findings that cost overruns and technical failures were rampant at the lab, such as the leaking nuclear waste drum at Los Alamos. "It's like a Laurel and Hardy movie, starring Bechtel-led LANS and NNSA," he told the Associated Press. "It happens again and again, on almost all projects." The nuclear labs began receiving heightened government and media scrutiny after several security lapses, especially including the brazen elderly nun who broke into the "Fort Knox of nuclear facilities: the Y-12 National Security Complex, which houses 300 to 400 metric tons of bomb-grade uranium," as the *Bulletin of the Atomic Scientists* reported the humiliating event. The amount of weapons-grade uranium needed to build a terrorist bomb with the equivalent explosive force of the Hiroshima bomb "could fit into a small gym bag," writer Eric Schlosser reported.

Using bolt cutters, Sister Megan Rice and two other activists managed to cut through three eight-foot-high security fences, hang protest
banners, light prayer candles, paint Bible verses on walls, and come
within twenty feet of nuclear material—all as a point of civil disobe-
dience to reveal how easily fissile materials could end up in the hands
of terrorists. The half-billion-dollar Highly Enriched Uranium Materials Facility at Y-12 was built after September 11, 2001, to protect the
nation's uranium stockpile. Yet the eighty-two-year-old nun from the
international ministry Society of the Holy Child Jesus triggered three
alarms before a lone guard arrived. She hoped her intrusion "would
begin the process of shutting down Y-12 and transforming the American empire from a source of bloodshed into one of world peace," wrote
Schlosser. Rice was convicted on charges of sabotage and spent two
years in a federal prison in Brooklyn before being released in May 2015.

The embarrassing break-in attracted widespread national and international attention—especially to the fact that private contractors,
including Bechtel, were managing the nation's nuclear enterprise. Even
though the US government owned the land and the facilities, corporations were running them. "The fact that an eighty-two-year-old nun
had broken into a high-security nuclear-weapons complex seemed un-
believable," reported the *New Yorker*.

Not surprisingly, the event prompted a DOE investigation of the
privatized management team of the nation's nuclear weapons complex. Mello welcomed the attention and oversight. He hoped it would
bring about a more enlightened government nuclear policy. But his
sanguinity faltered when his natural allies—the arms control and disarmament community, along with President Barack Obama—joined
in an agenda to modernize the nuclear enterprise at a cost of $31 bil-
lion per year. Mello saw the plan to "freshen up our bombs and cut
down the number of nuclear warheads," as a former presidential science advisor put it, as a red herring. He thought America was walking
"back down the limb we got ourselves out on with nuclear weapons."
Comparing the lab's confidence in the nuclear deterrent to confidence
in the tooth fairy, Mello wrote: "What with fallout, reactor meltdowns,

and nuclear winter, nuclear 'deterrence' amounts to a suicide vest for humanity. . . . The labs are political heroin. As long as our politicos remain addicted to them, they won't think straight."

Advocating for the nuclear mission to be minimized rather than maximized—to maintain existing facilities rather than expand them—Mello was up against an ever more potent force in Bechtel. The ubiquitous and long shadow of George Shultz would be unmistakable.

The Four Horsemen of the Apocalypse

"So today, I state clearly and with conviction America's commitment to seek the peace and security of a world without nuclear weapons." With great fanfare, Obama launched his doctrine for a nuclear-free world during his first foreign policy speech in April 2009. "I'm not naïve. This goal will not be reached quickly—perhaps not in my lifetime." Speaking to a cheering crowd of tens of thousands in Prague in the Czech Republic—a city symbolic for its peaceful toppling of Communism as the Cold War ended—Obama vowed to lead an international movement to reduce, and ultimately eliminate, nuclear weapons. "As a nuclear power, as the only nuclear power to have used a nuclear weapon, the United States has a moral responsibility to act."

Against the backdrop of Prague Castle, the president described how his administration planned to "put an end to Cold War thinking" by reducing both America's arsenal of warheads and stockpiles and the role of nuclear weapons in US national security strategy. In the speech, given less than three months after his inauguration, and just hours after a missile test by North Korea, Obama outlined his ambitious plans to negotiate a new Strategic Arms Reduction Treaty (New START) with Russia before the end of the year. He also promised to include "all nuclear weapons states"—Russia, the United Kingdom, France, China, India, Pakistan, and Israel—in this endeavor. He pledged to ratify a nuclear test ban treaty and to convene a global summit for the eventual elimination of nuclear stockpiles as part of his vision for a nuclear-free world.

This commitment to promoting "the peace and security of a world without nuclear weapons" was heady, even revolutionary, stuff. Obama's optimistic and stirring speech was greeted with excitement in the global arms community. No previous president had ever advanced a specific program for the ultimate elimination of nuclear arms. "He's been thinking about these issues for a long time," said one of his political science professors. New START was to be the first full-scale arms control treaty between the United States and Russia in two decades, reinvigorating a worldwide disarmament agenda that had grown stagnant.

It had been a dream of Obama's since he was a college student during the Cold War. As a senior at Columbia University in 1983, he wrote an article about his vision for a nuclear-free world and his abhorrence of the "first- versus second-strike capabilities" that furthered the interests of the military-industrial complex, with its "billion-dollar erector sets." Titled "Breaking the War Mentality," the story, published in a campus news magazine, revealed the prescience of the man who would become president twenty-six years later. Having come of age during the Reagan presidency, Obama disdained Reagan's characterization of the Soviet Union as "an evil empire" to justify the largest peacetime military buildup in history, and scorned the extreme ideology of some Reagan aides who posited the winnability of a nuclear war. When Obama's long-unnoticed article surfaced decades after it had been written—in July 2009—his conservative enemies attacked it as "naïve, anti-American, and blind to the Soviet threat."

The 2009 Prague speech was a crucial moment for Obama and his timing was critical. The nation's nuclear arsenal was aging and decaying in sixty-year-old, poorly maintained silos. Even though the United States had reduced its nuclear stockpile from 31,000 to about 4,800 as a result of the fall of the Soviet Union and various arms control treaties over the previous forty-five years, the average age of a US nuclear warhead was twenty-seven years, and many of the country's missiles, warheads, strategic bombers, and nuclear-powered submarines had not been maintained or stored safely. Many in the military thought the more serious nuclear threat to America was not an enemy strike but an accident. In the few years previous to Obama's speech, several near disasters had occurred. Four missile nose cones were accidentally sent to Taiwan, where they sat for two years before being discovered. It was but one incident in "a recent spate of hair-raising, Homer Simpson–style nuclear blunders," as a journalist described the terrifying scenario. Another potential catastrophe ensued when six nuclear missiles from a North Dakota facility were accidentally attached to an airplane's wings and flown across several states before being left unattended on a public tarmac. There were reports of air force officers falling asleep while guarding launch codes for nuclear weapons.

There was another chilling vulnerability: that of what was called the "insider threat." Epitomized by Edward Snowden, the private contractor working for the National Security Agency who gained access to the NSA's classified secrets, including the "launch codes for America's nuclear weapons but also for designing the equipment that decrypts the codes," the insider threat was far more sophisticated and opaque than in the days of the Manhattan Project.

That Obama, as president, manifested such a bold, far-reaching, and progressive nuclear-free vision at such a precarious moment was due in large part to his surprising and opportunistic alignment with George Shultz. The rabid anti-Communist hawk and longtime Bechtel principal had joined with three of the leaders in national security to campaign for global disarmament. Shultz, along with former secretary of state Henry Kissinger, onetime defense secretary William Perry, and former senator Sam Nunn, "had decided to campaign for the elimination of the nuclear arsenals they had built up and managed as cold warriors," as the New York Times depicted the turnabout.

The same man who had articulated in a 1978 speech that "the U.S. was losing its good standing in world trade . . . because of the [Jimmy] Carter administration's nuclear nonproliferation policies"—an argument he repeated and emphasized in his later nomination hearings for secretary of state—was now a senior US statesman in favor of nuclear nonproliferation. The consummate Cold Warrior and architect of Reagan's foreign policy of "peace through strength" and its hard-line nuclear deterrent doctrine was now leading a brigade of fellow formerly ardent nuclear proliferators in a global disarmament movement.

It had begun when Shultz's "Gang of Four," as they called themselves, penned an op-ed titled "A World Free of Nuclear Weapons" two years earlier. The jointly authored treatise was published in the *Wall Street Journal.* The four men who had all been "deeply immersed in the nuclear weapons establishment," as *Time* magazine pointed out, were now "united in a call to abolish the very weapons they once saw as projections of their nation's power." That at least two of the men had an extensive and long-standing relationship with Bechtel—one of the biggest purveyors of nuclear energy and weapons in the world, and which had just begun managing the nation's entire nuclear weapons complex—escaped notice by the national media. "All were veterans of America's cold-war security establishment, with impeccable credentials as believers in nuclear deterrence," observed the *Economist.* "They now asserted that far from making the world safer, nuclear weapons had become a source of intolerable risk."

The gist of the op-ed was that Russia was no longer the threat that the Soviet Union had once posed and that the dangerous leftover arsenals from both countries were finding their way into the hands of terrorists. Simplistically put, deterrence (though precarious) worked as long as there were only two nuclear superpowers, because, as the four elder statesmen described it, "America and the Soviet Union were diligent, professional, but also lucky that nuclear weapons were never used." But now, in the age of nuclear proliferation, "the growing number of nations with nuclear arms and differing motives, aims, and ambitions poses very high and unpredictable risks."

Dubbed "the four horsemen of the apocalypse" by the media— a futuristic analogy to the four horsemen in the Bible's book of Revelation that included pestilence, war, famine, and death—the band of "brothers" stunned the foreign policy community with their call to abolish the weapons they once so promulgated. "Detractors regarded [Shultz's] legacy with alarm, recalling what they saw as unremitting

nuclear brinkmanship and ideological anti-Communism," as one account put it. Still, these "Hawks Against the Bomb," as some critics
labeled them, continued a steady drumbeat with further op-eds, while
"an unlikely coterie of fellow Cold Warriors"—all once firm backers
of nuclear deterrence, and including sixteen top Reagan administration officials—joined the chorus. "Call it penance, or the desire for
absolution," wrote a *Time* magazine reporter, "but the four horsemen
had spoken, and warned of the continuing danger of nuclear apocalypse." The scholar and religious reformer James Carroll wrote bit-
ingly about the "sacrilegious renunciation of their nuclear faith" by the
"high priests of the cult of nuclear normalcy" and "former apostles of
nuclear *Realpolitik*."

Shultz's newfound belief that the only solution to avoiding nuclear
apocalypse was the elimination of nuclear weapons sparked debate
within and among governments and foreign-policy think tanks around
the world. "We all knew that there were a lot of close calls," Shultz replied in response to inquiries about his sudden and drastic change
in philosophy. "If there were a nuclear exchange between the Soviet
Union and the United States, it would basically wipe both countries
out and off the map. And if you think about a modern thermonuclear
weapon set off over New York City, say: What would it do? It would
incinerate Manhattan Island." Shultz also denied that his about-face
was either sudden or inconsistent, claiming to have supported nuclear
disarmament as far back as the 1986 Reykjavik Summit, when talks
between the United States and the Soviet Union collapsed. "Unfortunately, such figures had come to Jesus only after leaving office, when
they were exempt from the responsibility of matching their high-flown
rhetoric with the gritty work of making it real," wrote Carroll.

The Gang of Four lost no time in promoting their agenda despite
the fact that then president George W. Bush "never invited them to the
White House to make their case." But Democratic presumptive presidential nominee Obama embraced the four. He relished the political
cover they provided for a subject that would face powerful challenges
from the Right. "Ridding the world of nuclear weapons has long been a

cause of the pacifist left," according to the *Economist*. Shultz watched with satisfaction as Obama disseminated their talking points, "echoing their message in campaign speeches in places like Chicago and Denver and in Berlin," the *New York Times* reported.

"President Obama has taken up the issue very well," Shultz would later crow to *Time* about the plan's successful bipartisan support. Indeed, Obama had codified Shultz's recommendations as official foreign policy in his groundbreaking and history-making Prague speech. But Obama's vision of a nuclear-free world was quickly hamstrung, and his retreat from a nuclear-free policy disheartened his activist supporters. While it all seemed lofty at first, after the dust settled, many in the disarmament community saw more cynical, if not sinister, machinations at work. "It would all come to naught. Worse than naught," said an antinuclear activist who watched, disheartened and disbelieving, as the Obama administration spent the next six years diverting hundreds of millions of dollars from nuclear nonproliferation to nuclear warheads—with Bechtel profiting astronomically.

In the end, the president who had portrayed himself as an architect of disarmament shepherded the nation's skyrocketing nuclear weapons spending to levels unseen since the Reagan years, leaving many to speculate about what appeared increasingly to be a "devil's bargain" with Shultz and the "boys from Bechtel."

The Captain Ahab of Nuclear Weapons

Obama had been president for only twelve days when word leaked that he had been nominated for the Nobel Peace Prize—a choice that evoked outrage in the United States and abroad, considering the forty-seven-year-old's lack of foreign policy experience. Those close to the president said he was both humbled and embarrassed by the nomination and did not feel that he deserved it. There rose within the White House a desire to accomplish something tangible to justify the nomination, if not the prize. Expanding on his campaign speeches promoting the horsemen's nonproliferation agenda, Obama had refined his position, making it a centerpiece of his defense policy as he honed his speech for Prague.

His vision of "a world without nuclear weapons"—and America's moral obligation to lead the charge—became the cornerstone of his young presidency. He capitalized on what the *Atlantic* described as his "no-nukes push to the sky's-the-limit idealism that had electrified supporters" during his presidential campaign. Obama's backing of what arms control advocates had begun calling "global zero" was a bold and courageous step for an American president to take. Teaming up with Shultz and his three national security cohorts gave Obama "the cover he needed to endorse global zero and perhaps even paved the way for New START," according to one account.

After the Prague speech on April 5, 2009, the "president moved quickly to jump-start global efforts to secure loose nuclear weapons and poorly protected bomb-making materials, calling an unprecedented summit of forty-seven world leaders to address the problem," according to one account. It was the largest gathering of world leaders since the United Nations of 1945. All of the attending countries committed to safeguard loose nuclear material.

From the beginning, the president faced brutal and predictable opposition in Congress. "This is dangerous, wishful thinking," co-wrote Senator Jon Kyl, Republican of Arizona, and Richard Perle, Reagan-era Cold Warrior, in response to Obama's disarmament plan. They ridiculed the president's naïveté for miscalculating the "nuclear ambitions" of Kim Jong-il (North Korea) and Mahmoud Ahmadinejad (Iran). James Schlesinger, the former secretary of defense in the Nixon and Ford administrations, mocked Obama, referring to his blurred line "between vision and hallucination."

In the run-up to the Nobel Prize, which was scheduled to be awarded six months later, in October, White House pressure on Congress to attain the New START treaty was fierce—"no mean feat at a time when Republicans in Congress were opposing the administration on virtually every initiative it proposed," wrote William D. Hartung, the director of the nonprofit, Washington-based Center for International Policy, national security expert, and author of numerous books about the military-industrial complex. Senate ratification of major arms-control treaties was generally pro forma, but Obama was facing a galvanized body intent on thwarting him. "Extremist Republicans took Congress hostage, and Barack Obama found himself lashed, like Herman Melville's Captain Ahab, to the monomaniac incarnation of those malicious agencies which some deep men feel eating in them, till they are left living on half a heart and half a lung," author James Carroll drew a *Moby Dick* metaphor.

The president faced a tough battle in the US Senate. But his new-found strange bedfellows—the men who provided "the disarmament hook that Obama latched on to when he entered the White House," as one account put it—went into high gear on his behalf. Senate Majority Whip Kyl, ranked as one of the most conservative members of the

Senate, vowed to stop the New START. Against the backdrop of this intractable opposition in Congress, in October 2009 Obama won the Nobel Peace Prize for his "vision of and work for a world without nuclear weapons." The Nobel Committee faced withering criticism from around the world, and many political commentators, government officials, and international leaders denounced the prize, citing Obama's lack of concrete results toward nuclear nonproliferation. Even his New START treaty seemed dead.

"At this point, the pressure within the White House to attain a nuclear arms treaty must have soared 1000-fold," wrote a DOE insider using the pseudonym Dienekes—the namesake of a Spartan soldier noted for his bravery. It was clear to the administration that it needed the support of the Bechtel managers of the Los Alamos (LANS) and Livermore (LLNS) weapons labs to win Republican support of ratification. Bechtel and the labs had billions to lose if Obama's arms control initiatives curbed their long-term, multibillion-dollar financial commitments from the DOE. Greg Mello posed an obvious question: "Without nuclear weapons, what will LANS and LLNS do?" A smaller nuclear stockpile and no new projects to replace old warheads would constrain the weapons labs. So all the vested interests with a strong financial incentive to thwart Obama—Bechtel, NNSA, and the nuclear industry, along with the endorsement of Shultz and the Four Horsemen—redirected the rhetoric away from "disarmament" and toward "modernization."

Under intensive lobbying by Bechtel, the private contractors running the DOE nuclear weapons labs persuaded Kyl and a handful of Republicans to support the treaty in 2010. But that was accomplished only after Kyl, who was central to delivering Senate support, demanded that the White House put up $85 billion over ten years to maintain and modernize the weapons systems that had been designated obsolete. This modernization of the nation's nuclear arsenal, under the auspices of updating an outdated system, ushered in "a fullblown reinvention of the arms cache at an estimated future cost of more than a trillion dollars," according to one account. In a calculated quid pro quo, the president won a major foreign policy victory, while the nuclear enthusiasts and private contractors controlled the nation's nuclear policy once again. After Obama's "year of arms control," as two national security experts called it, "the topic receded in prominence on the presidential agenda."

Not only would progress on disarmament come to a standstill, but the US government also ramped up its modernization of nuclear warheads, delivery systems, and all the laboratories and facilities that designed, maintained, and manufactured the weapons. While the president's about-face mystified arms-control advocates, one element was thoroughly predictable: Bechtel would be the primary recipient of the lucrative DOE and DOD contracts resulting from the buildup.

Inextricably enmeshed in American foreign policy for seven decades, Bechtel proved powerful enough to hijack Obama's nuclear nonproliferation promises. "Obama fell for the Four Horsemen's propaganda," concluded Mello. "Now we have entered the twilight of the nuclear gods. This is not nuclear versus nonnuclear. It's sanity versus insanity. It's all about the new generation of every nuclear weapon." Global arms control advocates were stunned by the dramatic failure of the president's mission, disheartened and baffled at how Obama's global zero pledge had been so thoroughly derailed.

Not only would Obama go on to reduce "the size of the nation's atomic stockpile far less than did any of his three immediate predecessors, including both Presidents Bush," the *New York Times* reported, but he would also spend more than previous administrations to modernize the remaining arms and authorize "a new generation of weapons carriers." Cuts to the nuclear stockpile initiated by the Bush presidencies totaled 14,801 weapons. During Obama's entire eight years, reductions would stand at 507. The president's peaceful intentions retreated from center stage.

For their part, the Four Horsemen backpedaled away from "disarmament" and shifted to a return to the nuclear deterrence days of the Cold War. First Kissinger split from the other three, aligning with former national security advisor Brent Scowcroft in expressing concern that nuclear reductions would weaken US strategic stability. Soon Shultz, Perry, and Nunn joined in calling for "deterrence in the age of nuclear proliferation" instead of global zero. The "quartet barely make mention of abolition," *Time* magazine said of the turnaround. "One can't help notice that these opinion pieces are becoming increasingly chastened and unambitious as time goes on."

A Trial Lawyer Goes to Battle

Born in 1937 in Ogden, Utah, and raised throughout the American West, J. Gary Gwilliam came by his *David v. Goliath* passion honestly. From the roots of childhood abandonment, family dysfunction, and juvenile delinquency, from reckless adolescence and gang membership, from drug use and alcohol addiction, Gwilliam escaped his past to become a trial lawyer.

A descendant of nineteenth-century Mormon pioneers—Welsh sheep farmers on his paternal side and polygamist zealots on his maternal—Gwilliam fought from his earliest years to escape the oppression of the religious community. He watched as his peripatetic Mormon father dissolved into alcoholism while leaving his daring mother to seek a life for herself outside of Utah. Reared in Eugene, Oregon, and Seattle, Washington, Gwilliam's innate and inherited rebellious nature kicked in. By junior high, he was drinking and carousing, and by high school, he was tattooed and running around with "rougher and rougher guys." He pulled his long hair back into a ducktail, pegged his pants, and carried a switchblade. His anxious mother watched as her smart son's grades dipped below those acceptable for entry to a four-year college. When Gwilliam realized that only three kids in his gang of twenty would graduate from high school—and of those three, one went to prison and another committed suicide—he woke up. "Most of my friends were addicts, thieves, and lazy bums," he realized. His rescue came in the form of his family's Mormon matriarchy, which helped him relocate to Southern California to begin anew.

While holding down jobs at a nursery and Western Union, Gwilliam got serious about school, and in 1957, at twenty years old, he received an Associate of the Arts degree from Citrus Junior College in Glendora. Even though it was only a two-year college, Gwilliam recalled, "it was still a college degree." When he heard his name called to receive the award for "The Man Most Likely to Succeed," he put his wild past behind him and applied to Pomona College. "Have you ever thought of being a lawyer?" the venerated philosophy professor Fred Sontag asked Gwilliam one day. No one in Gwilliam's family had ever attended college, much less law school. "I had never met a lawyer. I had never seen a lawyer." But Sontag pressed. "You could be a great lawyer. You have a good mind, the gift of gab, and you get along well with people. You are able to think on your feet. You should give it a try."

Gwilliam considered it and dashed off applications to Harvard, the University of Chicago, and Boalt Hall at the University of California, Berkeley. He was accepted by all three. After graduating "just short of Phi Beta Kappa," he lit off for Berkeley, wanting to remain in California, where he joined "the most competitive, hardworking, anxious bunch of guys I had ever been around." He graduated in 1962 with a determination to become a trial lawyer and with the initial dream of pursuing a career as a prosecutor.

He was recruited by the Ventura County District Attorney's Office, which was one of the busiest prosecutors' offices in the Los Angeles area. He quickly advanced to the position of chief trial deputy. After four successful years as an assistant DA, Gwilliam decided to relocate to the San Francisco Bay Area with the hopes he could mend his struggling marriage. He leaped at the chance to join the Jesse Nichols law firm in the East Bay—the best-known plaintiffs' group in the region. "I didn't know much about plaintiffs work," Gwilliam later wrote, "but it seemed to me that it was fairly simple. As a prosecutor, I was carrying the burden of proof and going after the bad guys. The same seemed to be true with a plaintiff's attorney. But it turned out not to be that simple."

The firm gave him a string of small cases to try, and he fought some of the best insurance defense attorneys in the area. After losing his first five cases, his confidence faltered. But that changed with his first victory, and soon he had attained a reputation as a budding young trial lawyer. Over the next decade, that reputation grew. Eventually he formed a plaintiffs' firm with several colleagues, and as the senior partner would also be the rainmaker. In that role, he felt pressured to "win the big one," as he later put it, in a competitive legal environment.

Less than a decade later, his personal injury judgments had gained attention in the statewide legal community, and in 1987 he was elected president of the California Trial Lawyers Association. By then, his passion for the legal profession—and especially for the lawyer's role in helping people—had been galvanized by the adage "First, let's kill all the lawyers." The Shakespearean reference was much in vogue at the moment, tarnishing the entire profession as inhabited by unethical greed mongers. (In fact, the phrase, as used by Shakespeare, reflected positively on lawyers.) Gwilliam embraced a one-man crusade to counter that perception, setting forth the tenets of trial lawyers: "We don't cheat. We do not suborn. We do not fabricate. We do not lie to clients or for clients. We do not file frivolous suits, and we do not answer or defend against claims of merit with tricks or chicanery."

Citing the successful cases brought against the Ford Pinto, the Dalkon Shield intrauterine device, asbestos products, and more, Gwilliam saw the elevated role of the plaintiffs' attorney to bat "on behalf of the general public against the insensitive and uncaring [corporate defendants], removing from the marketplace . . . life-endangering products." Throughout the 1990s and into the twenty-first century, Gwilliam's legal victories would multiply, bringing national attention to his accomplishments and to the firm. Despite recurring bouts with the demons that had plagued him since childhood—alcoholism and work stress led to two divorces—he would become a role model for trial lawyers throughout the state of California dealing with the same pressures.

He became involved with Trial Lawyers for Public Justice: an organization consisting of three thousand of the most accomplished and revered lawyers in the nation. TLPJ "takes on issues that other lawyers won't," Gwilliam described it, "such as important environmental battles, consumer law matters, civil rights cases, and issues relating to court access." His life mission had become twofold: to "help the average person to pursue justice against the biggest and most powerful companies in the world," and to be an inspiration and advocate for trial lawyers. Finally finding marital happiness, he wrote a book about his deeply personal journey into sobriety and handling the lifestyle stress of the high-powered litigator, which led to requests for motivational lectures and legal ethics seminars throughout the state of California. That exposure, along with his numerous multimillion-dollar jury verdicts, made him a household name in legal circles.

By 2008, Gwilliam had tried more than 180 jury cases and had expanded his area of practice beyond personal injury into employment law, wrongful termination and employee discrimination and harassment, civil rights, and whistleblower protection. Some of his verdicts were the largest in California.

That spring, when Gwilliam learned that Bechtel had laid off 440 career employees at the Livermore Lab, he was prepared for the onslaught of phone calls. After forty years of practicing law, he was certain that he could not stand idly by, and that he would represent those employees. "I'm the only lawyer in the entire Bay Area who has ever taken on the Lab," Gwilliam said in an interview. "When this case came down, I was familiar to the plaintiffs' union, the Society of Professional Scientists and Engineers, so employees started calling the law office immediately. First, one called. Then another fifty. I was ultimately contacted by almost half of those laid off. The union was incensed, and there was almost a riot out there. The cases were very clear to me. They were wronged, and someone had to help them. Clearly, the federal government wasn't going to."

Of the 440 nuclear weapons scientists, researchers, assistants, and supervisors with long years of dedicated service, Gwilliam took on 130 as clients. "When they walked through our doors, most had lost more than just a paycheck. They had lost careers, sources of personal pride, and, in some cases, the very center of their lives. Their average age was fifty-four, and their average length of service was more than twenty years." An Alameda County superior judge in Oakland selected five of Gwilliam's clients to be test cases in a lawsuit involving all 130 plaintiffs with similar claims for wrongful termination. Each had additional claims for age discrimination—a phase of the case that would be tried later.

After a long five years during which Gwilliam's firm spent more than a million of its own dollars despite receiving no attorneys' fees— an Alameda County jury found in favor of the five plaintiffs on their contractual claims, deciding that LLNS had fired them without reasonable cause. The jury awarded them $2.7 million for lost wages and economic loss. With interest, the average award for each of the 130 employees was expected to be about $600,000—or an extrapolated value total of around $78 million. LLNS appealed the decision, and when it refused repeatedly to enter into settlement negotiations, Gwilliam accused it of using delaying tactics. "It's clear from the record the Bechtel Group is doing everything they can to delay it, block it, drag it out, because they want to squeeze the older clients. It is a blatant and obvious delay strategy to drive these older people to their knees. Many of them have already lost their houses, filed bankruptcy, and have challenging health problems, and the sad truth is that LLNS wants to delay until they're dead. The plaintiffs have gone through long depositions, extensive medical examinations, two trials lasting six weeks, in litigation that has dragged on for years. All they've won is what they lost in wages. And still, no one has yet seen a dime."

To further exacerbate the miscarriage of justice, according to Gwilliam, LLNS was "trying to pass the millions of dollars of damages for the illegal layoffs, as well as astronomical attorneys' fees, to the taxpayers through the DOE." Danielle Bryan, executive director of POGO, followed the case closely, "tracking the misuse of federal funds by government contractors to defend against lawsuits." Bryan testified that the government's reimbursement to private contractors for their attorneys' fees and costs "creates an incentive for contractors to litigate as long as possible—using federal funds—in order to avoid a finding of liability."

Gwilliam submitted requests to DOE under the Freedom of Information Act asking the amount the US government had paid LLNS's private San Francisco law firm in attorneys' fees—a figure that Gwilliam estimated to be at least $15 million. The firm, Orrick, Herrington, "frequently had as many as four to six lawyers for even routine motions," he observed. "The defense firm has two hundred times as many lawyers as I have. There are twelve hundred of them and six of us. Three of our lawyers, including my partner Randy Strauss and my associate Rob Schwartz, have devoted five years to working on this case. We're like commandos, and we're going to prevail," he said in 2015, with his conviction that "truth will out."

In October 2015, after seven years of litigation, the Lawrence Livermore Laboratory agreed to pay $37.25 million to 129 of its workers to settle their lawsuits. "As soon as the Lab was 'privatized' by the George W. Bush administration in 2007, they began plans to lay off their older, most experienced workers in order to save themselves money," said Gwilliam. "The evidence proved that this layoff was organized and implemented primarily by the Bechtel Corporation. There had not been a layoff there for thirty-five years before that." The company had won the trial relating to age discrimination claims, and under the terms of the settlement did not admit any wrongdoing had occurred.

CHAPTER FORTY

The Exxon of Space

"Bechtel is one of the great creations of California in the twentieth century, like Stanford University, like Kaiser Permanente, like Apple Computer," said California state historian Kevin Starr. "It's part of the establishment, part of the way America organizes itself." California journalist Mark Dowie wrote of "Bechtel's phenomenal metamorphosis from muleskinner to sovereign state"—a state that was "indistinguishable from the company itself."

By 2015, it was clear that Bechtel had its own foreign policy agenda, which the company relied upon and from which it benefitted. Bechtel routinely worked with public officials to write legislation that benefitted Bechtel. It kept its hand in the decision making of both public policy and foreign relations through its relationships in Congress. It gave robustly to the political campaigns that would further its interests. In one of the more recent political cycles, Bechtel Group spent $6.2 million in contributions and another $6.2 million on lobbyists. During the same cycle, Bechtel National spent $561,000 in political contributions and $4.3 million on lobbyists. While Bechtel's contributions have been distributed almost exclusively to Republicans, in recent years, it has doled out more money to an increasing number of high-level Democrats in states such as California and New Mexico, where the company hopes to limit government oversight of management at the national nuclear labs. Between 1999 and 2013, Bechtel entities received 4,108 government contracts, primarily from the Departments of Energy and Defense, totaling $40 billion.

Even though the jury trial in the Livermore wrongful termination lawsuit exposed the dark side of the for-profit model in the nation's nuclear weapons complex, Bechtel remained untouchable. Senator Dianne Feinstein, a longtime and fervent lab supporter and a top recipient over the past twenty years of Bechtel's financial largesse, seemed baffled to learn that Livermore had been privatized. Chair of the Intelligence Committee and the Appropriations Subcommittee that oversees NNSA's budget, Feinstein questioned the competency of the lab directors. "I am really concerned, because these labs used to be pristine," Feinstein, whose husband is on the University of California Board of Regents, remarked while criticizing the Bechtel-led team's long history of cost overruns. Like many of her colleagues in Congress, Feinstein expressed a lack of understanding of the degree of privatization involved in the nation's nuclear weapons laboratories. She expressed dismay that the lab directors behaved like corporate actors rather than government functionaries, only to be told that, in fact, they *were* corporate players.

In recent years, a string of government oversight investigations revealed egregious wrongdoing and safety violations at the Bechtel-managed sites. A congressional commission, led by former undersecretary of the army Norman Augustine and retired admiral Richard Mies, concluded in 2014 that the privatization of the nuclear weapons laboratories had resulted in a "dysfunctional management and operations relationship," and "uneven collaboration with customers"—the "customers" being the DOE.

Bechtel's multibillion-dollar contract to clean up the Hanford nuclear facility in eastern Washington came under fire by the federal government. Covering more than 580 square miles, the World War II–era plutonium production site was considered the most contaminated land in North America. Its nine nuclear reactors produced an estimated 43 million cubic yards of radioactive waste, and 475 billion gallons of radioactive wastewater were released into the ground. It is the biggest, most toxic nuclear-waste site in the Western Hemisphere. Hanford had changed from a nuclear weapons base to "the most costly environmental remediation the world has ever seen," according to one account. In 2000 Bechtel received the $4.3 billion deal for the cleanup, which the company estimated would cost $14 billion to complete. But eleven years later, with the job still uncompleted, Bechtel predicted that the final cost would be more than $120 billion.

Whistleblowers on the project complained to the Obama administration that Bechtel was "as toxic as the nuclear waste they're tasked to clean up," claiming that "Bechtel rushed through shoddy design plans in order to pocket some quick cash," according to the *Seattle Weekly*. Whistleblowers claimed that Frank Russo, Bechtel's director of the project and the so-called hatchet man who organized the Livermore layoffs, harassed and retaliated against them.

Dr. Walter Tamosaitis, a systems engineer employed for more than forty years by a Bechtel subcontractor, claimed Russo ordered him fired after he reported safety failures at the site. In 2014 the Ninth Circuit Court of Appeals reversed a lower court's decision and determined that Tamosaitis had a constitutional right to a jury trial in his legal case against the DOE, in which he claimed he was demoted for speaking out. "Hanford is a long-term threat to humanity," declared Tom Carpenter, head of a Hanford watchdog group based in Seattle.

After five years of litigation, Tamosaitis agreed in the summer of 2015 to a $4.1 million settlement of his federal whistleblower retaliation lawsuit. Called a "long overdue justice for a whistleblower who may have changed the course of history by preventing a nuclear tragedy," by a spokesman for the Government Accountability Project in Washington, the victory was lauded by antinuclear activists. "It was absolutely terrifying what Bechtel was planning at Hanford. It was a complete gamble with public health and safety, all to earn millions in bonus money for getting a job done, regardless of whether it was disastrous for the Pacific Northwest." Bechtel would be fined $800,000 after DOE investigations concluded the company had failed to follow safety guidelines it had agreed to more than a decade earlier. Also in 2014, the union representing the employees at Livermore requested a DOE investigation of LLNS for allegedly fabricating a $280 million budget shortfall to justify the 2008 employee layoffs. That year too the newly appointed head of NNSA, former air force lieutenant general Frank G. Klotz, received a waiver from DOE allowing him to make decisions involving and affecting Bechtel, even though his ties to the company involved consulting on billions of dollars' worth of NNSA contracts. "After consultation with the Office of the Counsel to the President, I have determined that it is in the public interest for you to participate in matters relating to Bechtel," wrote Susan Beard, the DOE assistant general counsel and ethics official, in response to complaints about the blatant revolving door. "Substantial national security challenges require your expertise and judgment in making sound decisions on major defense and public security programs, several of which involve Bechtel or one of its subsidiaries."

In what the media dubbed "the Valentine's day release," on the night of February 14, 2014, a drum of radioactive waste processed at Los Alamos leaked at the nation's only permanent repository. Stored in an underground salt cavern at the Waste Isolation Pilot Plant (WIPP) in Carlsbad, New Mexico, the fifty-five-gallon drum cracked and almost burst, contaminating twenty-one employees. The leak raised questions about the lack of safeguards taken by the Bechtel-led management team at the lab.

Still, Bechtel's fortunes in the nuclear industry continued to thrive. "Bechtel has designed or built more than half of this nation's nuclear power units, and worldwide has had a significant presence," said Bechtel Nuclear's president, Jim Reinsch. "Its procurement programs are world-class . . . its safety record in the nuclear field is second to none." Indeed, the company, and its numerous partnerships and consortiums, received millions from DOE to build, design, license, and deploy the world's first commercialized small modular nuclear reactors (SMRs). The Bechtel Marine Propulsion Corporation, a wholly owned subsidiary of the company, received a five-year contract from DOE to operate the Bettis and Knolls Atomic Power Laboratories. That project, worth between $6 and $9.7 billion, operates the navy's nuclear reactor–

powered warships, including aircraft carriers and submarines. The company completed a US Missile Defense Agency project in the Marshall Islands in 2013 and received a $7 billion contract for US Navy nuclear propulsion parts that same year. In 2015 Bechtel-led Consolidated Nuclear Security LLC teamed with NNSA and the US Army Corps of Engineers for the construction of the Uranium Processing Facility Site at the Y-12 National Security Complex. The $6.5 billion project was billed as NNSA's largest-ever construction project. A Bechtel corporate press release described it as a "multibuilding, state-of-the-art complex for enriched uranium operations related to nuclear security including assembly, disassembly, [and] dismantlement."

Meanwhile, the company further diversified its corporate footprint throughout the United States, with projects as disparate as commercializing space and solar power. Joining Google founder Larry Page and the company's executive chairman, Eric Schmidt, along with film director James Cameron, Bechtel invested heavily in Planetary Resources to set up fuel depots in space. "Mining is an industry they are involved a lot in on Earth," Eric Anderson, the founder of Planetary Resources, said of Bechtel. The company's goal is to search for water and mineral-rich asteroids. "We want to become the Exxon of space." The sixty-one-year-old Riley Bechtel declined to reveal details about the venture, except to describe the mission as "ambitious, but they've assembled a world-class team to succeed."

When Riley stepped down as chairman and CEO in 2014 after being diagnosed with early-stage Parkinson's disease, he turned over company control to his only son, Brendan Bechtel. Although Brendan, a graduate of Middlebury College in Vermont with a degree in geography, and with dual master's degrees from Stanford in business and construction engineering and management, was named president and COO, Riley fast-tracked longtime employee William N. Dudley as a placeholder CEO while the thirty-year-old Brendan gained experience—marking the first time in the company's 116-year history that a non–family member would hold the title of CEO.

It would be Brendan—the fifth generation of Bechtel men—who led the company back to its desert beginnings where, once again, it

was harnessing and distributing one of the nation's most valuable resources. The gigantic flagship project that rose in California's Mojave
Desert was the largest solar plant in the world. There, in 2014 in the
Ivanpah Valley, less than sixty miles from Hoover Dam—the project
that made the Bechtel Corporation a household name in the West—
Bechtel completed a $2.2 billion complex of three generating units.
Located on a six-square-mile swath of remote desert landscape owned
by the federal government, Ivanpah's technology included 350,000
mirrors, each one the size of a garage door. With its groundbreaking
thermal storage system, Ivanpah was expected to double the nation's
solar capacity, producing enough power for 140,000 homes.

Like all of Bechtel's projects, the government underwrote Ivanpah
generously, including a $1.6 billion loan guaranteed by the US Depart-
ment of Energy and funded by the Federal Financing Bank. "If California Energy Commission estimates are correct, the power figures
imply capital in play of between $15 billion and $500 billion," wrote
Nobel physicist and Stanford professor Robert B. Laughlin. Predict-
ably, Bechtel was once again positioned to be the leading construction
company in the privatizing of energy and natural resources.

The project's physical conspicuousness belied the stealth and secrecy with which it came to fruition. Its forty-story "power tower"
and 3,500-acre field of mirrors were in full view of a busy section of
the interstate that connects Las Vegas and Los Angeles. Still, it was
shrouded in mystery and controversy from the start. A long line of
cars carrying day and night laborers snaked toward the facility, each
vehicle inspected by a team of security guards. Considering the size
and historic nature of the development—and that taxpayers footed
close to 80 percent of the cost—Ivanpah received little publicity. Like
dozens, if not hundreds, of the company's high-profile projects that
managed to remain cloaked in the privately held company's bubble of
secrecy, the geothermal colossus escaped much scrutiny.

Characteristically, Bechtel managed to override what little environmental opposition to the project arose. Called a "$2.2 billion
bird-scorching solar project" by the *Wall Street Journal*, the massive

solar farm became the site of scores of dead birds that flew through the intense heat surrounding the towers that reached 1,000 degrees Fahrenheit. Bechtel mowed down thousands of desert plants and displaced thirty animal species, and dozens of state and federal environmental reviews concluded that the Mojave Desert was irretrievably scarred. "Despite its behemoth footprint, the Ivanpah project has slipped easily into place, unencumbered by lasting legal opposition or public outcry from California's boisterous environmental community," the *Los Angeles Times* reported. "Away from public scrutiny," a collaboration of solar developers, federal regulators, and a handful of environmentalists "sparked a wholesale remodeling of the American desert"—thanks to federal subsidies and allotments of public land.

It didn't stop there. In addition to building the massive Ivanpah solar farm, Bechtel became an equity investor in three California solar plants contracted to provide power to Pacific Gas and Electric and Southern California Edison. The company had come full circle back to its roots.

CHAPTER FORTY-ONE

A Nasty Piece of Work

In 2015, Jonathan Pollard began serving the thirtieth year of his life sentence in a US prison for spying on behalf of Israel. The previous year, Israeli president Shimon Peres announced that the US government was considering a deal to release Pollard. Part of a three-way arrangement between Washington, Jerusalem, and Ramallah to release Palestinian prisoners and salvage US-brokered peace talks between Israel and the Palestinians, Pollard's release seemed imminent. Peres admitted that he had discussed Pollard's case with President Obama, and that Obama promised that Attorney General Eric Holder would consider an "offer" Peres made to Obama. On his last official visit to Washington as president, in June 2014, Peres submitted an official request to the White House to advance Pollard's cause. "I made a specific offer, but I won't go into details," Peres told reporters, adding that he had discussed the proposal with Pollard family members before presenting it to Obama. "If I give too many details, it will just ruin things," Peres said. "I can't say that he responded positively on the spot. I don't want to add to what he said, which was that the US attorney general would become involved."

Senior American legal scholars wrote a letter coinciding with the Peres offer, petitioning Obama to commute Pollard's sentence. "Such commutation is more than warranted if the ends of justice are to be served, the rule of law respected, and simple humanity secured," the scholars wrote. Signatories to the letter included six Harvard Law

School professors, among them Alan Dershowitz, along with Canadian law professor emeritus and former minister of justice and attorney general of Canada Irwin Cotler. In the letter, the legal experts argued that Pollard's life sentence is "excessive, grossly disproportionate, unfair, and unjust," and noted the usual sentence for Pollard's offense of conveying classified information to a foreign government is six to eight years, with the average actual jail time standing at a mere two to four years. It was just the latest in a long line of entreaties to all American presidents since Ronald Reagan.

"My wife and I over the eight years of George W. Bush's presidency asked him a number of times for a commutation or pardon," Las Vegas casino magnate, billionaire, and fervent Zionist Sheldon Adelson recalled. "Each time he said he would consider it. The last time we asked him was in January 2009, at which point we thought he was sincere about seriously considering commuting the sentence, but something happened the next day in the media about [former Israeli Prime Minister Ehud] Olmert boasting that he personally convinced President Bush to create a positive outcome for something . . . that benefitted Israel." From that, Adelson inferred that Bush was no longer going to act on his request.

When Obama visited Jerusalem in 2013 he had been presented with a "Call for Clemency Campaign" petition containing 150,000 signatures. And upon his arrival at the Ben-Gurion Airport, two high-level government officials implored Obama to release the incarcerated spy.

At the time, Peres told the press that he intended to tell Obama "president to president" to release Pollard without delay on humanitarian grounds. Netanyahu weighed in as well, vowing to do whatever was necessary "to seek Jonathan's immediate release and repatriation to Israel." Since Pollard's confinement "the Israel lobby, said to be omnipotent and irresistible by so many people, has done everything in its power to spring him," according to an American journalist. And still, "he has rotted in jail. . . . The supposedly mighty and invincible 'Israel Lobby' is toothless when it comes to this case."

Obama had promised to review the case then as well. At that time, the top US officials who had joined the "Free Jonathan Pollard Now" bandwagon read like a who's who in American foreign policy. They included former president Jimmy Carter; former secretary of state Henry Kissinger; former CIA director R. James Woolsey, who reversed his original position; former and current senators Alan Simpson, Dennis DeConcini, John McCain, David Durenberger, and Charles Schumer Jr.; former national security advisor Robert McFarlane; and Nobel Laureate Elie Wiesel. Thirty-nine members of Congress signed a letter calling for his release, including Lee Hamilton, who served as chairman of the House Intelligence Committee at the time of Pollard's sentencing.

"The roster of the renowned passionately advocating for Pollard's release, or the overturn of his sentence, is nothing less than spectacular," according to one account. Pollard's cruel and excessive sentence outraged those who believed Pollard had simply passed to Israel intelligence that the United States should have shared in accordance with a memorandum of understanding between the two countries. In 1993 a thousand rabbis signed a full-page advertisement in the *New York Times* urging President Clinton to commute Pollard's sentence. Defining himself as a non-Zionist "secular Jew," apparently to remove any hint of bias in his reporting, venerable journalist Milton Viorst wrote that Pollard was imprisoned as "the result of a miscarriage of justice."

During the 1998 Middle East talks, Netanyahu had made Pollard's release a key bargaining point, telling Clinton he needed it in order to sell the peace agreement to the right wing of his coalition. "I could tell you for sure that I know that Bill Clinton was repeatedly asked by supporters of his to commute Jonathan Pollard's sentence or to pardon him," Adelson claimed. Clinton was apparently "impressed by the force of Netanyahu's arguments" on Pollard's behalf and was leaning toward fulfilling the request. But Clinton backed away from the incendiary issue when his CIA director, George Tenet, allegedly threatened to resign over the matter.

While Weinberger never relented in his spitefulness toward Pollard (Weinberger died in 2006), decades later Shultz softened his position toward the spy. "Dear Mr. President," Shultz wrote to Obama on January 11, 2011. "I am writing to join with many others in urging you to consider that Jonathan Pollard has now paid a huge price for his espionage on behalf of Israel and should be released from prison. I am impressed that the people who are best informed about the classified material he passed to Israel, former CIA Director James Woolsey and former Chairman of the Senate Intelligence Committee Dennis DeConcini, favor his release." The *Jerusalem Post* commented on the gravity of Shultz's reversal, given his seminal role in the case.

Citing anti-Semitism as a motivating force against Pollard, Woolsey gave numerous public statements and wrote formal requests for his release. "Forget that Pollard is a Jew," he wrote. "Pretend he's a Greek- or Korean- or Filipino-American and free him!"

Still, there are those who just as vehemently advocate that Pollard should die in jail for placing allegiance to Israel over loyalty to the United States. Such stalwarts include legendary investigative reporter Seymour Hersh, longtime editor of the *New Republic* Martin Peretz, and former secretary of state Hillary Clinton. Vice President Joe Biden has been particularly vocal on the subject. Responding in 2011 to a group of fifteen Florida rabbis who asked him why Pollard was still in jail, Biden said, "President Obama was considering clemency, but I told him, 'Over my dead body are we going to let him out before his time.' If it were up to me, he would stay in jail for life."

Typical of the schism among government officials that has defined the Pollard affair since its inception, Biden's resoluteness contrasted with Secretary of State John Kerry's flexibility. Striving toward conciliation, in late 2013 Kerry raised the possibility of releasing Pollard as part of a prisoner swap with Israel. But it soon became clear that Kerry had spoken without Obama's blessing.

The 2013 declassification of the CIA's top secret 1987 "Damage Assessment of the Pollard Case" revealed that the evidence does not support Weinberger's vitriolic assessment of the harm inflicted by Pollard's spying, as conveyed by Weinberger in his top secret sentencing memorandum to the judge. The intelligence agency fought for nearly three decades to withhold the report from public inspection. But the documents were eventually obtained and released by the National Security Archive. The CIA declassified the files under orders from a federal panel that determined the agency had no basis for continuing to maintain their secrecy. The documents rekindled questions about Weinberger's impulse to make sure that Pollard would never be released.

Though released to relatively little public notice, the declassified documents raised "doubts about whether the public was told the truth about Pollard, and the reasons he was prosecuted and given such a draconian prison term," as one account put it. Contrary to Weinberger's claims, the CIA report showed that the Israelis "never expressed interest in U.S. military activities, plans, capabilities, or equipment"—nor did Pollard procure any secrets about the United States.

Meanwhile, Weinberger's twenty-eight-year-old secret sentencing memorandum remained classified until key sections of the forty-nine-page document filed in federal court in Washington, DC, were released to Pollard's security-cleared legal counsel. "With little fanfare and no news media coverage, a dramatic, potentially game-changing development in the Jonathan Pollard spy case quietly occurred three months ago," wrote journalist Aaron Klein in February 2015. "The recent disclosures . . . show that the [US] government has been dishonestly hiding behind the mask of 'classified information' to materially mischaracterize the nature and extent of the harm caused by Mr. Pollard," Pollard's pro bono New York attorneys, Eliot Lauer and Jacques Semmelman, wrote in an op-ed for WND—the internet website successor to WorldNetDaily. The newly revealed material showed that "any harm that may have been caused by Mr. Pollard was in the form of short-term disruption in foreign relations between the United States and certain Arab countries," wrote the attorneys. "That is not at all the same thing as harm to US national security."

Weinberger's memorandum was seen as the basis for Pollard's unprecedented life sentence for spying for an ally and for his continued incarceration. One of the central figures in the Iran-Contra affair,

Weinberger's hostility toward Pollard "was surely inspired in large part by his deeply held animus toward the state of Israel," wrote former US national security advisor Robert C. "Bud" McFarlane in a letter in support of Pollard's release. "His extreme bias against Israel was manifested in recurrent episodes of strong criticism and unbalanced reasoning when decisions involving Israel were being made."

Many former Reagan administration officials who worked with Weinberger later came out in support of Pollard's release, most notably George Shultz. If Shultz had once agreed with Weinberger's loathing of Pollard, he later described Weinberger's malicious sentencing memorandum as "a nasty piece of work."

The pleas for clemency finally paid off, and on November 21, 2015, the sixty-one-year-old Pollard was finally paroled from his North Carolina prison. The following day marked the thirtieth anniversary of his arrest. The decision from the US Parole Commission to release Pollard came amid a sharp divide between the US and Israel over America's nuclear deal with Iran. Government officials with both governments denied that Pollard's release was an attempt to mollify Israel. Although Israel granted Pollard citizenship in the 1990s, his parole required that he remain in the US for five years—a constraint Pollard's attorneys asked President Barack Obama to overturn and allow him to move to Israel. But the White House quickly refused, citing the seriousness of Pollard's crimes.

The Kingdom of Bechtelistan

By the time Brendan Bechtel took over as president and COO in 2014, the company billed itself as the most respected engineering, procurement, and construction firm in the world. Its website boasted record revenues for ongoing projects worldwide. With forty permanent offices in fifty countries and nearly fifty-three thousand employees—and committed to remaining a privately held "family company"—Bechtel was as powerful and relevant in 2015 as at any time in its history. Claiming to have completed more than twenty-five thousand projects in 160 countries on all seven continents, Bechtel identified its areas of expertise as infrastructure; defense and security; environmental cleanup; oil, gas and chemicals; nuclear power; tanks; water; telecommunications; and mining and minerals.

Undertakings included "transforming" the infrastructure of the country of Gabon, including a soccer stadium for the Africa Cup of Nations; building a twenty-one-kilometer underground railway tunnel in London and expensive motorways in Romania, Croatia, and Albania; expanding a gigantic copper mine in Chile; erecting a $15 billion international airport and a $7 billion petrochemical plant in Qatar; new terminals in Dubai, Abu Dhabi, Riyadh, Jeddah, and Muscat; a $7.2 billion port and industrial zone at Abu Dhabi; a $1.4 billion LNG processing plant in Angola; the world's largest aluminum smelter in Saudi Arabia and another in Iceland; the Riyadh Metro; a dozen new gas pipelines in Thailand; one of the largest desalination plants in the world, located in Chile; an oil refinery in India; a gas pipeline in Algeria; a $1.3 billion 2015 contract to destroy chemical weapons of mass destruction at the Pueblo Chemical Agent-Destruction Pilot Plant at Pueblo, Colorado; and on and on. In 2015 Bechtel was among the first companies granted permission by the US Federal Aviation Administration (FAA) for commercial use of drones, or unmanned aerial vehicles.

Riley Bechtel was among a number of high-profile directors on the board of a controversial biotech sensation called Theranos that once included George Schultz and Henry Kissinger. The $9 billion private company claimed to have developed a device that could detect hundreds of medical issues with a pinprick. But in October 2015, Theranos came under fire amid allegations that the company had made numerous false claims to gain FDA approval.

Among the more fantastic ventures was the $500 million Magic World Theme Park in Dubai—a full-scale Arab entertainment zone of fantasy-based villages within a crater, including Legend Lagoon, Dino Canyon, and Techtown. Bechtel's concept for the park was based on a modern myth created for the project, in which a "fiery ball fell from the dark heavens." The meteorite crashed into a forgotten region of the Dubaian desert. "After the ash had settled and many years passed, life began to spring from this once barren land," as the marketing material described it.

C. David Welch, Bechtel's president for Europe, the Middle East, and Africa, told the press that at one point the company had forty thousand workers at the Doha airport construction site alone. A well-known figure in the region, Welch had been a US diplomat for more than thirty years—including assistant secretary of state for Near Eastern Affairs and US ambassador to Egypt. In 2008, prior to leaving the government and joining Bechtel the following year, Welch led negotiations under President George W. Bush to broker a deal to restore diplomatic relations between the United States and Libya's Mu'ammar Qaddafi. Once at Bechtel, Welch lobbied Congress on behalf of Bechtel's interests in Libya. In 2011 Welch brought unwanted attention to

Bechtel when it was reported that he was advising Qaddafi's regime on how to stay in power at a moment when the United States sought to depose the tyrant and while NATO air strikes were trying to oust him. Claiming to be acting as a go-between to the Obama administration and Congress, Welch met with senior Libyan officials at the Four Seasons Hotel in Cairo. He offered them assistance from Israeli intelligence and advised them to take advantage of the unrest in Syria. Welch's advice was "a clear contradiction of public demands from the White House that Qaddafi must be removed," according to Aljazeera news. The State Department claimed that Welch, a Bechtel employee, was not representing the US government, but was a private individual on a private mission. At the time, Bechtel had a contract to build power plants in Libya. Welch declined comment on the matter.

By 2015, Bechtel, which had been active in the Middle East for more than seventy-five years, was ranked the largest contractor in the world, with awards swelling past $100 billion. Welch described the company as a true multinational, with forces deployed throughout the world.

In an interview with an Egyptian newspaper, Welch announced that Bechtel was interested in assisting the Egyptian government with its infrastructure needs, including coal-fired plants and oil and gas facilities. Perhaps nowhere was the twenty-first-century iteration of international Bechtel more evident than in Kosovo, where the US ambassador there helped Bechtel win a contract to build a billion-dollar highway through neighboring Albania. Christopher Dell, a three-decade career diplomat, lobbied for the controversial project, dubbed the "Patriotic Highway," before taking a lucrative position with Bechtel. Peter Feith, the senior European Union diplomat in Kosovo when Bechtel and its partner, the Turkish behemoth Enka, secured the contract, criticized the way Dell spoke out in support of the project and then pushed through the deal. Calling for an inquiry, Feith questioned "the logic of an impoverished, nascent country undertaking such a huge infrastructure project," as the *Guardian* reported it. The highway project was mired in allegations of corruption on both sides of the border, as its estimated costs soared from $555 million to a final cost of $1.1 billion for a stretch of mountainous highway, costing $25 million per mile. Stretching across one of the poorest regions in southeastern Europe—where one in three Kosovars lives on less than $2.18 per day, and only one in seven owns a car—the completed state-of-the-art motorway was underused. "The highway's black vein of asphalt now stands out against the Balkan countryside, as if mocking the surrounding poverty like a cruel Dickensian joke," wrote journalist Matthew Brunwasser in *Foreign Policy* magazine.

The Balkan Investigative Reporting Network raised questions about the propriety of Dell's revolving door from the State Department to Bechtel after a one-year "cooling-off period" during which ambassadors are prohibited from lobbying the US government. Michelle Michael, a spokeswoman for Bechtel, said the suggestion that Dell "acted inappropriately or otherwise failed to meet his responsibility as a public servant is both unfair and offensive." Charlene Wheeless, Bechtel's vice president of global corporate affairs, went further, calling it "slanderous" to allege a conflict of interest between Dell's work as ambassador and any business he generated for Bechtel.

But the controversy didn't end there. "It isn't every day that a U.S. ambassador inspires a character in a comic strip," as Brunwasser put it. But that is what happened to Dell, who was satirized as the "Chief Pimp" in "The Pimpsons"—a Balkan cartoon strip depicting "the local political elite commandeering Kosovo's democracy and selling the country off to the highest bidder."

In one of the editions, published on Facebook, Dell the caricature was shown taking cash from Bechtel in exchange for helping the company get the billion-dollar contract for the forty-eight-mile, four-lane Kosovo Highway—the most expensive public works project in that country's history. While there are no real-life reports of such direct payments, a six-month investigation by the Investigative Reporting Program at the University of California at Berkeley Graduate School of Journalism in 2015 found that the Bechtel-built highways in the region "were boondoggles for the countries in which they were constructed, and that members of governments and international institutions often saw problems coming before Bechtel . . . even began work on the roads." And Dell the man had reportedly pressured the Kosovo government "not only to choose Bechtel but also to sign a contract with terms that were favorable to the corporation," according to the investigation, even though a coalition including the World Bank, numerous European embassies, and the International Monetary Fund opposed Bechtel's bid.

Bechtel did not suffer from either the allegations or the controversy. Instead, it was rewarded with more and bigger contracts throughout America and across the globe. Long-standing devotees of interventionist government, Bechtel is "*the* case study that explains how business is done between multinational construction giants and the governments that approve and fund the projects those giants engineer and build," according to *SF Weekly*.

Depending on one's interpretation, observers consider Bechtel either a brilliant triumph or an iconic symbol of grotesque capitalism. Driven by ideology as well as money, the Bechtel corporate insiders embrace a fixed perception of America—and the path that it needs to follow—as part of a particular worldview. "Bechtel plays politics because it cares about government," William Greider once wrote. "Especially about who is running the government." Veteran journalist Lisa Davis agreed. One could view the company "as either a shining success or a horrific monster," she wrote. "But it can't be seen as a rogue firm playing outside the rules. Bechtel is the textbook example of business as usual." Indeed, in May 2015 Bechtel was named the top-ranked US contractor for the seventeenth year running by *Engineering News-Record*, the leading publication for the engineering and construction industry. In addition to ranking number one on the annual list of the top four hundred contractors, it ranked in the top twenty petroleum, transportation, power, industrial, and hazardous waste firms.

The Bechtel family political philosophy tends toward conservative, in some respects libertarian, anti-big government even as their company made billions from government contracts. The company has a long history of taking taxpayer money for deals with governments of strategic interest to the United States. "Bechtel is a mighty component in this great industrial defense complex, which in effect has been determining policy for our country," remarked a Texas congressman on the House floor. Even though it is an engineering and construction firm, "profits are reported as personal income by individual owners," according to the *Nation*.

Like the Koch brothers and others in their political milieu, the Bechtel Foundation and its individual family members contribute to the Heritage Foundation, the antienvironmentalist Pacific Legal Foundation, American Enterprise Institute, Georgetown University Center for Strategic and International Studies, and other conservative think tanks. The firm subscribes to former vice president Dick Cheney's Energy Policy task force promoting energy policy to benefit the private sector. Its political contributions tilt more toward its business interests than its ideology, as do the foundation's charitable gifts, "often going to the universities with engineering schools that accept and then graduate Bechtel employees," according to one account. Philip M. Smith, one of the most experienced science policy professionals in the United States—and science advisor to four US presidents—described Bechtel's political leanings as a continuation of the old energy paradigm that began with the Cold War. "Neither Steve Bechtel Sr. nor Steve Jr. had any interest in national affairs unless it benefitted their company."

Likewise, both the corporation and the Bechtel family philanthropy is "outside the realm of what might be considered business-related fraternizing," according to *SF Weekly*. The Bechtels "remain virtually off the social radar" and are not among the regular benefactors of San Francisco's charity fetes, galas, and balls. Stephen Bechtel Jr.'s favorite philanthropy is the $439 million Boy Scout camp—the Summit Bechtel Family National Scout Reserve—located in Mount Hope, West Virginia.

The company's public relations stance is aggressive, even hostile, toward critical news reporters and authors. "Bechtel has a three-point PR strategy," according to one reporter. "Trashing journalists who report critically on the company, spinning financial institutions who lend the company money, and bending the truth."

When Ralph King, a former banking reporter for the *Wall Street Journal*, wrote a 4,700-word exposé of Bechtel that was published in a San Francisco–based magazine, "company spinmeisters promptly ran a background check on him," searched internal phone and email records in an attempt to find who was leaking information to him, and charged that the story was inaccurate and unbalanced. After the *Boston Globe*'s explosive investigation of Bechtel's cost overruns for the Big Dig, the company compiled and circulated an eighteen-page memo accusing the newspaper of failing to understand the construction trade. Following widespread national and international media criticism for how it landed the massive Iraq reconstruction contract, Bechtel compiled a point-by-point refutation of the allegations against it, which it distributed to the press and company partners and posted on the firm's website. Among their refutations, Bechtel denied that politics played any role in procuring the contract, claiming the company "engages in the political process legally, openly, and appropriately," and stating the company balanced its political campaign contributions more fairly between Republicans and Democrats than most other construction industry PACs. "The implication that Bechtel wins business or succeeds in a highly competitive marketplace through political connections is misguided and false."

When journalist and author Laton McCartney published *Friends in High Places: The Bechtel Story—The Most Secret Corporation and How It Engineered the World* in 1988—a book highly critical of Bechtel—corporate executives pressured his New York publisher with threats of litigation. "The first thing they did was get a copy of the book and demand corrections," McCartney recalled. Caspar Weinberger called for all references to him to be omitted. When McCartney's publisher, Simon & Schuster—also the publisher of this book—stood behind its author, Bechtel representatives then obtained a copy of McCartney's publicity schedule for his book tour. McCartney said that every time he was on a live radio interview show, someone from Bechtel would call in to lambaste him. As a last resort, after the publisher refused to back down in response to the company's threats, Bechtel published a fifteen-page alternative edition entitled "The Real Story," which it distributed to the media and circulated among company employees.

Bechtel accused McCartney of committing "errors on more than 100 pages" and making up events that never occurred, and asserted that McCartney's book was full of fabrications, falsehoods, and innuendo.

McCartney prevailed against the onslaught against his professionalism and factual accuracy. Bechtel did admit that it would be "preposterous for us to say we haven't built good relationships with important people"—relationship building the company described as mere "networking."

In the *New York Times* review of the book, and the clash, Stephen Labaton wrote the obvious: By either Bechtel's or McCartney's standards, it was "corporate networking of unparalleled dimensions."

The Bechtel story is most important for how the company embodied the rise of a corporate capitalism forged in the American West that over the decades took the world by storm—a capitalism much more in line with cronyism than free market ideology. Bechtel pioneered the revolving door system that now pervades both US politics and the American economic system—a door that came to shape foreign policy not always in the interest of the nation and its citizens, but for the interests of multinational corporations.

In the end, this is the ugly, untold story of America. A story not of the triumph of laissez faire capitalism, but of Profiteers whose sole client was government itself.

ACKNOWLEDGMENTS

This book would not exist if not for the incomparable Donald S. Lamm, consummate editor and literary agent. Its genesis was spawned by Lamm, who saw behind the opacity of Bechtel to envision one of the great, untold stories of American history and invention. That he saw me as Bechtel's natural and long-needed chronicler—a perfect union of author and subject—was my personal good fortune. But he didn't stop there. He shepherded the book through the process of pairing me with the skilled and enthusiastic Ben Loehnen at Simon & Schuster. And then continued as the book's unofficial steward through its years of research and writing. I am profoundly grateful for his belief and commitment, and for the team he and his fellow agent, Christy Fletcher, mustered to bring it forth.

Many archivists, librarians, academics, policy advisors, activists, and colleagues contributed to my research and understanding of Bechtel and its relationship with the US government and its role in the world. I wish to thank Scott Armstrong, Stephen Bates, Sid Blumenthal, Matthew Brunwasser, Tom Carpenter, Phillip Coyle, Matt Davis, Mark Feldstein, Peyton George, Hugh Gusterson, Gary Gwilliam, Todd Edward Holmes, Todd Jacobson, Walter Kirn, John Mankiewice, Jonathan Marshall, Laton McCartney, Greg and Trish Mello, Bob Moss, Judith Nies, Virginia Scharff, Tick Segerblom, Elisa Rivlin, Jeff Smith, Russ Wellen, and Valerie Plame Wilson.

Once again, I am thankful to the many friends who continually sustain me through the long, often grueling process of writing a book. The usual suspects who pepper the acknowledgment pages of my previous seven books are here once again. Charmay Allred, Shaune

Bazner, Sandy Blakeslee, Maxine Champion, Nancy Cook, Frankie Sue Del Papa, Dan Flores, Bonnie Goldstein and Jim Grady, Felice Gonzales, Michael Green and Deborah Young, Joanna Hurley, Judy Illes, Don and Jean Lamm, Roger Morris, Jim and Julie Anne Overton, Ellen Reiben, Bob Samuel, Tick Segerblom, Sam Smith, Jamey Stillings, and Greg and Barbara Wierzynski. I am sorry that my dear friend Phil Smith—one of the most eminent science policy experts in America—did not live to see this book come to fruition. He was an early and stalwart champion of the project and lent his insight and expertise to me, as well as providing introductions to key sources.

In the friendship category, I owe a special debt of gratitude to Mike and Terri Jerry, who essentially adopted my dog, Fremont, for months at a time during my peripatetic research schedule. And to Kathy Kinsella and Ed James, who welcomed me into their stunning Cleveland Park, DC, home for an entire four months while I conducted intensive research at the Library of Congress. Famous for their hospitality, Ed and Kathy host a steady stream of writers, lawyers, entrepreneurs, labor leaders, artists, activists, and journalists, all the while plying everyone with gourmet meals and fine wine and ongoing, enlightening conversation, all unpretentiously reminiscent of the historic Washington salons of earlier eras.

I am grateful for my four months of research at the John W. Kluge Center at the Library of Congress—an opportunity that not only enhanced my life in unexpected ways but also deepened my understanding of the world Bechtel made, while broadening my scope into previously unimagined territories. Librarians Thomas Mann and Janice Herd were indefatigable in their pursuit of documents and databases, primary sources and obscure archives. Gulnar Nagashybayeva, the library's Business Reference Specialist, taught me how to navigate the inscrutable ocean of the "Deep" or "Hidden" web, which opened a whole new world to me—a world where Bechtel operated that didn't crop up on a Google search. My intern, Mary Ahearn, was thorough and resourceful. Mary Lou Reker, Travis Hensley, and Jason Steinhauer made a daunting task manageable. They provided the community of scholars at Kluge with a social and intellectual vibrancy that was infectious. I am thankful for the support I encountered at that extraordinary venue during my Kluge/Black Mountain Institute fellowship.

It is not an exaggeration to say that the Black Mountain Institute at the University of Nevada, Las Vegas, literally made this book possible. The BMI dream team, under the helm of Carol Harter and Richard Wiley, fostered a magical haven of creativity and academic excellence. The collegial and sustaining environment of BMI was unlike anything I had previously experienced in my twenty-five years of book writing. Many thanks go to Carol and Richard for helping make the past couple of years the best of my life. Thanks also to my BMI colleagues: Maile Chapman, Joe Langdon, and Maritza White. Special appreciation as well to Chris Hudgins, the Dean of UNLV's College of Liberal Arts, for his unwavering support of the institute, and to Beverly Rogers, whose recent $30 million gift to the newly rechristened Beverly Rogers and Carol C. Harter Black Mountain Institute guarantees that it will remain among the preeminent literary establishments in America for years to come.

Once again, I owe the world to my mother, Sara Denton, and my three sons, Ralph, Grant, and Carson Samuel. I wish with all my heart that my father, Ralph Denton, had lived to read this book. He never wavered in his pride about me, but this particular endeavor touches on many aspects of American life, culture, and politics that were of utmost concern to him.

Finally, thanks to John Smith, the ever-witty and patient journalist, who was there in the trenches to watch my back.

Sally Denton
November 27, 2015

NOTES

Although I didn't know it, the inspiration for this book began five decades ago. As a fourth-generation Nevadan—raised in the Boulder City home built by one of the engineers on the Hoover Dam—I have been fascinated by Bechtel all of my life. To me, the company has always embodied the best and worst of American capitalism. Riddled as the company has been with the influence peddling and cronyism endemic to such multinational empires, it has always intrigued me as a very human story of entrepreneurship, of American homegrown ingenuity and technological genius.

My reporting on Bechtel began formally in 2011, when Americans seemed to be reaching an apex of concern about corporate accountability and responsibility. Because of the historic and public nature of some of the subjects of this book, there exists a wealth of information in various collections and locales. I relied extensively on primary and secondary sources in institutions such as the Library of Congress in Washington, DC. The vast collections at the Library of Congress were by far the most all-encompassing and enlightening—from the various libraries within (the Jefferson, the Madison, and the Adams), to the incomparable worldwide databases and periodicals to which the Library subscribes.

This book is based on thousands of pages of confidential and public government and corporate records, as well as dozens of interviews with government officials and corporate players. Unfortunately, I was denied access to Caspar Weinberger's papers, which, though housed at the Manuscript Division of the Library of Congress, are controlled by Weinberger's son, Caspar Weinberger Jr., who personally rejected my inquiry. Likewise, the Hoover Institution Journalism Program denied my request for a journalism fellowship because my area of reporting did not include "overlap with Hoover Institution scholars' area of research and expertise." The Hoover-affiliated scholars whom I identified as of interest to me, and who are seminal to my book, included Stephen Bechtel Jr., along with the "four horsemen of the apocalypse," George Shultz, Henry Kissinger, William Perry, and Sam Nunn.

Because of the private corporate status of the company, combined with Bechtel's long-standing tradition of privacy and secrecy, information that would be in the public domain for a publicly traded company was not available. Neither the Department of Energy nor NNSA was helpful or forthcoming. My freedom of information requests to DOE and NNSA regarding Bechtel contracts were denied in their entirety. Still, despite being handicapped by the secrecy and privacy of Bechtel, I was able to shine a light on many of its opaque activities in order to present a balanced picture of the company.

Bechtel's media relations department responded to my request to submit questions in writing regarding the company's history and current projects by directing me to the company's online press kit. And in fact, their website along with corporate histories provided a wealth of information. The company's website is brimming with financial and technical details about its worldwide megaprojects throughout history. The three corporate-sponsored company histories—*The Bechtel Story*, *A Builder and His Family*, and *Bechtel in Arab Lands*—were a veritable treasure trove of family and company history. John Simpson's obscure, privately printed autobiography, *Random Notes: Recollections of My Early Life*, was starkly revealing of the milieu of the Cold War intrigues of the Bechtel-McCone era. I was fortunate to have worked for Jack Anderson, the legendary investigative reporter, on the heels of his famous exposés of John McCone and ITT, the assassination of Salvador Allende, and McCone's role in the CIA investigation of the John F. Kennedy assassination. Anderson's files, as well as those of his predecessor, the equally legendary Drew Pearson, added wonderful context and color to an opaque subject.

I also drew on a wide range of private documents and conducted dozens of interviews with well-placed informants in Washington, California, and abroad. I have relied on published histories and stories by first-rate journalists working in the United States, Europe, Central and South America, and throughout the Middle East. I have culled and analyzed dozens of congressional hearings, court documents, conference papers, graduate theses, white papers, think-tank analyses, declassified State Department and CIA cables, and memoranda, as well as congressional and inspector general investigations.

I reviewed the papers of numerous individuals who appear in these pages, including Allen Dulles, John Foster Dulles, James Forrestal, John Simpson, John McCone, Richard Nixon, Edwin Meese, Donald Rumsfeld, Ronald Reagan, among many other public and private figures.

Some of my interviews were conducted on "background," meaning I could rely upon the information they provided in order to independently verify it but I agreed not to identify them. There are no anonymous quotations in the book.

All direct quotations come from either primary sources, including historical and legal documents; firsthand accounts; audiovisual transcripts; scholarly papers; and especially government cables, memoranda, reports, and legal or congressional hearings; or secondary sources used to analyze the primary sources. The vast number of secondary sources came from numerous libraries and repositories in California, Nevada, New Mexico, and Washington, DC. Those sources include published works, articles from books and journals, documentaries, dissertations, reports, blogs, and manuscripts.

ix *"These capitalists generally act harmoniously and in concert, to fleece the people"*: Abraham Lincoln. Speech in the Illinois Legislature. Jan. 11, 1837. http://quod .lib.umich.edu/l/lincoln/lincoln1/1:92?rgn=div1;view=fulltext.

ix *"If you can't trust a man's word"*: Robert L. Ingram, *The Bechtel Story: Seventy Years of Accomplishment in Engineering and Construction* (San Francisco: Ingram, 1968), 33.

ix *"We're more about making money than making things"*: Bechtel, quoted in Jeffrey St. Clair, "Bechtel, More Powerful Than the U.S. Army," *Axis of Logic*, May 15, 2005, 7. http://www.axisoflogic.com/artman/publish/Article_17669.shtml.

ix *"There's no reason for people to hear of us. We're not selling to the public"*: Jim Riccio, "Incompetence, Wheeling & Dealing: The Real Bechtel," *Multinational Monitor* 10, no. 10 (October 1989).

ix *"We will never be a conglomerate"*: www.bechtel.com/BAC-Chapter-7.html.

ix *"The company's goal has always been to be the best"*: www.bechtel.com.

PREFACE: MISSION ACCOMPLISHED

The account of the major combat operations in Iraq—and Bechtel's role in it—draws on extensive American and international contemporaneous newspaper accounts. The facts about the rise of Bechtel were gleaned primarily from the company website, the company's three officially sponsored histories and news stories written by California authors.

1 *"This place is surreal"*: James Cox and Gary Strauss, "Iraq Work Puts Bechtel in Spotlight: Private Contractor Juggles Restoration with Controversy," *USA Today*, June 19, 2003.

2 *"Saddam's 'I'm-on-crack'"*: Peter Van Buren, *We Meant Well: How I Helped Lose the Battle for the Hearts and Minds of the Iraqi People* (New York: Metropolitan Books, 2011).

2 *"Sinatra's Vegas"*: Ibid., 167.

3 *"script"... "imagined Americans"*: Ibid., 6.

3 *"What did work out"*: Walter Hickey, "The U.S. Embassy in Baghdad Cost a Staggering $750 Million," Business Insider, March 20, 2013, http://www.business insider.com/750-million-united-states-embassy-iraq-baghdad-2013-3.

4 *"The World's Largest"... "We placed"*: Van Buren, *We Meant Well*, 154.

4 *"the world's worst bar scene"*: Ibid., 159.

4 *"the biblical Eden"*: Ibid., 110.

4 *"hideous modernist bunker"... "scowls at the world"... "an insult"*: Martin Kemp, "Diplomacy Has No Place in This Monstrous Bunker," Guardian.com, May 23, 2007, www.theguardian.com/artanddesign/artblog/2007/may/23/diplomacyhas noplaceinthis.

5 *"War began last week"*: Elizabeth Rosenberg, Anthony Allesandrini, and Adam Horowitz, "Iraq Reconstruction Tracker," *Middle East Report* 33 (Summer 2003), www.merip.org/mer/mer227/iraq-reconstruction-tracker.

5 *"We were the ones"*: Van Buren, *We Meant Well*, 3.

5 *"exceptionally maladroit"... "only well-connected"*: Thomas A. Fogarty, "Companies Bid on Rebuilding Iraq—Halliburton, Bechtel Benefit from Experience and Political Ties," *USA Today*, March 26, 2003.

6 *"build anything"*... *"The bigger, the tougher"*: *Fortune*, March 1951, quoted in Laton McCartney, *Friends in High Places: The Bechtel Story—The Most Secret Corporation and How It Engineered the World* (New York: Ballantine Books, 1988), 55.

6 *"wheeling and dealing"*: *Newsweek*, December 29, 1975.

7 *"an entity so powerful"*: Kevin Starr, *Endangered Dreams: The Great Depression in California* (New York: Oxford University Press, 1996), 297.

7 *"Wild West capitalism"*: Robert B. Laughlin, *Powering the Future: How We Will (Eventually) Solve the Energy Crisis and Fuel the Civilization of Tomorrow* (New York: Basic Books, 2011), 98.

7 Re: Bechtel's ranking among private companies, see www.forbes.com/pictures /eggh45efje/4-bechtel-5.

8 *"What appears to an outsider"*: Mark Dowie, "The Bechtel File: How the Master Builders Protect Their Beachheads," *Mother Jones*, September/October 1978, 33.

8 Re: petitioning to have family voter records sealed, see Lisa Davis, "It's a Bechtel World: Think That a $680 Million Iraq Contract Is a Big Deal? You Don't Know Bechtel," *SF Weekly*, June 18, 2003.

8 *"In fact, if they had their way"*: Dowie, "Bechtel File," 33.

9 *"multiyear megaprojects"*... *"markets"*... *"signature projects"*... *"tens of thousands"*... *"a third of the world's"*... *"many of the largest"*... *"global leader in design"*: www.bechtel.com.

10 *"to industrial standards"*: Gary Gwilliam press release, interview with author.

10 *"the U.S. Nuclear Security Enterprise"*: www.bechtel.com.

11 *Bechtel was in it for the money*: Hugh Gusterson, "The Assault on Los Alamos National Laboratory: A Drama in Three Acts," *Bulletin of the Atomic Scientists* (November/December 2011).

11 *"a playground for political patronage"*: Upton.

11 *"a deep-pocketed"*: Ralph King and Charlie McCoy, "Bechtel's Power Outage," *Business 2.0*, March 2004.

11 *"Bechtel espouses"*: William Greider, "The Boys from Bechtel: Will Ronald Reagan Reverse U.S. Policy on Nuclear Proliferation?" *Rolling Stone*, September 2, 1982, http://www.rollingstone.com/politics/news/the-boys-from -bechtel-19820902.

11 *"There's no reason for people to hear of us. We're not selling to the public"*: Riccio, quoted in *Newsweek*.

12 *Bechtel achievement*... *"frequent discouragements"*... *"showed what men could do"*: Robert L. Ingram, *A Builder and His Family, 1898–1948: Being the Historical Account of the Contracting, Engineering & Construction Career of W. A. Bechtel and of How His Sons and Their Associates Have Carried Forward His Principles in Their Many Activities* (San Francisco: privately printed, 1949), xii.

12 *"The California settlement"*: Joan Didion, *Where I Was From* (New York: Alfred A. Knopf, 2003), 24.

12 *"Western builders will build"*: *Pacific Builder,* quoted in Peter Wiley and Robert Gottlieb, *Empires in the Sun: The Rise of the New American West* (Tucson: University of Arizona Press, 1982), 16.

12 *"single most remarkable achievement"*: Ibid.

PROLOGUE: THE SPY WITH A FAN CLUB

The Jonathan Pollard account is drawn from the many authors and journalists who covered the Pollard case, including Mark Shaw, Milton Viorst, and Jeff Stein. Outlets included *Washingtonian,* the *Los Angeles Times,* *Newsweek,* and *Wall Street Journal.*

13 *The Spy with a Fan Club*: *Washingtonian,* quoted in Mark Shaw, *Miscarriage of Justice: The Jonathan Pollard Story* (Saint Paul, MN: Paragon House, 2001), 153.

> The journalism pool present at President Obama's speech reported the references to Pollard. The *New York Times* reported that the Hebrew-speaking heckler was an Arab-Israeli activist calling for the liberation of Palestine. But Jennifer Bendery of the *Huffington Post* and other journalists stood by the pool report: www.huffingtonpost.com/2013/03/21/obama-heckled_n_2924127.html, http://abcnews.go.com/blogs/politics/2013/03/who-is-jonathan-pollard-obama -heckled-over-spy-for-israel.

13 *"the endless Pollard intrigues"*: Black.

14 *"Year of the Spy"* . . . *"last gasps"*: Federal Bureau of Investigation.

14 *"The Spy with a Fan Club"*: *Washingtonian,* quoted in Shaw, *Miscarriage of Justice,* 153.

14 *"Whoever has studied"* . . . *" 'Catch-22' Plight"*: Milton Viorst, "The 'Catch-22' Plight of Imprisoned Spy Jonathan Pollard: The U.S. Has Shown a Key Memo to Its Attorneys 25 Times but Denied It to the Defense as Irrelevant and Top Secret," *Los Angeles Times,* September 19, 2003.

14 *"bullying tactics"* . . . *"Even Pollard Deserves"*: Gordon L. Crovitz, "Even Pollard Deserves Better Than Government Sandbagging," *Asian Wall Street Journal,* September 27, 1991.

15 *"Israel has been caught"*: Jeff Stein, "Israel Flagged as Top Spy Threat to U.S. in New Snowden/NSA Document," *Newsweek,* August 4, 2014.

PART ONE: WE WERE AMBASSADORS WITH BULLDOZERS, 1872–1972

The history of Bechtel's first hundred years has been thoroughly chronicled, beginning first with the extensive, in-depth and revealing three-part, 1943 series in *Fortune* called "The Earth Movers." The story of Six Companies, the construction of Hoover Dam, and the politics of water in the American West have all been the subject of numerous full-length and definitive works, including Mark Reisner's *Cadillac Desert,* Michael Hiltzik's *Collossus,* Judith Nies's *Unreal City,* Peter Wiley's and Robert Gottlieb's *Empires in the*

Sun, and Joseph E. Stevens's *Hoover Dam*. Guy Rocca's biography of Frank Crowe was particularly insightful, as was Dennis McBride's history of Boulder City. Any interpretation of the Bechtel-McCone company's participation in World War II maritime construction, as well as the early seminal pipeline construction projects in the Middle East, owes a primary debt to Laton McCartney's groundbreaking company history, *Friends in High Places*. Again, the Bechtel-sponsored corporate histories by Robert L. Ingram were enormously helpful—especially Richard Finnie's *Bechtel in Arab Lands*, as was John L. Simpson's rare and hard-to-find autobiography of his life as a Bechtel family member operating in the clandestine postwar world of the Dulles brothers.

As for the origins of the OSS and CIA, works by authors Burton Hersh, Stephen Kinzer, and Anthony Cave Brown, among many others, were particularly helpful. The rise of John McCone from shipbuilder to Chairman of the AEC to Director of the CIA was charted in his nomination hearings before the US Congress, and, especially, in the investigative reporting of national syndicated columnists, Drew Pearson and Jack Anderson. The account of the death of Bechtel Senior Vice President George Colley in 1958 in Baghdad was reported by the *Associated Press*, as well as in US State Department cables.

A vast bibliography exists about McCone's role as CIA Director in the events leading up to the Kennedy assassination and the investigation of the crime, including books and journalism by acclaimed writers and reporters Jefferson Morley, Jack Anderson, and Curt Gentry, and a treasure trove of declassified government documents obtained by Tom Blanton's indefatigable researchers at the National Security Archive at George Washington University.

Many newspaper and magazine stories have been published over several decades about Bohemian Gove, as well as several sociological studies, including works by William G. Domhoff, Peter Martin Phillips, Joan Didion, and John van der Zee.

The CIA's attempt to oust Chilean President Salvador Allende has been widely reported, contemporaneously by investigative columnist Jack Anderson and in Victor Marchetti's and John Marks's definitive book, *The CIA and the Cult of Intelligence*, and later by Peter Kornbluh in *The Pinochet File*, among many published sources.

17 *We Were Ambassadors with Bulldozers*: Richard Finnie, *Bechtel in Arab Lands: A Fifteenth-Year Review of Engineering and Construction Projects* (San Francisco: Bechtel Corporation, 1958), 50.

17 *"This extreme reliance"*: Didion, *Where I Was From*, 24.

CHAPTER ONE: GO WEST!

19 *"tall, beefy man"*: Fortune 28, I.

19 *"at a time when he saw"*: Judith Nies, *Unreal City: Las Vegas, Black Mesa, and the Fate of the American West* (New York: Nation Books, 2014, advance uncorrected proof), 147.

20   *"Either the music of the ladies' band"*: *New York Times*, August 28, 1933.

21   *"Having mastered these, gather up your family"*: www.gilderlehrman.org/history
     -by-era/development-west/resources/horace-greeley-"go-west"-1871.

21   *"I landed in Reno"*: Ingram, *Builder and His Family*, 3.

21   *"He was learning"*: Ibid., 4.

21   *"a horse-drawn fresno-scraper"*: *Fortune 28*, I.

21   *"Many of the old-timers"*: McCartney, *Friends in High Places*, 21.

22   *"Still largely undeveloped"*: Davis, "It's a Bechtel World."

23   *"whose trek to California"*: Joseph E. Stevens, *Hoover Dam: An American Adventure* (Norman: University of Oklahoma Press, 1988), 35.

23   *"Might as well ask him in"*: Wattis, quoted in McCartney, *Friends in High Places*, 23.

23   *"coming of age"* . . . *"I never expected"*: Ingram, *Builder and His Family*, 13.

24   *"near misses, the bad judgment calls"* . . . *"It is difficult to connect"*: Heather Zwicker, " 'To Build a Better World': Bechtel, a Family Company," in *Cultural Critique and the Global Corporation*, ed. Purnima Bose and Laura E. Lyons (Bloomington: Indiana University Press, 2010), 110.

24   *"and still fancying himself"*: McCartney, *Friends in High Places*, 25.

26   *"egomaniacal small-time"*: Marc Reisner, *Cadillac Desert: The American West and Its Disappearing Water* (New York: Viking, 1986), 131.

26   *"It sounds a little ambitious"*: *Fortune 28*, I.

CHAPTER TWO: FOLLOW THE WATER

28   *"the most fateful transformation"*: Reisner, *Cadillac Desert*, 172.

28   *"The Colorado has always been best known"*: Michael Hiltzik, *Colossus: Hoover Dam and the Making of the American Century* (New York: Free Press, 2010), 3.

29   *"unequivocally announced"*: Starr, *Endangered Dreams*, 294–95.

29   *"Two were aging Mormons"*: *Fortune 28*, I.

30   *"Hocking everything but their shirts"*: Reisner, *Cadillac Desert*, 132.

30   *"put in motion"*: Nies, *Unreal City*, 149.

31   *"wild to build this dam"*: *Fortune 28*, I.

32   *"When the last bills are paid"* . . . *"The U.S. is willing"*: *Fortune*, quoted in Sally Denton, "Hoover's Promise: The Dam That Remade the American West Celebrates Its 75th Anniversary," *Invention & Technology* 25, no. 2 (Summer 2010): 14.

33   *"In All the President's Men"*: Wiley and Gottlieb, xvi.

CHAPTER THREE: HOBO JUNGLE

34   *"unleash a flood"*: Denton, "Hoover's Promise."

34   *"We were all scared stiff"*: Stevens, *Hoover Dam*, 35.

35   *"like a general"*: Al M. Rocca, *America's Master Dam Builder: The Engineering Genius of Frank T. Crowe* (Langham, MD: University Press of America, 2001), 190.

35 *"When one set of tracks"*: Dennis McBride, *In the Beginning: A History of Boulder City, Nevada* (Boulder City: Hoover Dam Museum, 1992), 16.

35 *"He knew it would take"*: Rocca, *America's Master Dam Builder*, 190.

35 *rock bottom*: Manchester, I:I.

35 *"hobo jungle"*: Rocca, *America's Master Dam Builder*, 190.

35 *"Instead of the young miners"*: Nies, *Unreal City*, 149.

36 *"This will be a job for machines"*: Denton, "Hoover's Promise."

37 *"The structure spanned ideology"*: Roger Morris, *Richard Milhous Nixon: The Rise of an American Politician* (New York: Henry Holt, 1990), 11.

CHAPTER FOUR: THAT HELLHOLE

38 *"bête noir"*: McCartney, *Friends in High Places*, 45.

38 *"resembled a battlefield"*: Hiltzik, *Colossus*, 216.

39 *"pocketed an additional"*: McCartney, *Friends in High Places*, 39.

39 *"Besides the hazards of the construction"*: Reisner, *Cadillac Desert*, 133.

40 *"That siren—oh, it scared you"*: Helen Holmes, quoted in Rocca, *America's Master Dam Builder*, 196.

40 *"exempt from the prying attentions"* . . . *"showed up in Las Vegas"* . . . *"quickly, quietly, and privately"*: Hiltzik, *Colossus*, 218–19.

41 *"We feel it's a crime"*: McCartney, *Friends in High Places*, 39.

41 *"They will have to work"*: Wattis, quoted in Stevens, *Hoover Dam*, 72.

41 *"In the town"*: Ibid., 173.

42 *"crisis-filled narrative"*: T. H. Watkins, *Righteous Pilgrim: The Life and Times of Harold L. Ickes, 1874–1952* (New York: Henry Holt, 1990), 383.

42 *"coaxed and manipulated"*: Wiley and Gottlieb, *Empires in the Sun*, 20.

42 *"a telegraphic bombardment"*: Ickes, quoted in Watkins, *Righteous Pilgrim*, 384.

42 *"Flooded gorges"*: Denton and Morris, 96.

42 *"This is a good time"*: Ingram, *Builder and His Family*, 36.

43 *"an overdose of a medicine"*: "W. A. Bechtel Dies in Moscow Hotel," *New York Times*, August 29, 1933, 17.

43 *"Fumbling with a syringe"*: McCartney, *Friends in High Places*, 45. For details of Warren Bechtel's death and the count Zucatur, see McCartney, 45 ff., and 244, notes for chapter 4.

44 *"Coming at the time it did"*: Steve Bechtel interview, Stevens, *Hoover Dam*, 258.

CHAPTER FIVE: WARTIME SOCIALISTS

45 *"Warren Bechtel was a very successful"*: www.bechtel.com.

45 *"aggressive, boisterous"*: McCartney, *Friends in High Places*, 46.

45 *"They wanted me to lead"*: Ibid., 49.

46 *"on the job"*: *New York Times*, March 16, 1989.

46 *"burning up the French countryside"*: www.bechtel.com.

46 *"The incident"..."There was no explanation"*: McCartney, *Friends in High Places*, 47.

47 *"went east to talk"... "As a newcomer"*: Ingram, *Builder and His Family*, 27.

47 *"more sophisticated and worldly"*: McCartney, *Friends in High Places*, 49.

47 *"The ancient Western dream"*: Bernard De Voto, "The Anxious West," *Harper's*, December 1946.

47 *"lusty, uninhibited"*: Fortune 28, I.

48 *"Steve's vision was of energy"*: Ingram, *Builder and His Family*, 41.

48 *"Steve and I shared a sense"... "Not just pipelines"*: McCone, quoted in McCartney, *Friends in High Places*, 53.

49 *"it was a success"*: Fortune 28, II.

50 *"jaunty fellow"*: Fortune 28, I.

50 *"hard-boiled"... "molten temper"*: "Nominations of McCone, Korth, and Harlan." U.S Senate. *Hearing Before the Committee on Armed Services*. 87th Cong., 2nd Sess. January 18, 1962.

50 *"the perfect material"... "a real grind"*: Warren Kozak, "The American Defender Stop: John McCone Helped Thwart a Cuban Missile," *Investor's Business Daily*, April 10, 2012.

50 *"great foresight"... "Like others"*: Ingram, *Builder and His Family*, 45.

50 *"seemed about ripe"*: Fortune 28, II.

51 *"the American Onassis"*: McCartney, *Friends in High Places*, 109.

51 *"Japs"*: Ingram, *Builder and His Family*, 72.

51 *"the mountains are nameless"*: Service, quoted in Ingram, *Builder and His Family*, 72.

52 *"just begun to fight!"*: Ibid., 50.

52 *"strengthening the nation's sinews"*: Ibid., 70.

52 *"the war would have been lost"*: Ibid., 55.

52 *"built the ships"*: Admiral Howard L. Vickery, paraphrased in McCartney, *Friends in High Places*, 70.

52 *"I daresay"*: Casey, quoted in David Wise and Thomas B. Ross, *The Invisible Government* (New York: Random House, 1964), 193.

52 *"cast up a worthwhile profit-and-loss"*: Fortune 28, III.

CHAPTER SIX: PATRIOT CAPITALISTS

53 *"We're not worried"*: Fortune 28, III.

53 *"Nobody around here wanted to go foreign"*: www.bechtel.com.

53 *"quasi-industrialists"*: Fortune 28, III.

53 *"Size can work to your advantage"*: Church, "Stephen Bechtel."

53 *"a series of shrewd"*: McCartney, *Friends in High Places*, 71.

54 *"the birth of the modern Bechtel Corporation"*: www.bechtel.com/BAC-Chapter-3.html.

54 *"the company took off like a rocket"*: Bridges, quoted in McCartney, *Friends in High Places*, 73.

54 *"hardworking WASP"*: Ibid., 73.

54 *"They are not always the easiest"*: Clayton Hirst, "The World's at Bechtel's Beck and Call," *Independent* (London), April 20, 2003.

55 *"determined the entire future course"*: John L. Simpson, *Random Notes: Recollections of My Early Life. Europe Without a Guidebook, 1915–1922* (Printed privately, 1969), ii.

55 *"full of virtue"*: Ibid., 1.

55 *"Everything followed"*: Ibid., ii.

55 *"who had some sort"*: Ibid., 39.

55 *"actor in"... "interpreter of"*: Ibid., 60.

55 *"a rather Machiavellian scheme"... "At this point"... "It was rough"*: Ibid., 39–40.

56 *"making history"*: Ibid., 60.

56 *"saving the world"*: Ibid., 63.

56 *"An intelligence agency"*: Allen Dulles, *The Secret Surrender* (New York: Harper & Row, 1966), 9.

57 *"major politics, finance"*: Ingram, *A Builder and His Family*, 77.

58 *"Fast friends"... "shanking irons"*: Jeffrey St. Clair, "Straight to Bechtel," *Counterpunch*, May 9, 2005.

58 *"America's unadvertised"*: Burton Hersh, *The Old Boys: The American Elite and the Origins of the CIA* (New York: Charles Scribner's Sons, 1992), 2.

58 *"those lucrative thickets"*: Stephen Kinzer, *The Brothers: John Foster Dulles, Allen Dulles, and Their Secret World War* (New York: Times Books, 2013), 33.

58 *"forward-looking monarch"... "a tight circle"*: www.bechtel.com/BAC-Chapter-3.html.

58 *"globe-girdling behemoth"*: Alexander Taylor, "A Secretive Construction Giant Enters the Limelight," *Time*, June 12, 1982.

58 *"the rise of the notoriously potent"*: McCartney, *Friends in High Places*, 12.

58 *"In the Middle East program"*: Ingram, *Builder and His Family*, 95.

CHAPTER SEVEN: THE LARGEST AMERICAN COLONY

59 *"Bechtel Corporation, which is"*: Rebecca Solnit, "Dry Lands," *London Review of Books*, December 3, 2009.

59 *"modernize this ancient region"*: Finnie, *Bechtel in Arab Lands*, 7.

59 *"even a Bedouin camp"... "This thirty-inch"*: www.bechtel.com/BAC-Chapter-3.html.

60 *"Europe's back door"... "the largest American colony"*: Ingram, *Builder and His Family*, 96.

60 *"one of the most extraordinary"*: Finnie, *Bechtel in Arab Lands*, 88.

61 *"For all their obvious differences"*: McCartney, *Friends in High Places*, 85.

61 *"possess any plant, firm, or branch"*: July 18, 1974, agreement between International Bechtel Incorporated and the Egyptian government, quoted in McCartney, *Friends in High Places*, 185. McCartney writes: "The exclusion of Jews from Bechtel projects was quietly sanctioned by the State Department, which at the time did not employ Jews in Saudi Arabia either. Nor were any Jews employed by Aramco." McCartney, *Friends in High Places*, 87.

61 *"part of the corporate-intelligence"*: John Loftus and Mark Aarons, *The Secret War Against the Jews: How Western Espionage Betrayed the Jewish People* (New York: St. Martin's Press, 1994), 244.

61 *"everything from pipelines"*: Finnie, *Bechtel in Arab Lands*, 39.

61 *"STEPHEN BECHTEL INFORMED ME TODAY"*: US minister J. Rives Childs cable to Sec. of State, 2/17/47, quoted in McCartney, *Friends in High Places*, 86.

61 *"Camel Legionnaires"*: Ingram, *Builder and His Family*, 99.

62 *"a payment or bribe"*: Dispatch, Francis E. Meloy to Division of Near Eastern Affairs, 9/29/48, quoted in McCartney, *Friends in High Places*, 86.

62 *"The king and his advisers"*: Steve Coll, *The Bin Ladens: An Arabian Family in the American Century* (New York: Penguin Press, 2008), 40.

62 *"came down to take a look"*: Steve Bechtel, quoted in McCartney, *Friends in High Places*, 96.

62 *"city-state that existed"*: Finnie, *Bechtel in Arab Lands*, 119.

62 *"gangs of Arabs"*: Ibid., 117.

62 *"may have been descendants"*: Ibid., 119.

62 *"apart from a few brackish wells"*: Ibid., 91.

62 *"life easier"* . . . *"As one well"*: Ibid., 87.

63 *"In this business"*: Steve Bechtel, quoted in McCartney, *Friends in High Places*, 96.

63 *"was of such volume"*: Finnie, *Bechtel in Arab Lands*, 43.

63 *"As oil flowed"*: Coll, *Bin Ladens*, 48.

64 *"an elite East Coast Ivy League"*: Hersh, *Old Boys*, book jacket.

64 *"weakness for old-boy"*: Ibid., 155.

64 *"threats to corporate interests"*: Adam LeBor, "Overt and Covert," review of *The Brothers*, by Stephen Kinzer, *New York Times*, November 8, 2013.

64 *"a great political force"*: Kennan, quoted in Kinzer, *Brothers*, 81.

64 *"multinational corporation"*: McCartney, *Friends in High Places*, 115.

65 *"I have talked this over with Steve"*: Simpson to Dulles, December 15, 1952, quoted in McCartney, 116.

65 *"political forces"*: Daniel Yergin, *The Prize: The Epic Quest for Oil, Money and Power* (New York: Simon & Schuster, 1991), photographic insert between 512–13.

65 *"Persia's oil petroleum"*: Roger Morris, "Robert Gates: The Specialist" (Part One), TomDispatch.com, June 19, 2007, www.tomdispatch.com/dialogs/print/?id =174812.

65 *"Bechtel's 12-volume"*: Dowie, "Bechtel File," 38.

CHAPTER EIGHT: GOING NUCLEAR

66 *"New 'Cold War' Plan"*: *Boston Globe*, quoted in Kinzer, *Brothers*, 89.

66 *"favored his friends"*: Background Investigation of John Alex McCone. US Department of Justice, Federal Bureau of Investigation. May 5, 1954.

66 *"which put planes"*: Nies, *Unreal City*, 195.

67 *"The strong-willed, stern-looking"*: Wise and Ross, *Invisible Government*, 192.

67 *"We are the inheritors"*: Swanberg.

67 *"men of great mental vigor"*: Ibid., 317.

68 *"It was only after"*: Denton, *The Pink Lady: The Many Lives of Helen Gahagan Douglas* (New York: Bloomsbury Press, 2009), 95.

69 *"Mr. President"*: Kai Bird and Martin J. Sherwin, *American Prometheus: The Triumph and Tragedy of J. Robert Oppenheimer* (New York: Vintage, 2006), 332.

69 *"the impossibility of any defense"*: Ibid., 324.

70 *"two permanently opposed"*: Ibid., 424.

70 *"More horrific"*: Ibid., 418.

70 *"I do not know how the Third World War"*: Walter Isaacson, *Einstein: His Life and Universe* (New York: Simon & Schuster, 2007), 489.

70 *"Your statement is obviously designed"*: "Nomination of John A. McCone to Be a Member of the Atomic Energy Commission." 15.

70 *"conservative who believes"*: Arthur Lack, "McCone Unlikely to Change AEC's Nuclear Power Policies Significantly," *Wall Street Journal*, June 9, 1958.

71 *"Going nuclear"*... *"Nuclear power was a mechanism"*... *"was a considered move"*: Davis, quoted in McCartney, *Friends in High Places*, 102.

71 *"will not bring undue"*: Davis, quoted in Ronald Brownstein and Nina Easton, *Reagan's Ruling Class: Portraits of the President's Top 100 Officials* (Washington, DC: Presidential Accountability Group, 1982), 150.

71 *"helped finance"*: Dowie, "Bechtel File," 35.

71 *"the largest, most efficient"*: Ibid., 32.

72 *"ignored the legal opinion"*: Pearson, April 28, 1959.

72 *"pattern of business links"*: Ibid., January 17, 1962.

72 *"merely on leave of absence"*: Drew Pearson, quoted in McCartney, *Friends in High Places*, 108.

72 *"so incestuous"*: Ibid., 104.

72 *"McCone said he had done"*: Pearson, January 17, 1962.

72 *"big bomb"*: Pearson, December 3, 1961.

72 *"telling the public one thing"*: Ibid., July 3, 1960.

72 "world's last chance": Ibid., March 28, 1960.

73 "McCone was positively rabid": McCartney, Friends in High Places, 111.

CHAPTER NINE: MCCONEY ISLAND

74 "discuss implications": Memorandum for the Record.

75 "Steve Bechtel is the kind of American": Eisenhower to Bechtel, November 5, 1958, quoted in McCartney, Friends in High Places, 112.

75 "There were many chores": Ibid.

75 "two oil men" . . . "Soviet economic warfare" . . . "very bad": Memorandum for the Files.

75 "the intelligence structure": Memorandum of Meeting With the President.

75 "roll back the dark forces": http://coldwarradios.blogspot.com/2013/03/march-12-1951-original-radio-free-asia.html.

76 "the unofficial board of directors": G. William Domhoff, quoted in Paretsky, 32.

76 "dashing figure": McCartney, Friends in High Places, 119.

76 "in charge of all affairs": Bechtel to Suleiman, October 1, 1950, quoted in McCartney, Friends in High Places, 121.

76 "With the assistance of Snodgrass": Ibid., 124.

77 "inequitable modernization": Roger Morris, "Robert Gates: The Specialist" (Part 2), June 21, 2007, http://www.tomdispatch.com/dialogs/print/?id=174813.

77 "MY FRIENDS REPORT": Dulles cable to Simpson, July 20, 1958, quoted in McCartney, Friends in High Places, 117.

77 "buried in a common grave": Bishop, 57. For the account of Colley's death, see also Stan Carter, "How Iraq Mob Slew Americans," Associated Press, July 22, 1958. Colley's life had been risked in a Bechtel venture seventeen years earlier, in 1941, when Bechtel was building installations on the Philippines' Manila Bay. When enemy forces attacked, Colley, his wife, Marjorie, and another Bechtel couple made a run for it in a small boat heading for Australia, according to official Bechtel accounts. They were caught near Borneo, imprisoned at nearby Kuching where ten prisoners were executed, and held for four years before Australians rescued them.

78 "The Agency and the company": St. Clair, "Straight to Bechtel."

78 "hard-nosed executive": Wise and Ross, Invisible Government, 243.

78 "splinter the CIA": New York Times, April 21, 1966. See also Tom Wicker et al., "C.I.A.: Maker of Policy, or Tool?" New York Times, April 25, 1966.

78 "With his paper-thin mandate": Tuchman, 286.

78 "at a time when the agency was expanding": Dowie, "Bechtel File."

79 "He shuns the press" . . . "tauter, more efficient": Jack Anderson, "John McCone: Secrecy Is His Business," Boston Globe, December 16, 1962.

79 "disciple of massive retaliation": Tuchman, 286.

79 *"all-out"* . . . *"wrapped in an armor"* . . . *"disseminating false"*: Andrew J. Bacevich, *Washington Rules: America's Path to Permanent War* (New York: Metropolitan Books, 2010), 40–41.

79 *"to occupy the country"*: McCone, quoted in Seymour Hersh, *The Dark Side of Camelot* (Boston: Little, Brown, 1997), 349.

80 *"Central Intrigue Agency"*: Pearson, June 17, 1962.

80 *"a damned Murder Inc."*: LBJ quoted by Leo Janos, "The Last Days of the President: LBJ in Retirement," *Atlantic Monthly* 232, no. 1 (July 1973): 35–41.

80 *"twenty-six-year-old Tikriti"*: Roger Morris, "The Undertaker's Tally: Sharp Elbows" (Part One), TomDispatch.com, February 13, 2007, www.tomdispatch.com /post/165669.

80 *"Make sure we had no one"*: Helms, quoted in Jefferson Morley, *Our Man in Mexico: Winston Scott and the Hidden History of the CIA* (Lawrence: University of Kansas Press, 2008), 206. See also "Memorandum for the Record: Discussion with President Johnson," November 25, 1963. John McCone Memoranda.

80 *"McCone's agency had been trying"*: Jack Anderson with Daryl Gibson, *Peace, War, and Politics: An Eyewitness Account* (New York: Forge, 1999), 115. Jack Anderson would contend that his sources told him that McCone "anguished with Bobby over the terrible possibility that the assassination plots sanctioned" by Bobby may have backfired.

Seymour Hersh wrote that there was no evidence that McCone knew about the plots against Castro. "The murder attempts, prodded by Bobby Kennedy, probably went on behind his back." Hersh, *Dark Side of Camelot*, 278. See also Nies, *Unreal City*, n. 197: "In an oral interview at the Kennedy Library, the interviewer did not ask McCone about Oxcart because the project was still secret information. He also claimed no knowledge of Operation Mongoose, the secret plot to destabilize the Cuban government and assassinate Castro. The operation was organized during the Kennedy administration and involved the CIA's recruitment of American gangsters such as Sam Giancana and Santo Trafficante."

LBJ feared the assassination would force him to wage war on Cuba or the Soviet Union if Oswald's connections to the Communists were exposed. He pushed McCone to find everything possible about Oswald's contacts with the Communists in Mexico City. "[LBJ] might be facing a communist dirty trick or a rightwing provocation from those who hated Kennedy for the Bay of Pigs fiasco." (See Morley, *Our Man in Mexico*, 216.) According to Morley, both Bobby and Jackie Kennedy knew "that Castro's charge that the assassination was a provocation by Kennedy's rightwing foes was all too plausible." Ibid., 227.

80 *"walked back and forth"*: Arthur M. Schlesinger, *Journals: 1952–2000* (New York: Penguin Press, 2007), 288.

80 *"Did you kill my brother?"*: Curt Gentry, *J. Edgar Hoover: The Man and the Secrets* (New York: W. W. Norton, 1991), 557n. See also Bryan Bender and Neil Swidey,

"Robert F. Kennedy Saw Conspiracy in JFK's Assassination," *Boston Globe*, November 24, 2013.

81 *"Castro was behind the assassination"*: Anderson and Gibson, *Peace, War, and Politics*, 116.

81 *"had also gone to the Cuban consulate"*: Morley, *Our Man in Mexico*, 216.

    Six days after the assassination, McCone told LBJ about Oswald's visit to the Soviet embassy and Cuban consulate in Mexico City and shared an intelligence report that an agent of the Nicaraguan Secret Police had infiltrated the Cuban embassy and had seen an embassy employee give $6,500 to Oswald to "kill the president" (Peter Kornbluh). Just hours later, McCone notified the president that the intelligence report was bogus. The informant had confessed to making up the story, claiming that it was "a fabrication designed to provoke the U.S. into kicking Castro out of Cuba" (Kornbluh). "Kennedy's Last Act/Reaching Out to Cuba," National Security Archive, November 20, 2013.

81 *"McCone thought there were two people"*: Moyers, quoted in Schlesinger, *Journals*, 184.

81 *"to dispel the swirling allegations"*: Kornbluh, "Kennedy's Last Act."

81 *"a Machiavellian plot"* ... *"immediately an aggressive policy"*: Castro, ibid.

81 *"mission of peace"* ... *"This is terrible"* ... *"There goes"*: Declassified CIA files, quoted in ibid.

82 *"most limited Washington discussions"*: McCone in secret memo to White House, May 1, 1963, ibid.

82 *"tighten the tourniquet"*: From CIA Director John McCone to President Lyndon Johnson, April 28, 1965.

82 *"The two firms built"* ... *"had billed the government"*: Nies, *Unreal City*, 200.

82 *"the greatest organizer"*: Anderson, "John McCone."

CHAPTER TEN: WEAVING SPIDERS

83 *"In the councils of government"*: Eisenhower speech, televised farewell address to the nation, January 17, 1961.

83 *"Rarely does a big Pentagon construction project surface"*: St. Clair, "Straight to Bechtel."

84 *"possible consequences of the loss"*: Eisenhower, quoted in Wiley and Gottlieb, *Empires in the Sun*, 37.

84 *"powerhouse gateway"*: Wolfe, "BART: Bechtel's Baby."

84 *"the Co-ordination of Motives"*: Weldon B. Gibson, *SRI, the Founding Years: A Significant Step at the Golden Time* (Los Altos, CA: Publishing Services Center, 1981), 117.

    Stephen Bechtel's relationship with SRI as a "founding director" can be found in Gibson, *SRI*, 156.

84 *"SRI's Pacific Rim strategy"... "war in Vietnam"*: Wiley and Gottlieb, *Empires in the Sun*, 37–38.

84 *" 'doubled and doubled' "*: Gibson, *SRI*, 156.

85 *"Among its many programs"*: McCartney, *Friends in High Places*, 78n.

85 *"hobnobbing with kings"*: Church, "Stephen Bechtel."

85 *"In his overseas dealings"... "to buzz a group"*: John van der Zee, *The Greatest Men's Party on Earth: Inside the Bohemian Grove* (New York: Harcourt Brace Jovanovich, 1974), 98.

85 *"more relaxed"... "would fly to London"*: Bechtel vice president Jerome Komes, quoted on company website, www.bechtel.com/BAC-Chapter-3.html.

86 *"If you want me to take over"... "began working on"... "Energy use"*: www.bechtel.com/BAC-Stephen-D-Bechtel-Jr.html.

87 *"hush-hush"... "alleged socialist"... "With all the secrecy"... "'gratuities' to Mexican aviation"... "would have made the uninformed"*: Anderson, February 19, 1966.

88 *"The world's most prestigious"*: *Newsweek*, August 2, 1982.

88 *"the greatest men's party"*: Peter Martin Phillips, "A Relative Advantage: Sociology of the San Francisco Bohemian Club" (dissertation, Office of Graduate Studies, University of California, Davis, 1994), 2.

88 *"that swinging Bohemian"*: William G. Domhoff, *The Bohemian Grove and Other Retreats: A Study in Ruling-Class Cohesiveness* (New York: Harper & Row, 1974), 57.

88 *"virtual personification"*: Didion, *Where I Was From*, 86.

88 *"Here, shielded from intrusion"*: McCartney, *Friends in High Places*, 13.

88 *"The all-maleness of the Club"*: Phillips, "Relative Advantage," 152.

89 *"I knew that I was in Bohemia"*: Van der Zee, *Greatest Men's Party*, 82.

89 *"Nixon declared that most"*: Wiley and Gottlieb, *Empires in the Sun*, 38.
        For the agreement between Reagan and Nixon, see Phillips, "Relative Advantage," 95. See also Domhoff, *Bohemian Grove*, 42. Domhoff's 1974 study revealed that more than 90 percent of Bohemians' political contributions went to Republicans (Phillips, "Relative Advantage," 99).

89 *"faltered"*: Larry Kramer, "Bohemian Grove: Where Big Shots Go to Camp," *New York Times*, August 14, 1977.

CHAPTER ELEVEN: COVERT CORPORATE COLLABORATION

91 *"The biggest challenge"*: Jones.

91 *"It's very unusual"*: Brechin, quoted in David Streitfeld, "A Quiet Ambition at Work; Bechtel Prides Itself on Discretion, But Its Projects, Such as the $680 Million Contract to Rebuild Iraq, Give It a High Profile," *Los Angeles Times*, June 8, 2005.

91 *"He was in a terribly difficult position"*: McCartney, *Friends in High Places*, 140.

92   *"permits common men"*: Julie Pitta, "Building a New World," *World Trade* 16, no. 8 (August 2003).

92   *"steady at the helm"*... *"function well"*... *"scout oath and laws"*... *"value of a dollar"*... *stake puncher*: Bechtel, 148.

92   *"everything a Bechtel wife"*: McCartney, *Friends in High Places*, 131.

93   *"fierce"*: Bechtel, 150.

94   *"environmentalism, globalism"*: www.bechtel.com/BAC-Stephen-D-Bechtel-Jr.tml.

94   *"Of all the business relationships"*: McCartney, *Friends in High Places*, 143.

94   *"Although ben Halim was held in high disgrace"*: Dowie, "Bechtel File," 33.

94   *"used Bechtel to build the line"*: Christopher Rand, *Making Democracy Safe for Oil: Oilmen and the Islamic East* (Boston: Little, Brown, 1975), 257.

95   *"Anyone on that committee"*: *Engineering News Record*, February 21, 1974, quoted in McCartney, *Friends in High Places*, 154.

96   *"The Indonesian Affair"*: Alan A. Block and Constance A. Weaver, *All Is Clouded by Desire: Global Banking, Money Laundering, and International Crime* (Westport, CT: Praeger, 2004), 13.

96   *"all Western interests"*: John K. Cooley, *Libyan Sandstorm* (New York: Holt, Rinehart and Winston, 1982), 13–14.

96   *"meaning independent nationalism"*: Chomsky.

97   *"covert corporate collaboration"*: Peter Kornbluh, *The Pinochet File* (New York: New Press, 2004), 97.

97   *"hammered home"*: Jack Anderson interviewed by Connie Chung on *CBS Morning News*, March 21, 1972, quoted in Mark Feldstein, *Poisoning the Press: Richard Nixon, Jack Anderson and the Rise of Washington's Scandal Culture* (New York: Farrar, Straus and Giroux, 2010), 271. See also Anderson, *Peace, War, and Politics*, 193ff.

97   *"that he had played the key role"*: Victor Marchetti and John D. Marks, *The CIA and the Cult of Intelligence* (New York: Alfred A. Knopf, 1974), 18.

       For McCone's meeting with Helms and Kissinger, see Feldstein, *Poisoning the Press*, 276.

97   *"the gentlemanly planner of assassinations"*: Thomas Powers, quoted in Morley, *Our Man in Mexico*, and in *Slate*. For Helms's claims that Nixon had ordered him to instigate the coup, see Richard Helms and William Hood, *A Look over My Shoulder: A Life in the Central Intelligence Agency* (New York: Random House, 2003), 405.

97   *"The only sin in espionage"*: Helms, quoted in Annie Jacobsen, *Area 51: An Uncensored History of America's Top Secret Military Base* (New York: Little, Brown, 2011), 252.

98   *"Kissinger asked that the plan"*: "New FRUS Volume."

98   *"In the heady days"*: Jack Devine, "What Really Happened in Chile: The CIA, the Coup Against Allende, and the Rise of Pinochet," *Foreign Affairs*, July/August 2014.

98 *"virus"* . . . *"spread contagion"*: Chomsky.

98 *"a stretch of the geopolitical imagination"*: Marchetti and Marks, *CIA and Cult of Intelligence*, 19.

99 *"Why should you care?"*: Ibid., 18.

99 *"The revolving door spins so fast"*: Greider, "Boys from Bechtel."

99 *"For a top job at Bechtel"*: Hirst, "World's at Bechtel's Beck and Call."

99 *"Washington, to bring up"*: Robert Baer, *Sleeping with the Devil: How Washington Sold Our Soul for Saudi Crude* (New York: Crown, 2003), 50.

99 *"Over the years"*: "Bechtel Responds to Inaccuracies in Media Coverage of the USAID Iraq Infrastructure Reconstruction Program Award," April 29, 2003, www.bechtel.com/2003-04-29.html.

CHAPTER TWELVE: THE ENERGY-INDUSTRIAL COMPLEX

100 *"the greatest departure"* . . . *"moved quickly in the Middle East"*: Wiley and Gottlieb, *Empires in the Sun*, 40.

101 *"twenty-year chemical fertilizer deal"*: Cooley, *Libyan Sandstorm*, 293.

101 *"of oilfield and fertilizer technology"*: Rand, *Making Democracy Safe for Oil*, 255.

102 *"You must be out of your cotton-pickin' mind"*: Jackson, quoted in McCartney, *Friends in High Places*, 161.

102 *"Any company which purchases"*: Kearns, quoted in ibid., 160.

102 *"Obviously Bechtel's firm"*: Aspin, quoted by William Clairborne, "Conflict of Interest Laid to Former Ex-Im Bank Figure," *Washington Post*, February 26, 1974, A2.

102 *"an Algerian construction project"*: Ibid.

103 *"complex web of relationships"*: Wiley and Gottlieb, *Empires in the Sun*, 38.

104 *"what may be the largest"*: Jonathan Kwitny, *The Crimes of Patriots: A True Tale of Dope, Dirty Money, and the CIA* (New York: W. W. Norton, 1987), and *Wall Street Journal*, November 2, 1975, quoted in McCartney, *Friends in High Places*, 199.

104 *"cover the Colorado Plateau"*: Wiley and Gottlieb, *Empires in the Sun*, 41.

104 *"disastrous rise"*: Eisenhower speech.

104 *"the U.S. government has not had"*: Bechtel, 162.

104 *" 'private sector' "* . . . *"can easily lead"*: Ibid., 164.

105 *"the most faggy goddamned thing"*: Watergate tape, on YouTube, www.youtube.com/watch?v=dPb-PN9F2Pc.

105 *"Hiring people in high places"*: Dowie, "Bechtel File," 34.

PART TWO: THE BECHTEL CABINET, 1973–1988

The role of Bechtel principals in the Ronald Reagan presidency is a richly documented history, especially regarding Secretary of State George Shultz and Defense Secretary Caspar Weinberger. The overview of the years 1973 to 1988 is drawn from a vast array of sources, including nonfiction books, national and international journalism, as well as thousands of pages of US government cables, scholarly papers, State Department and Defense Department memoranda, court filings, and congressional and legal hearings. Additionally, I conducted dozens of interviews with knowledgeable government and private industry sources, most notably in California and Washington, DC.

The Iran-Contra scandal has been scrutinized by numerous respected journalists and authors, and the investigations by the Justice Department, the independent counsels, and various congressional committees have resulted in a massive archive of official records.

107   *Bechtel Cabinet*: Greider, "Boys from Bechtel."

107   *"Every gun that is made"*: Eisenhower, quoted in Stephen Ambrose, *Eisenhower: Soldier and President* (New York: Simon & Schuster, 1990), 325.

CHAPTER THIRTEEN: BECHTEL'S SUPERSTAR

109   *Bechtel's Superstar*: *San Francisco Examiner*, quoted in McCartney, *Friends in High Places*, 219.

109   *"If I could choose one American"*: Kissinger, quoted in Bernard Gwertzman, "The Shultz Method," *New York Times*, January 2, 1983.

109   *"a Nixon-inspired boondoggle"*: Dowie, "Bechtel File," 34. Re: Shultz's denial of his lobbying efforts on behalf of Uranium Enrichment Associates, see: "Nomination of George P. Shultz," July 13, 1982, 54. "But in the early days of the Nixon administration, in an effort to privatize things, a decision was made—I was not a part of it . . . to encourage private companies to undertake the job of enriching uranium for the use of nuclear powerplants."

110   *"It was not"*: Thomas C. Hayes, "Bechtel: A Reclusive Giant," *New York Times*, July 8, 1982.

110   *"I understand through Secretary Shultz"*: Vasiliy F. Garbuzov to Arthur F. Burns, Chairman of the Board of Governors, Federal Reserve System. "Memorandum of Conversation," Office of the Minister, Ministry of Finance of the USSR, May 8, 1974.

110   *"The president is a very determined"*: Arthur F. Burns to Vasiliy F. Garbuzov, ibid.

110   *"mortally stricken"*: Morris, "Specialist" (Part 2).

111   *"one painstaking rung"*: McCartney, *Friends in High Places*, 170.

111   *"Buddha-like"*: Gwertzman, "Shultz Method."

112   *"just look at each other"*: Jack Lynch, quoted in McCartney, *Friends in High Places*, 171.

112   *"the leading political organization"*: Paretsky, 34.

113   *"tightly interlocked"*: Paretsky, 37.

113 *"for reforming the institutions"*: Ibid., 152.

113 *"who worship at the altar"*: Baer, Online review of *Hoodwinked*.

114 *"An echo of long"* . . . *"collisions at the tips"*: Hedrick Smith, *The Power Game: How Washington Works* (New York: Random House, 1988), 569.

114 *"Shultz and Weinberger were long-distance runners"*: Lou Cannon, *President Reagan: The Role of a Lifetime* (New York: Public Affairs, 2000), 352.

114 *"difficult to tell"*: Edmund Morris, *Dutch: A Memoir of Ronald Reagan* (New York: Random House, 1999), 463.

115 *"arguing with him"*: Smith, *Power Game*, 581.

115 *"all sails up"*: Colin Powell, quoted in Cannon, *President Reagan*, 353.

CHAPTER FOURTEEN: CAP THE KNIFE

116 *"valuable shares of Bechtel stock"*: Caspar W. Weinberger with Gretchen Roberts, *In the Arena: A Memoir of the 20th Century* (Washington, DC: Regnery, 2001), 255.

116 *"on the same political fast track"*: McCartney, *Friends in High Places*, 175.

117 *"The recruiting process"*: Weinberger with Roberts, *In the Arena*, 255.

117 *"On religious matters"*: Ibid., 16.

117 *"the year the United States"*: Ibid., 1.

117 *"sunny, optimistic"*: Ibid., 12.

118 *"he suffered"*: McCartney, *Friends in High Places*, 176.

118 *"alphabet soup of programs"* . . . *"best government was the least"*: Weinberger with Roberts, 25.

118 *"defeated the radical"*: Ibid., 126.

119 *"Peace, Prosperity, Progress"*: Ibid., 127.

119 *"splendid redwood trees"*: Ibid., 254.

119 *"As seemed to be the case"*: Ibid., 259.

120 *"like a men's club"*: McCartney, *Friends in High Places*, 191. In 1979 Bechtel settled the sex discrimination case, paying its suing female employees $1.3 million. The company settled the race discrimination case the previous year.

120 *"about potential operating"* . . . *"errors in design"*: Dowie, "Bechtel File," 35. Bechtel settled with Consumers Power for $14 million in cash and a promise to remedy the plant.

120 *"there is likely to be"*: Dr. Stephen Hanauer, quoted in McCartney, *Friends in High Places*, 199. The problems with Tarapur were first reported by Paul Jacobs, journalist, activist, and one of the founders of *Mother Jones* magazine. See Paul Jacobs, "What You Don't Know May Hurt You," *Mother Jones*, February 1976.

121 *"doesn't own the plants"*: Dowie, "Bechtel File," 35.

121 *"Bechtel sometimes likes"*: Ibid., 35–36.

122 *"a builder is measured"*: www.bechtel.com/BAC-Stephen-D-Bechtel-Sr.html.

122 *"No longer would utilities"*: Nies, *Unreal City*, 202. The FTC issued an order and decision that Kennecott's purchase of Peabody violated federal antitrust laws, putting too much control of the nation's coal reserves in the hands of a single company. Kennecott was ordered to divest itself of all interests in Peabody in June 1971. Then, in April 1974, the US Supreme Court declined to review the decision of the US Court of Appeals that upheld the FTC's order that Kennecott divest itself of Peabody. In June 1977 the FTC approved Kennecott's sale of Peabody Coal to Peabody Holding Company, a consortium made up of Newmont Mining Company (27.5 percent), Williams Companies (27.5 percent), Bechtel Corporation (15 percent), Boeing company (15 percent), Fluor Corporation (10 percent), and Equitable Life Insurance Company (5 percent).

 For the company's version of Jubail, see the Bechtel website, www.bechtel.com /BAC-Chapter-5.html.

122 *"What you* really *need"*: Weinberger with Roberts, *In the Arena*, 258.

123 *"a myriad of closely held"*: Dowie, "Bechtel File," 30.

123 *"In all the expansive"*: *Time*, July 12, 1982, quoted in McCartney, *Friends in High Places*, 208.

CHAPTER FIFTEEN: THE ARAB BOYCOTT

124 *"He's a Jewish fellow"*: McCartney, ibid., 184.

124 *"ran deep with Aryan blood"*: Margaret Lucas Montgomery, quoted in McCartney, 183.

125 *"who repeatedly"*: Ibid., 184.

125 *"by the loss of old Jerusalem"*: Robert Lacey, *The Kingdom* (New York: Harcourt Brace, 1981).

126 *"It will do grave damage"*: Kissinger, quoted in Memorandum of Telephone Conversation.

126 *"The Jews would oppose you"*: Kissinger, quoted in Memorandum of Conversation, January 7, 1976.

126 *"It amazes me"*: Ford, quoted in ibid.

127 *"in areas and in ways"*: *Washington Post.* "The Boycott Issue."

128 *"The Saudis have thrown"*: *Jewish Telegraphic Agency*, May 9, 1978.

 For details about the "Church Committee" hearings and published volumes, see the Assassination Archives and Research Center, www.aarclibrary.org/publib /church/reports/contents.htm.

 For details about "The Family Jewels," see the 1992 declassified documents obtained by the nongovernmental National Security Archive, "Family Jewels." Memorandum for Executive Secretary, CIA Management Committee, May 16, 1973, declassified June 2007, National Security Archive.

128 *"Despite its [Bechtel's] prominent"*: Thomas J. Lueck, "Bechtel Loses Another Officer to Reagan's Cabinet," *New York Times*, June 26, 1982.

The case brought by Attorney General Edward Levi was eventually settled by consent decree, although Congress considered—unsuccessfully—going further and imposing criminal penalties against companies and executives who observed the boycott.

129 *"With the benefit of hindsight"*: Bechtel.

CHAPTER SIXTEEN: THE PACIFIC REPUBLIC

130 *"Reputed to be"* . . . *"grandfather of corporate"*: Paretsky, 107–8.

131 *"What John Connally stands for"*: Ibid., 113.

131 *"we create a United States oil company"*: Ibid.

131 *"aimed mainly"*: Paul Burka, "The Truth About John Connally," *Texas Monthly,* November 1979.

131 *"candidate of the oil interests"* . . . *"smacks of trading"* . . . *"more like an energy program"* . . . *"represents a fundamental shift"* . . . *"is not a bargaining chip"* . . . *"rehashing the stale"*: *Jewish Telegraphic Agency,* October 15, 1979.

132 *had become "acute"*: Cannon, *President Reagan,* 202.

133 *"how the federal government worked"*: Shultz, quoted in ibid., 202.

133 *"Cap's being at Bechtel"*: Mayman, quoted in McCartney, *Friends in High Places,* 218.

134 *"Republicans as well as Democrats"*: Hedrick Smith, *Who Stole the American Dream* (New York: Random House, 2012), 8.

134 *"The lack of a US energy"*: www.bechtel.com/BAC-Chapter-5.html.

134 *"We found ourselves"*: Catherine Austin Fitts, "Dillon, Read & Co. Inc. and the Aristocracy of Stock Profits," 2006, www.dunwalke.com/introduction.htm.

135 *"little acorns"*: www.bechtel.com/BAC-Chapter-6.html.

135 *"We can afford"*: Shultz, quoted in *Forbes,* December 7, 1981. (See McCartney, *Friends in High Places,* 220.)

135 *"less often mentioned"* . . . *"Through the holding"* . . . *"The booklet is long"*: "Bechtel's Dance of the Seven Veils," *Economist,* May 18, 1981.

136 *"Pacific Republic"*: Wiley and Gottlieb, *Empires in the Sun,* 76.

136 *"Ronald Reagan represented"* . . . *"The West was"*: Ibid., 304.

136 *"Republican presidents"*: "The Workhorse Returns," *Economist,* July 3, 1982.

CHAPTER SEVENTEEN: THE BECHTEL BABIES

137 *"When Reagan named"* . . . *"the hard-eyed"* . . . *"He is one of the few"*: Brownstein and Easton, *Reagan's Ruling Class,* 433–34.

138 *"had heard"*: Gwertzman, "Shultz Method."

138 *"not really one company"*: Mark Dowie et al., "Bechtel: A Tale of Corruption," *Multinational Monitor* 5, no. 5 (May 1984).

138 *"Literally at the moment"*: Alan Friedman, *Spider's Web: The Secret History of How the White House Illegally Armed Iraq* (New York: Bantam Books, 1993), xvi.

139 *"In an administration"*: H. W. Brands, *The Devil We Knew: Americans and the Cold War* (New York: Oxford University Press, 1993), 169.

139 *"pro-Arab disposition"*: Stephan B. Zatuchni and Daniel B. Drooz, "Back Door to the PLO," *Los Angeles Herald Examiner*, August 2, 1982.

139 *"seemed to go out of his way"*: Oliver North with William Novak, *Under Fire: An American Story* (New York: HarperCollins, 1991), 154–55.

139 *"Caspar Weinberger has reversed"*: Biden, quoted in Zatuchni and Drooz, "Back Door to the PLO."

139 *"Weinberger had almost a visceral dislike"*: Hilary Leila Krieger, "Former Senior U.S. Defense Official Korb to Make Case for Pollard's Release at Knesset," *Jerusalem Post*, December 19, 2010.

139 *"predilection to support Saudi Arabia"*... *"Weinberger believes"*: Zatuchni and Drooz, "Back Door to the PLO."

139 *"Weinberger's anti-Israel tilt"*: Joe Conason, " 'Most Antagonistic' Toward Israel? That Would Be Ronald Reagan's Defense Secretary," Creators Syndicate, January 10, 2013, https://www.creators.com/liberal/joe-conason/-most-antagonistic-toward-israel-that-would-be-ronald-reagan-s-defense-secretary.html.

139 *"Others believed it was more complicated"*: Ibid.

140 *"redirect"*... *"seem to have differing assessments"*... *"of being hostile"*... *"neglected its ties"*: Bernard Gwertzman, "Reagan Aides at Odds," *New York Times*, February 15, 1982.

140 *"Bechtel oil group"*: Kondracke, quoted in *Jewish Telegraphic Agency*, August 18, 1981.

140 *"Cap, you talk about"*: Kirkpatrick, quoted in Howard Teicher and Gayle Radley Teicher, *Twin Pillars to Desert Storm: America's Flawed Vision in the Middle East from Nixon to Bush* (New York: William Morrow, 1993), 204.

141 *"The AWACS deal"*: Bechtel letter, quoted in McCartney, *Friends in High Places*, 223. See also "Nomination of George P. Shultz."

141 *"This was a policy in which"*: Angelo M. Codevilla, a former senior staff member of the Senate Intelligence Committee and professor of international relations at Boston University, quoted in Rebekah Israel, "American Responses to Israeli Foreign Policy Initiatives" (unpublished paper presented at the annual meeting of the Southern Political Science Association, Hotel Intercontinental, New Orleans, LA, January 7, 2009), http://citation.allacademic.com/meta/p273901_index.html.

141 *"the Bechtel Babies"*: Shaw, *Miscarriage of Justice*, 129.

142 *"the sale to Iraq"*: Michael Dobbs, "U.S. Had Key Role in Iraq Buildup: Trade in Chemical Arms Allowed Despite Their Use on Iranians, Kurds," *Washington Post*, December 30, 2002.

142 *"activist CIA director"*... *"the Israelis began"*: Joseph J. Trento, *The Secret History of the CIA* (New York: MJF Books, 2001), 445–46.

142 *"the boys from Bechtel"*: Greider, "Boys from Bechtel."

142 *"tough-talking"*: Shultz, quoted in John Boykin, *Cursed Is the Peacemaker: The American Diplomat Versus the Israeli General, Beirut 1982* (Washington, DC: Applegate Press, Diplomats and Diplomacy Series, 2002), xii.

142 *"There may be a change"* . . . *"Yes, but I have to wait"* . . . *"George, you have thirty-six hours"*: Miller Center.

143 *"It's not a good idea"*: George P. Shultz, *Turmoil and Triumph: My Years as Secretary of State* (New York: Charles Scribner's, 1993), 3.

143 *"I was shocked"*: *Newsweek*, July 12, 1982, quoted in McCartney, *Friends in High Places*, 222.

143 *"Bill, I want you to tell President Reagan"* . . . *"My experience was"*: William P. Clark, quoted in Miller Center.

143 *"sniping or guerrilla warfare"*: Nixon, quoted in McCartney, *Friends in High Places*, 222.

144 *"Reagan seems to have had"* . . . *"As it turned out"*: Cannon, *President Reagan*, 352.

CHAPTER EIGHTEEN: THE REAGANAUTS

145 *"There are too many people from Bechtel in this administration"*: *Washington Post*, December 14, 1982.

145 *"providing artful"*: Greider, "Boys from Bechtel."

145 *"a company with a long history"*: Wiley and Gottlieb, *Empires in the Sun*, 308.

146 *"I . . . took some jabs"* . . . *"A hot issue"*: Shultz, *Turmoil and Triumph*, 19.

146 *"If I have any differences"*: Shultz, quoted in Hayes, "Bechtel: A Reclusive Giant."

146 *"We did not go around twisting arms"*: Shultz in "Nomination of George P. Shultz," 51.

146 *" 'the entire gamut' "* . . . *"curb the spread"* . . . *"weakened our diplomatic efforts"*: "Nomination of George P. Shultz," 55–56.

147 *"Cranston took me on"* . . . *"stand up"*: Shultz, *Turmoil and Triumph*, 19.

147 *"smear against Bechtel"* . . . *"Well, now, wait a minute"* . . . *"ever . . . undercut"*: "Nomination of George P. Shultz," 56.

147 *"pervasive"*: Metzenbaum, quoted in *Jewish Telegraphic Agency*, July 19, 1982.

147 *"very, very serious matter"*: Boykin, *Cursed Is the Peacemaker*, 179.

147 *"actively lobbies"*: *New York Times*, July 26, 1982.

148 *"an employee or consultant"* . . . *"beware"*: "Bechtel Responds to Inaccuracies in Media Coverage of the USAID Iraq Infrastructure Reconstruction Program Award," April 29, 2003, www.bechtel.com/2003-04-29.html. The *International Directory of Company Histories*, Vol. 99, also identifies Casey as a Bechtel consultant.

148 *"Bechtel is controlling"*: Candidate George Sheldon, quoted in Boykin, *Cursed Is the Peacemaker*, 180.

148 *"gave the stink little thought"* . . . *"understanding with George"* . . . *"about the facts of life"*: Ibid.

148 *"implication of any conflict"*: New York Times, July 26, 1982.

148 *"having Lebanese blood"*: Boykin, Cursed Is the Peacemaker, 180.

148 *"The essential point"*: Greider, "Boys from Bechtel."

148 *"insinuations about"... "rising tide"*: www.bechtel.com/BAC-Chapter-6.html.

149 *"the most hawkish"*: Naomi Oreskes and Erik M. Conway, Merchants of Doubt (New York: Bloomsbury Press, 2010), 38.

149 *"The antinuclear propaganda"*: Teller, quoted in the Wall Street Journal, June 16, 1979. See McCartney, Friends in High Places, 225.

149 *"became obsessed with proving"*: Bechtel executive, quoted in McCartney, 224.

150 *"as more than a propaganda"... "What its slick"*: Howard Kurtz, "Hiding a Lobby Behind a Name: Why Not Truth in Labeling for Interest Groups?" Washington Post, January 27, 1985.

150 *"pride and joy"*: Michael J. Graetz, The End of Energy: The Unmaking of America's Environment, Security, and Independence (Cambridge: Massachusetts Institute of Technology Press, 2011), 148.

151 *"If the Reagan administration"*: Brownstein and Easton, Reagan's Ruling Class, 144.

151 *"the story goes"*: Fehner, 1.

151 *"few megaprojects"*: www.bechtel.com/BAC-Chapter-6.html.

151 *"For one thing"*: Nies, Unreal City, 200.

151 *"We have to approach"... "bailout teams"*: www.bechtel.com/BAC-Chapter-6.html.

152 *"Winning FUSRAP"... "It gave us"*: www.bechtel.com/2007-07-13.html.

CHAPTER NINETEEN: A WORLD AWASH IN PLUTONIUM

153 *"sufficiently alarmed"... "Bechtel Cabinet"... "their private interests"*: Greider, "Boys from Bechtel."

153 *"Four Horsemen of the Non-Apocalypse"... "as a threat to the world"*: The Four Horsemen are former secretary of state George Shultz; former US senator Sam Nunn; former secretary of state Henry Kissinger; and former secretary of defense William Perry, as part of the Nuclear Security Project created in 2007, www.nuclearsecurityproject.org.

154 *"a legitimate need"*: Greider, "Boys from Bechtel."

154 *"the Antichrist"*: Amory Lovins, quoted in Brownstein and Easton, Reagan's Ruling Class, 153.

155 *"open secret"*: McCartney, Friends in High Places, 226.

156 *"When the average person"... "Shaped the way"*: Fehner, 1.

156 *"was a separate state"*: Marks, quoted in Richard Rhodes, Dark Sun: The Making of the Hydrogen Bomb (New York: Simon & Schuster, 1995), 231.

157 *"Bechtel was the poster child"*: Interview, David Hill, August 13, 2013.

158 *"a market Bechtel had"*: McCartney, Friends in High Places, 228.

158 *"Employing former government officials"*: Bechtel, 161–62.

159 *"It's more effective"*: McCartney, 156.

CHAPTER TWENTY: IT WOULD BE A TERRIBLE MESS

160 *"size of the Soviet buildup"*: Weinberger, quoted in Brownstein and Easton, *Reagan's Ruling Class*, 434. For discussion of the US miscalculations regarding the Soviet buildup, see Ronald Powaski's *March to Armageddon* and James Lebovic's *Flawed Logics*.

161 *"To paraphrase Will Rogers"*: Congressman Les Aspin, quoted in ibid., 451.

161 *"The government has a long history"* . . . *"government-subsidized"*: Dan Briody, *The Iron Triangle: Inside the Secret World of the Carlyle Group* (Hoboken, NJ: John Wiley & Sons, 2003), 42.

161 *"Our long-term goal"*: Weinberger, quoted in Brownstein and Easton, *Reagan's Ruling Class*, 451.

161 *"from virtually every domestic"*: Ibid., 450.

162 *"is really running things"*: Meese, quoted in ibid., 645.

162 *"swamp"*: David Stockman, quoted in ibid., 453.

163 *"Reagan and Weinberger"*: Norris, quoted in ibid., 455.

163 *"The only purposes"* . . . *"It is difficult to see"*: Smith, quoted in ibid., 455.

163 *"Cold War cabal"*: Robert Scheer, *With Enough Shovels: Reagan, Bush and Nuclear War* (New York: Random House, 1982), 5.

163 *"threat inflators"* . . . *"dourly predict"*: Ibid., 38.

164 *"My idea of American policy"*: Reagan, quoted in Donald Rumsfeld, *Known and Unknown* (New York: Sentinel, 2011), 12. For details about Reagan's anti-nuclear proliferation stance, see Paul Lettow, *Ronald Reagan and His Quest to Abolish Nuclear Weapons*.

164 *"I have read the book of Revelation"*: Weinberger, quoted in Scheer, *With Enough Shovels*, 2.

164 *"rightist suspicions"*: Ibid., 41.

164 *"It would be a terrible mess"*: Louis Onorato Giuffrida, quoted in ibid., 3.

164 *"This would kill"*: Oreskes and Conway, *Merchants of Doubt*, 49.

165 *"the boys from Bechtel"* . . . *"As long as policy making"* . . . *"commercialism"* . . . *"economic greed"*: Churba, quoted in *Jewish Telegraphic Agency*, January 19, 1983.

165 *"the administration is suffering"*: George Arzt, "Cap Calls Saudi Story 'Fabrication,' " *New York Post*, August 19, 1983.

165 *"I would like to confirm"* . . . *"tryout"* . . . *"model is not"* . . . *"appalled"* . . . *"access to information"*: George Arzt, "Koch Blasts Caspar," *New York Post*, August 18, 1983.

166 *"hostility to the State"* . . . *"a secret supergovernment"* . . . *"fabrication"* . . . *"not to reveal details"*: "The Koch-Weinberger Letters: An Exchange of Rejoinders on the Mideast," *New York Times*, November 9, 1983.

CHAPTER TWENTY-ONE: ULTIMATE INSIDERS

167 *"young pup" . . . "feet" . . . "cluster of geniuses"*: Rumsfeld, quoted in Naomi Klein, *The Shock Doctrine: The Rise of Disaster Capitalism* (New York: Picador, 2007), 65. See also Klein, 611, n. 5.

167 *"preference for uniformed"*: Morris, "Undertaker's Tally" (Part 1).

168 *"After the Iranian"*: St. Clair, "Bechtel, More Powerful Than the U.S. Army," 7.

168 *"unpaid government employee" . . . "simply wanted to be helpful"*: Rumsfeld, *Known and Unknown*, 13.

168 *"almost daily use"*: Julian Borger, "Rumsfeld 'Offered to Help Saddam': Declassified Papers Leave the White House Hawk Exposed over His Role During the Iran-Iraq War," *Guardian* (Manchester, UK), December 31, 2002.

168 *"We believed the Iraqis"*: Rick Francona, quoted in ibid.

A United Nations team provided the first outside confirmation that Iraq used chemical weapons in a March 26, 1984, report, "which was released the same day that Rumsfeld met with Aziz to repitch the pipeline plan," according to Jim Vallette, with Steve Kretzmann and Daphne Wysham, *Crude Vision: How Oil Interests Obscured U.S. Government Focus on Chemical Weapons Use by Saddam Hussein*, 2nd ed. (Washington, DC: Institute for Policy Studies, August 13, 2003), 11.

168 *"whatever was necessary and legal"*: Borger, "Rumsfeld 'Offered to Help Saddam.' "

169 *"Acting as a special White House"*: David Lindorff, "Secret Bechtel Documents Reveal: Yes, It Is About Oil," *Counterpunch*, April 9, 2003.

The State Department memoranda were declassified in February 2003 by the National Archives and published by IPS, *Washington Post*, and other journalism and public outlets.

169 *"I said I could understand"*: Rumsfeld declassified memo, quoted in Bob Herbert, "Ultimate Insiders," *New York Times*, April 14, 2003.

169 *"the revolving door" . . . "shaped and implemented" . . . "bent many rules"*: Vallette with Kretzmann and Wysham, *Crude Vision*, 2.

169 *"sordid tale" . . . "focused on getting a pipeline" . . . "Hussein's troops"*: Vallette, quoted on *Smiley*.

169 *"a bagman for Bechtel"*: Vallette, quoted in Lindorff, "Secret Bechtel Documents Reveal."

169 *"ruthless little bastard"*: Nixon, quoted in Klein, *Shock Doctrine*, 357.

170 *"As Saddam was gassing the Kurds"*: "Rumsfeld's Dealings with Saddam: Were Trips to Iraq Meant to Secure Pipeline Deal?" *Village Voice*, April 1, 2003.

According to Vallette, when United Nations weapons inspectors arrived in Iraq in 1991, they declared the industrial complex PC-2 was a major part of the "smoking gun" that proved Iraq was pursuing a Weapons of Mass Destruction program. Vallette with Kretzmann and Wysham, *Crude Vision*, 7.

170 *"went on to talk glowingly"*: Barry M. Lando, *Web of Deceit: The History of Western Complicity in Iraq, from Churchill to Kennedy to George W. Bush* (New York: Other Press, 2007), 69.

170 *"He was there to beg"*: St. Clair, "Bechtel, More Powerful Than the U.S. Army."

170 *"at State's invitation"*: Vallette with Kretzmann and Wysham, *Crude Vision*, 13.

170 *"Out of public view"* . . . *"composed Donald Rumsfeld's pipeline pitch"*: Ibid., 3.

170 *"were withheld from me at the time"*: Shultz, *Turmoil and Triumph*, 238n.

170 *"The problem now is for Iraq"* . . . *"support and sanctuary"*: "Briefing Notes for Rumsfeld Visit to Baghdad," Cable from Secretary of State George Shultz to American Embassy in Sudan, Secret, March 27, 1984, declassified November 14, 1996, w2.gwu.edu/~nsarchiv/NSAEBB/NSAEBB82/iraq48.pdf.

In a memorandum dated May 3, 1985, Bechtel executive Eugene Moriarty explained to a Jordanian official: "Although Mr. Shultz has isolated himself from the pipeline project because of Bechtel's involvement, if HRH [King Hussein] or any of his staff initiate a discussion about Jordan's petroleum development and the related pipeline project, Mr. Shultz may not react directly, but his staff will be aware of the situation and will be in a position to do so on his behalf." 17.

For his part, Rumsfeld would write in his memoir that he discussed with Saddam "a proposal to funnel Iraqi oil" through the Aqaba pipeline "at the State Department's request." Rumsfeld, *Known and Unknown*, 6–7.

Another news account contradicts Shultz's claims that he had recused himself from all Bechtel-related matters. According to Jeffrey St. Clair, Shultz "closely reviewed a top secret State Department cable which spelled out Saddam's fears regarding Israeli sabotage and speculated about ways in which they might be addressed by the Reagan administration. In response to Rumsfeld's interest in seeing Iraq increase oil exports, including through a possible new pipeline across Jordan to Aqaba, Saddam suggested Israeli threat to security of such a line was major concern and US might be able to provide some assurances in this regard.'" St. Clair, "Bechtel, More Powerful Than the U.S. Army," 8.

171 *"Contrary to mistaken critics"*: www.bechtel.com. April 29, 2003. Jonathan Marshall, Bechtel's then media relations director, maintained that Shultz's name appeared on the State Department cables as a matter of "formality" because "all outgoing State Department memos carry the name of the top ranking department officer in Washington." Vallette, Kretzmann, and Wysham, *Crude Vision*, 16.

For the role of George H. W. Bush in lobbying for the pipeline, see Mark Hosenball, "The Odd Couple," *New Republic*, June 1, 1992.

171 *"Stocked as it was"*: St. Clair, "Bechtel, More Powerful Than the U.S. Army," 8.

171 *"an insurance company"*: Allard.

171 *"Bechtel, U.S. government officials"*: Vallette, Kretzmann, and Wysham, *Crude Vision*, 14.

171 *"I cannot emphasize enough"*: Bechtel executive H. B. Scott, quoted in Lindorff, "Secret Bechtel Documents Reveal."

172 *"the ways in which oil interests"*: Vallette, Kretzmann, and Wysham, *Crude Vision*, 9.

172 *"worked hand-in-glove"*: Ibid., 12.

172 *"company was virtually an unofficial expediter"*: Friedman, *Spider's Web*, 29.

172 *"Whatever misgivings we had"*: Rumsfeld, *Known and Unknown*, 4.

172 *"prepare a plan of action"*: "Pipeline Project" (Washington, DC: Government Printing Office, 1988); "Measures to Improve U.S. Posture and Readiness to Respond to Developments in the Iran-Iraq War," Top Secret National Security Decision Directive 139, April 5, 1984, declassified August 18, 1994, www2.gwu.edu/~nsarchiv/NSAEBB/NSAEBB82/iraq53.pdf.

172 *"I hope they kill each other"*: Kissinger, quoted in Lando, *Web of Deceit*, 48.

173 *"My meeting with Saddam"*: Rumsfeld, *Known and Unknown*, 6.

173 *"no mention"*: Borger, "Rumsfeld 'Offered to Help Saddam.' "

173 *"No one seemed concerned"*: Herbert, "Ultimate Insiders."

CHAPTER TWENTY-TWO: A WITCH'S BREW

174 *"Jews were overly sensitive"*: Pollard, "First Memorandum In Aid of Sentencing," 15. Declassified November 13, 2014, http://www.archives.gov/declassification/iscap/pdf/2013-084-doc2.pdf.

   When exactly Pollard began spying for Israel remains a matter of dispute. Pollard told the US Justice Department that he began spying in July 1984 and that he offered his services rather than having been recruited. Investigative journalist Seymour Hersh reported that Pollard "offered to supply Israel with intelligence as early as 1980, but was not recruited as an operative until the fall of 1981, three years earlier than he and the Israeli government have admitted." Seymour Hersh, *The Samson Option: Israel's Nuclear Arsenal and American Foreign Policy* (New York: Random House, 1991), 285. The CIA Damage Assessment of the Pollard case states that his spying began in June 1984. *The Jonathan Jay Pollard Espionage Case: A Damage Assessment.* Authors Loftus and Aarons, who have written extensively about Pollard, claim that he was recruited in 1984 by "a group of right-wing Israeli politicians." Loftus and Aarons, *Secret War*, 473.

174 *"To Pollard, that comment"*: Shaw, *Miscarriage of Justice*, 1. Jonathan Marshall, a classmate of Pollard's at Stanford who, ironically, would go on to become Media Relations Manager for Bechtel, described Pollard to the *New York Times* as "a committed Zionist, but fairly liberal" on Middle East politics. Marshall, quoted in Wolf Blitzer, *Territory of Lies: The Exclusive Story of Jonathan Jay Pol-*

lard: The American Who Spied on His Country for Israel and How He Was Betrayed (New York: Harper & Row, 1989), 36.

174 *"The US Navy"*: "Defendant Jonathan J. Pollard's First Memorandum," 14.

174 *"short but intensive"*... *"technological Pearl Harbor"*: *The Jonathan Jay Pollard Espionage Case*, v–viii.

174 *"the details of Iraq's"*: Blitzer, *Territory of Lies*, 166.

174 *"Amalek Complex"*: Pollard, quoted in Bernard R. Henderson, *Pollard: The Spy's Story* (New York: Alpha Books, 1988), 196.

175 *"the focus of American strategic concern"*: Blitzer, *Territory of Lies*, 208.

175 *"a witch's brew"*: William Blum, *Killing Hope: U.S. Military and CIA Interventions Since World War II* (Monroe, ME: Common Courage Press, 1995). See also *United States Export Policy*.

175 *"It wasn't just a tilt"*: Ted Koppel, "How U.S. Arms and Technology Were Transferred to Iraq," *Nightline*, ABC News, September 13, 1991.

175 *"higher-than-secret"*: Bernard R. Henderson, *Pollard: The Spy's Story* (New York: Alpha Books, 1988), 11, ff.

175 *"was to be the pride"*: Friedman, *Spider's Web*, 117.

176 *"We were hired"*: Tom Flynn, a senior vice president at Bechtel, quoted by Alan Friedman, "Warning Forced Bechtel out of Iraq Chemical Project," *Financial Times*, February 21, 1991.

176 *"fuel air explosive bombs"*: *United States Export Policy*, 71.

176 *"direct encouragement"*: Flynn, quoted by Friedman, "Warning Forced Bechtel."

176 *"I watched the threats"*: "Defendant Jonathan J. Pollard's First Memorandum," 16.

176 *"As Diaspora Jews"*: Bernard Henderson, 42.

177 *"My parents never ceased"*... *"The first flag"*: *The Jonathan Jay Pollard Espionage Case* (Personal History).

177 *"he had begun dreaming"*: Ibid., iv.

177 *"had traveled with his father"*: Bernard Henderson, 11 ff.

177 *"growing determination"*... *"managed to gain the respect"*... *"temperamental genius"*... *"outstanding"*: *Jonathan Jay Pollard Espionage Case*.

177 *"looked like a blueprint"*: IMRA.

177 *"It was widely known"*: Pollard, quoted in Blitzer, *Territory of Lies*, 209.

179 *"to provide Israel"*... *"collection requirements"*: *Jonathan Jay Pollard Espionage Case*, v–viii. According to a 2013 author interview with investigative reporter Seymour Hersh, who has written about the Pollard Affair, Pollard's handler, Eitan, was trading Pollard's classified information with the Soviet Union in exchange for help in getting Jews out of Russia.

Kurt Lohbek, Pollard's friend and, according to Pollard, fellow spy, described Eitan as "the former deputy chief of operations for the Mossad who was involved in the Adolph Eichmann affair." At the time he was Pollard's handler, according to Lohbeck, Eitan "headed a small, highly covert intelligence section of the Israeli Defense Ministry called 'Lakam.' Passed over for promotion as head of the Mossad, he was described as having a 'score to settle with Mossad.' " Kurt Lohbeck, *Holy War, Unholy Victory: Eyewitness to the CIA's Secret War in Afghanistan* (Washington, DC: Regnery Gateway, 1993), 132. Pollard also claimed that Eitan was involved in "some type of intense bureaucratic competition with the Mossad." Shaw, *Miscarriage of Justice*, 99.

CHAPTER TWENTY-THREE: THE TERRITORY OF LIES

180   *The Territory of Lies*: Pollard, quoted in Blitzer, *Territory of Lies*.

180   *"known and appreciated"*: *Jonathan Jay Pollard Espionage Case*, v–viii.

180   *"the urgency of their requests"*: Blitzer, *Territory of Lies*, 102.

180   *"shocked the hell out of them"*: Pollard, quoted in Elliot Goldenberg, *The Hunting Horse: The Truth Behind the Jonathan Pollard Spy Case* (New York: Prometheus Books, 2000), 213.

180   *"Everything I seemed"*: Blitzer, *Territory of Lies*, 102.

For more about the chemical warfare complex, see Goldenberg, *Hunting Horse*, 211.

181   *"What was I supposed to do?"*: Pollard, quoted in Barouch Levy, "Pollard and the U.S. Government: A Polity of Amorality," *Arutz Sheva*, November 28, 2014.

181   *"together with U.S."*: Wesley Phelan, "The True Motives Behind the Sentencing of Jonathan Pollard" (interview with Angelo Codevilla), *Washington Weekly*, January 11, 1999.

181   *"were of a number"*: Crovitz, "Even Pollard Deserves."

Lohbeck would contend that he never purchased any classified documents from Pollard, but rather was used by Pollard as a "red herring to throw [FBI agents] off the trail of the Israeli agent" who had bought the documents. Pollard identified Lohbeck as "a recognized liaison to the [Afghan] mujahideen" who had access to classified documents. Also see Erwin Knoll, "Journalistic Jihad: Holes in the Coverage of a Holy War," *Progressive*, May 1990, 17–22.

181   *"Jay laughed"*: Lohbeck, 133.

181   *"Wiping away beaded perspiration"* . . . *"You must leave!"* . . . *"get out"*: Shaw, *Miscarriage of Justice*, 37–38.

182   *"told his parents"*: Ibid., 62. The movie *Three Days of the Condor* is based upon the 1974 spy thriller written by investigative reporter James Grady.

182   *"deliver the knockout punch"*: Ibid., 127.

182   *"to conceive of a greater harm"*: Supplemental Declaration.

182   *"severe punishment"* . . . *"magnitude of the treason"*: Declaration of the Secretary, 45.

182   *"As secretary of state"*: Gil Hoffman, "George Shultz Urges Obama to Free Pollard," *Jerusalem Post*, January 12, 2011.

183 *"a slender child"*: Ronald J. Olive, *Capturing Jonathan Pollard: How One of the Most Notorious Spies in American History Was Brought to Justice* (Annapolis, MD: Naval Institute Press, 2006), 7.

183 *"mama's boy"*: Shaw, *Miscarriage of Justice*, 48.

183 *"sounded like something"*: Letter from Pollard to his father, quoted in Shaw, *Miscarriage of Justice*, 149.

183 *"I would rather spend"*: Pollard, quoted in Levy, "Pollard and the U.S. Government."

183 *"Jews judging Jews"*: Shaw, *Miscarriage of Justice*, 153.

183 *"American counterpart"*: Levy, "Pollard and the U.S. Government."

183 *"should have been shot"*: Weinberger, quoted in Blitzer, *Territory of Lies*, 238.

184 *"contradicted what the US government"*: Phelan, "True Motives Behind Sentencing of Jonathan Pollard."

184 *"Year of the Spy"*: The CIA dubbed 1985 the Year of the Spy because fourteen Americans were arrested and/or convicted of spying for the Soviet Union and its allies, as well as for Israel, China, and Ghana. Included were John Walker, Edward Lee Howard, Aldrich Ames, and Robert Hanssen.

185 *"busted the most secret"* . . . *"Neither Pollard nor the government"*: Loftus and Aarons, *Secret War*, 402. Loftus and Aarons contend that by fixing the beginning date for Iran-Contra in 1985 rather than in 1984, as Pollard contended, the Reagan administration attempted to scapegoat Israel. "In its rush to conclude the Iran-Contra inquiry in just three months, Congress ignored several leads to the 1984 French connection and started its investigation with the Israeli involvement in 1985. As a result, Congress missed the beginning of the Iran-Contra affair by a full year. No one even asked [coconspirators] North, or Bush, or Gregg, or McFarlane what he was doing in 1984 and before. Congress fell for the cover story and assumed that the Israelis began the first arms-for-hostages deal in the summer of 1985." Loftus and Aarons, *Secret War*, 455.

    As scholars Block and Weaver put it, "neither the commission, nor the independent counsel, nor the congressional committees that investigated the ensuing scandals, got it right. The US sale of weapons to Iran was assuredly begun prior to the hostage taking in Lebanon. There is some intimation of this in a congressional research service paper written by Richard M. Preece in January 1984 and updated that August. Preece noted that by 1983, a considerable illicit traffic in U.S. arms to Iran had developed." Block and Weaver, *All Is Clouded by Desire*, 89.

    Block and Weaver contend that the idea of clandestine sales of US weapons to Iran "originated in summer 1984, when international arms dealers—Adnan Khashoggi, and most importantly Manucher Ghorbanifar, a former Savak officer (Iranian intelligence organization under the shah)—desired to move the United States and Iran into an 'arms relationship.' " Ibid., 87.

185 *"Joseph DiGenova"* . . . *"He has argued"*: Goldenberg, *Hunting Horse*, 16.

185 *"The Hunting Horse"*: Ibid., 2.

185 *"History proved"*: Shaw, *Miscarriage of Justice*, 129. Regarding Reagan's speech denying Weinberger's culpability, see Shaw, *Miscarriage of Justice*, 147.

186 *"With my eyes shut"*: Pollard, "First Memorandum In Aid of Sentencing," August 20, 1986. Classified "Secret." Declassified November 13, 2014, *U.S. National Archives.*

A 2014 book based upon tens of thousands of pages of recently declassified documents obtained by the National Security Archive placed Reagan at the center of the 1980s Iran-Contra scandal. The book, *Iran-Contra: Reagan's Scandal and the Unchecked Abuse of Presidential Power* by Malcolm Byrne (University Press of Kansas), shows that Reagan "stood at the epicenter of the scandal both in terms of his willingness to break the law in order to free American hostages in Lebanon and his failure to take account of the costs and consequences of his decisions, including the illicit conduct of numerous aides." National Security Archive Electronic Briefing Book No. 483, posted September 5, 2014, www2.gwu.edu/~nsarchiv /NSAEBB/NSAEBB483.

CHAPTER TWENTY-FOUR: A TANGLED SCHEME

187 *"the most dangerous breach"*: Lawrence E. Walsh, *Firewall: The Iran-Contra Conspiracy and Cover-Up* (New York: W. W. Norton, 1997), jacket copy.

187 *"At the time"*: Ibid., xiv.

188 *"One of the most complicated"*: www.washingtonpost.com/wp-srv/politics/special /clinton/frenzy/iran.htm.

188 *"a tangled scheme"*: Dwyer et al., quoted in Loftus and Aarons, *Secret War*, 489.

188 *"Saddam may have been"*: St. Clair, "Bechtel, More Powerful Than the U.S. Army," 8.

188 *"offended"* ... *"underlying hostility"*: Malcolm Byrne, "Saddam Hussein: More Secret History," National Security Archive, George Washington University's Gelman Library, www2.gwu.edu/~nsarchiv/NSAEBB/NSAEBB107.

189 *"the depth of Iraqi feeling"* ... *"global lobbying blitz"*: Dwyer et al., "Bechtel's Iraqi Pipe Dream Could Land It in Hot Water," *BusinessWeek*, February 22, 1988, 33.

189 *"surfaced in several"*: Block and Weaver, *All Is Clouded by Desire*, 71. Rappaport had also played a key role in the CIA's secret financial aid to the Afghan rebels fighting Soviet troops, "a program constructed by Casey when he became the Agency's director." Ibid., 27.

189 *"In a project where the lines"*: Vallette, Kretzmann, and Wysham, *Crude Vision*, 21.

189 *"a reduction worth $650 million"*: *New York Times*, February 25, 1988.

189 *"I am following with great interest"*: Peres, quoted in Block and Weaver, *All Is Clouded by Desire*, 78–79.

190 *"anything of value"*: George Lardner, "Pipeline Promoter to Aid in Probe: Special Counsel Gives Rappaport Immunity in Meese Investigation," *Washington Post*, March 5, 1988.

At the same time that McKay and Walsh were investigating the machinations surrounding the Aqaba pipeline, the FBI was targeting Bechtel in a probe involving the bribery of South Korean officials in possible violation of the 1977 Foreign Corrupt Practices Act. "A whistleblower who was highly placed in Bechtel and familiar with the alleged corruption has told the FBI that he has reason to believe that Weinberger knew about it," according to a team of investigative reporters who examined the events that occurred between 1978 and 1980, while Weinberger and Shultz were top executives at Bechtel. In 1977 the Seoul government announced plans to build twenty-one nuclear plants, and President Jimmy Carter dispatched John L. Moore, head of Ex-Im Bank, to South Korea "to convey the bank's support for the newly installed military regime." A short time later, Bechtel lured Moore away from Ex-Im with the creation of a new position for him as executive vice president for financing services. See Dowie et al., "Bechtel: A Tale of Corruption."

190 *"most derided"*: Shultz, *Turmoil and Triumph*, 834.

190 *"The twists and turns"*: George Lardner, "Iraqi Pipeline: Exploiting Security, Project Illustrates Use of U.S. Interests by Business Promoters," *Washington Post*, February 1, 1988.

190 *"a protection racket"*: Lardner, "Pipeline Promoter to Aid in Probe."

190 *"use of under-the-table"*: Michael Wines and Ronald J. Ostrow, "Pipeline Deal: How Private Citizens Use Public Power," *Los Angeles Times*, February 7, 1988.

191 *"quid pro quo"*: Rappaport, quoted in Vallette, Kretzmann, and Wysham, *Crude Vision*, 6.

191 *"What is clear"*: Joan Mower, "Clash of Interests: Iran-Contra, Pipeline Scandals Strain U.S.-Israeli Ties," *Sun-Sentinel* (Fort Lauderdale, Florida), March 27, 1988.

191 *"That unwelcome attention"*: Stephen Labaton, "Role in Scuttled Iraqi Pipeline Brings U.S. Probe to Bechtel," *Globe and Mail* (Toronto), February 25, 1988.

191 *"becoming an object"*: St. Clair, "Bechtel, More Powerful Than the U.S. Army," 10.

192 *"Though the pipeline"*: Block and Weaver, *All Is Clouded by Desire*, 80.

192 *"any illegality"* . . . *"tried to distance themselves"*: *New York Times*, February 24, 1988. See also Labaton, "Role in Scuttled."

192 *"though rich and successful"*: Block and Weaver, *All Is Clouded by Desire*, 90–91.

192 *"choking with rage"* . . . *"Israel agreed"*: *Jewish Telegraphic Agency*, February 2, 1988.

192 *"had been bending over backward"*: Loftus and Aarons, *Secret War*, 489.

193 *"American and foreign businessmen"*: Lando, *Web of Deceit*, 2.

For details of the Aqaba pipeline, see also James C. McKay, *Report of Independent Counsel: In Re: Edwin Meese III*. "Part Seven, Aqaba Pipeline Project" (Washington, DC: Government Printing Office, 1988). See also Christopher Drew,

"President Has Faith in Meese," *Chicago Tribune*, February 24, 1988, for details about E. Robert Wallach's 1985 memo to Meese confirming the arrangement for $65 million to $75 million a year for ten years to Peres.

193 *"lengthy diatribe"... "fulminated"... "part of a Zionist"... "vented his spleen"... "turn to non-U.S. suppliers"*: "Minister of Industry Blasts Senate Action."

PART THREE: DIVIDING THE SPOILS, 1989–2008

The modern era of Bechtel—1989–2008—received more public attention than any of the previous decades, especially the company's involvement in the lead up to the US war on Iraq and the toppling of Saddam Hussein. Bechtel's massive contract for Iraqi reconstruction was the subject of dozens of books and hundreds of news articles throughout the world, as well as Inspector General and congressional investigations.

195 *"War began last week"*: Diana B. Henriques, "Which Companies Will Put Iraq Back Together?" *New York Times*, March 23, 2003.

CHAPTER TWENTY-FIVE: A DEAL WITH THE DEVIL

197 *Deal with the Devil*: Gonzales, quoted in Peter Mantius, *Shell Game: A True Story of Banking, Spies, Lies, Politics—and the Arming of Saddam Hussein* (New York: St. Martin's Press, 1995), 12.

197 *"by all accounts"*: McCartney, *Friends in High Places*, 236.

197 *"The U.S. embassy"... "thought nothing"*: Friedman, *Spider's Web*, 117.

198 *"the company never knew"*: Friedman, "Warning Forced Bechtel."

198 *"able to acquire"... "There was no way"*: Koppel, "How U.S. Arms."

198 *"the mother of all foreign policy"... "run-of-the-mill"*: Gonzalez, "Lesson No. 4."

199 *"executive branch, working with"*: Mantius, *Shell Game*, 5.

199 *"When it comes to governmental relations"*: St. Clair, "Bechtel, More Powerful Than the U.S. Army," 5.

199 *"fevered imaginings"... "mixing their private"*: Greider, "Boys from Bechtel."

199 *"slid back and forth"*: Roger Morris, *Partners in Power: The Clintons and Their America* (New York: Henry Holt, 1996), 345.

199 *"something is going to go"*: Shultz, quoted in Friedman, *Spider's Web*, 118.

200 *"world gray market"*: "Iraqgate: Saddam Hussein, U.S. Policy and the Prelude to the Persian Gulf War, 1980–1994," http://nsarchive.chadwyck.com/marketing/about.jsp.

200 *"The United States spent"*: Crogan, Part II.

200 *"Hitler revisited"*: Lando, *Web of Deceit*, 148.

200 *"Many trace the breakdown"*: Antonia Juhasz, "The Corporate Invasion of Iraq," *LeftTurn*, August/September 2003.

201   *"American officials tolerated"*: Crogan, Part III.

201   *"in ways far removed"* . . . *"tents on a corner"* . . . *"Within, in gardens"*: John F. Burns, "Confrontation in the Gulf—Baghdad's U.S. Hostages: Escape Plans and Anger," *New York Times*, October 7, 1990.

202   *"Riley Bechtel essentially camped"* . . . *"every Bechtel person"* . . . *"quietly with Kuwaiti officials"* . . . *"As the Desert Storm"* . . . *"The destruction"*: Bechtel website, www.bechtel.com/BAC-Chapter-7.html.

        See also Richard Lelby, "Iraqi Hostage Seeks Justice," *Washington Post*, December 1, 2002, for details of hostage taking.

202   *"walked across the zone"* . . . *"The wells were extinguished"*: Streitfeld, "Quiet Ambition at Work."

CHAPTER TWENTY-SIX: THE GIANT LAND OF BECHTEL

204   *"The white hope, the brains"*: McCartney, *Friends in High Places*, 236.

204   *"Not only was he"*: Ibid., 235.

205   *"number three dog"*: www.bechtel.com/BAC-Riley-P-Bechtel.html.

206   *"One Bechtel"*: www.bechtel.com/BAC-Chapter-7.html.

206   *"closed-cycle process"* . . . *"An emphasis"* . . . *"the world's most"*: Ibid.

206   *"Bechtel engineers for years"* . . . *"There is no way"*: Arnold. See also Baker, "Big Dig Tragedy."

207   *"This is a pretty small job"* . . . *"If total expenditures"* . . . *"Rather than depress"* . . . *"having the equivalent"*: Nies, "Bechtel in Boston and Black Mesa" (unpublished manuscript).

207   *"With a cadre"*: Raphael Lewis and Sean P. Murphy, "Lobbying Translates into Clout," *Boston Globe*, February 11, 2003.

207   *"as the costs"* . . . *"a remarkable run"*: Nies, "Bechtel in Boston."

208   *"Big Dig chain of command"*: David S. Bernstein, "A Handy Guide to the Big Dig Screw-Up," *Phoenix*, July 27, 2006.

208   *"Steve Sr. had so many times"* . . . *"If we don't have a client"*: www.bechtel.com /BAC-Chapter-6.html.

209   *"Ethnic, religious, and territorial"*: Steve Coll, *Private Empire: ExxonMobil and American Power* (New York: Penguin Press, 2012), 17–18.

209   *"human needs"*: www.bechtel.com/BAC-Chapter-6.html.

209   *"the largest American colony"*: Ingram, *Builder and His Family*, 96.

210   *"become a signal"* . . . *"There is a sense"* . . . *"Working with Bechtel"*: Matthew Brunwasser, "Steamrolled: A Special Investigation into the Diplomacy of Doing Business Abroad," *Foreign Policy*, January 30, 2015.

CHAPTER TWENTY-SEVEN: SOME FOUND THE COMPANY ARROGANT

211   *"from Dubai to Dallas"* . . . *"core competencies"* . . . *"Most conglomerates ultimately falter"* . . . *" 'homegrown' "* . . . *"formalize and clarify"* . . . *"eliminating cor-*

porate waste"... *"The company now needed"*... *"matrix fashion"*... *"Regions"*...
"The center of Bechtel's": www.bechtel.com/BAC-Chapter-7.html.

213 *"more of a militarylike"*: Seth Lubove, "A Piece of the Action," *Forbes*, May 31, 1999.

213 *"the perception of Bechtel"*... *"Bechtel, some thought"*: www.bechtel.com/BAC
     -Chapter-7.html.

214 *"The year 1992"*: Weinberger with Roberts, *In the Arena*, 347.

214 *"a pawn in a clearly political game"*... *"vindictive wretch"*: Special Prosecutor
     James Brosnahan responded to Weinberger: "Our case was breathtakingly sim-
     ple. It had nothing to do with policy. It had nothing to do with politics. It had to
     do with the secretary of defense being asked questions and giving answers which
     the grand jury found were false. That was the case." Bensky, "End Game."

214 *"Weinberger gave a little glimpse"*... *"breathtaking and poisonous"*: Mary
     McGrory, quoted in Shaw, *Miscarriage of Justice*, 132.

214 *"When confronted with scandals"*: Walsh, *Firewall*, 490–91.

     It was widely reported that the only thing Shultz and Weinberger ever agreed
     upon was that the Iran-Contra affair was misguided, and both opposed sending
     arms to Iran. Both men "thought that if it ever became [public], it would look like
     we were trading arms for hostages," Reagan later said. Cannon, *President Rea-
     gan*, 590. But neither took any action or threatened to resign. In its obituary of
     Weinberger, the *Economist* referred to a lie Weinberger had told regarding the
     magazine. He "always said, with great charm, that he had also been an occasional
     correspondent for the *Economist*. Embarrassingly, this was a claim that our rec-
     ords could not corroborate." Ibid.

215 *"Regulators and the regulated"*: Coll, *Private Empire*, 4.

215 *"enjoyed access to the administration"*: Ibid., 68.

215 *"help preserve the peace"*: www.bechtel.com.

216 *"as part of an ambitious"*: www.bechtel.com/1998-04-03.html.

216 *"In a world increasingly long"*... *"powerful competitive tools"*: www.bechtel.com
     /BAC-Chapter-7.html.

216 *"Don't just build things"*: King and McCoy, "Bechtel's Power Outage."

CHAPTER TWENTY-EIGHT: GLOBAL REACH WITH A LOCAL TOUCH

217 *"Leading the Way to Change"*... *"Building a Century"*: www.bechtel.com/BAC
     -Chapter-7.html.

217 *"Global Reach with a Local Touch"*: www.bechtel.com/BAC-Chapter-8.html.

218 *"world-class ownership"*... *"USGen took off"*: www.bechtel.com/BAC-Chapter-7
     .html.

218 *"were eager"*... *"zealously guarded"*: King and McCoy, "Bechtel's Power Outage."

218 *"does not release"*: Jude P. Laspa, quoted in ibid.

219 *"The family reputation"*: Ibid.

219 *"Staffed by MBA hotshots"*: Ibid.

219 *"invest in privatization"* . . . *"renowned for its financial designs"*: Lubove, "Piece of the Action."

220 *"Ownership is private"*: Jane Mayer, "The Contractors," *New Yorker*, May 5, 2003.

220 *"It's a long way"*: Lubove, "Piece of the Action."

220 *"Enough of this waiting around"*: ibid.

220 *"It's been so successful"*: Unruh, quoted in ibid.

221 *"dot-com-era folly"* . . . *"He was seen as the Einstein"* . . . *"Red flags"* . . . *"Telecoms and dot-coms"*: King and McCoy, "Bechtel's Power Outage."

221 *"Someone wasn't telling"*: Dennis Connell, quoted in ibid.

222 *"As vexing"* . . . *"fled the nation"* . . . *"World Bank–controlled"*: Raphael Lewis and Sean P. Murphy, "Building a Reputation: Bechtel Has Never Shied Away from Big Construction Projects, but Worldwide Achievements Are Accompanied by Controversy," *Boston Globe*, February 28, 2003.

222 *"expropriated assets"*: Jim Shultz, "Riley Bechtel."

222 *"The fact that a World Bank"*: U.S. Newswire, "Three Hundred Citizen Groups Call on Secret World Bank Trade Court to Open Up Bechtel Case Against Bolivia," August 29, 2002. A wide range of groups joined in the demand to open up the legal case for public scrutiny, including labor, environmental groups, research and consumer organizations, and religious institutions. Among those joining were the Canadian Labour Congress, Public Services International, Friends of the Earth, Public Citizen, the Institute for Policy Studies, the Transnational Institute, the Maryknoll Fathers and Brothers, and the American Friends Service Committee. The Cochabamba case was explored in the 2003 documentary film *The Corporation* and in the 2010 Spanish film *Even the Rain*.

223 *"For Bechtel Enterprises"*: Jim Shultz, "Riley Bechtel."

223 *"marriage between"*: Vallette, Kretzmann, and Wysham, *Crude Vision*, 14.

223 *"In Bolivia"*: Jim Shultz, quoted in Lewis and Murphy, "Building a Reputation."

223 *"controls water rates"*: Jeff Berger, quoted ibid.

CHAPTER TWENTY-NINE: A LICENSE TO MAKE MONEY

225 *"economic equivalent"*: Klein, *Shock Doctrine*, 343.

225 *"the world's biggest"*: *New York Times*, quoted in ibid., 347.

226 *"worth a fraction"* . . . *"In late 2001"* . . . *"gave coal-fired plants"* . . . *"We knew Bechtel"* . . . *"One of the most tightly"*: King and McCoy, "Bechtel's Power Outage."

227 *"If this were a public company"*: Riley Bechtel, quoted in ibid.

227 *"No one on the engineering"*: Bechtel partner Dennis Connell, quoted in ibid.

227 *"fiendishly hardworking"* . . . *"Their big reward"* . . . *"The old boy is asking"*: Ibid.

228 *"Seemingly innocent disclosures"*: Adrian Zaccaria, quoted in ibid.

228 *"twin themes"*: Russ Hoyle, *Going to War: How Misinformation, Disinformation, and Arrogance Led America into Iraq* (New York: Thomas Dunne Books, 2008), 26.

229 *"The same men"*: Vallette, Kretzmann, and Wysham, *Crude Vision*, 2.

229 *"I would be surprised"* ... *"Iraq ruled by Saddam Hussein"*: Shultz, quoted in Hoyle, *Going to War*, 83.

230 *"committed to moving"*: Bob Herbert, "Ask Bechtel What War Is Good For: A License to Make Money," *International Herald Tribune*, April 22, 2003.

230 *"People will say there will be chaos"*: Weinberger, quoted in George Packer, *The Assassin's Gate: America in Iraq* (New York: Farrar, Straus and Giroux, 2005), 53.

230 *"The more we gave Saddam"*: Gary Milhollin, "Building Saddam Hussein's Bomb: They Are Pouring Concrete as We Speak," *New York Times*, March 8, 1992.

230 *"a license to make money"* ... *"Bechtel in the driver's seat"*: Herbert, "Ask Bechtel What War Is Good For."

230 *"The Danger Is Immediate"* ... *"if there is a rattlesnake"*: Shultz in the *Washington Post*, September 6, 2002.

230 *"Since his role was at arm's length"*: Klein, *Shock Doctrine*, 403.

231 *"remove the remains"*: John Broder, "In Storm's Ruins, a Rush to Rebuild and Reopen for Business," *New York Times*, September 10, 2005.

CHAPTER THIRTY: MORE POWERFUL THAN THE US ARMY

232 *"Every so often Bechtel emerges a little"*: *Economist*.

232 *"mother contract"*: Dan Baum, "Nation Builders for Hire," *New York Times*, June 22, 2003.

232 *"of the billing"*: Tom Engelhardt, "Everything's Private," *Mother Jones*, November 4, 2003.

232 *"The rush to secure contracts"*: Joshua Chaffin and Andrew Hill, "The Rush to Secure Contracts to Rebuild Iraq and the Awarding of the First Wave of Deals Is Causing as Much Debate as the Decision to Wage War," *Financial Times*, April 28, 2003.

233 *"competitive"*: Project on Government Oversight.

233 *"incentive for corporations"*: Public Citizen, 14.

233 *"It's a relatively small club"*: Baum, "Nation Builders for Hire."

233 *"that the government seems"*: Michael Liedtke, "D.C. Ties Help Bechtel Tie Up Iraqi Reconstruction Work," *South Florida Sun-Sentinel*, April 19, 2003.

233 *"I ran the Big Dig"* ... *"It is charged"*: Koppel, "Assistance for Iraq," *Nightline*, ABC News, April 23, 2003.

233 *"in charge of the biggest"*: Brian, quoted in David Streitfeld and Mark Fineman, "U.S. Engineers Working Under the Gun in Iraq," *Los Angeles Times*, October 26, 2003.

234 *"Only a handful"* ... *"So we went"*: Koppel, "Assistance for Iraq."

234 *"I think some senators"*: Henriques, "Which Companies."

234 *"Perhaps Bechtel's institutional"*: Crogan, "The Dishonor Role."

234 *"legitimate commercial"*: Benjamin Pimentel, "Iraq Got Bay Area Boost in '80s," *San Francisco Chronicle*, January 26, 2003.

234 *"conventional weapons"*: UN report, excerpted in *Corpwatch*.

234 *"relative routineness"*: Davis, "It's a Bechtel World."

235 *"once party central"* . . . *"to a squadron"*: Cox and Strauss, "Iraq Work Puts Bechtel in Spotlight."

235 *"Rumsfeld has sat"*: Rep. Marcy Kaptur, quoted in "Old Men's Oil Wars."

235 *"A motley assortment"*: T. Christian Miller, *Blood Money* (New York: Little, Brown, 2006), 4.

235 *"We should have a separation"*: Jim Vallette, quoted in Liedtke, "D.C. Ties Help Bechtel."

235 *"The U.S. comes in"* . . . *"I mean, Bechtel"*: Baker, October 3, 2003.

235 *"Within hours"*: Davis, "It's a Bechtel World."

236 *"the corporate invasion"*: Streitfeld, "Quiet Ambition at Work."

236 *"Also vocal"* . . . *"Vulture! Vulture!"*: Cox and Strauss, "Iraq Work Puts Bechtel in Spotlight."

236 *"We are a tiny"*: Illich, quoted in Streitfeld, "Quiet Ambition at Work."

236 *"Executives forcefully reject"*: Ibid.

236 *"Everyone says Iraq is a gravy train"*: Bechtel vice president Jim Illich, quoted in ibid.

236 *"Even for Bechtel"*: Ibid.

236 *"If a project goes financially wrong"*: Hirst, "World's at Bechtel's Beck and Call."

237 *"eliminates the substantial"*: Bechtel, 160.

237 *"More powerful than the U.S. Army"*: St. Clair, "Bechtel, More Powerful Than the U.S. Army."

237 *"maintained a cloak of secrecy"*: Taylor, "Secretive Construction Giant."

237 *"I don't know that Bechtel"*: Shultz, quoted in Bob Herbert, "War Hawks Are Circling In," *Oakland Tribune*, April 13, 2003.

CHAPTER THIRTY-ONE: THE HYDRA-HEADED AMERICAN GIANT

238 *"Bechtel arrived in Iraq quietly"*: *Public Citizen*, 2.

238 *"amateurish and vainglorious"*: Maureen Dowd, "Jeb Bush's Brainless Trust," *New York Times*, February 22, 2015.

238 *"policy engine"* . . . *"Bechtel has positioned itself"*: *Public Citizen*, 12.

Three months after the invasion, Saddam's sons, Uday and Qusay, were killed in a gunfight with US forces, and Saddam was placed at the top of the US list of most-wanted Iraqis. Bremer announced his capture in December 2003 during the American assault Operation Red Dawn, presented video footage of the Iraqi leader wearing a full beard and long hair, and reported plans to put him on trial.

239 *"not solely by controlling"*: Stephen C. Pelletiere, "A War Crime or an Act of War?" *New York Times*, January 31, 2003.

239 *"has two rivers"*: Antonia Juhasz, "Bechtel Bails on Iraq," AlterNet, November 13, 2006.

    For the estimated percentage of subcontracts awarded by Bechtel, see Diana B. Henriques, "Bechtel Set to Rely on Iraqi Labor," *International Herald Tribune*, April 21, 2003.

239 *"hydra-headed"* . . . *"golden keys"*: Baum, "Nation Builders for Hire."

239 *"every businessman's"* . . . *"institutional strengthening"*: Betool Khedairi, "Meeting Mr. Bechtel," *Guardian* (Manchester, UK), September 2, 2003.

240 *"God-invoking Bushies"*: Michael Hirsh, "Paul Bremer Was Just Following Instructions," *Washington Monthly*, March 2006.

240 *"The Iraqi public"*: Ed Harriman, "Cronyism and Kickbacks," *London Review of Books*, January 26, 2006, www.lrb.co.uk/v28/n02/ed-harriman/cronyism-and-kickbacks.

240 *"military hardmen, diplomats"*: Neil Mackay, "Gulf War 2 Part Three: Carving Up the New Iraq," *Sunday Herald* (Glasgow, UK), April 13, 2003.

240 *"new Gilded Age"*: Engelhardt, "Everything's Private."

240 *"on an urgent basis"* . . . *"insufficient fuel"*: Ed Harriman, "The Least Accountable Regime in the Middle East," *London Review of Books*, November 2, 2006, www.lrb.co.uk/v28/n21/ed-harriman/the-least-accountable-regime-in-the-middle-east.

240 *"task and delivery"*: *Project on Government Oversight.*

241 *"clearly met"* . . . *"support costs"* . . . *"a large miscellaneous"* . . . *"Other"*: SIGIR, quoted in Ed Harriman, "Burn Rate: Ed Harriman Writes About Making Money and Losing Ground in Iraq," *London Review of Books*, September 7, 2007. Bechtel disagreed with the SIGIR findings, with Bechtel spokesman Jonathan Marshall telling NBC News that "there is almost nothing in the audit that is critical of Bechtel's performance," and blaming USAID. See Aram Roston, "Federal Audit Rips Iraqi Reconstruction," *NBC Nightly News*, July 25, 2007.

241 *"Pity the poor Iraqis"*: Harriman, "Burn Rate."

241 *"battalions of earth-moving"*: Klein, *Shock Doctrine*, 526.

241 *"USAID had cooked the books"*: Harriman, "Burn Rate."

242 *"undeserved reputation"*: Cox and Strauss, "Iraq Work Puts Bechtel in Spotlight."

242 *"Had Iraq been"*: Baker, "Bechtel Pulling Out."

242 *"corporate-friendly"*: Juhasz, "Bechtel Bails on Iraq."

242 *"drew from an insurgency"*: Dowd, "Jeb Bush's Brainless Trust."

242 *"Iraqi companies"*: Juhasz, "Bechtel Bails on Iraq."

242 *"If you're going to Iraq"*: Cox and Strauss, "Iraq Work Puts Bechtel in Spotlight."

242 *"hero culture"* . . . *"Eat Dirt"*: Streitfeld, "Quiet Ambition at Work."

242 *"Resembling over-wide"*: Streitfeld and Fineman, "U.S. Engineers."

243 *"Bechtel—which charged"*: Baker, "Bechtel Pulling Out."

243 *"the pretexts"* . . . *"complex chain"* . . . *"tricky politically"*: James Glanz, "U.S. Ousts Iraq Hospital Contractor: Cost Overruns and Delays Under Bechtel Doomed Project," *New York Times*, July 29, 2006.

243 *"legacy of waste"*: Liz Sly, "A U.S. 'Legacy of Waste' in Iraq," *Los Angeles Times*, August 29, 2010.

243 *"opened"*: Van Buren, *We Meant Well*, 214.

244 *"It is a simple fact"*: Barlett and Steele.

244 *"parallel disaster economy"*: Klein, *Shock Doctrine*, 526.

244 *"The world is a messy place"*: Rice, quoted in ibid., 431. See also n. 1, 645.

CHAPTER THIRTY-TWO: PROFITING FROM DESTRUCTION

245 *"there too early"*: Laton McCartney, quoted in David Whelan, "San Francisco Contractor Bechtel Is No Stranger to Iraq," Knight Ridder Tribune News Service, June 4, 2003.

245 *"disaster capitalism"*: Klein, *Shock Doctrine*, 6.

245 *"grand guru"*: Ibid., 5.

245 *"waiting for a major crisis"*: Ibid., 7.

246 *"Within weeks"*: Ibid., 519.

246 *"indefinite delivery"*: Sheila Carapico, "Forecasting Mass Destruction, from Gulf to Gulf," *Middle East Report*, September 29, 2005.

246 *"Baghdad's Green Zone"*: Klein, *Shock Doctrine*, 519.

246 *"hollowed out"*: Chideya, Griff Witte interview. "The outsourcing of government began in earnest really in the Clinton administration with the reinventing government initiatives of Vice President Al Gore. That was a major initiative of the Clinton administration. It was something that they took great pride in, that they were reducing the number of overall federal employees, that they were giving work to the private sector where it was warranted." Ibid.

246 *"rushing to cash in"*: Broder, "In Storm's Ruins."

246 *"They are throwing"*: James Albertine, quoted in ibid.

246 *"working under an informal"* . . . *"as well as mess halls"*: Ibid.

247 *"Political contributions"*: Menaker, quoted in ibid.

247 *"This landmark public-private"* . . . *"This partnership"*: Riley Bechtel, quoted in PR Newswire, "Business Roundtable Announces Initiative to Spur Construction Training and Bring Jobs to Thousands of Gulf Region Residents," July 28, 2006.

247 *"the first line of defense"*: Richard Lardner: "Auditors Go Easy on Contractors," *Huffington Post*, December 11, 2008.

247 *"We cannot allow greed"*: "Waste, Fraud, and Abuse in Hurricane Katrina Contracts," U.S. House of Representatives, *Prepared for Committee on Government Reform—Minority Staff Special Investigations Division*, August 2006.

248 *"the slowest responding"* . . . *" 'chronic failure' to provide"*: Richard Lardner, "Auditors Go Easy."

248 *"ballooned from approximately"* . . . *"mismanagement"* . . . *"wasteful spending"*: "Waste, Fraud, and Abuse."

PART FOUR: FROM MULESKINNER TO SOVEREIGN STATE, 2009–2015

The case of Wen Ho Lee has been thoroughly reported in news reports—in the US and abroad—and in books, papers, audiovisual accounts, congressional and legal hearings, and investigation documents. Among the most insightful was the work of Hugh Gusterson, the anthropologist who calls himself "the Margaret Mead of the Weapons Labs." Also important is *A Convenient Spy* by Dan Stober and Ian Hoffman.

In the case of the laid off employees against LLNS, I watched the entire first jury trial in Alameda County court in Oakland, California, and perused thousands of pages of motions, depositions, and court filings. I also interviewed five of the 140 plaintiffs represented by attorney J. Gary Gwilliam.

249 *From Muleskinner to Sovereign State*: Dowie, "Bechtel File," 37.

249 *"When the modern corporation"*: John Kenneth Gailbraith, from an address delivered in Toronto, December 29, 1972, and published in *American Economic Review*, March 1973. Quoted in Richard J. Barnet, *Roots of War* (New York: Atheneum, 1972), 6.

CHAPTER THIRTY-THREE: A CONVENIENT SPY

251 *"egged on the hapless endeavor"* . . . *"triangular relationship"*: Gusterson, "Assault on Los Alamos."

252 *"plowing much"*: Gusterson, "Assault on Los Alamos."

252 *"the Margaret Mead of the weapons labs"*: Ibid.

252 *"China Stole"*: James Risen and Jeff Gerth, "China Stole Nuclear Secrets for Bombs, US Aides Say," *New York Times*, March 6, 1999.

252 *"hoping for a glimpse"* . . . *"Convoys of FBI"* . . . *"FBI agents descended"*: Gusterson, "Assault on Los Alamos."

254 *"Reporters and congressmen"*: Stober and Hoffman, *Convenient Spy*, 209.

254 *"I am truly sorry"* . . . *"As a member"*: James Parker, quoted in Wen Ho Lee, *My Country Versus Me: The First-Hand Account by the Los Alamos Scientist Who Was Falsely Accused of Being a Spy* (New York: Hachette, 2002), 2.

254 *"convenient spy"*: Stober and Hoffman, *Convenient Spy*, book title.

254 *"Wen Ho Lee was an invented crisis"*: Author interview with Greg Mello.

255 *"The way he was hung"*: Hecker, quoted in Stober and Hoffman, *Convenient Spy*, 347.

255 *"Regardless of Lee's motives"*: Stober and Hoffman, *Convenient Spy*, 347.

255   *review recommendations*: Broad, "California Is Surprise Winner."

255   *"quite confident"*: D'Agostino, quoted in ibid.

255   *"fortified, forested"*: Ibid.

255   *"The greatest irony"*: Kennette Benedict, "The U.S. Nuclear Weapons Complex Needs a New Role," *Bulletin of the Atomic Scientists*, April 10, 2014.

255   *"The Cold War"*: Author interview with Mello.

CHAPTER THIRTY-FOUR: PRIVATIZE THE APOCALYPSE

256   *"Privatize the Apocalypse"*: Frida Berrigan, "Privatizing the Apocalypse," Tom Dispatch.com, March 30, 2006, www.tomdispatch.com/post/72765.

256   *the US Nuclear Security Enterprise*: www.bechtel.com.

257   *"sent Los Alamos"* . . . *"What do we do"* . . . *"the urge to privatize"*: Berrigan, "Privatizing the Apocalypse."

       For more on the Bush agenda for privatization, see also Jon D. Michaels, "Beyond Accountability: The Constitutional, Democratic, and Strategic Problems with Privatizing War," *Washington University Law Quarterly* 82 (March 29, 2005): 1001.

257   *"deeply wounded"*: Author interview with Mello.

257   *"The need is clear"*: DOD Posture Review.

257   *"Washington should oversee"*: Stepp et al., 11.

257   *"scientific discovery"*: Ibid., 5.

257   *"A recipe for the enrichment"*: Author interview with Mello.

258   *"corporatization"* . . . *"self-serving"* . . . *"an anachronism"*: Memorandum from Robert Civiak to G. Gary Gwilliam in *Andrews v. LLNS* litigation.

258   *"After initial US and Russian"*: Benedict, U.S. Nuclear Weapons Complex.

258   *"Bechtel leveraged"*: Author interview with Todd Jacobson.

258   *"Everybody thought"*: Stockton, quoted in Upton, "Employee Lawsuit."

259   *"Bechtel gets nuclear"*: Gary Gwilliam on law firm website, https://giccb.com/privatization-of-lawrence-livermore-lab-bechtel-gets-nuclear-lab-taxpayers-foot-the-bill/.

259   *"There was a social contract"*: Jeff Garberson, "National Report: Broken Relationship Quality at LLNL," *Livermore Independent*, February 17, 2012.

259   *"are no longer to be"*: Berrigan, "Privatizing the Apocalypse."

260   *"zero tolerance"* . . . *"these facilities"*: O'Leary, quoted in Chris Berdik, "The Department of Energy's War on Whistleblowers," *Mother Jones*, January 17, 2001.

260   *"using taxpayer dollars"* . . . *"Keep your mouth shut"*: Ibid.

260   *"In wars in Iraq"*: Benedict, U.S. Nuclear Weapons Complex.

260   *"powerful as one of its"*: Streitfeld, "Quiet Ambition at Work."

261   *"none of the thirty-one nations"*: Hore-Lacy, quoted in "Our Aging Nuclear Arsenal," *Week*, January 23, 2015.

CHAPTER THIRTY-FIVE: NUKES FOR PROFIT

Details about Bechtel's federal contracts, by agency and date, as well as company revenues and lobbying power can be found in numerous locations—on oversight organization websites, government agencies, and business and trade journals, as well as on the Bechtel company's website, including:

https://www.usaspending.gov/Pages/Default.aspx

http://influenceexplorer.com

http://www.beyondnuclear.org

http://nucleardiner.com

http://www.enr.com

http://thebulletin.org

http://www.arabianoilandgas.com

http://www.govconwire.com

http://www.forbes.com/search/?q=bechtel

http://www.contractormisconduct.org

262 *"Private interests"*: "Nomination of George P. Shultz," 104.

262 *"From Los Alamos to Kwajalein"*: Western States Legal Foundation.

263 *"the ultimate white-collar"*: David Hobson (R-OH), quoted in Berrigan, "Privatizing the Apocalypse."

263 *"Profits and nuclear weapons"*: Tyler Przybylek, quoted in Benedict, U.S. Nuclear Weapons Complex.

263 *"creeping privatization"... "unwise"*: Bruce Held, quoted in "U.S. Nuclear Weapons Agency to Delay Work on Interoperable Warhead," *Global Security Newswire*, February 18, 2014.

263 *"Bechtel and its partners"*: Author interview with Gary Gwilliam.

264 *"In the classic slash-and-burn"*: Author interview with fired employee.

264 *"hatchet man"*: Author interview with Gary Gwilliam.

264 *"kitchen cabinet"*: Liedle video deposition in *Elaine Andrews et al. vs. Lawrence Livermore National Security, LLC, et al.*, February 17, 2011.

264 *"through their limited liability"*: Author interview with Gary Gwilliam.

264 *"intentionally overstated its budget problems"... "At OMB"*: Robert L. Civiak affidavit, *Andrews vs. LLNS*, December 15, 2011.

265 *"The sheriff was there"*: Author interview with Marian Barraza.

265 *"corporate takeover"*: Livermore employee Art Wong, trial testimony, *Andrews vs. LLNS*, March 21, 2013.

265 *"LLNS put everything into NIF"*: Author interview with Gusterson.

265 *"stadium-sized laboratory"... "an era of carbon-free"*: John Upton, "Fusion Experiment Faces New Hurdles," *New York Times*, June 24, 2011.

265 *"[w]e are assigned missions"... "So those four committees"*: Videotaped deposition of George Miller in *Andrews v. LLNS*, January 4, 2011.

266 *"giant array of lasers"*: Upton, "Fusion Experiment."

266 *"People don't know"*: Greg Mello, quoted in Roger Snodgrass, "Activist's Experience, Passion Culminate in LANL Project Delay," *Santa Fe New Mexican*, March 9, 2012.

266 *"far more intelligent"*: Author interview with Mello.

CHAPTER THIRTY-SIX: THE BUDDHIST AND THE BOMB

267 *"None of my friends"* . . . *"Basically, by 1970"* . . . *"Nixon wanted me"*: Author interview with Mello.

267 *"strong sense"*: Mello, quoted in Snodgrass, "Activist's Experience."

267 *"I was disgusted"* . . . *"apprentice activists"* . . . *"He was just a teacher"* . . . *"I didn't fit the Harvard mold"* . . . *"economic hit men"*: Author interview with Mello.

269 *"the Cold War permeated"* . . . *"Essentially a monk"*: Ibid.

269 *"I realized that the Cold War"*: Mello, quoted in Snodgrass, "Activist's Experience."

269 *"Our idea"*: Author interview with Mello.

270 *"have made standing up"*: Carolyn Carlson, "Greg Mello and Trish Williams-Mello," *Alibi*, April 19–25, 2012.

270 *"a gigantic self-licking"*: Greg Mello, quoted in Jeri Clausing and Matthew Daly, "LANL, Other Nuke Facilities Under Renewed Scrutiny," Associated Press, September 12, 2013.

270 *"strange bedfellows"*: Snodgrass, "Activist's Experience."

270 *"Greg has always been"*: Masco, quoted in Snodgrass, "Activist's Experience."

270 *"Few realized"* . . . *"Just as the country"*: Author interview with Mello.

271 *"an antinuclear complex"*: Snodgrass, "Activist's Experience."

271 *"Now we have the threatened extinction"*: Author interview with Mello.

271 *"It's like a Laurel and Hardy"*: Jeri Clausing, "Management of LANL Waste Facility Faulted," Associated Press, September 12, 2013.

271 *"Fort Knox of nuclear facilities"*: Peter Stockton, "Security at Y-12 Nun Too Good," *Bulletin of Atomic Scientists*, October 2, 2012.

271 *"could fit into a small gym bag"* . . . *"would begin the process"* . . . *"The fact that"*: Eric Schlosser, "Break-In at Y-12: How a Handful of Pacifists and Nuns Exposed the Vulnerability of America's Nuclear-Weapons Sites," *New Yorker*, March 9, 2015. At the time of Sister Megan's break-in at Y-12 during the summer of 2012, Wackenhut Services, Inc. was responsible for security at the site. A onetime American company, Wackenhut had been acquired by a Group 4 Falck, a British company. G4S, as it was called, was the third-largest private employer in the world, operating private prisons, defending American embassies, and providing security at rock concerts. In July 2014 a consortium headed by Bechtel and Lockheed Martin took over as the operator of Y-12.

As of March 2015, Sister Megan was incarcerated at the Metropolitan Detention Center in Brooklyn, where, at eighty-five years old, she was serving out her sentence for her intrusion at Y-12.

272 *"freshen up our bombs"*: Author interview with Philip M. Smith.

272 *"back down the limb"*: Snodgrass, "Activist's Experience."

272 *"What with fallout"*: Greg Mello, "Udall Promotes Labs at Expense of New Mexico," *Santa Fe New Mexican*, August 17, 2014.

CHAPTER THIRTY-SEVEN: THE FOUR HORSEMEN OF THE APOCALYPSE

274 *"So today, I state clearly"* . . . *"I'm not naïve"* . . . *"As a nuclear power"* . . . *"put an end to Cold War thinking"* . . . *"all nuclear weapons states"*: Remarks by President Obama.

275 *"the peace and security"*: Ibid.

275 *"first- versus second-strike"* . . . *"billion-dollar"* . . . *"Breaking the War Mentality"*: Obama's March 1983 article that appeared in *Sundial*. Quoted in William J. Broad and David E. Sanger.

275 *"naïve, anti-American"*: Ibid. See also "Obama's Youth Shaped His Nuclear-Free Vision," *New York Times*, July 5, 2009.

276 *"a recent spate"*: Zachary Roth, "Global Zero: Obama's Distant Goal of a Nuclear-Free World," *Atlantic*, September 29, 2011.

276 *"insider threat"* . . . *"launch codes"*: Schlosser, "Break-In at Y-12."

276 *"had decided"*: Broad and Sanger, "Obama's Youth."

276 *"the U.S. was losing"*: Greider, "Boys from Bechtel."

277 *"A World Free"*: Shultz et al., *Wall Street Journal*, January 4, 2007.

277 *"deeply immersed"*: Eben Harrell, "The Four Horsemen of the Nuclear Apocalypse," *Time*, March 10, 2011.

277 *"All were veterans"*: "The Growing Appeal of Zero: Banning the Bomb Will Be Hard, but Not Impossible," *Economist*, June 16, 2011.

277 *"America and the Soviet Union"* . . . *"the growing number"*: Shultz et al., *Wall Street Journal*, March 7, 2011.

277 *"Detractors regarded"* . . . *"an unlikely coterie"*: Tyler Wigg-Stevenson, "Hawks Against the Bomb," *Sojourners*, November 2009.

278 *"Call it penance"*: Eben Harrell, "The Four Horsemen of the Nuclear Apocalypse: In Conversation," *Time*, May 20, 2011.

278 *"sacrilegious renunciation"* . . . *"high priests"* . . . *"former apostles"*: James Carroll, "Why President Obama Needs to Revive His Pledge for a Nuclear-Free World," *Nation*, December 11, 2014.

278 *"We all knew"*: Wigg-Stevenson, "Hawks Against the Bomb."

278 *"Unfortunately, such figures"*: Carroll, "Why President Obama Needs to Revive."

278 *"never invited them"*: Broad and Sanger, "Obama's Youth."

278 *"Ridding the world"*: "Growing Appeal of Zero."

279 *"echoing their message"*: Broad and Sanger, "Obama's Youth."

279 *"President Obama has taken"*: Harrell, "Four Horsemen . . . In Conversation."

279 *"It would all come"*: Author interview with antinuclear activist.

279 *"devil's bargain"*: Carroll, "Why President Obama Needs to Revive." For Obama's nuclear modernization program, see Mecklin.

CHAPTER THIRTY-EIGHT: THE CAPTAIN AHAB OF NUCLEAR WEAPONS

280 *Captain Ahab*: Carroll.

280 *"a world without"*: Remarks by President Obama.

280 *"no-nukes push"* ... *"cover he needed"*: Roth, "Global Zero."

280 *"president moved quickly"*: William D. Hartung, "Cut Nukes Now," *Huffington Post*, April 15, 2013.

281 *"This is dangerous"* ... *"nuclear ambitions"*: Broad and Sanger, "Obama's Youth."

281 *"between vision"*: Roth, "Global Zero."

281 *"no mean feat"*: Hartung, "Cut Nukes Now."

281 *"Extremist Republicans"*: Carroll, "Why President Obama Needs to Revive."

281 *"the disarmament hook"*: Emily B. Landau and Shimon Stein, "From Prague to Berlin: The Decline of the U.S. Nuclear Disarmament Agenda and Its Implications for the Middle East," James Martin Center for Nonproliferation Studies (CNS), August 21, 2013, http://wmdjunction.com/1308021_disarmament _agenda_decline_mideast.htm.

282 *"vision of and work for"*: www.nobelprize.org/nobel_prizes/peace/laureates/2009 /press.html.

282 *"At this point, the pressure"*: Dienekes. Remarks published on LASG website.

282 *"Without nuclear weapons"*: Author interview with Mello. Details of Bechtel lobbying Kyl were revealed by Mello in author's interview.

282 *"a full-blown reinvention"*: Carroll, "Why President Obama Needs to Revive."

283 *"year of arms control"*: Landau and Stein, "From Prague to Berlin."

283 *"Obama fell"* ... *"Now we have entered"*: Author interview with Mello.

283 *"the size of the nation's"* ... *"a new generation"*: William J. Broad, "Which President Cut the Most Nukes?" *New York Times*, November 1, 2014.

284 *"deterrence in the age"*: Henry Kissinger et al., "Deterrence in the Age of Nuclear Proliferation," *Wall Street Journal*, March 7, 2011.

284 *"quartet barely make mention"*: Harrell, "Four Horsemen."

CHAPTER THIRTY-NINE: A TRIAL LAWYER GOES TO BATTLE

285 *"rougher and rougher"*: G. Gary Gwilliam, *Getting a Winning Verdict: A Trial Lawyer Finds His Soul* (Walnut Creek, CA: Pavior, 2007), 46.

285 *"Most of my friends"*: Ibid., 57.

286 *"it was still a college degree"*: Ibid., 69.

286 *"Have you ever thought"* ... *"I had never met"* ... *"You could be"*: Ibid., 88–89.

286 *"just short"* ... *"the most competitive"*: Ibid., 95.

286 *"I didn't know"*: Ibid., 113.

287 *"win the big one"*: Ibid., 127.

287 *"We don't cheat"* . . . *"on behalf of the general"*: Ibid., 170–71.

288 *"takes on issues"* . . . *"help the average"*: Ibid., 269.

288 *"I'm the only lawyer"* . . . *"When this case"* . . . *"It's clear"* . . . *"trying to pass"*: Author interview with Gary Gwilliam.

290 *"tracking the misuse"*: Declaration of Danielle Bryan.

290 *"frequently had"*: Author interview with Gary Gwilliam.

> In 2013 the author filed a Freedom of Information Act request with the Department of Energy, National Nuclear Security Administration. The request was specific and limited: "1. The adverse impact analysis of the 2008 workforce restructuring at Lawrence Livermore National Laboratory, submitted by Lawrence Livermore National Security, LLC (LLNS) to the Department of Energy (DOE) and/or its National Nuclear Security Administration (NNSA) in or about May 2008. 2. All attorney's fees and expenses paid by DOE and/or NNSA for the representation of LLNS in *Andrews et al. v. Lawrence Livermore National Security, LLC, et al.*, Alameda County Superior Court Case No. RG09453596."
>
> After a two-year wait, on April 9, 2015, the office of the General Counsel of NNSA finally responded by redacting nearly five hundred pages of material in its entirety. The exemptions cited by NNSA included protection of "trade secrets and commercial or financial information" and the attorney-client privilege between the US government, LLNS, and private attorneys retained by LLNS (and paid by the US government).

290 *"As soon as the Lab"*: Author interview with Gary Gwilliam.

CHAPTER FORTY: THE EXXON OF SPACE

291 *"Bechtel is one of the great creations"*: Starr, quoted in Streitfeld, "Quiet Ambition at Work."

291 *"Bechtel's phenomenal"* . . . *"indistinguishable"*: Dowie, "Bechtel File," 37.

291 *In one of the more recent political cycles* Political cycle cited here was 2011–2012.

292 *"I am really concerned"*: Feinstein, in US Senate Appropriations Subcommittee on Energy and Water, April 24, 2013. For Feinstein's contributions from Bechtel and the nuclear industry lobby, see Center for Public Integrity, "Are Nuclear Weapons Contractors' Millions in Campaign Contributions Buying Favors?" June 6, 2012, www.publicintegrity.org.

292 *"dysfunctional management"*: Benedict, U.S. Nuclear Weapons Complex.

293 *"the most costly"* . . . *"as toxic"* . . . *"Bechtel rushed"*: Joshua Frank, "Hanford's Nuclear Option: Department of Energy Scientists Allege Catastrophic Mismanagement of the Costliest Environmental Cleanup in World History," *Seattle Weekly,* October 18, 2011.

293 *"Hanford is a long-term"*: Carpenter, quoted in Alexander Nazaryan, "America's Fukushima?" *Newsweek,* November 20, 2013.

293 *a "long overdue justice"* . . . *"It was absolutely terrifying"*: Malone.

294 *"After consultation"*: Susan Beard, quoted by Munger, February 4, 2015, http://knoxblogs.com/atomiccity/2015/02/04/nnsa-defends-klotz-waiver/. Also see Smallberg for Klotz-Bechtel relationship.

294 *"Bechtel has designed"*: *World Generation Class of 2002*.

295 *"multibuilding"*: www.yournuclearnews.com/bechtel+praises+completion+of +first+step+toward+building +vital+national+security+facility_113970.html.

295 *"Mining is an industry"* . . . *"We want to become"* . . . *"ambitious"*: Mark Odell, "Bechtel Adds Grit to Space-Mine Mission," *Financial Times*, April 22, 2013.

296 *"If California Energy"*: Laughlin, *Powering the Future*, 98.

296 *"$2.2 billion bird-scorching"*: Cassandra Sweet, "The $2.2 Billion Bird-Scorching Solar Project," *Wall Street Journal*, February 12, 2014.

297 *"Despite its behemoth"* . . . *"Away from public"* . . . *"sparked a wholesale"*: Julie Cart, "Sacrificing the Desert to Save the Earth," *Los Angeles Times*, February 5, 2012.

CHAPTER FORTY-ONE: A NASTY PIECE OF WORK

298 *A Nasty Piece of Work*: *Baltimore Sun*, October 2, 1990.

298 *"I made a specific offer"* . . . *"If I give too many details"* . . . *"Such commutation"* . . .

299 *"excessive, grossly disproportionate"*: Gil Ronen, "Jonathan Pollard Turns 60 Behind Bars," Israel National News, August 7, 2014.

299 *"My wife and I"*: Author email exchange with Sheldon Adelson, November 15, 2014.

299 *"Call for Clemency Campaign"*: *Jewish Link*.

299 *"president to president"* . . . *"to seek Jonathan's"*: Ibid.

299 *"the Israel lobby"*: Walter Russell Mead, "The Spy Who Didn't Walk," *American Interest*, April 24, 2012.

300 *"secular Jew"* . . . *"the result of a miscarriage of justice"*: Viorst, " 'Catch-22' Plight."

300 *"I could tell you for sure"*: Author email exchange with Adelson.

300 *"impressed by the force"*: *New York Times News Service*.

301 *"Dear Mr. President"*: http://voices.washingtonpost.com/right-turn/2011/01 /exclusive_george_p_shultz_call.html.

301 *"Forget that Pollard"*: Woolsey, quoted in Klein, *Shock Doctrine*.

301 *"President Obama was considering clemency"*: Helene Cooper, "Obama Turns to Biden to Reassure Jewish Voters, and Get Them to Contribute Too," *New York Times*, September 30, 2011.302 *"doubts"*: Baker, *WhoWhatWhy*, March 7, 2013.

302 *"never expressed interest"*: *The Jonathan Jay Pollard Espionage Case*.

302 *"With little fanfare"*: Aaron Klein, "Exposed: Secret Memo Reveals Pollard Sentence a Sham," *WND*, February 23, 2015.

302 *"The recent disclosures"* . . . *"any harm that may"*: Lauer and Semmelman op-ed, www.wnd.com/2015/02/feds-lied-for-30-years-about-jonathan-pollard/.

303 *"was surely inspired"*: McFarlane, February 9, 2012, letter in support of Pollard's release, quoted in Klein, *Shock Doctrine.*

303 *had once agreed: Economist*, "Caspar Weinberger."

CHAPTER FORTY-TWO: THE KINGDOM OF BECHTELISTAN

305 *"fiery ball"*... *"After the ash"*: Quoted from marketing material of Magic World, www.exlinedesign.com/entertainment/portfolio/theme/magiworl.htm.

306 *"a clear contradiction"*: Jamal Elshayyal, "Secret Files: US Officials Aided Gaddafi," *Aljazeera*, August 31, 2011.

307 *"the logic of an impoverished"*: Paul Lewis, "U.S. Ambassador to Kosovo Hired by Construction Firm He Lobbied For," *Guardian* (Manchester, UK), April 14, 2014.

307 *"The highway's black vein"*: Brunwasser, "Steamrolled."

307 *"acted inappropriately"*: Lewis, "U.S. Ambassador to Kosovo."

307 *"slanderous"*: Brunwasser, "Steamrolled."

307 *"It isn't every day"*... *"the local political elite"*... *"were boondoggles"*... *"not only to choose"*: Ibid.

308 *"the case study"*: Davis, "It's a Bechtel World."

308 *"Bechtel plays politics"*: Greider, "Boys from Bechtel."

308 *"as either a shining success"*: Davis, "It's a Bechtel World."

309 *"Bechtel is a mighty"*: Rep. Henry Gonzalez, Remarks made in the US House of Representatives, 1992.

309 *"often going to the universities"*: Davis, "It's a Bechtel World."

309 *"Neither Steve"*: Author interview with Philip M. Smith.

309 *"outside the realm"*: Davis, "It's a Bechtel World." In 2014, the S.D. Bechtel Jr. Foundation, which is not part of the Bechtel Group Foundation, gave $25 million to the Golden Gate National Parks Conservancy as part of its plan to spend down its assets by 2020. Meanwhile, the company became a visible sponsor of some National Public Radio stations, including KNPR in Las Vegas and KQED in San Francisco, and in 2015, the Bechtel-led team at the Hanford, Washington vitrification site donated more than $590,000 to local community organizations.

309 *"Bechtel has a three-point"*... *"company spinmeisters"*: A. C. Thompson, "Inside Bechtel's Spin Machine," ZNET Communications, May 10, 2004, www.zcommunications.org.

310 *"engages in the political process"*... *"The implication that Bechtel"*: www.Bechtel.com, April 29, 2003.

310 *"The first thing they did"*: Author interview with Laton McCartney.

311 *"errors on more"*... *"preposterous"*... *"corporate networking"*: Labaton, "Role in Scuttled."

BIBLIOGRAPHY

BOOKS

Agee, Philip. *On the Run*. Secaucus, NJ: Lyle Stuart, 1987.

Ambrose, Stephen. *Eisenhower: Soldier and President*. New York: Simon & Schuster, 1990.

Anderson, Jack, with Daryl Gibson. *Peace, War, and Politics: An Eyewitness Account*. New York: Forge, 1999.

Anderson, Jack, with James Boyd. *Fiasco: The Real Story Behind the Disastrous Worldwide Energy Crisis—Richard Nixon's "Oilgate."* New York: Times Books, 1983.

Bacevich, Andrew J. *Washington Rules: America's Path to Permanent War*. New York: Metropolitan Books, 2010.

Baer, Robert. *Sleeping with the Devil: How Washington Sold Our Soul for Saudi Crude*. New York: Crown, 2003.

Bamford, James. *Body of Secrets: The National Security Agency—From the Cold War Through the Dawn of the New Century*. New York: Doubleday, 2001.

Barnet, Richard J. *Roots of War*. New York: Atheneum, 1972.

Bird, Kai, and Martin J. Sherwin. *American Prometheus: The Triumph and Tragedy of J. Robert Oppenheimer*. New York: Vintage, 2006.

Blitzer, Wolf. *Territory of Lies. The Exclusive Story of Jonathan Jay Pollard: The American Who Spied on His Country for Israel and How He Was Betrayed*. New York: Harper & Row, 1989.

Block, Alan A., and Constance A. Weaver. *All Is Clouded by Desire: Global Banking, Money Laundering, and International Crime*. Westport, CT: Praeger, 2004.

Blout, Elkan, ed. *The Power of Boldness: Ten Master Builders of American Industry Tell Their Success Stories*. Washington, DC: A Joseph Henry Book, 1996.

Blum, William. *Killing Hope: U.S. Military and CIA Interventions Since World War II*. Monroe, ME: Common Courage Press, 1995.

Boykin, John. *Cursed Is the Peacemaker: The American Diplomat Versus the Israeli General, Beirut 1982.* Washington, DC: Applegate Press, Diplomats and Diplomacy Series, 2002.

Brands, H. W. *The Devil We Knew: Americans and the Cold War.* New York: Oxford University Press, 1993.

Brennglass, Alan C. *The Overseas Private Investment Corporation: A Study in Political Risk.* U.S.: Praeger Special Studies, 1983.

Briody, Dan. *The Iron Triangle: Inside the Secret World of the Carlyle Group.* Hoboken, NJ: John Wiley & Sons, 2003.

Brookstone, Jeffrey M. *The Multinational Businessman and Foreign Policy: Entrepreneurial Politics in East-West Trade and Investment.* U.S.: Praeger Special Studies, 1976.

Brown, Anthony Cave. *Wild Bill Donovan: The Last Hero.* New York: Times Books, 1982.

Brownstein, Ronald, and Nina Easton. *Reagan's Ruling Class. Portraits of the President's Top 100 Officials.* Washington, DC: The Presidential Accountability Group, 1982.

Brunn, Stanley D. *Engineering Earth: The Impacts of Megaengineering Projects.* New York: Springer, 2001.

Byrne, Malcolm. *Iran-Contra: Reagan's Scandal and the Unchecked Abuse of Presidential Power.* Lawrence: University Press of Kansas, 2014.

Cannon, Lou. *President Reagan: The Role of a Lifetime.* New York: Public Affairs, 2000.

Claire, Rodger W. *Raid on the Sun: Inside Israel's Secret Campaign That Denied Saddam the Bomb.* New York: Broadway Books, 2004.

Coll, Steve. *The Bin Ladens: An Arabian Family in the American Century.* New York: Penguin Press, 2008.

_____. *Private Empire: ExxonMobil and American Power.* New York: Penguin Press, 2012.

Collins, Catherine, and Douglas Frantz. *Fallout: The True Story of the CIA's Secret War on Nuclear Trafficking.* New York: Free Press, 2011.

Colodny, Len, and Tom Shachtman. *The Forty Years War: The Rise and Fall of the Neocons, from Nixon to Obama.* New York: Harper, 2009.

Cooley, John K. *Libyan Sandstorm.* New York: Holt, Rinehart and Winston, 1982.

_____. *Unholy Wars: Afghanistan, America and International Terrorism.* London: Pluto Press, 1999.

Corera, Gordon. *Shopping for Bombs: Nuclear Proliferation, Global Insecurity, and the Rise and Fall of the A. Q. Khan Network.* New York: Oxford University Press, 2006.

Crile, George. *Charlie Wilson's War.* New York: Atlantic Monthly Press, 2003.

Cull, Nicholas J. *The Cold War and the United States Information Agency: American Propaganda and Public Diplomacy, 1945–1989.* Cambridge: Cambridge University Press, 2009.

Denton, Sally. *The Pink Lady: The Many Lives of Helen Gahagan Douglas.* New York: Bloomsbury Press, 2009.

Didion, Joan. *Where I Was From.* New York: Alfred A. Knopf, 2003.

Domhoff, G. William. *The Bohemian Grove and Other Retreats: A Study in Ruling-Class Cohesiveness.* New York: Harper & Row, 1974.

Duelfer, Charles. *Hide and Seek: The Search for Truth in Iraq.* New York: Public Affairs, 2009.

Dulles, Allen. *The Secret Surrender.* New York: Harper & Row, 1966.

Eisenhower, Dwight D. *Mandate for Change: The White House Years.* Garden City, NY: Doubleday, 1963.

Eveland, Wilbur Crane. *Ropes of Sand: America's Failure in the Middle East.* New York: W. W. Norton, 1980.

Feldstein, Mark. *Poisoning the Press: Richard Nixon, Jack Anderson and the Rise of Washington's Scandal Culture.* New York: Farrar, Straus and Giroux, 2010.

Finnie, Richard. *Bechtel in Arab Lands: A Fifteenth-Year Review of Engineering and Construction Projects.* San Francisco: Bechtel Corporation, 1958.

Fitzgerald, Frances. *Way Out There in the Blue: Reagan, Star Wars and the End of the Cold War.* New York: Simon & Schuster, 2000.

Flynn, Jean. *Henry B. Gonzalez: Rebel with a Cause.* Austin, TX: Eakin Press, 2004.

Foster, Mark S. *Henry J. Kaiser: Builder in the Modern American West.* Austin: University of Texas Press, 1989.

Friedman, Alan. *Spider's Web: The Secret History of How the White House Illegally Armed Iraq.* New York: Bantam Books, 1993.

Gentry, Curt. *J. Edgar Hoover: The Man and the Secrets.* New York: W. W. Norton, 1991.

Gibson, Weldon B. *SRI, The Founding Years. A Significant Step at the Golden Time.* Los Altos, CA: Publishing Services Center, 1981.

Goldenberg, Elliot. *The Hunting Horse: The Truth Behind the Jonathan Pollard Spy Case.* New York: Prometheus Books, 2000.

_____. *The Spy Who Knew Too Much: The Government Plot to Silence Jonathan Pollard.* New York: SPI Books, 1993.

Graetz, Michael J. *The End of Energy: The Unmaking of America's Environment, Security, and Independence.* Cambridge: Massachusetts Institute of Technology Press, 2011.

Grose, Peter. *Gentleman Spy: The Life of Allen Dulles.* New York: Houghton Mifflin, 1994.

Gusterson, Hugh. *Nuclear Rites: A Weapons Laboratory at the End of the Cold War.* Berkeley: University of California Press, 1996.

_____. *People of the Bomb: Portraits of America's Nuclear Complex.* Minneapolis: University of Minnesota Press, 2004.

Gwilliam, G. Gary. *Getting a Winning Verdict: A Trial Lawyer Finds His Soul.* Walnut Creek, CA: Pavior, 2007.

Halberstam, David. *The Best and the Brightest*. New York: Random House, 1969.

Hartung, William D. *How Much Are You Making on the War, Daddy? A Quick and Dirty Guide to War Profiteering in the Bush Administration*. New York: Nation Books, 2003.

_____. *Prophets of War: Lockheed Martin and the Making of the Military-Industrial Complex*. New York: Nation Books, 2011.

Helms, Richard, and William Hood. *A Look over My Shoulder: A Life in the Central Intelligence Agency*. New York: Random House, 2003.

Henderson, Bernard R. *Pollard: The Spy's Story*. New York: Alpha Books, 1988.

Henderson, Paul. *The Unlikely Spy: Paul Henderson, Former Managing Director of Matrix Churchill*. New York: Bloomsbury, 1995.

Hersh, Berton. *The Old Boys: The American Elite and the Origins of the CIA*. New York: Charles Scribner's Sons, 1992.

Hersh, Seymour. *The Dark Side of Camelot*. Boston: Little, Brown, 1997.

_____. *The Samson Option: Israel's Nuclear Arsenal and American Foreign Policy*. New York: Random House, 1991.

Hiltzik, Michael. *Colossus: Hoover Dam and the Making of the American Century*. New York: Free Press, 2010.

Hochschild, Adam. *King Leopold's Ghost: A Story of Greed, Terror, and Heroism in Colonial Africa*. Boston: Houghton Mifflin, 1998.

Hoyle, Russ. *Going to War: How Misinformation, Disinformation, and Arrogance Led America into Iraq*. New York: Thomas Dunne Books, 2008.

Ingram, Robert L. *The Bechtel Story: Seventy Years of Accomplishment in Engineering and Construction*. San Francisco: Ingram, 1968. (Official Company History.)

_____. *A Builder and His Family, 1898–1948: Being the Historical Account of the Contracting, Engineering & Construction Career of W. A. Bechtel and of How His Sons and Their Associates Have Carried Forward His Principles in Their Many Activities*. Privately Printed. San Francisco, 1949.

Isaacson, Walter. *Einstein: His Life and Universe*. New York: Simon & Schuster, 2007.

Isaacson, Walter, and Evan Thomas. *The Wise Men: Six Friends and the World They Made*. New York: Simon & Schuster, 1987.

Isikoff, Michael, and David Corn. *Hubris: The Inside Story of Spin, Scandal, and the Selling of the Iraq War*. New York: Crown, 2006.

Jacobsen, Annie. *Area 51: An Uncensored History of America's Top Secret Military Base*. New York: Little, Brown, 2011.

Jamail, Dahr. *Beyond the Green Zone: Dispatches from an Unembedded Journalist in Occupied Iraq*. Chicago: Haymarket Books, 2007.

Johnson, Chalmers. *The Costs and Consequences of American Empire*. New York: Metropolitan Books, 2000.

Juhasz, Antonia. *The Bush Agenda: Invading the World, One Economy at a Time*. New York: ReganBooks, 2006.

Kaplan, Robert D. *The Arabists: The Romance of an American Elite*. New York: Free Press, 1993.

Kelly, Cynthia C. *The Manhattan Project*. New York: Black Dog & Leventhal, 2007.

Kennan, George F. *Memoirs: 1950–1963*. Boston: Little, Brown, 1972.

Kinzer, Stephen. *All the Shah's Men: An American Coup and the Roots of Middle East Terror*. Hoboken, NJ: John Wiley & Sons, 2008.

_____. *The Brothers: John Foster Dulles, Allen Dulles, and Their Secret World War*. New York: Times Books, 2013.

_____. *Overthrow: America's Century of Regime Change from Hawaii to Iraq*. New York: Times Books, 2006.

Kissinger, Henry. *White House Years*. Boston: Little, Brown, 1979.

Klein, Naomi. *The Shock Doctrine: The Rise of Disaster Capitalism*. New York: Picador, 2007.

Kornbluh, Peter. *The Pinochet File*. New York: New Press, 2004.

Krass, Allan S., Peter Boskma, Boelie Elzen, and Wim A. Smit. *Uranium Enrichment and Nuclear Weapon Proliferation*. New York: International Publications Service, 1983.

Kwitny, Jonathan. *The Crimes of Patriots: A True Tale of Dope, Dirty Money, and the CIA*. New York: W. W. Norton, 1987.

Lacey, Robert. *The Kingdom*. New York: Harcourt Brace, 1981.

Lando, Barry M. *Web of Deceit: The History of Western Complicity in Iraq, from Churchill to Kennedy to George W. Bush*. New York: Other Press, 2007.

Langewiesche, William. *The Atomic Bazaar: The Rise of the Nuclear Poor*. New York: Farrar, Straus and Giroux.

Laughlin, Robert B. *Powering the Future: How We Will (Eventually) Solve the Energy Crisis and Fuel the Civilization of Tomorrow*. New York: Basic Books, 2011.

Lebovik, James H. *Flawed Logics: Strategic Nuclear Arms Control from Truman to Obama*. Baltimore: Johns Hopkins University Press, 2013.

Lee, Mordecai. *Nixon's Super-Secretaries. The Last Grand Presidential Reorganization Effort*. College Station: Texas A & M University Press, 2010.

Lee, Wen Ho. *My Country Versus Me: The First-Hand Account by the Los Alamos Scientist Who Was Falsely Accused of Being a Spy*. New York: Hachette, 2002.

Lettow, Paul. *Ronald Reagan and His Quest to Abolish Nuclear Weapons*. New York: Random House, 2005.

Loftus, John, and Mark Aarons. *The Secret War Against the Jews: How Western Espionage Betrayed the Jewish People.* New York: St. Martin's Press, 1994.

Lohbeck, Kurt. *Holy War, Unholy Victory: Eyewitness to the CIA's Secret War in Afghanistan.* Washington, DC: Regnery Gateway, 1993.

Manchester, William. *The Glory and the Dream.* 2 vols. Boston: Little, Brown, 1973.

Mangold, Tom. *Cold Warrior: James Jesus Angleton—The CIA's Master Spy Hunter.* New York: Simon & Schuster, 1991.

Mansfield, Peter. *The New Arabians.* Chicago: J. G. Ferguson, 1981.

Mantius, Peter. *Shell Game: A True Story of Banking, Spies, Lies, Politics—and the Arming of Saddam Hussein.* New York: St. Martin's Press, 1995.

Marchetti, Victor, and John D. Marks. *The CIA and the Cult of Intelligence.* New York: Alfred A. Knopf, 1974.

McBride, Dennis. *In the Beginning: A History of Boulder City, Nevada.* Boulder City: Hoover Dam Museum, 1992.

McCartney, Laton. *Friends in High Places: The Bechtel Story—The Most Secret Corporation and How It Engineered the World.* New York: Ballantine Books, 1988.

Melman, Seymour. *Pentagon Capitalism: The Political Economy of War.* New York: McGraw-Hill, 1970.

Miller, T. Christian. *Blood Money.* New York: Little, Brown, 2006.

Mintz, Morton, and Jerry S. Cohen. *Inc.: Public and Private Rules and How to Make Them Accountable.* New York: Viking Press, 1976.

Moran, Theodore H. *Reforming OPIC for the 21st Century.* Washington, DC: Institute for International Economics, May 2003.

Morley, Jefferson. *Our Man in Mexico: Winston Scott and the Hidden History of the CIA.* Lawrence: University of Kansas Press, 2008.

Morris, Edmund. *Dutch: A Memoir of Ronald Reagan.* New York: Random House, 1999.

Morris, Roger. *Partners in Power: The Clintons and Their America.* New York: Henry Holt, 1996.

_____. *Richard Milhous Nixon: The Rise of an American Politician.* New York: Henry Holt, 1990.

Nader, Ralph, and John Abbots. *The Menace of Atomic Energy.* New York: W. W. Norton, 1977.

Nies, Judith. *Unreal City: Las Vegas, Black Mesa, and the Fate of the American West.* New York: Nation Books, 2014. (Advance Uncorrected Proof.)

Nixon, Richard. *RN: The Memoirs of Richard Nixon.* New York: Grosset & Dunlap, 1978.

North, Oliver, with William Novak. *Under Fire: An American Story.* New York: HarperCollins, 1991.

Olive, Ronald J. *Capturing Jonathan Pollard: How One of the Most Notorious Spies in American History Was Brought to Justice.* Annapolis, MD: Naval Institute Press, 2006.

Oreskes, Naomi, and Erik M. Conway. *Merchants of Doubt.* New York: Bloomsbury Press, 2010.

Packer, George. *The Assassin's Gate: America in Iraq.* New York: Farrar, Straus and Giroux, 2005.

Pearson, Graham S. *The Search for Iraq's Weapons of Mass Destruction: Inspection, Verification and Non-Proliferation.* New York: Palgrave MacMillan, 2005.

Peck, James. *Washington's China: The National Security World, the Cold War, and the Origins of Globalism.* Amherst: University of Massachusetts Press, 2001.

Pemberton, Miriam, ed., and William D. Hartung. *Lessons from Iraq: Avoiding the Next War.* Boulder, CO: Paradigm Publishers, 2008.

Perkins, John. *Confessions of an Economic Hit Man: The Shocking Inside Story of How America Really Took Over the World.* London: Ebury Press, 2005.

_____. *Hoodwinked: An Economic Hit Man Reveals Why the World Financial Markets Imploded—and What We Need to Do to Remake Them.* New York: Broadway Books, 2009.

Phillips-Fein, Kim. *Invisible Hands.* New York: W. W. Norton, 2009.

Powaski, Ronald E. *March to Armageddon: The United States and the Nuclear Arms Race, 1939 to the Present.* Oxford: Oxford University Press, 1989.

Prouty, L. Fletcher. *JFK: The CIA, Vietnam, and the Plot to Assassinate John F. Kennedy.* New York: Skyhorse, 2009.

_____. *The Secret Team: The CIA and Its Allies in Control of the United States and the World.* Englewood Cliffs, NJ: Prentice Hall, 1973.

Rand, Christopher. *Making Democracy Safe for Oil: Oilmen and the Islamic East.* Boston: Little, Brown, 1975.

Rapoport, Roger. *The Great American Bomb Machine.* New York: E. P. Dutton, 1971.

Reisner, Marc. *Cadillac Desert: The American West and Its Disappearing Water.* New York: Viking, 1986.

Rhodes, Richard. *Dark Sun: The Making of the Hydrogen Bomb.* New York: Simon & Schuster, 1995.

Richelson, Jeffrey T. *Civilians, Spies, and Blue Suits. The Bureaucratic War for Control of Overhead Reconnaissance, 1961–1965.* www2.gwu.edu/~nsarchiv/monograph/nro/nromono.pdf.

_____. *Spying on the Bomb: American Nuclear Intelligence from Nazi Germany to Iran and North Korea*. New York: W. W. Norton, 2006.

Ritter, Scott. *Iraq Confidential*. Clevedon, UK: Tauris, 2005.

Rocca, Al M. *America's Master Dam Builder: The Engineering Genius of Frank T. Crowe*. Lanham, Maryland: University Press of America, Inc., 2001.

Rothkopf, David. *Power, Inc. The Epic Rivalry Between Big Business and Government—and the Reckoning That Lies Ahead*. New York: Farrar, Straus and Giroux, 2012.

Rumsfeld, Donald. *Known and Unknown*. New York: Sentinel, 2011.

Russell, Dick. *The Man Who Knew Too Much*. New York: Carroll and Graf, 1993.

Sampson, Anthony. *The Seven Sisters: The Great Oil Companies and the World They Made*. New York: Viking Press, 1975.

_____. *The Sovereign State: The Secret History of ITT*. London: Hodder and Stoughton, 1974.

Savas, E. S. *Privatization and Public-Private Partnerships*. New York: Chatham House, 2000.

Scheer, Robert. *With Enough Shovels: Reagan, Bush and Nuclear War*. New York: Random House, 1982.

Schlesinger, Arthur M., Jr. *Journals: 1952–2000*. New York: Penguin Press, 2007.

Schulman, Daniel. *Sons of Wichita: How the Koch Brothers Became America's Most Powerful and Private Dynasty*. New York: Grand Central, 2014.

Shaw, Mark. *Miscarriage of Justice: The Jonathan Pollard Story*. St. Paul, MN: Paragon House, 2001.

Shawcross, William. *Allies: Why the West Had to Remove Saddam*. New York: Public Affairs, 2004.

Shorrock, Tim. *Spies for Hire: The Secret World of Intelligence Outsourcing*. New York: Simon & Schuster, 2008.

Shultz, George P. *Turmoil and Triumph: My Years as Secretary of State*. New York: Charles Scribner's, 1993.

Shultz, George P., and Kenneth W. Dam. *Economic Policy Beyond the Headlines*. Chicago: University of Chicago Press, 1998.

Sick, Gary. *October Surprise: America's Hostages in Iran and the Election of Ronald Reagan*. New York: Times Books, 1991.

Simpson, John L. *Random Notes: Recollections of My Early Life. Europe Without a Guidebook. 1915–1922*. (Printed privately.) San Francisco, 1969.

Singer, P. W. *Corporate Warriors: The Rise of the Privatized Military Industry*. Ithaca, NY, and London: Cornell University Press, 2008.

Smith, Hedrick. *The Power Game: How Washington Works*. New York: Random House, 1988.

_____. *Who Stole the American Dream?* New York: Random House, 2012.

Smith, Richard Harris. *OSS: The Secret History of America's First Central Intelligence Agency.* Berkeley: University of California Press, 1972.

Starr, Kevin. *Endangered Dreams: The Great Depression in California.* New York: Oxford University Press, 1996.

Stephenson, James. *Losing the Golden Hour: An Insider's View of Iraq's Reconstruction.* Washington, DC: Potomac Books, 2007.

Stevens, Joseph E. *Hoover Dam: An American Adventure.* Norman: University of Oklahoma Press, 1988.

Stober, Dan, and Ian Hoffman. *A Convenient Spy: Wen Ho Lee and the Politics of Nuclear Espionage.* New York: Simon & Schuster, 2002.

Swanberg, W. A. *Luce and His Empire.* New York: Charles Scribner's Sons, 1972.

Taubman, Philip. *Secret Empire: Eisenhower, the CIA, and the Hidden Story of America's Space Espionage.* New York: Simon & Schuster, 2003.

Teicher, Howard, and Gayle Radley Teicher. *Twin Pillars to Desert Storm: America's Flawed Vision in the Middle East from Nixon to Bush.* New York: William Morrow, 1993.

Thomas, Evan. *Ike's Bluff: President Eisenhower's Secret Battle to Save the World.* New York: Little, Brown, 2012.

Trento, Joseph J. *Prelude to Terror: The Rogue CIA and the Legacy of America's Private Intelligence Network.* New York: Carroll & Graf, 2005.

_____. *The Secret History of the CIA.* New York: MJF Books, 2001.

Van Buren, Peter. *We Meant Well: How I Helped Lose the Battle for the Hearts and Minds of the Iraqi People.* New York: Metropolitan Books, 2011.

Van der Zee, John. *The Greatest Men's Party on Earth: Inside the Bohemian Grove.* New York: Harcourt Brace Jovanovich, 1974.

Wallop, Malcolm, and Angelo Codevilla. *The Arms Control Delusion.* San Francisco: Institute for Contemporary Studies, 1988.

Walsh, Lawrence E. *Firewall: The Iran-Contra Conspiracy and Cover-Up.* New York: W. W. Norton, 1997.

Watkins, T. H. *Righteous Pilgrim: The Life and Times of Harold L. Ickes, 1874–1952.* New York: Henry Holt, 1990.

Weinberg, Steve. *Armand Hammer: The Untold Story.* Boston: Little, Brown, 1989.

Weinberger, Caspar W., with Gretchen Roberts. *In the Arena: A Memoir of the 20th Century.* Washington, DC: Regnery, 2001.

Weiner, Tim. *Blank Check: The Pentagon's Black Budget.* New York: Warner Books, 1990.

Wiley, Peter, and Robert Gottlieb. *Empires in the Sun: The Rise of the New American West.* Tucson: University of Arizona Press, 1982.

Wilford, Hugh. *America's Great Game: The CIA's Secret Arabists and the Shaping of the Modern Middle East.* New York: Basic Books, 2013.

Wise, David, and Thomas B. Ross. *The Espionage Establishment.* New York: Random House, 1967.

_____. *The Invisible Government.* New York: Random House, 1964.

Woodward, Bob. *Veil: The Secret Wars of the CIA, 1981–1987.* New York: Pocket Books, 1987.

Yergin, Daniel. *The Prize: The Epic Quest for Oil, Money and Power.* New York: Simon & Schuster, 1991.

Zwicker, Heather. " 'To Build a Better World': Bechtel, a Family Company," In *Cultural Critique and the Global Corporation,* edited by Purnima Bose and Laura E. Lyons, 9–127. Bloomington: Indiana University Press, 2010.

JOURNALS, ARTICLES, DISSERTATIONS, REPORTS,
BLOGS, AND MANUSCRIPTS

Alvarez, Robert. "Who Should Manage the Nuclear Weapons Complex?" *Bulletin of the Atomic Scientists,* December 12, 2012.

American Small Business League. *ASBL Report: Small Business Contract Recipients FY 2009.* www.asbl.com.

Anderson, Jack. "John McCone: Secrecy Is His Business." *Boston Globe.* December 16, 1962.

_____. "The Washington Merry-Go-Round." *Boston Globe.* February 19, 1966.

Anderson, Sarah. *Nation.* April 16, 2012.

Arabian Oil & Gas Staff. "World's 10 Largest Oil and Gas Contractors." www.arabianoilandgas.com/article-5773-worlds-10-largest-oil-and-gas-contractors. November 20, 2013.

Arkin, William M. "Nuclear Warfare: Secret Plan Outlines the Unthinkable." *Los Angeles Times.* March 10, 2002.

Armstrong, Scott. "The $200 Billion Secret." *Mother Jones,* November/December 1991.

Arnold, Chris. "Most Large-Scale Public Works Projects Go Well over Budget." NPR. *All Things Considered.* April 10, 2003.

Arzt, George. "Cap Calls Saudi Story 'Fabrication.' " *New York Post,* August 19, 1983.

_____. "Koch Blasts Caspar." *New York Post,* August 18, 1983.

Associated Press. "Ex-Handler Says Jonathan Pollard Bungled '85 Escape Plan—Takes Responsibility for Pollard Being Thrown Out of Embassy," December 1, 2014.

Baer, Robert. "The Fall of the House of Saud." *Atlantic.* May 2003.

_____. Online Amazon review of *Hoodwinked,* by John Perkins. www.amazon.com/Hoodwinked-Economic-Reveals-Economy-IMPLODED/dp/030

7589943/ref=sr_1_2?s=books&ie=UTF8&qid=1406406900&sr=1-2
&keywords=hoodwinked.

Bagdikian, Ben H. "Unsecretive Report on the C.I.A." *New York Times*, October 27, 1963.

Baker, David R. "The Bechtel Breed." *San Francisco Chronicle*. October 3, 2003.

_____. "Bechtel Pulling Out After 3 Rough Years of Rebuilding Work." *San Francisco Chronicle*, November 1, 2006.

_____. "Bechtel's 2003 Revenue Breaks Company Record." *San Francisco Chronicle*, April 20, 2004.

_____. "Big Dig Tragedy Could Stain Bechtel's Name: Delays, Cost Overruns, Leaks and Now a Death in Boston Puts Spotlight on S.F. Construction Giant—and Some of Its Other Mammoth Projects." *San Francisco Chronicle*, July 19, 2006.

_____. "Little Scrutiny for Firms In Iraq/SF's Bechtel Among Most Prominent Ones." *San Francisco Chronicle*, November 14, 2006.

Baker, Russ. "The Jonathan Pollard Spy Case: Plot Thickens." *WhoWhatWhy*, March 7, 2013. www.whowhatwhy.com.

Barber, Lionel, and Alan Friedman. "A Fatal Attraction: Under the Nose of the White House, Kickbacks and Illegal Deals Funded Saddam." *Financial Times*, May 3, 1991.

Barlett, Donald L., and James B. Steele. "Washington's $8 Billion Shadow." *Vanity Fair*, March 2007.

Barlow, Maude. "Water Is a Basic Human Right." *Peace Research*, November 2000.

Baum, Dan. "Nation Builders for Hire." *New York Times*, June 22, 2003.

BBC News. "Iraqi Resident Holds Talks with Ex-US Assistant Secretary of State," January 21, 2010.

Bechtel, Stephen D., Jr. "Reflections on Success." *Dædalus* 125, no. 2 (Spring 1996): 147–66.

Beglov, I. "California Tycoons." *International Affairs* 11, no. 11 (1965): 28–35.

Beglov, M., and S. Veglov. "Guardians on the Potomac." *International Affairs* 32, no. 7 (1986): 122–29.

Bender, Bryan, and Neil Swidey. "Robert F. Kennedy Saw Conspiracy in JFK's Assassination." *Boston Globe*, November 24, 2013.

Benedict, Kennette. "The U.S. Nuclear Weapons Complex Needs a New Role." *Bulletin of the Atomic Scientists*, April 10, 2014.

Bennett, Brian, and Michael Weisskopf. "The Sum of Two Evils." *Time*, May 25, 2003.

Bensky, Larry. "End Game." *California Lawyer*, January 1993.

Berdik, Chris. "The Department of Energy's War on Whistleblowers." *Mother Jones*, January 17, 2001.

Bernstein, David S. "A Handy Guide to the Big Dig Screw-Up." *Phoenix*, July 27, 2006.

Berrigan, Frida. "Privatizing the Apocalypse." tomdispatch.com, March 30, 2006. www.tomdispatch.com/post/72765.

Bischoff, Glenn. "Master of the Megaproject." *Telephony* 242, no. 22 (June 3, 2002).

Bishop, Elizabeth. " *'Blown Away by the Winds Like Ashes'*: Biopower in Egypt's #25 Jan. and Iraq's 14 Tammuz." (In "The Arab Spring: Comparative Perspectives and Regional Implications," ed. Philipp O. Amour, Special Issue. *Alternatives: Turkish Journal of International Relations* 12, no. 3 (Fall 2013): 47–65.

Black, Edwin. "Why Jonathan Pollard Is Still in Prison." *Jewish Journal*, July 4, 2002.

Blum, William. "Anthrax for Export: U.S Companies Sold Iraq the Ingredients for a Witches' Brew." *Progressive*, April 1998.

Booth, Robert, Owen Gibson, and Pete Pattisson. "Qatar Under Pressure over Migrant Labour Abuse." *Guardian* (Manchester, UK), September 26, 2013.

Borderland Beat Forum. "Border Patrol Opposes Cross-Border Energy Project," November 26, 2012.

Borger, Julian. "Rumsfeld 'Offered to Help Saddam': Declassified Papers Leave the White House Hawk Exposed over His Role During the Iran-Iraq War." *Guardian* (Manchester, UK), December 31, 2002. *Boston Globe*. "Memos Prove U.S. Knew Iraq Was Pursuing Nukes." July 5, 1992.

Bowman, M. E. "Keep Pollard Behind Bars." *New York Times*, January 14, 2014.

Braden, Tom. "The Nuclear Export Fight." *Washington Post*, July 24, 1976.

Broad, William J. "California Is Surprise Winner in Bid to Run Los Alamos." *New York Times*, December 22, 2005. http://www.nytimes.com /2005/12/22/us/california-is-surprise-winner-in-bid-to-run-los -alamos.html?_r=0.

———. "Which President Cut the Most Nukes?" *New York Times*. November 1, 2014.

Broad, William J., and David E. Sanger. "Obama's Youth Shaped His Nuclear-Free Vision." *New York Times*, July 4, 2009. http://www.nytimes .com/2009/07/05/world/05nuclear.html?pagewanted=all&_r=0.

Broder, John. "In Storm's Ruins, a Rush to Rebuild and Reopen for Business." *New York Times*, September 10, 2005.

Brownfield, Allan C. "The Ongoing Campaign to Secure the Release of Convicted Spy for Israel, Jonathan Pollard." *Washington Report on Middle East Affairs* 31, no. 7 (October 2012): 50–51.

Brunwasser, Matthew. "Steamrolled: A Special Investigation into the Diplomacy of Doing Business Abroad." *Foreign Policy*, January 30, 2015.

_____. "That Crush at Kosovo's Business Door? The Return of U.S. Heroes." *New York Times*, December 11, 2012.

Burka, Paul. "The Truth About John Connally." *Texas Monthly*, November 1979.

Burke, Jason. "Indian Labourers Working on Construction Sites in Qatar Reveal Abuse." *Guardian. September 27, 2013*. www.theguardian.com /world/2013/sep/27/indian-labourers-construction-site-qatar-abuse -revealed-guardian. November 9, 2013.

Burns, John F. "Confrontation in the Gulf—Baghdad's U.S. Hostages: Escape Plans and Anger." *New York Times*. October 7, 1990.

Business Monitor News & Views. "U.S. Construction Company Bechtel Capitalising on Changing Opportunities," November 5, 2014.

Business Wire. "Army Sued for Refusing to Release Bechtel Contracting Data, According to the American Small Business League," March 2, 2011.

Byrne, Malcolm. "Saddam Hussein: More Secret History." www2.gwu.edu/~ns archiv/NSAEBB/NSAEBB107/.

Carapico, Sheila. "Forecasting Mass Destruction, from Gulf to Gulf." *Middle East Report*, September 29, 2005. www.merip.org/mero/mero 092905.

Carlson, Carolyn. "Greg Mello and Trish Williams-Mello." *Alibi*, April 19–25, 2012.

Carlton, Jim. "Venerable Builder Bechtel Gets a New Lift from the Dot-Com Boom: It Signs Huge Construction Deals as E-Commerce Companies Race to Build Infrastructure. *Wall Street Journal*, March 1, 2000.

Carroll, James. "Why President Obama Needs to Revive His Pledge for a Nuclear-Free World." *Nation*, December 11, 2014.

Cart, Julie. "Sacrificing the Desert to Save the Earth." *Los Angeles Times*, February 5, 2012.

Carter, James M. "War Profiteering from Vietnam to Iraq." *CounterPunch*, December 11, 2003.

Carter, Stan. "How Iraq Mob Slew Americans." Associated Press, July 22, 1958.

Center for Public Integrity. "Are Nuclear Weapons Contractors' Millions in Campaign Contributions Buying Favors?" June 6, 2012. www.public integrity.org.

_____. "How an 82-Year-Old Exposed Security Lapses at Nuclear Facilities." September 12, 2012. www.publicintegrity.org.

_____. "Obama Proposes Shifting Funds from Nuclear Nonproliferation to Nuclear Weapons." April 9, 2013. www.publicintegrity.org.

Chaffin, Joshua, and Andrew Hill. "The Rush to Secure Contracts to Rebuild Iraq and the Awarding of the First Wave of Deals Is Causing as Much Debate as the Decision to Wage War." *Financial Times*, April 28, 2003.

Chatterjee, Pratap. "Bechtel's Nuclear Nightmares." *CorpWatch*. May 1, 2003. www.corpwatch.org/article.php?id=6669&printsafe=1.

Chen, Edwin. "Bush Aims to Privatize Many Federal Jobs: About 850,000 Civilian Workers Would Face Competition. Unions, Democrats Decry Move." *Los Angeles Times*, November 15, 2002.

Chesler, Phyllis. "Is Pollard Caspar Weinberger's Revenge on the Jews?" *Jewish Chronicle*, February 3, 2011.

Chomsky, Noam. "Should We Stop Talking About National Security?" www .tomdispatch.com/blog/175863/.

Church, George J. "Stephen Bechtel." *Time* (cover), December 7, 1998.

Clairborne, William. "Conflict of Interest Laid to Former Ex-Im Bank Figure." *Washington Post*, February 26, 1974, A2.

Clausing, Jeri. "Management of LANL Waste Facility Faulted." Associated Press, September 12, 2013.

Clausing, Jeri, and Matthew Daly. "LANL, Other Nuke Facilities Under Renewed Scrutiny." Associated Press, September 12, 2013.

Cockburn, Alexander, and Jeffrey St. Clair. "The Truth About the Bohemian Grove." *Counterpunch*, June 19, 2001. www.counterpunch.org/2001/06 /19/the-truth-about-the-bohemian-grove/print.

Conason, Joe. " 'Most Antagonistic' Toward Israel? That Would Be Ronald Reagan's Defense Secretary." Creators Syndicate, January 10, 2013. https://www.creators.com/liberal/joe-conason/-most-antagonistic -toward-israel-that-would-be-ronald-reagan-s-defense-secretary .html.

Cooper, Helene. "Obama Turns to Biden to Reassure Jewish Voters, and Get Them to Contribute Too." *New York Times*, September 30, 2011.

Corpwatch, Global Exchange and *Public Citizen*. "Bechtel: Profiting from Destruction. Why the Corporate Invasion of Iraq Must be Stopped." June 2003. www.corpwatch.org.

Cox, James, and Gary Strauss. "Iraq Work Puts Bechtel in Spotlight: Private Contractor Juggles Restoration with Controversy." *USA Today*, June 19, 2003. http://usatoday30.usatoday.com/money/world/iraq/2003-06-18 -bechtel_x.htm.

Crabtree, Susan. "Obama Heckled During Speech to Israelis." *Washington Times*, March 21, 2013.

Crogan, Jim. "The Dishonor Role: America's Corporate Merchants of Death in Iraq." *LA Weekly*, May 1, 2003. Part 3.

_____. "Made in the USA: A Guide to Iraq's Weapons of Mass Destruction." *LA Weekly*, March 21–27 and April 25–May 1, 2003. Parts 1 and 2.

Crovitz, L. Gordon. "Even Pollard Deserves Better Than Government Sandbagging." *Asian Wall Street Journal*, September 27, 1991.

_____. "Pollard Was a Victim of U.S. Sandbagging." *Wall Street Journal*, September 9, 1991.

Crow, Robert Thomas. "The Business Economist at Work: The Bechtel Group." *Business Economics* 29, no. 1 (January 1994): 46.

Davis, Lisa. "It's a Bechtel World: Think That a $680 Million Iraq Contract Is a Big Deal? You Don't Know Bechtel." *SF Weekly*, June 18, 2003. http://www.sfweekly.com/sanfrancisco/its-a-bechtel-world/Content?oid=2148387.

_____. "The World According to Bechtel. There Are Well-Connected Companies. Then There's Bechtel." *SF Weekly*, June 18, 2003. http://www.sfweekly.com/sanfrancisco/the-world-according-to-bechtel/Content?oid=2148394.

Defense Industry Daily Staff. "The U.S. Navy's Nuclear Propulsion Contracts." *Defense Industry Daily*. www.defenseindustrydaily.com/the-us-navys-nuclear-propulsion-contracts-04752/.

Denton, Sally. "Hoover's Promise: The Dam That Remade the American West Celebrates Its 75th Anniversary." *Invention & Technology* 25, no. 2 (Summer 2010): 14.

Devine, Jack. "What Really Happened in Chile: The CIA, the Coup Against Allende, and the Rise of Pinochet. *Foreign Affairs*, July/August 2014. www.foreignaffairs.com/articles/141453/jack-devine/what-really-happened-in-chile.

De Voto, Bernard. "The Anxious West." *Harper's*, December 1946.

Dobbs, Michael. "U.S. Had Key Role in Iraq Buildup: Trade in Chemical Arms Allowed Despite Their Use on Iranians, Kurds." *Washington Post*, December 30, 2002.

Domhoff, G. William. "Where the Elite Meet." *Washington Post*. August 17, 1975.

Dowd, Maureen. "Jeb Bush's Brainless Trust." *New York Times*, February 22, 2015.

Dowie, Mark. "The Bechtel File: How the Master Builders Protect Their Beachheads." *Mother Jones*, September/October 1978.

Dowie, Mark, Peter Hayes, Tim Shorrock, and Lyuba Zarsky. "Bechtel: A Tale of Corruption." *Multinational Monitor* 5, no. 5 (May 1984). http://multinationalmonitor.org/hyper/issues/1984/05/dowie.html.

Dreazen, Yochi. "Cleaning Up Assad's Chemical Weapons Is the New Mideast Gold Rush." www.thecable.foreignpolicy.com/posts.

Drew, Christopher. "President Has Faith in Meese." *Chicago Tribune*, February 24, 1988.

Dreyfuss, Robert. "The CIA Crosses Over." *Mother Jones*, January 1, 1995.

Drozdiak, William. "State-Run Energy Firm Filled Italian Parties' Coffers." *Washington Post*, July 25, 1993.

Dwyer, Paula, et al. "Bechtel's Iraqi Pipe Dream Could Land It in Hot Water." *BusinessWeek*, February 22, 1988, 33.

Economist. "Another Fine Meese He's Gotten Himself Into." February 6, 1988.

_____. "Bechtel's Dance of the Seven Veils." May 18, 1981.

_____. "Building with Bechtel." November 13, 1997.

_____. "Caspar Weinberger." April 1, 2006.

_____. "The Growing Appeal of Zero: Banning the Bomb Will Be Hard, but Not Impossible." June 16, 2011.

_____. "Hubbub over Habib." July 31, 1982.

_____. "Portrait of a Corporation." September 4, 1982.

_____. "The Workhorse Returns." July 3, 1982.

Eisler, Peter. "Energy Office Wants Contractor Relieved in Nuclear Cleanup." *USA Today*, January 13, 2013.

Elshayyal, Jamal. "Secret Files: US Officials Aided Gaddafi." *Aljazeera*, August 31, 2011.

Energy Global. "Bechtel Capitalising on Changing Opportunities." December 11, 2014.

Engelhardt, Tom. "Everything's Private." *Mother Jones*, November 4, 2003.

Engineering News Record. "Bechtel Awash in Complaints." September 23, 2002.

ENP Newswire. "B & W and Bechtel Form Alliance to Commercialize World's First Generation III++SMR Nuclear Plant." July 16, 2010.

Falk, Richard. "Reviving Global Justice, Addressing Legitimate Grievances." *Middle East Report* 33 (Winter 2003). www.merip.org/mer/mer229/reviving-global-justice-addressing-legitimate-grievances.

Fang, Lee. "Grover Norquist, Lobbyist." *Nation*, January 21, 2013.

Fatsis, Stefan. "Bechtel Group Inc. to Play a Major Role in Rebuilding Kuwait." Associated Press, April 1, 1991.

Federal Bureau of Investigation. "Famous Cases and Criminals: The Year of the Spy." fbi.gov/about-us/history/famous-cases/the-year-of-the-spy.

Feinberg, Lawrence. "A-Plant Aide Draws Perjury Term." *Washington Post*, October 14, 1975.

Fidler, Stephen, and Thomas Catan. "Private Companies on the Frontline." *Financial Times*, August 11, 2003.

Fitts, Catherine Austin. "Dillon, Read & Co. Inc. and the Aristocracy of Stock Profits," 2006. www.dunwalke.com/introduction.htm.

Flalka, John J., and Peter Truell. "Pandora's Box: Bush Administration's Ties to Iraq Loan Scandal Grow." *Asian Wall Street Journal*, October 12, 1992.

_____. "The Plot Thickens: As 'Iraqgate' Unfolds, New Evidence Raises Questions of Cover-Up—Once-Obscure Bank Scandal Keeps Unwanted Focus on Bush's Saddam Policy—Altered Lending Documents." *Wall Street Journal, Europe*, October 12, 1992.

Fogarty, Thomas A. "Companies Bid on Rebuilding Iraq—Halliburton, Bechtel Benefit from Experience and Political Ties." *USA Today*, March 26, 2003.

Fortune 28. "The Earth Movers I." August 1943: 99–107, 210–14.

_____. "The Earth Movers II." September 1943: 119–22, 219–26.

_____. "The Earth Movers III." October 1943: 139–44, 193–99.

FOX News. "Bechtel Leaves Iraq After Losing 52 Workers in 3 Years." November 2, 2006.

Frank, Joshua. "Hanford's Nuclear Option: Department of Energy Scientists Allege Catastrophic Mismanagement of the Costliest Environmental Cleanup in World History." *Seattle Weekly*, October 18, 2011.

_____. "Whistleblower Will Finally Have Day in Court: The Case of Hanford Contractor Walter Tomosaitis." *Counterpunch*, November 11, 2014.

Frantz, Douglas. "Bush Exercised Hands-On Role in Iraq Aid Effort." *Los Angeles Times*, April 26, 1992.

Friedman, Alan. "Warning Forced Bechtel out of Iraq Chemical Project." *Financial Times*, February 21, 1991.

Garberson, Jeff. "Analyst Sees Lasting Damage to Los Alamos, Livermore Labs." *Livermore Independent*, December 3, 2011.

_____. "Congressional Testimony Reinforces Picture of Damage to Labs from Federal Micromanagement." *Livermore Independent*, February 24, 2012.

_____. "National Report: Broken Relationship Quality at LLNL." *Livermore Independent*, February 17, 2012.

Garner, Dwight. "Oil's Dark Heart Pumps Strong." *New York Times*, April 26, 2012.

Gendzier, Irene. "Democracy, Deception and the Arms Trade: The U.S., Iraq and Weapons of Mass Destruction." *Middle East Report* 35 (Spring 2005). www.merip.org/mer/mer234/democracy-deception-arms-trade.

Gerew, Gary. "Los Alamos Management Gets Contract Extension Despite Low Score." *New Mexico Business Weekly*, January 17, 2013.

Ginsburg, Mitch. "Peres and Rabin Knew Pollard Was Planted in U.S. Armed Forces." *Times of Israel*, November 30, 2014.

Glanz, James. "Auditor in Iraq Finds Job Gone After Exposes: House GOP Quietly Is Closing Agency." *New York Times*, November 3, 2006.

_____. "Bechtel Meets Goals on Fewer Than Half of Its Iraq Rebuilding Projects, U.S. Study Finds." *New York Times,* July 26, 2007.

_____. "Idle Contractors Add Millions to Iraq Rebuilding." *New York Times,* October 25, 2006.

_____. "Series of Woes Mar Iraq Project Hailed As Model: U.S. Drops Top Company." *New York Times,* July 28, 2006.

_____. "Star Wars: The Next Version." *New York Times,* May 4, 2004.

_____. "U.S. Ousts Iraq Hospital Contractor: Cost Overruns and Delays Under Bechtel Doomed Project." *New York Times,* July 29, 2006.

Global Security Newswire. "U.S. Nuclear Weapons Agency to Delay Work on Interoperable Warhead." February 18, 2014.

Goldman, Yoel. "Kerry Offers to Release Jonathan Pollard." *Times of Israel,* December 27, 2013.

Gondo, Nancy. "Bechtel, Builder of Giants Dig Deep: The Hoover Dam Was Part of His Project Load." *Investor's Business Daily,* June 4, 2012.

Goodnough, Abby. "2 Big Dig Companies to pay $407 Million for Repairs." *New York Times,* January 24, 2008.

Gordon, Michael R. "U.S. Nuclear Plan Sees New Targets and New Weapons: Contingencies for North Korea, Iraq, Iran, Syria and Libya." *New York Times,* March 10, 2002.

Government of Israel. "The Iraqi Nuclear Threat—Why Israel Had to Act." *Ministry of Foreign Affairs and the Atomic Energy Commission (Office of the Prime Minister).* Jerusalem, 1981.

Greenberg, Eric J. "Hillary Eyeing Move on Pollard: Talks with Dems Hinge on Release of Secret Weinberger Memo." *New York Jewish Week,* September 22, 2000.

Greider, William. "The Boys from Bechtel: Will Ronald Reagan Reverse U.S. Policy on Nuclear Proliferation?" *Rolling Stone,* September 2, 1982. http://www.rollingstone.com/politics/news/the-boys-from-bechtel -19820902.

Gusterson, Hugh. "The Assault on Los Alamos National Laboratory: A Drama in Three Acts." *Bulletin of the Atomic Scientists,* November/December, 2011.

_____. "An Open Letter to the Tea Party." *Bulletin of the Atomic Scientists,* October 29, 2010.

_____. "Weapons Labs and the Inconvenient Truth." *Bulletin of the Atomic Scientists,* February 28, 2012.

Gwertzman, Bernard. "Reagan Aides at Odds." February 15, 1982.

_____. "The Shultz Method." *New York Times,* January 2, 1983.

Hadar, Leon T. "Reading Clinton's Mideast Crystal Ball: Where Realities May Prevail." *Washington Report on Middle East Affairs,* January 31, 1993.

Hall, Mark Everett. "Pioneers of the Private Cloud." *Computerworld* 43, no. 35 (December 21, 2009).

Harrell, Eben. "The Four Horsemen of the Nuclear Apocalypse." *Time,* March 10, 2011.

_____. "The Four Horsemen of the Nuclear Apocalypse: In Conversation." *Time,* May 20, 2011.

Harriman, Ed. "Burn Rate: Ed Harriman Writes About Making Money and Losing Ground in Iraq." *London Review of Books,* September 7, 2007. www.lrb.co.uk/v29/n17/ed-harriman/burn-rate.

_____. "Cronyism and Kickbacks." *London Review of Books,* January 26, 2006. www.lrb.co.uk/v28/n02/ed-harriman/cronyism-and-kickbacks.

_____. "The Least Accountable Regime in the Middle East." *London Review of Books,* November 2, 2006. www.lrb.co.uk/v28/n21/ed-harriman/the -least-accountable-regime-in-the-middle-east.

Harris, Shane, and Matthew M. Aid. "Exclusive: CIA Files Prove America Helped Saddam as He Gassed Iran. The U.S. Knew Hussein Was Launching Some of the Worst Chemical Attacks in History—and Still Gave Him a Hand. *Foreign Policy,* August 26, 2013.

Hartung, William D. "Cut Nukes Now." *Huffington Post,* April 15, 2013.

Hayes, Thomas C. "Bechtel: A Reclusive Giant." *New York Times,* July 8, 1982.

Hedgpeth, Dana. "Bechtel's Projects Lacking in Iraq: Less Than Half of Jobs Complete, Report Concludes." *Washington Post,* July 26, 2007.

Henriques, Diana B. "Bechtel Set to Rely on Iraqi Labor." *International Herald Tribune,* April 21, 2003.

_____. "Which Companies Will Put Iraq Back Together?" *New York Times,* March 23, 2003.

Herbert, Bob. "Ask Bechtel What War Is Good For: A License to Make Money." *International Herald Tribune,* April 22, 2003.

_____. "War Hawks Are Circling In." *Oakland Tribune,* April 13, 2003.

_____. "War Hawks' History Neat Fit with Present." *South Florida Sun Sentinel,* April 17, 2003.

_____. "Ultimate Insiders." *New York Times,* April 14, 2003.

Hersh, Seymour M. "Huge CIA Operation Reported in U.S. Against Antiwar Forces, Other Dissidents in Nixon Years." *New York Times,* December 22, 1974.

_____. "The Iran Pipeline: A Hidden Chapter; U.S. Said to Have Allowed Israel to Sell Arms to Iran." *New York Times,* December 8, 1991.

Hickey, Walter. "The U.S. Embassy in Baghdad Cost a Staggering $750 Million." Business Insider, March 20, 2013. www.businessinsider.com/750 -million-united-states-embassy-iraq-baghdad-2013-3.

Hildyard, Nicholas. "Snouts in the Trough: Export Credit Agencies, Corporate Welfare and Policy Incoherence." Corner House. June 30, 1999. www .thecornerhouse.org.uk/resource/snouts-trough.

Hirsh, Michael. "Paul Bremer Was Just Following Instructions." *Washington Monthly*, March 2006.

Hirst, Clayton. "The World's at Bechtel's Beck and Call." *Independent* (London), April 20, 2003.

Hochschild, Adam. "Well-Oiled Machine." *New York Times*, June 10, 2012.

Hoffman, Gil. "George Shultz Urges Obama to Free Pollard." *Jerusalem Post*, January 12, 2011.

_____. "Korb: Declassify Documents That Incriminated Pollard." *Jerusalem Post*, October 31, 2010.

Hosenball, Mark. "The Odd Couple." *New Republic*, June 1, 1992.

Human Rights Watch. Letter to Bechtel. May 15, 2012. www.hrw.org.

_____. "Qatar: Migrant Construction Workers Face Abuse." www.hrw.org/print /news/2012/06/12.

_____. "U.S. Corporation Complicit in Abuses in India: Report Charges U.S. and Indian Governments Also Overlook Human Rights Violations." January 25, 1999. www.hrw.org.

IMRA. "Back Door to the PLO: More Light on Shepherdstown, Pollard, and the US-Israel Special Relationship." *Independent Media Review & Analysis*. January 8, 2000. www.jonathanpollard.org/2000/010800.htm.

Independent (London). "Iraq the Dossier: Part 1. Iraq's Chemical, Biological, Nuclear and Ballistic Missile Programmes," September 25, 2002.

Jacobs, Paul. "What You Don't Know May Hurt You." *Mother Jones*, February 1976.

Janos, Leo. "The Last Days of the President: LBJ in Retirement." *Atlantic Monthly* 232, no. 1 (July 1973): 35–41.

Jekowski, Jack. "Weathering the Perfect Storm: Implications of 2012 Events on the Nuclear Security Enterprise (NSE)." *Innovative Technology Partnerships, LLC*.

Jewish Link of Bergen County. "Young Israel Launches 'Call for Clemency Campaign.'" March 25, 2013.

Jewish Telegraphic Agency. "Behind the Headlines New Helmsman in Troubled Waters." July 19, 1982.

_____. "Churba: Economic Greed Rules U.S. Policy in the Mideast." January 19, 1983.

_____. "Congress, Administration Still at Loggerheads over Mideast Plane Deal." May 9, 1978.

_____. "Connally Under Fire." October 15, 1979.

_____. "Focus on Issues a Most Unusual Development." August 18, 1981.

_____. "Peres Angrily Denies Being Offered Bribe on Pipeline." February 2, 1988.

_____. "Supreme Court Orders Bechtel to Honor Anti-boycott Agreement." December 2, 1981.

Jilani, Zaid. "Bush Official and Bechtel VP Who Normalized Relations with Qaddafi Plotted with Dictator to Undermine Rebels." August 31, 2011. http://thinkprogress.org/security/2011/08/31/309166/bush-official-qaddafi-rebels-nato/.

Jones, Del. "Tough to Follow Father's Footsteps." *USA Today*, December 4, 2009.

Jones, William H. "Bechtel Denies Conflict." *Washington Post*, December 6, 1975.

_____. "Bechtel Settles Suit with Pledge to Stop Arab Boycott Role." *Washington Post*, January 11, 1977.

Juhasz, Antonia. "Bechtel Bails on Iraq." AlterNet, November 13, 2006.

_____. "The Corporate Invasion of Iraq." *LeftTurn*, August/September 2003.

Kahn, Joseph. "Bechtel Tests Waters for Big Jobs in China." *Wall Street Journal*, May 1, 1995.

Kanellos, Michael. "Top Ten Green Giants." *Greentech Media*, April 19, 2010.

Kemp, Martin. "Diplomacy Has No Place in This Monstrous Bunker." Guardian.com, May 23, 2007. www.theguardian.com/artanddesign/artblog/2007/may/23/diplomacyhasnoplaceinthis.

Kenney, Charles. "Analysts Divided on Shultz' Mideast Tilt." *Boston Globe*, June 27, 1982.

Khedairi, Betool. "Meeting Mr. Bechtel." *Guardian* (Manchester, UK), September 2, 2003.

King, Neil, Jr. "Bush Officials Draft Broad Plan for Free-Market Economy in Iraq." *Wall Street Journal*, May 1, 2003.

_____. "U.S. Prepares for Rebuilding of Iraq—Initial Plan Could Spend as Much as $900 Million on Repairs After a War." *Wall Street Journal*, March 10, 2003.

King, Ralph, and Charlie McCoy. "Bechtel's Power Outage." *Business 2.0*, March 2004.

Kissinger, Henry A., Sam Nunn, William J. Perry, and George P. Shultz. "Deterrence in the Age of Nuclear Proliferation." *Wall Street Journal*, March 7, 2011.

Klein, Aaron. "Exposed: Secret Memo Reveals Pollard Sentence a Sham." *WND*, February 23, 2015.

Knoll, Erwin. "Journalistic Jihad: Holes in the Coverage of a Holy War." *Progressive*, May 1990, 17–22.

Koppel, Ted. "Assistance for Iraq." *Nightline*. ABC News, April 23, 2003.

_____. "How U.S. Arms and Technology Were Transferred to Iraq." *Nightline*. ABC News, September 13, 1991.

Kornbluh, Peter. "Kennedy's Last Act: Reaching Out to Cuba." November 20, 2013. http://nsarchive.wordpress.com/2013/11/20/kennedys-last-act -reaching-out-to-cuba/.

Kozak, Warren. "The American Defender Stop: John McCone Helped Thwart a Cuban Missile War." *Investor's Business Daily*, April 10, 2012.

Kramer, Larry. "Bohemian Grove: Where Big Shots Go to Camp." *New York Times*, August 14, 1977.

Krieger, Hilary Leila. "Former Senior U.S. Defense Official Korb to Make Case for Pollard's Release at Knesset." *Jerusalem Post*, December 19, 2010.

_____. "Romney Plays Israel Card with Talk of Upcoming Visit." *Jerusalem Post*, April 7, 2012.

Kulkov, I. "CIA in the Service of Monopolies and Reaction." *International Affairs* 30, no. 10 (1984): 97–105.

Kurtz, Howard. "Hiding a Lobby Behind a Name: Why Not Truth in Labeling for Interest Groups?" *Washington Post*, January 27, 1985.

Labaton, Stephen. "Government by Bechtel." *New York Times*, May 22, 1988.

_____. "Role in Scuttled Iraqi Pipeline Brings U.S. Probe to Bechtel." *Globe and Mail* (Canada), February 25, 1988.

Lack, Arthur. "McCone Unlikely to Change AEC's Nuclear Power Policies Significantly." *Wall Street Journal*, June 9, 1958.

Lake, Eli. "Ex-envoy, Bechtel Gain From Revolving Door." *The Washington Times*, February 20, 2009.

Landau, Emily B., and Shimon Stein. "From Prague to Berlin: The Decline of the U.S. Nuclear Disarmament Agenda and Its Implications for the Middle East." James Martin Center for Nonproliferation Studies (CNS), August 21, 2013. http://wmdjunction.com/1308021_disarmament _agenda_decline_mideast.htm.

Langewiesche, William. "The Mega-Bunker of Baghdad." *Vanity Fair*, November 2007.

Lardner, George. "How Iraq Pipeline's Backers Pulled Strings." *San Francisco Chronicle*, February 2, 1988.

_____. "Iraqi Pipeline: Exploiting Security, Project Illustrates Use of U.S. Interests by Business Promoters." *Washington Post*, February 1, 1988.

_____. "Pipeline Promoter to Aid in Probe: Special Counsel Gives Rappaport Immunity in Meese Investigation." *Washington Post*, March 5, 1988.

Lardner, Richard. "Auditors Go Easy on Contractors." *Huffington Post*, December 11, 2008.

LeBor, Adam. "Overt and Covert." Review of *The Brothers*, by Stephen Kinzer. *New York Times*, November 8, 2013.

Lelby, Richard. "Iraqi Hostage Seeks Justice." *Washington Post*, December 1, 2002.

Levine, Yasha. "The Billionaire Brothers Behind America's Predator Drones—And Their Very Strange Past." Alternet, April 24, 2013. www.alternet .org/investigations/billionaire-brothers-behind-americas-predator -drones-and-their-very-strange-past.

LeVine, Mark. "The Peace Movement Plans for the Future." *Middle East Report*, July 2003. www.merip.org/mero/interventions/peace-movement -plans-future.

Levy, Barouch. "Pollard and the U.S. Government: A Polity of Amorality." *Arutz Sheva*, November 28, 2014.

Lewis, Paul. "U.S. Ambassador to Kosovo Hired by Construction Firm He Lobbied For." *Guardian* (Manchester, UK), April 14, 2014.

Lewis, Raphael, and Sean P. Murphy. "Building a Reputation: Bechtel Has Never Shied Away from Big Construction Projects, but Worldwide Achievements Are Accompanied by Controversy." *Boston Globe*, February 28, 2003.

———. "Lobbying Translates into Clout." *Boston Globe*, February 11, 2003.

Liedtke, Michael. "D.C. Ties Help Bechtel Tie Up Iraqi Reconstruction Work." *South Florida Sun-Sentinel*, April 19, 2003.

Lindorff, David. "Secret Bechtel Documents Reveal: Yes, It Is About Oil." *Counterpunch*, April 9, 2003.

Lubove, Seth. "A Piece of the Action." *Forbes*, May 31, 1999.

Lueck, Thomas J. "Bechtel Loses Another Officer to Reagan's Cabinet." *New York Times*, June 26, 1982.

Mackay, Neil. "Gulf War 2 Part Three: Carving Up the New Iraq." *Sunday Herald* (Glasgow, UK), April 13, 2003.

Maline, Morris. Op-Ed. *Jewish Press* 72, no. 17 (December 23, 1994): 4.

———. Op-Ed. *Jewish Press* 72, no. 18 (December 30, 1994): 4.

Malone, Patrick. "Nuclear Cleanup Project Haunted by Legacy of Design Failures and Whistleblower Retaliation." *The Center for Public Integrity*, September 1, 2015.

Malkin, Elisabeth. "At World Forum, Support Erodes for Private Management of Water." *New York Times*, March 20, 2006.

Marshall, Jonathan. "The Perils of Saudi Arabia Bankrolling U.S. Foreign Policy." *Huffington Post*, September 12, 2012.

Mathiason, Nick. "Has Bechtel Shot Its Bolt in Britain?" *Observer* (UK), September 11, 2005.

Matlock, Staci. "Tracing Waste Drum's Journey from LANL to Leak." *Santa Fe (NM) New Mexican*, June 7, 2014.

Matthews, Kay. "Bechtel and Los Alamos National Laboratory: The Privatization of the Nuclear Industry." *La Jicarita*, March 30, 2012.

Mayer, Jane. "The Contractors." *New Yorker*, May 5, 2003.

McGeehan, Nicholas. " 'Modern-day Slavery' in Qatar: There's Bad and Good News." www.theguardian.com/commentisfree/2013/sep/27/qatar -modern-day-slavery-world. November 9, 2013.

McKenna, Arin. "LANL Still Looking for Answers." *Los Alamos (NM) Monitor*, August 22, 2014.

McMahon, Jeff. "Bechtel Incompetent to Complete Hanford Nuclear Waste Cleanup." *Forbes*, August 29, 2012.

Mead, Walter Russell. "The Spy Who Didn't Walk." *American Interest*, April 24, 2012.

Mecklin, John. "Disarm and Modernize." *Foreign Policy*, March 24, 2015.

Meed Middle East Economic Digest. "Bechtel to Manage $7.4 Billion Doha Petrochemicals Project: The Complex Will Produce More Than 3 Million Tons a Year of Chemicals," 57, no. 23 (June 7, 2013): http://search .rdsinc.com/texis/rds/suite/+wdeAkHce5xbtqziw5r+X96Xewxlqmrw wwewhan.

Mello, Greg. "Udall Promotes Labs at Expense of New Mexico." *Santa Fe New Mexican*, August 17, 2014.

Melman, Yossi. "To Help a Spy." *Jerusalem Report*, April 4, 1991.

Meotti, Giulio. "J'accuse on Pollard." *Jerusalem Post*, August 22, 2011.

Michaels, Jon D. "Beyond Accountability: The Constitutional, Democratic, and Strategic Problems with Privatizing War." *Washington University Law Quarterly* 82 (March 29, 2005): 1001.

Middle East Economic Survey. "Bechtel Awarded Petrochemical Consultancy Contract." Vol. 31, no. 45. August 15, 1988. http://archives.mees.com /issues/1243/articles/43546.

_____. "Iraq Plans an Additional TDI Unit at Petrochemical Complex No. 2." Vol. 33, no. 3. October 23, 1989. http://archives.mees.com/issues/1099 /articles/39567.

_____. "Iraq Resumes Work on Petrochemical Complex No. 2." Vol. 36, no. 2. October 12, 1992. http://archives.mees.com/issues/943/articles /35117.

Milhollin, Gary. "Building Saddam Hussein's Bomb: They Are Pouring Concrete as We Speak." *New York Times*, March 8, 1992.

Miller, Merle. "One Man's Long Journey—From a One-World Crusade to the 'Department of Dirty Tricks.' " *New York Times*, January 7, 1973.

Mitchell, Timothy. "America's Egypt: Discourse of the Development Industry." *Middle East Report.* www.merip.org/mer/mer169/americas -egypt.

Morgan, Oliver. "Contract Killings: Bechtel Makes Friends, and Deals, a Private Affair. The U.S. Firm Has Maneuvered Itself into a Key Role in Britain's Nuclear Industry." *Observer* (UK), February 6, 2005.

Morley, Jefferson. "The Gentlemanly Planner of Assassinations." *Slate*, November 1, 2002. www.slate.com/articles/news_and_politics/obit/2002/11/the_gentlemanly_planner_of_assassinations.html.

Morris, Roger. "The Specialist: Robert Gates and the Tortured World of American Intelligence." Part 1. www.tomdispatch.com/dialogs/print/?id=174812.

_____. "The Specialist: The CIA and the Politics of Counterrevolution," Part 2. www.tomdispatch.com/dialogs/print/?id=174813.

_____. "The Specialist: The Rise and Rise of Robert Gates." Part 3. www.tomdispatch.com/dialogs/print/:id=174814.

_____. "A Tyrant 40 Years in the Making." *New York Times*, Op-Ed, March 14, 2003.

_____. "The Undertaker's Tally: Sharp Elbows." Part 1. www.tomdispatch.com/post/165669.

_____. "The Undertaker's Tally: The Power and the Glory." Part 2. www.tomdispatch.com/dialogs/print/?id=165346.

Mower, Joan. "Clash of Interests: Iran-Contra, Pipeline Scandals Strain U.S.-Israeli Ties." *Sun Sentinel* (Fort Lauderdale, Florida), March 27, 1988.

Munger, Frank. "NNSA Defends Klotz Waiver." Knoxblogs.com. http://knoxblogs.com/atomiccity/2015/02/04/nnsa-defends-klotz-waiver/.

Nazaryan, Alexander. "America's Fukushima?" *Newsweek*, November 20, 2013.

New York Times. "Bechtel Asia Unit Is Habib Employer." July 26, 1982.

_____. "Bechtel's Link to the Pipeline." February 24, 1988.

_____. "The Koch-Weinberger Letters: an Exchange of Rejoinders on the Mideast." November 9, 1983.

_____. "Peres Aide Says Bechtel Offered Oil At Reduced Price for Pipeline Pledge." February 25, 1988.

_____. "Stephen D. Bechtel: Master Builder in Many Lands." March 16, 1989.

_____. "W. A. Bechtel Dies In Moscow Hotel." August 28, 1933.

_____. "W. A. Bechtel Dies in Moscow Hotel." August 29, 1933.

_____. (Bechtel as private co.) January 18, 1979.

_____. (Bechtel) December 5, 1980.

_____. (Reagan Cabinet) July 15, 1982.

_____. (Habib) July 26, 1982.

New York Times News Service. "CIA Director Threatened to Resign If Spy Was Released; In Key Bargaining Point at Wye Talks, Netanyahu Sought Pollard's Freedom." November 11, 1998.

Newsweek. (Bechtel Corporate Culture.) March 18, 1968.

Nies, Judith. "Bechtel in Boston and Black Mesa." (Unpublished manuscript.)

Norton-Taylor, Richard. "Nuclear States Developing New Weapons in Defiance of Treaty, Report Claims." *Guardian* (Manchester, UK), June 3, 2013.

Nuclear Weapons & Materials Monitor. Exchange Monitor Publications, Inc. May 17, 2013.

_____. February 15, 2013.

_____. November 22, 2013.

Odell, Mark. "Bechtel Adds Grit to Space-Mine Mission." *Financial Times*, April 22, 2013.

O'Toole, Thomas. "Ford Urges A-Fuel Role for Industry." *Washington Post*, June 27, 1975.

Paretsky, Nick. "Policy-Planning Organizations and Capitalist Support for Industrial Policy, 1970-1984." A Dissertation Presented to the Faculty of the Graduate School, University of Missouri-Columbia. December 2003.

Paterson, Tony. "Leaked Report Says German and U.S. Firms Supplied Arms to Saddam: Baghdad's Uncensored Report to UN Names Western Companies Alleged to Have Developed Its Weapons of Mass Destruction." CommonDreams, December 18, 2002. www.commondreams.org/headlines 02/1218-06.htm.

PBS Frontline. "Bolivia: Leasing the Rain." June 2002.

Pearson, Drew. "The Washington Merry-Go-Round." April 28, 1959.

_____. March 28, 1960.

_____. July 3, 1960.

_____. December 3, 1961.

_____. January 17, 1962.

Pelletiere, Stephen C. "A War Crime or an Act of War?" *New York Times*, January 31, 2003.

Perl, Peter. "The Spy Who's Been Left in the Cold." *Washington Post*, July 5, 1998.

Phelan, Wesley. "The True Motives Behind the Sentencing of Jonathan Pollard." (Interview with Angelo Codevilla.) *Washington Weekly*, January 11, 1999.

Phillips, Peter Martin. "A Relative Advantage: Sociology of the San Francisco Bohemian Club." Dissertation, Office of Graduate Studies, University of California, Davis, 1994.

Pilisuk, Marc, and Jennifer Achord Rountree. "Not Quite a Conspiracy: Networks of Power." *Peace Magazine*, July–September 2008.

Pimentel, Benjamin. "Iraq Got Bay Area Boost in '80s." *San Francisco Chronicle*, January 26, 2003.

Pinkus, Walter. "Troops Have Withdrawn from Iraq, but U.S. Money Hasn't." *Washington Post*, June 27, 2012.

Pitta, Julie. "Building a New World." *World Trade* 16, no. 8 (August 2003).

Polaris Institute. "Bechtel—Corporate Profile." www.polaris.com.tw/Portal /pages/content/Report.aspx?Node=55484676-a851-4e18-906e-38faf 9cd1d2c&Show=LIST.

Pollard, Carol. "Pollard Caused No Harm; Jews Must Press for Parole." *Jewish Bulletin of Northern California* 144, no. 23 (June 9, 1995): 21.

PR Newswire. "Bechtel Telecommunications Expands to Provide Telecom and Wireless Carriers with Full Range of Technical and Engineering Services from Planning to Network Cutover." May 29, 2001.

_____. "Business Roundtable Announces Initiative to Spur Construction Training and Bring Jobs to Thousands of Gulf Region Residents." July 28, 2006.

Project on Government Oversight (POGO). "Federal Contracting and Iraq Reconstruction." March 11, 2004.

Public Citizen, with Dahr Jamail. "Bechtel's Dry Run: Iraqis Suffer Water Crisis." *A Special Report by Public Citizen's Water for All Campaign.* April 2004. www.wateractivist.org.

Public Library of U.S. Diplomacy. www.wikileaks.com.

Remnick, David. "War Without End?" *New Yorker*, April 21, 2003.

Riccio, Jim. "Incompetence, Wheeling & Dealing: The Real Bechtel." *Multinational Monitor* 10, no. 10 (October 1989).

Rich, Spencer. "Senate Kills Measure on Enriched Uranium." *Washington Post*, October 1, 1976.

Richardson, John H. "Stuart Bowen: The Man Charged with Auditing the Iraq Reconstruction Finds He's Fighting His Own Kind of War." *Esquire*, November 30, 2006.

Richardson, Joseph. "Blacklisting: An Age-old Scandal." *Counterpunch*, January 31, 2013. www.counterpunch.org/2013/01/31/englands-war -on-whistleblowers.

Ridgeway, James. "Corporate Colonialism." *Village Voice*, April 22, 2003.

Risen, James, and Jeff Gerth. "China Stole Nuclear Secrets for Bombs, US Aides Say." *New York Times*, March 6, 1999.

Robbins, Brian. "West Could Never Kick Weapons Sales Habit." *Sydney (Australia) Morning Herald*, December 15, 2003.

Robbins, Tom. "Cleaning Up at Ground Zero: A Billion-Dollar Award Looms for GOP Ally." *Village Voice*, November 27, 2001.

Rollo, William. "Row Over Asbestos Found at LNG Plant." *ABC News Australia*, August 2, 2012.

Ronen, Gil. "Jonathan Pollard Turns 60 Behind Bars." Israel National News, August 7, 2014.

Rosenberg, Elizabeth, Anthony Allesandrini, and Adam Horowitz. "Iraq Reconstruction Tracker." Middle East Report 33 (Summer 2003). www.merip.org/mer/mer227/iraq-reconstruction-tracker.

Roston, Aram. "Federal Audit Rips Iraqi Reconstruction." NBC Nightly News, July 25, 2007.

Roth, Zachary. "Global Zero: Obama's Distant Goal of a Nuclear-Free World." Atlantic, September 29, 2011.

Sahimi, Mohammad. "Iran's Nuclear Program, Part 1: Its History." Payvand Iran News, October 2, 2003. www.payvand.com/news/03/oct/2025.html.

St. Clair, Jeffrey. "Bechtel, More Powerful Than the U.S. Army." Axis of Logic, May 15, 2005. www.axisoflogic.com/artman/publish/Article_17669.shtml.

———. "Straight to Bechtel." Counterpunch, May 9, 2005.

Saunders, Debra J. "Bohemian Grove—Men Only." www.sfgate.com/opinion/sauders/article/Bohemian-Grove-men-only-2355089.php.

Scahill, Jeremy. "The Saddam in Rumsfeld's Closet." CommonDreams, August 2, 2002. www.commondreams.org.

Scherer, Michael. "K Street on the Tigris." Mother Jones, November 1, 2003.

Schlosser, Eric. "Break-In at Y-12: How a Handful of Pacifists and Nuns Exposed the Vulnerability of America's Nuclear-Weapons Sites." New Yorker, March 9, 2015.

Sciolino, Elaine. "A Budding Scandal, in Brief: A Primer on the B.N.L. Affair." New York Times, October 18, 1992.

Sherwell, Philip. "Uday's Idea of a Good Party." Telegraph (UK), April 20, 2003. www.telegraph.co.uk/news/worldnews/middleeast/iraq/1428026/Udays-idea-of-a-good-party.html.

Shultz, George P. "Act Now: The Danger Is Imminent. Saddam Hussein Must Be Removed." Washington Post, Op-Ed, September 6, 2002.

Shultz, George P., William J. Perry, Henry A. Kissinger, and Sam Nunn. "How to Protect Our Nuclear Deterrent: Maintaining Confidence in Our Nuclear Arsenal Is Necessary as the Number of Weapons Goes Down." Wall Street Journal, January 19, 2010.

———. "A World Free of Nuclear Weapons." Wall Street Journal, January 4, 2007.

Shultz, Jim. "Bolivian Uprisings Flow from Bechtel's Greed." San Francisco Examiner, April 19, 2000.

———. "Worldbeaters . . . Riley Bechtel." New Internationalist, April 2002.

Silverstein, Ken, and Chuck Neubauer. "Consulting and Policy Overlap: Advisor Perle Has Given Seminars on Ways to Profit from Possible Conflicts

Discussed by Defense Board He Sits On." *Los Angeles Times*, May 7, 2003.

Slabodkin, Gregory. "The Enemy Is . . . US." *Jerusalem Report*, May 19, 1994.

Sly, Liz. "A U.S. 'Legacy of Waste' in Iraq." *Los Angeles Times*, August 29, 2010.

Smallberg, Michael. "Nuclear Official Allowed to Oversee Former Client." The Project on Government Oversight. February 4, 2015.

Smith, R. Jeffrey, and Marc Fisher. "German Firms Primed Iraq's War Machine Series. Sending Equipment to Iraq: Anatomy of a Deal." *Washington Post*, July 23, 1992.

_____. "How an 82-Year-Old Nun Exposed Security Lapses at Nuclear Facilities." *Mother Jones*, September 14, 2012.

Snodgrass, Roger. "Activist's Experience, Passion Culminate in LANL Project Delay." *Santa Fe New Mexican*, March 9, 2012. http://www.lasg.org/press/2012/SFNM_10Mar2012.html.

Solnit, Rebecca. "Dry Lands." *London Review of Books*, December 3, 2009.

Staff Report. "Arms Sales to Iraq. Ministerial Evidence to the Scott Inquiry." *Gulf Centre for Strategic Studies*. April 1994.

Stein, Jeff. "Hustlers, Con Men and Dupes Cashing In on the War on Terror." *Newsweek*, October 20, 2014.

_____. "Israel Flagged as Top Spy Threat to U.S. in New Snowden/NSA Document." *Newsweek*, August 4, 2014.

Steinle, Mia. "Stuck in the Past? DOE's Cold War Mindset." *Project on Government Oversight*. www.pogo.org.

Stevenson, Richard W. "The Incredible Shrinking Government, Bush Style." *New York Times*, December 8, 2002.

Stockton, Peter. "Security at Y-12 Nun Too Good." *Bulletin of Atomic Scientists*, October 2, 2012.

Street, Chriss W. "Majority of Theranos Board Gone After FDA Report." Breitbart.com. October 29, 2015.

Streitfeld, David. "A Quiet Ambition at Work; Bechtel Prides Itself on Discretion, But Its Projects, Such as the $680-Million Contract to Rebuild Iraq, Give It a High Profile." *Los Angeles Times*, June 8, 2005.

Streitfeld, David, and Mark Fineman. "U.S. Engineers Working Under the Gun in Iraq." *Los Angeles Times*, October 26, 2003.

_____. "War with Iraq: Rebuilding a Country." *Los Angeles Times*, April 18, 2003.

Sweet, Cassandra. "The $2.2 Billion Bird-Scorching Solar Project." *Wall Street Journal*, February 12, 2014.

Tassava, Christopher James. "Multiples of Six: The Six Companies and West Coast Industrialization, 1930–1945." Dissertation, Department of History at Northwestern University, 2003. http://muse.jhu.edu/journals/enterprise_and_society/v004/4.1tassava.html.

Taub, Stephen. "Multinationals Take Anti-Bribery Pledge." *CFO.com.* http://
ww2.cfo.com/risk-compliance/2005/01/multinationals-take-anti
-bribery-pledge.

Taylor, Alexander. "A Secretive Construction Giant Enters the Limelight."
Time, June 12, 1982.

Taylor, Paul. "Pressler Urges Habib to Quit as U.S. Envoy." *Washington Post*,
July 26, 1982.

Thompson, A. C. "Inside Bechtel's Spin Machine." ZNET Communications,
May 10, 2004. www.zcommunications.org. *Time*. "Korean Thermonuclear Plants." October 4, 1954.

Timmerman, Kenneth R. "Pollard's Weinberger Problem." *Forward*, October 30, 1997.

Toensing, Chris. "Another 'Historic Day' Looms in Iraq." *Middle East Report*,
January 28, 2005. www.merip.org/mero/mero012805.

Traynor, Ian. "Barack Obama Launches Doctrine for Nuclear-Free World."
Guardian (Manchester, UK), April 5, 2009.

Twersky, David. "New Weinberger Bombshell: Judge Asked for Pollard Memo."
Jewish News, September 30, 1999.

Unger, Craig. "Saving the Saudis." *Vanity Fair*, October 2003.

Upton, John. "Employee Suit Exacerbates Lab's Issues." *New York Times*, September 11, 2011.

———. "Fixes Fall Short at Nuclear Lab." *Bay Citizen*, September 10, 2011.

———. "Fusion Experiment Faces New Hurdles." *New York Times*, June 24,
2011.

Vallette, Jim, with Steve Kretzmann and Daphne Wysham. *Crude Vision: How
Oil Interests Obscured U.S. Government Focus on Chemical Weapons
Use by Saddam Hussein*. 2nd ed. Washington, DC: Institute for Policy
Studies, August 13, 2003.

Vartabedian, Ralph. "Manager Says Safety Issues Are Ignored at Hanford Nuclear Site." *Los Angeles Times*, February 13, 2013.

Village Voice. "Rumsfeld's Dealings with Saddam: Were Trips to Iraq Meant to
Secure Pipeline Deal?" April 1, 2003.

Viorst, Milton. "The 'Catch-22' Plight of Imprisoned Spy Jonathan Pollard; the
U.S. Has Shown a Key Memo to Its Attorneys 25 Times but Denied It
to the Defense as Irrelevant and Top Secret." *Los Angeles Times*, September 19, 2003.

Von Hoffman, Nicholas. "Contract Killers: How Privatizing the U.S. Military
Subverts Public Oversight." *Harper's Magazine*, June 2004.

Vulliamy, Ed. "Appointment in Samarra: William Shawcross's Defence of Pax
Americana Would Have Benefited from First-Hand Experience." *Observer* (London), December 28, 2003.

Waas, Murray, and Craig Unger. "Annals of Government—How the U.S. Armed Iraq." *New Yorker*, November 2, 1992.

Waas, Murray, and Douglas Frantz. "Bush Had Long History of Support for Iraq Aid." *Los Angeles Times*, February 24, 1992.

Walshe, Shushannah. "Who Is Jonathan Pollard? Obama Heckled over Spy for Israel." *ABC News*, March 21, 2013. http://abcnews.go.com/blogs /politics/2013/03/who-is-jonathan-pollard-obama-heckled-over-spy -for-israel.

Washington Post. "The Boycott Issue." January 26, 1976.

Week. "Our Aging Nuclear Arsenal." January 23, 2015.

Weinstein, Henry. "Loans to Iraq May Have Funded Arms, U.S. Alleges Indictment: The Justice Department Says $4 Billion in Illegal Financing Through an Italian Bank's Atlanta Branch May Have Contributed to Baghdad's Arsenal." *Los Angeles Times*, March 1, 1991.

Wellen, Russ. "Despite Funneling Money to the Corporations That Run the Nuclear Labs, the Administration Finds Itself in Their Debt." *Foreign Policy in Focus* (blog), April 2, 2013.

Western States Legal Foundation. "The Bechtel Corporation: San Francisco's Engineers of Empire." Summer 2012. www.wslfweb.org.

Whelan, David. "San Francisco Contractor Bechtel Is No Stranger to Iraq." Knight Ridder Tribune News Service, June 4, 2003.

Wherry, Rob. "Contacts for Contracts." *Forbes*, June 23, 2003.

Wigg-Stevenson, Tyler. "Hawks Against the Bomb." *Sojourners*, November 2009.

Williams, Thomas D. "Firms Sued over Gulf War Illnesses: Veterans Say Iraqis Had Help Developing Chemical Weapons." *Hartford Courant*, June 15, 1994.

Williams, Timothy. "U.S. Companies Join Race on Iraqi Oil Bonanza." *New York Times*, January 14, 2010.

Wines, Michael, and Ronald J. Ostrow. "Pipeline Deal: How Private Citizens Use Public Power." *Los Angeles Times*, February 7, 1988.

Wolfe, Burton H. "BART: Bechtel's Baby." *San Francisco Bay Guardian*, February 14, 1973. *World Generation Class of 2002*. "Jim Reinsch." www .world-gen.com/class3/reinsch.html.

Wright, Susan. "Terrorists and Biological Weapons: Forging the Linkage in the Clinton Administration." *Politics and the Life Sciences* 25, nos. 1–2 (March–September 2006).

Yermachenkov, I. "Playing with Fire Near Oil Wells." *Current Digest of the Russian Press* 36, no. 31 (August 29, 1984). http://dlib.eastview.com/browse /doc/19982533.

Zatuchni, Stephan B., and Daniel B. Drooz. "Back Door to the PLO." *Los Angeles Herald Examiner*, August 2, 1982.

Zoll, Daniel. "Soaking the Poor." *San Francisco Bay Guardian*, December 13, 2000.

Zonana, Victor F. "Tough Slog: Megabuilder Bechtel Tries to Stay on Top by Being Aggressive—As Huge Jobs Grow Fewer, It Drums Up New Work and Stresses Financing—A Dynasty Among Dynasties." *Wall Street Journal*, October 16, 1984.

AUDIO/VISUAL

Arnold, Chris. "Profile: Most Large-Scale Public Works Projects Go Well over Budget." NPR: *All Things Considered*. April 10, 2003.

Chideya, Farai. "News and Notes." NPR News. "Interview: Griff Witte on Post-Katrina Contractors in the Gulf Region." September 21, 2005.

Conan, Neal. "Reconstruction and privatization in postwar Iraq." NPR. *Talk of the Nation.* September 3, 2003.

Goodman, Amy. "The Most Important Journalist You've Never Heard Of: Remembering William Worthy." www.democracynow.org/2014/5/19/the _most_important_journalist_youve_never.

Schalch, Kathleen. "Bechtel wins contract to help rebuild Iraq.": *All Things Considered.* April 17, 2003.

Smiley, Tavis. NPR. "Interview: Jim Vallette discusses the Institute for Policy Studies's new report suggesting oil is the main reason behind the war in Iraq." April 16, 2003.

U.S. Newswire. "Three Hundred Citizen Groups Call on Secret World Bank Trade Court to Open Up Bechtel Case Against Bolivia." August 29, 2002.

Vallette, Jim, Steve Kretzmann, and Daphne Wysham. "Crude Vision: How Oil Interests Obscured U.S. Government Focus on Chemical Weapons Use by Saddam Hussein." Investigative report prepared for the Sustainable Energy and Economy Network/Institute for Policy Studies. August 13, 2003.

YouTube Video: "Top U.S. Officials: Free Jonathan Pollard Now!" Uploaded February 22, 2012. www.youtube.com/watch?v=5e_OqB0lQeM.

PAPERS

Ahrari, M.E, with James Beal. "The New Great Game in Muslim Central Asia." McNair Paper, 47. Institute for National Strategic Studies, National Defense University. January 1996.

Burrows, Anne Platt, Paul Kucik; William Skinnyhorn; and John Straigis. "A Systems Analysis of the A.Q. Khan Network." Social Sciences Seminar, December 8, 2005. Presented at the Freeman Spogli Institute for International Studies at Stanford University. Authors: "Competition—or Collusion? Privatization and Crony Capitalism in the Nuclear Weapons Complex: Some Questions from New Mexico." Los Alamos Study Group. Authors: Damon Hill and Greg Mello. May 30, 2006.

Fehner, Terrence R. "The U.S. Department of Energy and the Cold War." Presented at the Conference on The Power of Free Inquiry and Cold War International History at the National Archives at College Park, Maryland. September 26, 1998.

Israel, Rebekah. "American Responses to Israeli Foreign Policy Initiatives." Unpublished Paper presented at the annual meeting of the Southern Political Science Association, Hotel Intercontinental, New Orleans, LA, January 7, 2009. http://citation.allacademic.com/meta/p273901 _index.html.

Miller Center. (2005). *Interview with William P. Clark.* Charlottesville, VA: University of Virginia. Retrieved from http://millercenter.org-/president /reagan/oralhistory/william-clark. August 17, 2003.

Stepp, Matthew, Sean Pool, Nick Loris, and Jack Spencer. "Turning the Page: Reimagining the National Labs in the 21st Century Innovation Economy." *Nonpartisan Policy Reforms from the Information Technology and Innovation Foundation, the Center for American Progress, and the Heritage Foundation.* June 2013.

Swanson, Sandra A. "A Closer Look." *Project Management Institute, Publications Division.* February 2010, Vol. 24, Issue 2.

GOVERNMENT CABLES, MEMORANDA, REPORTS, PAPERS, COURT FILINGS, AND HEARINGS

"Afghanistan: Soviet Invasion and the U.S. Response." *By the Afghanistan Task Force, Foreign Affairs and National Defense Division.* The Library of Congress Congressional Research Service. Issue Brief I550006. January 1, 1980.

"A major battle of principle and policy has been joined by the Justice Department's civil suit charging the San Francisco–based Bechtel Corporation with supporting the Arab Boycott of Israel." January 28, 1976. Declassified May 4, 2006. From Secretary of State, Washington, DC, to Embassies at Abu Dhabi, Amman, Baghdad, Beirut, Cairo, Damascus, Doha, Jidda, Khartoum, Kuwait, Manama, Muscat, Sana, Tripoli, Algiers, Rabat, Tel Aviv, Tunis. Subject: "Arms Control. U.S. Efforts to Control the Transfer of Nuclear-Capable Missile Technology." *Report to the Honorable Dennis DeConcini, U.S. Senate.* United States General Accounting Office June 1990.

Background Investigation of John Alex McCone. U.S. Department of Justice, Federal Bureau of Investigation. May 5, 1954.

"Banca Nazionale del Lavoro (BNL)." U.S. Congress. *Hearing before the Committee on Banking, Finance and Urban Affairs. House of Representatives.* 102nd Cong., 1st Sess. April 9, 1991. Declassified July 3, 1996.

"Bechtel Projects in Saudi Arabia." February 9, 1976. Declassified May 4, 2006. *From American Embassy in Jidda to Secretary of State, Washington, DC.*

"Briefing Notes for Rumsfeld Visit to Baghdad." Cable from Secretary of State George Shultz to American Embassy in Sudan. Secret. March 24, 1984. Declassified November 14, 1996. w2.gwu.edu/~nsarchiv/NSAEBB/NSA EBB82/iraq48.pdf.

"Church Committee Reports." http://aarclibrary.org/publib/contents/contents _church.htm.

"CIA Director John McCone recommends to President Johnson deploying additional troops to Vietnam and increasing air action against North Vietnam." Reproduced in *Declassified Documents Reference System.* Farmington Hills, Mich.: Gale, 2013.

"Comprehensive Report of the Special Advisor to the DCI [Director Central Intelligence] on Iraq's WMD With Addendums." Washington, DC: *U.S. Government Printing Office.*

"Declaration of Danielle Brian Supporting Plaintiffs' Supplemental Brief in Support of Motion for Attorneys' Fees." Elaine Andrews et al. vs. Lawrence Livermore National Security, LLC, et al., *Superior Court of the State of California, County of Alameda.* Case No: RG09453596. December 15, 2014.

"Declaration of the Secretary of Defense Caspar W. Weinberger" sentencing memorandum in the Jonathan Pollard case. http://ww2.gwu.edu /~nsarchiv/NSAEBB/NSAEBB407/docs/EBB-PollardDoc6.pdf. September 30, 2004. Vols. I–III.

Declassified Documents Reference System. Farmington Hills, Michigan: Gale, 2013.

Defendant Jonathan J. Pollard's First Memorandum in Aid of Sentencing. Exhibit B. Declassified 2013. *U.S. National Archives.* http://www.archives .gov/declassification/iscap/pdf/2013-084-doc2.pdf.

Defendant Jonathan J. Pollard's Second Memorandum in Aid of Sentencing. March 23, 1987. Partially declassified October 26, 2012. *National Security Archive. Ibid.*

"Department of State Action Memorandum. Issue for Decision: Whether to instruct USINT Baghdad to raise issue of Iraqi CW use and urge cessation." From Jonathan T. Howe to Lawrence S. Eagleburger. *National Security Archive.* November 21, 1983. Declassified May 20, 1994.

"DOD Agreement Sheds Light on NNSA Problems." *Union of Concerned Scientists*. August 20, 2012. Author: Stephen Young.

"DOJ Request for Record of McCone/ITT Contacts." CIA Memorandum for the Record. September 16, 1975. Declassified, July 23, 1987. Reproduced in *Declassified Documents Reference System*. Farmington Hills, Mich.: Gale, 2013.

Donald Rumsfeld Papers. *Manuscript Division, Library of Congress*. Washington, DC. Elaine Andrews et al. vs. Lawrence Livermore National Security, LLC, et al. *Superior Court of the State of California, County of Alameda*. Case No: RG09453596.

"Export-Import Bank. OMB's Method for Estimating Bank's Loss Rates Involves Challenges and Lacks Transparency." *Report to Congressional Committees*. Government Accountability Office. September 2004.

"Family Jewels." Memorandum for Executive Secretary, CIA Management Committee. May 16, 1973. Declassified June 2007. *National Security Archive*.

From Alfred L. Atherton, Jr., to Secretary of State. Department of State Action Memorandum. From CIA Director John McCone to President Lyndon Johnson. April 28, 1965. Declassified January 3, 1986.

Hill, Damon, and Greg Mello. "Competition—or Collusion? Privatization and Crony Capitalism in the Nuclear Weapons Complex: Some Questions from New Mexico." *Los Alamos Study Group*. May 30, 2006.

"Iran-Contra Investigation. Testimony of George P. Shultz and Edwin Meese, III." U.S. Congress. Joint Hearings Before the Senate Select Committee on Secret Military Assistance to Iran and the Nicaraguan Opposition and the House Select Committee to Investigate Covert Arms Transactions with Iran. 100th Cong., 1st Sess. July 23, 24, 28, and 29, 1987.

"Iran-Contra Investigation. Testimony of Donald T. Regan and Caspar W. Weinberger." *Joint Hearings before the House Select Committee to Investigate Covert Arms Transactions with Iran and Senate Select Committee on Secret Military Assistance to Iran and the Nicaraguan Opposition*. 100th Cong., 1st Sess. July 30, 31, and August 3, 1987.

"Iraq Stabilization and Reconstruction." *Hearing Before the Committee on Foreign Relations*. Telegram from American Embassy Baghdad to Secretary of State, Washington, DC, Re: "Iraqgate: Saddam Hussein, U.S. Policy and the Prelude to the Persian Gulf War, 1980-1994. http://nsarchive .chadwyck.com/marketing/about.jsp.

"Iraqi anger expressed to Bechtel representatives over U.S. Senate's passage of act invoking economic sanctions against Iraq for use of chemical weapons against the Kurds." *The Genocide Bill, calling it part of Zionist conspiracy to undermine Iraq.* September 13, 1988. U.S. Senate. 109th Cong., 2nd Session. February 8, 2006.

"Iraqi Attitude Toward an Israeli Embarace [*sic*] on the Aqaba Pipeline." April 16, 1984. http://www2.gwu.edu/~nsarchiv/NSAEBB/NSAEBB107/.

"Lesson No. 4: War and Oil." Henry B. Gonzalez. U.S. House of Representatives. *Congressional Record.* February 21, 1991.

McKay, James C. *Report of Independent Counsel: In Re: Edwin Meese III.* "Part Seven, Aqaba Pipeline Project." Washington, DC: Government Printing Office, 1988.

"Measures to Improve U.S. Posture and Readiness to Respond to Developments in the Iran-Iraq War. Top Secret National Security Decision Directive 139. April 5, 1984. Declassified August 18, 1994. http://www2.gwu.edu/~nsarchiv/NSAEBB/NSAEBB82/iraq53.pdf.

"Memorandum for: Mr. William E. Colby. Subject: Special Activities." *Central Intelligence Agency.* June 1, 1973.

"Memorandum for the Files." Department of State. April 21, 1958. *Declassified Documents Reference System.* Farmington Hills, Michigan. Gale, 2013.

"Memorandum for the Record." White House. May 19, 1958. Declassified October 17, 1983.

"Memorandum for the Record: Discussion with President Johnson," November 25, 1963. John McCone Memoranda, Meetings with the President, Box I, File 23 November 1963–27 December 1963. LBJ Papers. LBJ Library. Austin, Texas.

"Memorandum of Conversation." Office of the Minister, Ministry of Finance of the U.S.S.R. May 8, 1974. *Declassified Photocopy from Gerald R. Ford Library.* http://galenet.galegroup.com/servlet/DDRS?vrsn=1.0&view=image&slb=FT&locID=loc.

"Memorandum of Conversation." President Ford, Henry Kissinger, Donald Rumsfeld, Brent Scowcroft. January 7, 1976. *Declassified Documents Reference System.*

"Memorandum of Conversation." Secretary of State Henry Kissinger's Meeting with the General Advisory Committee on Arms Control and Disarmament. January 6, 1976. Classified "Secret." Declassified April 5, 2000.

"Memorandum of Meeting with the President. White House. Top Secret." Bureau of the Budget to Study the Intelligence Structure of the Government. February 3, 1960. Declassified October 28, 1981. *Declassified Documents Reference System.* Farmington Hills, Michigan: Gale, 2013.

"Memorandum of Telephone Conversation." *Kissinger Telephone Conversations.* January 6, 1976. Digital National Security Archive. Item Number: KA14486.

"Minister of Industry Blasts Senate Action." *Confidential Cable from American Embassy, Baghdad, to Secretary of State.* September 13, 1988. National Security Archive. http://nsarchive.chadwyck.com/cat/display ItemImages.do?queryType=cat&ResultsID=14.

"Modernizing the Nuclear Security Enterprise. Observations on NNSA's Options for Meeting Its Plutonium Research Needs." *Report to the Committee on Armed Services, U.S. Senate.* U.S. Government Accountability Office. September 2013.

"Multinational Corporations and United States Foreign Policy." U.S. Senate. *Hearings before the Subcommittee on Multinational Corporations of the Committee on Foreign Relations.* 94th Cong., 2nd Sess. August 9, Executive Session, and September 10, 13, 15, and 27, 1976.

"New FRUS Volume on the U.S.-Supported Overthrow of Chilean President Salvador Allende. U.S. Covert Intervention in Chile: Planning to Block Allende Began Long Before September 1970 Election." *National Security Archive Electronic Briefing Book No. 470.* National Security Archive. May 23, 2014.

"Nomination of Caspar W. Weinberger to be Secretary of Defense." U.S. Senate. *Hearing before the Committee on Armed Services.* 97th Cong., 1st Sess. January 6, 1981.

"Nomination of George P. Schultz [sic] to Be Secretary of the Treasury." *Hearing Before the Committee on Finance.* U.S. Senate. 92nd Cong., 2nd Sess. May 25, 1972.

"Nomination of George P. Shultz." U.S. Senate. *Hearings Before the Committee on Foreign Relations. Nomination of George P. Shultz, of California, to be Secretary of State.* 97th Cong., 97th Sess. July 13 and 14, 1982.

"Nomination of John A. McCone to be a Member of the Atomic Energy Commission." U.S. Congress. *Hearing before the Senate Section of the Joint Committee on Atomic Energy.* 85th Cong., 2nd sess. July 2, 1958.

"Nominations of McCone, Korth, and Harlan." U.S Senate. *Hearing Before the Committee on Armed Services.* 87th Cong., 2nd Sess. January 18, 1962.

"Nuclear Energy Agreement for Cooperation with Iran." December 6, 1974. "Iraqi Illegal Use of Chemical Weapons." Department of State Briefing Paper. November 16, 1984. National Security Archive, Declassified April 6, 2007.

"Nuclear Proliferation. Failed Efforts to Curtail Iraq's Nuclear Weapons Program." U.S. House of Representatives. *Hearing Before the Subcommit-*

tee on Oversight and Investigations of the Committee on Energy and Commerce. 102nd Cong., 1st Sess. April 24, 1991. "Modernizing the Nuclear Security Enterprise."

"Observations on DOE's Management Challenges and Steps Taken to Address Them." *Testimony Before the Subcommittee on Oversight and Investigations, Committee on Energy and Commerce, House of Representatives.* U.S. Government Accountability Office. July 24, 2013.

"Old Men's Oil Wars." Representative Marcy Kaptur on the floor of Congress. *Congressional Record.* May 8, 2003.

"Oversight of the Private Sector Activities of the Overseas Private Investment Corporation and the Agency for International Development's Bureau for Private Enterprise." *Hearing Before the Subcommittee on International Economic Policy and Trade of the Committee on Foreign Affairs.* U.S. House of Representatives. 99th Cong., 2nd Sess. September 10, 1986.

"Public Statements of Caspar W. Weinberger, Secretary of Defense." U.S. Library of Congress. Vol. IV, 1983.

"Remarks by President Barack Obama." Hradcany Square. Prague, Czech Republic. April 5, 2009. www.whitehouse.gov/the_press_office/Remarks -By-President-Barack-Obama-In-Prague-As-Delivered.

"Renewing OPIC and Reviewing Its Role in Support of Key U.S. Objectives." U.S. Congress. *Hearing Before the Committee on International Relations.* 108th Cong., 1st Sess. June 10, 2003.

Report of Independent Counsel In Re Edwin Meese, III. Washington, DC, July 5, 1988. U.S. Government Printing Office.

"Review of Bechtel's Spending Under Its Phase II Iraq Reconstruction Contract." *Office of the Special Inspector General for Iraq Reconstruction.* SIGIR-07-009. July 24, 2007.

"Search of Files for Materials Relevant to Assassination Plans." *Commission on CIA Activities Within the United States. Memorandum to the White House.* An examination of the personal files of John McCone from November 29, 1961, through December 31, 1964 . . . "and the files relating to MONGOOSE and ZRRIFLE relevant to plans to assassinate Castro." May 1, 1975. Declassified June 17, 1996. Reproduced in *Declassified Documents Reference System.* Farmington Hills, Mich.: Gale, 2013.

"Special Activities." *Memorandum for Mr. William E. Colby.* June 1, 1973.

"Structure of Corporate Concentration: Institutional Shareholders and Interlocking Directorates Among Major U.S. Corporations. A Staff Study." U.S. Senate. *Committee on Government Affairs.* Vol. 1. December 1980.

"Summary of Facts and Conclusions." The Independent Prosecutor's

Report on Meese. (Excerpt from the McKay Report published by *New York Times*. July 19, 1988.)

Supplemental Declaration of Caspar W. Weinberger, Secretary of Defense. *United States of America v. Jonathan Jay Pollard. U.S. District Court for the District of Columbia*. Criminal No. 86-0207. March 3, 1987.

"The Atomic Energy Commission." By Alice Buck. U.S. Department of Energy, 1983. http://energy.gov/sites/prod/files/AECHistory.pdf.

"The Banca Nazionale del Lavoro (BNL) Scandal and the Department of Agriculture's Commodity Credit Corporation (CCC) Program for Iraq. Parts I and II." U.S. Congress. Hearing Before the Committee on Banking, Finance and Urban Affairs. House of Representatives. 102nd Cong., 2nd Sess. May 21, 1992.

"The Foreign Trade Practices Act." U.S. Congress. *Hearings before the Subcommittee on International Economic Policy and Trade of the Committee on Foreign Affairs*. 98th Cong., 1st Sess. April 18, 25; July 12; October 6, 1983.

"The Intelligence Community's Involvement in the Banca Nazionale Del Lavoro (BNL) Affair." Report Prepared by the Staff of the Select Committee on Intelligence. U.S. Senate. 103rd Cong., 1st Sess. February 1993.

"The International Petroleum Cartel, the Iranian Consortium and U.S. National Security." U.S. Senate. *Prepared for the Use of Subcommittee on Multinational Corporations of the Committee on Foreign Relations*. February 21, 1974.

"The International Telephone and Telegraph Company and Chile, 1970–71." U.S. Senate. Report to the Committee on Foreign Relations by the Subcommittee on Multinational Corporations. June 21, 1973.

"The Jonathan Jay Pollard Espionage Case: A Damage Assessment." Prepared by the Foreign Denial and Deception Analysis Committee. October 30, 1987. Released by the CIA in 2006. *National Security Archive*. Electronic Briefing Book. Posted December 14, 2012. Updated January 9, 2013. http://www2.gwu.edu/~nsarchiv/NSAEBB/NSAEBB407/.

"The New START Treaty." *Testimony of Dr. Michael R. Anastasio, Laboratory Director, Los Alamos National Laboratory*. U.S. Senate Committee on Foreign Relations. July 15, 2010.

"The Overseas Private Investment Corporation's Investment Funds Program." *Briefing Report to the Chairman and the Ranking Minority Member, Subcommittee on Foreign Operations, Committee on Appropriations*. U.S. Senate. Government Accountability Office. May 2000.

"The U.S. Policy Regarding United Nations Inspections of Iraqi Chemical Sites." *Joint Hearing Before the Committee on Foreign Relations and*

Committee on Armed Services. U.S. Senate. 105th Cong., 2nd Sess. September 3, 1998.

"The Weapons of Mass Destruction Program of Iraq." U.S. Senate. *Hearing Before the Subcommittee on Emerging Threats and Capabilities of the Committee on Armed Services.* 107th Cong., 2nd Sess. February 27, 2002.

"U.N. Inspections of Iraq's Weapons of Mass Destruction Programs: Has Saddam Won?" *Hearing Before the Committee on International Relations.* U.S. House of Representatives. 106th Cong., 2nd Sess. September 26, 2000.

"United States Export Policy Toward Iraq Prior to Iraq's Invasion of Kuwait. Did U.S. Exports Aid Iraq's Military Capabilities and Did the Administration Accurately Disclose Its Licensing of Dual-Use Exports to Iraq?" U.S. Senate. *Hearing Before the Committee on Banking, Housing, and Urban Affairs.* October 27, 1992.

"U.S. Chemical and Biological Warfare–Related Dual Use Exports to Iraq and Their Possible Impact on the Health Consequences of the Persian Gulf War." *A Report of Chairman Donald W. Riegle, Jr., and Ranking Member Alfonse M. D'Amato of the Committee on Banking, Housing and Urban Affairs with Respect to Export Administration.* U.S. Senate. May 25, 1994. Telegram from Secretary of State, Washington, DC, to USINT Baghdad.

"U.S. Chemical Shipment to Iraq." March 4, 1984. Excised, September 18, 1996. *Telegram from Secretary of State, Washington, DC, to USINT Baghdad.*

"U.S. Oil Companies and the Arab Oil Embargo: The International Allocation of Constricted Supplies." U.S. Senate. *Prepared for the Use of Subcommittee on Multinational Corporations of the Committee on Foreign Relations by the Federal Energy Administration's Office of International Energy Affairs.* January 27, 1975.

Walsh, Lawrence E. *Iran/Contra: The Final Report.* New York: Times Books, 1994.

"Waste, Fraud, and Abuse in Hurricane Katrina Contracts." U.S. House of Representatives. *Prepared for Committee on Government Reform— Minority Staff Special Investigations Division.* August 2006.

"White House Efforts to Thwart Congressional Investigations of Pre-War Iraq Policy: The Case of the Rostow Gang." U.S. Congress. *Hearing Before the Committee on Banking, Finance and Urban Affairs.* 102nd Cong., 2nd Sess. May 29, 1992.

INDEX

ABC News, 164, 175, 198, 233

Abu Dhabi projects, United Arab Emirates, 304

Adelson, Sheldon, 299, 300

AEC. *See* Atomic Energy Commission

Afghanistan, 260

Aguas del Tunari, 222

Ahmadinejad, Mahmoud, 281

airport construction projects, 5, 9, 10, 58, 60, 61, 122, 127, 208, 211, 235, 304, 305

Aitken, Robert, 269

Albania, 304, 306

Alexander, Donald A., 261

Algeria, 9, 78, 95, 101, 102, 103, 123, 305

Allard, Wayne, 171

Allende, Salvador, 97, 98, 118

Al Qaeda, 3, 228, 231, 242

American Enterprise Institute, 239, 309

American exceptionalism, 24, 74

American Federation of Labor (AFL), 41

Americans for Tax Reform, 11

Anderson, Eric, 295

Anderson, Jack, 79, 80, 82, 87, 97, 318, 329n80

Anti-Defamation League (ADL), 125, 126

Anti-Terrorist Alert Center (ATAC), 181

antiwar protests, 84, 126, 267

Aqaba pipeline proposal
  investigation of, 191
  Iran-Contra affair and, 191–92
  Rumsfeld as Shultz's envoy to Saddam to lobby for, 168–71, 172–73, 188

Saddam's rejection of, 192, 194, 197, 200–01, 202, 213

Arabian American Oil Co. (Aramco), 53, 62, 63, 131

Arab League, 125, 127

Arab Spring, 5, 96

Arco, Idaho, National Reactor Testing Station, 10

Argentina, 98, 225

Armour Research Foundation, 84

Asian Development Bank, 112

Aspin, Les, 102, 161

Associated General Contractors of America, 27

Associated Press, 147, 271

Association of Southeast Asian Nations (ASEAN), 209

Athens, Greece, subway system, 208

Atlantic (magazine), 280

Atomic Energy Commission (AEC), 68, 70–71, 72, 74, 104, 105, 120, 153, 154, 156, 157

Augustine, Norman, 292

Aziz, Tariq, 169

B-1 bombers, 160

Bacevich, Andrew J., 79

Baer, Robert, 99, 113

Baker, Howard, 131

Balfour, Guthrie and Company, 56

Balkan Investigative Reporting Network, 307

Banca Nazionale del Lavoro (BNL), 197–99, 200, 201

Barcelona, Summer Olympics (1992) in, 208

Barlett, Donald L., 244

Barraza, Marian, 264–65

Baum, Dan, 233

Bay Area Rapid Transit (BART) system, California, 9, 87

Bay of Pigs invasion, Cuba, 78

Beard, Susan, 294

Becon Construction, 135, 204

Bechtel, Alice Elizabeth, 8, 23, 43–44

Bechtel, Brendan
  background of, 295
  as Bechtel head, 9, 295–96, 304

Bechtel, Clara Alice West, 20, 21, 43, 45–46

Bechtel, Elizabeth Bentz, 19

Bechtel, Elizabeth ("Betty") Hogan, 92, 93

Bechtel, Gary, 93, 204, 207

Bechtel, John Moyer, 19

Bechtel, Kenneth, 8, 21, 22, 45, 53, 117

Bechtel, Laura Adeline Peart, 46, 55

Bechtel, Lauren, 93, 204–05

Bechtel, Nonie, 93, 205

Bechtel, Riley P., 93
  ASEAN countries and, 209–10
  background of, 205
  Bechtel Enterprises Holdings (BEn) and, 218–19, 221, 225, 227
  as Bechtel head, 9, 192, 197, 200, 204
  Bechtel's image and, 213
  Bechtel stock value decline and, 226–28
  biotech company Theranos and, 305
  Boston's Big Dig project and, 207, 208, 221–22
  business philosophy of, 209
  Clinton administration and, 214–15
  criticism of, 223–24
  diversification plan of, 217, 219
  employees as hostages in Iraq and, after US invasion, 202
  Export Council membership of, 229
  hurricane Katrina cleanup and, 246, 247
  international business sought by, 208–09
  Iraq projects and, 192, 197, 200

Kuwait reconstruction and, 202–03
  organizational changes by, 204–05, 212–13, 217–18, 219
  partnerships and, 220–21
  planetary exploration and, 295
  privatization and, 202–03, 216–17
  son Brendan as successor to, 9, 295
  success of, 211
  telecom and Internet start-ups and, 221, 226
  wealth of, 9, 262

Bechtel, Shana, 93, 204

Bechtel, Stephen Davison ("Steve Sr.")
  ant-Communist views of, 64, 75, 84
  anti-Jewish sentiment of, 124–25
  as Bechtel head, 8, 44, 45, 50
  Bechtel-McCone Corporation formed by, 49–50
  birth and childhood of, 20, 21, 22, 45–46
  business philosophy of, 49, 53, 59, 74, 85, 86, 109
  business reputation of, 47, 95
  as business visionary, 46–47, 49
  as chief administrator of Six Companies, 47
  Casey and, 132
  Cold War arms race and, 70
  college traffic accident and, 46
  Colley's murder in Iraq and, 77
  cost-plus model of business contract invented by, 49, 262
  death of, 204
  difference between father and, 47
  energy industry as focus of, 46–47, 48–49
  Export-Import Bank position of, 95, 101, 102
  father's death and, 44
  government contacts of, 58, 68, 74, 105
  government regulation and, 149
  growth of Bechtel under, 86
  Hoover Dam construction and, 6, 38, 48
  intelligence community and, 8, 61, 64, 65, 75–76

international business sought by, 53, 58, 59, 85, 208–09, 215

King Faisal of Iraq and, 5

marriage and family of, 46, 204

McCone's bond with, 48, 49–50, 68, 82

military contracts and, 47–48, 83

military-industrial complex and, 83

Nixon and, 75, 95, 101

nuclear energy and, 70, 71

oil industry and, 48–49, 58, 59, 60, 62, 63, 124

Pacific Rim strategy of, 84

personality of, 45, 49–50

relationship between US presidents and, 8

Saudi Arabian projects and, 58, 59–62, 63, 75, 124, 209

Shultz and, 109, 112, 129, 135

son Steve Jr. as successor to, 8, 86

son Steve Jr. compared to, 91–92

son Steve Jr.'s relationship with, 93

SRI's research and, 84

stock investments of, 53–54, 59, 219

turnkey contract used by, 49

wartiime experience of, 46, 47

Weinberger and, 117

Bechtel, Steve Jr., 11–12

antilabor stance of, 87

background and education of, 86, 92–93

as Bechtel head, 8–9, 86, 91–92, 93–94, 138, 143

business philosophy of, 91–92, 97, 104–05, 150, 159, 212, 213, 220, 309

Casey and, 132

Connally's campaign against Reagan and, 130–32

Dad Bechtel's biography as a self-made man embraced by, 11–12

energy industry as focus of, 86–87

father Steve Sr. compared to, 91–92

father Steve Sr.'s relationship with, 93

government contacts of, 99, 104–05

Iran-Contra affair and, 192

Iraq pipeline project and, 192

Jubail new city project, Saudi Arabia, and, 122–23

Libya and, 94

marriage and children of, 92, 93, 197, 204

Middle East projects and, 87

multinational approach to projects under, 151–52, 153

Nixon and, 87–88, 89, 90, 104, 143

nuclear plant contracts under, 151

nuclear power safety and, 149–50

personality of, 86, 91, 92, 212

Reagan and, 130, 133, 135, 143, 150, 152, 151, 158–59, 214

rebuff of an interview request by, 11

retirement of, 204

revolving door with Washington and, 148–49, 152, 158–59

Shultz and, 110, 113–14, 121–22, 127, 129, 135, 143, 148

son Riley as successor to, 9, 192, 197, 200, 204

stock ownership by, 227

Treasury Department position of, 95

wealth of, 262

Weinberger and, 117, 119, 148

Bechtel, Warren Augustine ("Dad")

background and childhood of, 19–20

birth of the modern Bechtel company and, 22, 23

business reputation of, 25–26, 38, 42, 47

cattle business and, 20, 23

children and family life of, 20, 21, 22, 23–24, 45–46

death of, 8, 43–44

difference between son Steve Sr. and, 47

early construction work of, 19, 20, 21, 22

first railroad subcontract of, 22–23

founding of Bechtel by, 8

Hoover Dam project and, 26–27, 38, 40, 41, 42

Horatio Alger–like biography of being a self-made man used for, 11–12, 24

marriage of, 20

move west by, 20–22

Bechtel, Warren Augustine ("Dad") (*cont.*)
  new western industrialism and, 12,
    22–23
  oil and gas construction contracts of, 26
  partners of, 22–23, 26
  railroad construction work of, 19, 20–23,
    24, 26, 47, 217
  road and highway construction by,
    24–26, 46, 53, 60, 61, 122, 306–07, 308
  son Steve Sr. as successor to, 8, 44, 45
  Southern Pacific Railroad job of, 20, 21
  Soviet visit of, 42–44
  success of, 23–24, 26, 45
Bechtel, Warren Jr., 8, 20, 21, 22, 45
Bechtel (Bechtel corporation in general)
  American exceptionalism belief of, 24,
    74
  antiregulatory, antigovernment stance
    of, 11
  Arab boycott of trade with Israel and,
    125–27, 128–29, 146
  bad publicity for, 120–21, 123–24, 127,
    147–49, 213
  as company that can "build anything,
    any place, any time," 6
  conflict-of-interest questions about, 72,
    102, 103, 147–49, 173, 192, 199, 207,
    237, 307
  cost-plus model of business contract
    used by, 49, 63, 233, 262
  criminal cases connected with
    employees of, 120
  Dad Bechtel's first subcontract and birth
    of, 22
  Dad Bechtel's biography as a self-made
    man embraced in, 11–12, 24
  employee and contractor market
    divisions in, 9
  founding of, 8
  government ties used by, 6, 11, 12,
    47–48, 55, 57–58, 72, 74–75, 76, 105,
    110, 113, 120, 148–49, 152, 157–59,
    160, 166, 172
  Hoover Dam as signature project for, 6,
    29, 44

  as leading engineering and construction
    firm, 6, 12, 44
  links to US presidents by, 6, 8, 74–75,
    87–88, 90, 95, 104, 113
  lobbying used by, 27, 41–42, 76, 104, 113,
    128, 130, 141, 146, 148, 149, 150, 162,
    173, 189–90, 202, 207, 211, 218, 224,
    257, 261, 282, 291, 307
  move into international work by, 53, 57,
    59
  multiyear megaproject specialization
    of, 9
  "mystique" as member of global power
    elite held by, 11
  overview of Bechtel family at, 7–9
  private ownership structure of, 45, 52,
    227, 237, 219, 318
  revolving door between US government
    and, 6, 7, 54, 72, 99, 105, 148–49, 158,
    169, 223, 294, 307
  sex and race discrimination charges
    against, 120, 126–27
  size of, 7–8, 47, 53
  turnkey contract used by, 49
  US foreign policy at odds with, 7
  venture capital used by, 95, 135
  workers in. *See* Bechtel workforce
  World War II contracts and, 50–52
Bechtel Cabinet, 153, 157
Bechtel Civil and Minerals, Inc., 134
Bechtel Corporation
  alliance with Hammer in Libya, 94
  change of name to Bechtel Group, 134
  formation of, 54
  government contracts for, 57
  Helms and Kissinger as consultants for,
    99
  Ivanpah, California, solar facility and,
    296
  Iraq pipeline project with Saddam and,
    170
  Iraq reconstruction and, 238
  Livermore management by, 290
  Peabody purchase by, 336n122
  Saudi Arabian contracts of, 59, 62, 63

Shultz as president of, 114, 170
Steve Jr. at, 92
Weinberger at, 134
Bechtel Enterprises (BEn), 218–19, 220,
    221, 225, 227, 233
Bechtel Enterprises Holdings, Inc., 95, 218
Bechtel family
    Bohemian Grove membership of, 87, 88,
        89, 114, 184
    domination in business through five
        successive generations of, 6–7
    overview of Bechtel succession with, 7–9
    political beliefs of, 11
    preoccupation with being out of public
        eye in, 8, 11, 46
    private ownership structure and, 45, 135,
        227, 237, 318
    secrecy about operations maintained by,
        6, 46, 57, 76, 87, 213, 219, 223, 227, 237,
        296, 318
    transition between generations in, 8–9,
        44, 45, 86, 91, 192, 197, 200, 295
    western beginnings of, 7
Bechtel Financing Services Inc., 216, 218
Bechtel Group, 111
Bechtel Group of Companies, 138
Bechtel in Arab Lands (Finnie), 63
Bechtel Ltd., 197, 205
Bechtel Marine Propulsion Corporation,
    294–94
Bechtel-McCone Corporation
    allegations of wartime profiteering
        lodged against, 52
    Pearson on revolving door between
        government and, 72, 79, 148
    defense contracts of, 51, 52, 53
    focus of, 50
    formation of, 49–50
    national laboratories and AEC contracts
        and, 68, 72
    number of employees in, 50
    Steve Jr.'s work at, 86
Bechtel National Inc., 5
Bechtel Nuclear, 294
Bechtel Petroleum Inc., 134

Bechtel Power Corporation, 114, 134
Bechtel workforce
    CIA agents in, as cover, 76, 78
    Colley's murder in Iraq and, 77, 192
    on Dad Bechtel's railroad projects in
        California, 25
    deaths on Libyan pipeline projects and,
        94
    as hostages in Iraq, after US invasion,
        201–02
    Hoover Dam construction and, 35, 42,
        317
    Jewish workers excluded from, 61,
        124–25
    on Jubail new city project, Saudi Arabia,
        123
    Philippines as source of, 123
    in Saudi Arabia, 61–62
    Steve Jr.'s antilabor stance on, 87
Belgian Relief, 55
Belgium, 121
Benedict, Kennette, 255, 258
ben Halim, Mustafa, 94
Berger, Jeff, 223
Berlin Wall, 257, 269
Berrigan, Frida, 257, 259–60
Bettis Atomic Power Laboratory, West
    Mifflin, Pennsylvania, 294–95
Biden, Joe, 139, 301
Bin Laden Construction, 58, 59
bin Laden family, 219–20
Bird, Kai, 70
Black Canyon, 28, 31, 35, 37, 39–40
Blackwater, 4
Blitzer, Wolf, 174, 178
Boeing Company, 122
Bohemian Grove, California, 88–89, 100,
    117, 184, 224
    Bechtel family's Mandalay Lodge at, 88,
        89, 97, 105, 114
Bolivia, 98, 222–23
Boston Central Artery/Tunnel Project
    ("Big Dig"), 9, 206–08, 222, 233–24,
    310
Boston Globe, 66, 207, 222, 310

Boston *Phoenix* (newspaper), 208
Boulder Canyon Project Act, 32–33
Boulder City, Nevada, 38, 40, 41, 318
Boulder Dam. *See* Hoover Dam
Boykin, John, 148
Boy Scouts, 54, 92, 309
Brady, Nicholas F., 225
Brazil, 80, 95, 121, 146, 158, 225
"Breaking the War Mentality" (Obama), 275
Brechin, Gray, 91
Bremer, L. Paul ("Jerry") III, 238, 239–40, 242, 356n238
Brezhnev, Leonid, 101
bridge projects, 5, 9, 22, 208, 235
Broder, John, 246
Briody, Dan, 161
British Petroleum, 62, 65, 85
Brown, Jerry, 136
Brown, Ronald H., 215–16
Brown and Root, 82
Brunwasser, Matthew, 307
Bryan, Danielle, 234, 290
Bryza, Matthew, 210
Brzezinski, Zbigniew, 132
Buckley, William F., 88
Burns, Arthur, 110, 133
Bush, Barbara, 2
Bush, George H. W., 13, 88, 89
    Aqaba pipeline proposal and, 171, 200
    Bechtel's relationship with, 199, 206, 211, 212
    election of, 199
    Iraqi policy of, 198, 200
    Operation Desert Storm and, 202
Bush, George W., 89
    Bechtel's relationship with, 232
    environmental of, 226
    initial US invasion of Iraq and, 3
    Iran-Contra affair and, 184–85
    Iraq reconstruction plans of, 5
    Iraq War and, 1, 2, 3
    Middle East Free Trade Area (MEFTA) created by, 244

nuclear warhead industry and, 10
    Pollard affair and, 299
    Qaddafi in Libya and, 305–06
    reconstruction of Iraq by, 5, 232, 242
    September 11, 2001, terrorist attacks and, 3, 228
Bush, Jenna, 2
Bush, Laura, 241, 243
Business Advisory Council, 74
Business Council, 57, 76, 112–13
Business Roundtable, 112–13, 130, 247
Business 2.0 (magazine), 218, 221
BusinessWeek (magazine), 188, 189
BWX Technologies (BWXT), 258
Byrne, Malcolm, 348n186

California
    Bechtel's first federal highway contract in, 25
    Dad Bechtel's move to, 21–24
    Hoover Dam development and need for water in, 30–31
    Reagan Revolution and, 136
California Institute of Technology (Caltech), 70
Calvert Cliffs, Maryland, nuclear plant, 120
Cameron, James, 295
Canada, 9, 51, 87, 95
Canavan, Francis, 306
Cannon, Lou, 114, 132
CANOL project, 51
Carnegie, Andrew, 86
Carpenter, Tom, 293
Carroll, James, 278, 281
Carter, Jimmy
    arms control efforts of, 163
    administration of
    election of, 116, 130
    energy policy of, 150
    foreign policy of, 160
    Iran hostage crisis and, 133, 138–39
    nuclear nonproliferation policy of, 153, 276
    nuclear power plant and, 153

Pollard affair and, 132, 300
Reagan's defeat of, 133, 136, 139
Shultz's criticism of, 153
Carus, W. Seth, 176
Casey, Ralph E., 52
Casey, William
background of, 132
Bechtel's relationship with, 147–48
as CIA director, 142, 147, 175, 189
Israel and, 175, 178
Reagan and, 132–33, 172
Shultz's friendship with, 132
Castro, Fidel
Kennedy's assassination and, 81, 82
plots against, 78, 80
possible rapprochement with, during
Kennedy administration, 81–82
Center for Defense Information, 163
Center for Strategic and International
Studies, Georgetown University,
309
Central Artery/Tunnel Project ("Big Dig"),
Boston, 9, 206–08, 222, 233–24,
310
Central Intelligence Agency (CIA)
Allende coup in Chile and, 97, 98–99
Bechtel's employment of agents from, to
provide cover, 76, 78
Bechtel officers' moving to, 7
Bechtel's relationship with, 75–77, 94,
99, 128
Casey as director of, 142, 147
Church Committee investigation of
abuses in, 128
Colley's murder in Iraq and, 77
covert plots of, 79–80, 95, 96, 97–99,
128, 175
creation of, 64, 67
Cuban plots of, 78, 79
Helms as director of, 80, 97–99, 162
Indonesian coup and, 95–96
intelligence-gathering by, 63
Israel's request for information from,
178
Kennedy's assassination and, 78, 81–82

Libyan pipeline project and, 94
McCone's tenure at, 74, 78–82, 95, 97
Middle East policy and, 4–5, 63, 65
Mossadegh's overthrow in Iran and, 65
Nixon's use of, 95, 96, 97
Pollard's application for fellowship from,
183
Pollard spy case and, 174, 175, 177, 184
Soviet Union and, 79
Steve Sr.'s relationship with, 75–76
transfer to Iraq of US-manufactured
weapons and, 175
Year of the Spy cases and, 184
Channel Tunnel, 9
Chao, Daniel, 229
Chappel, H. G., Jessie, and Elizabeth, 46
chemical plant construction projects, 50,
58, 87. See also PC2 petrochemicals
complex, Iraq
chemical weapons
Bechtel's contract to build Iraqi plant
for, 198–99, 230
Bechtel's contract to destroy, 305
Iraq's production facilities for, 174, 176,
180–81
Pollard's intelligence on, 180
proposed sanctions against Iraq for use
of, 193
Saddam's use of, 168, 169–70, 173, 193,
200, 230
Shultz 's policy on, 237
Weinberger's policy on, 161
Cheney, Dick, 309
Chernobyl nuclear disaster, Ukraine, 10,
216
Childs, J. Rives, 61
Chile, 95, 97–99, 304, 305
China
Bechtel projects in, 122, 158, 208, 209,
211
Nixon and, 89, 100
nuclear technology sales to, 158, 274
spying for, 252, 253
US foreign policy and, 83
China Syndrome, The (film), 149

Chomsky, Noam, 96
Christiansen, Thor, 1–2
Churba, Joseph, 165
Church, Frank, 128
Church Committee, Senate, 128
Churchill, Winston, 118
CIA. *See* Central Intelligence Agency
Civiak, Robert, 258, 264
Civil War, 19
Clark, William P., 142–43, 162, 172, 189
Clinton, Bill, 207, 214–16, 246, 254, 300
Clinton, Hillary, 301
coal industry, 7, 30, 87, 103, 104, 121–22, 158
Coalition Provisional Authority (CPA), Iraq, 238, 239–40
coal-slurry pipelines, 103, 121–22
Cochabamba, Bolivia, water system privatization, 222–23
Cohen, Danny, 178
Cold War, 14, 64, 69–70, 110–11, 156
Coll, Steve, 62, 63, 209, 215
Colley, George Jr., 64–65, 77, 192
Colombia, 218
Colorado River
  description of, 28
  damming of. *See* Hoover Dam
  state partnerships to divide water rights from, 30–31
Colorado River Compact, 31
Committee for Nuclear Responsibility, 268
Committee for the Liberation of Iraq, 229
Commission for Relief in Belgium, 55
Committee on the Present Danger, 130–31, 163
Commodity Credit Corporation (CCC), 197
Commonwealth Edison, 121
Communism
  domino theory on, 75
  Eisenhower's concerns about, 75, 83–84
  JFK's stance on, 78
  Nixon's stance on, 87

Condor II ballistic missiles, 197
conflict-of-interest questions, and Bechtel contracts, 72, 102, 103, 147–49, 173, 192, 199, 207, 237, 307
Congo, Democratic Republic of, 80
Congress
  financing for Bechtel projects and, 110
  Hoover Dam construction and, 31, 32, 33, 34, 41
  Iran-Contra inquiry by, 185, 347n185
  lobbying for Bechtel projects in, 128
  nonproliferation legislation of, 153
  Obama's New START proposal in, 281–82
  Shultz nomination as Reagan's secretary of state in hearings before, 145–47
  Weinberger's defense budget and, 162
  World War II contracts and, 51–52
Congressional Budget Office, 82
Connally, John, 130–31, 132
Connelly, Ross J., 229
Consolidated Nuclear Security LLC, 295
Consolidated Steel Inc., 48
Consumers Power, 120, 335n120
Continental Gas, Inc., 26, 47, 48
Coolidge, Calvin, 89, 118, 214
Cooperative Threat Reduction (CTR) program, 215
cost-plus contracts, 49, 63, 233, 262
Cotler, Irwin, 299
Council on Foreign Relations (CFR), 113
Cranston, Alan, 146–47
Croatia, 215, 216, 304
Crogan, Jim, 201, 234
Crowe, Frank T., 47
  background of, 32
  Hoover Dam construction and, 34–36, 38
  idea for Hoover Dam from, 31–32
  workers and, 39, 40
Crude Vision: How Oil Interests Obscured U.S. Government Focus on Chemical Weapons Use by Saddam Hussein (Vallette, Kretzmann, and Wysham), 169, 229

Cuba
Bay of Pigs invasion and, 78
CIA operations about, 78, 79, 81
Guantanamo Bay facility and, 231
Kennedy's assassination and, 81–82
possible rapprochement with, 81, 82
US foreign policy and, 81–82
Cutler, Lloyd, 145

Dachs, Alan, 204
Dachs, Lauren Bechtel, 93, 204–05
Dædalus (journal), 104
D'Agostino, Tom, 255
dams
in Soviet Union, 43
in United States, 22. *See also* Hoover
Dam
Dart, Justin W., 88
Davis, John, 118
Davis, Lisa, 236, 308
Davis, W. Kenneth, 71, 153–55, 156, 157
Deaver, Michael, 137–38
DeConcini, Dennis, 300, 301
Defense Contract Audit Agency (DCAA),
247–48
defense contracts
audits of, 247
Bechtel and, 47–48, 58, 83, 85, 160, 215,
232, 247, 294, 304
McCone and, 66, 82, 83
in Middle East, 58
Weinberger in Department of Defense
and, 139, 160–62
defense industry
Bechtel in, 309
military-industrial complex and, 83, 88,
275
national security and, 294
SRI research for, 85
US foreign policy and influence of, 83
defense policy
McCone's role in developing, 66
nuclear weapon use and, 163
Obama administration and, 280
Truman administration and, 66

Defense Policy Board, 229
Dell, Christopher, 306–08
Dershowitz, Alan M., 185, 299
desalination plant projects, 122, 304–05
De Voto, Bernard, 47
Didion, Joan, 12, 17, 88
DiGenova, Joseph, 182, 185
Dillon, C. Douglas, 57, 75, 112
Dillon, Read & Company, 57, 112, 134–35,
220, 225
disaster relief projects, 217
hurricane Katrina and, 244, 245–48,
262
Dole, Robert, 131
domino theory, 75, 84, 87, 98, 100
Donovan, William ("Wild Bill"), 56, 57, 64
Doomsday Machine, 164
Douglas, Helen Gahagan, 118
Dowd, Maureen, 238
Dowie, Mark, 8, 65, 94, 105, 121, 291
Draper, William III, 171
Dresden, Illinois, Nuclear Power Plant, 10
drones, 305
Dubai, 211, 304, 305
Dudley, William N., 295
Dugas, Dennis, 235
Dulles, Allen Welsh, 56–57, 58, 59, 63, 64,
66, 67, 77, 78, 89
Dulles, John Foster, 56, 57
Dulles Corridor Metrorail Extension,
Washington, DC, 9
Durenberger, David, 300

Eban Report, 182
Eccles, David, 23
Eccles, Marriner, 23
Economist (magazine), 135, 136, 232, 277,
279
Edwards, James, 155
Egypt
Bechtel projects in, 9, 60, 95, 101, 125,
139, 306
Israel and, 141, 168
Eichmann, Adolf, 178
Einstein, Albert, 68, 70

Eisenhower, Dwight D. ("Ike"), 107, 119
    "Atoms for Peace" speech (1953), 69
    Bechtel's relationship with, 6, 74, 75
    domino theory on Communism of, 75
    McCone's influence on, 67, 68, 71, 74, 75
    military-industrial complex and, 83, 88,
        99, 104
    nuclear weapons policy of, 69, 70, 71, 72,
        73
    presidency of, 57, 89, 130
Eitan, Rafael, 178–79, 182, 346n178
El Paso Natural Gas, 101
Engelhardt, Tom, 240
Engineering News-Record (magazine), 308
Enka, 211, 216, 306–07
Enron, 226, 227
environmental cleanup projects, 158, 206,
        217, 231, 293, 304
    audits of, 247
    hurrican Katrina and, 244, 245–48, 262
    after nuclear power plant accidents, 10,
        149–50, 152, 216
Equitable Life Insurance Company,
        336n122
Eubanks, Alice Elizabeth Bechtel, 8, 23
Eubanks, Brantley M., 8
Export Council, 229
Export-Import Bank of the United States
        (Ex-Im Bank; EXIM)
    Aqaba pipeline proposal and, 170, 171,
        188
    Bechtel's financing using, 216, 229,
        349n190
    Casey as head of, 132
    Croatian roadway project and, 216
    Indian power plant project and, 226
    Iraq projects and, 170, 171, 188, 200
    Russian loans from, 100, 101–02, 110
    nuclear energy facilities and, 102
    Sausi Arabia and, 61
    Steve Sr.'s position with, 95, 101
    Taiwan projects and, 157

F-15 jet fighter bombers, 127–28, 165
Faisal, King of Saudi Arabia, 58, 122, 125

Faisal II, King of Iraq, 1, 5
Farley, Terry, 242
Federal Aid Road Act, 25
Federal Bureau of Investigation (FBI)
    Bechtel's South Korean project and,
        349n190
    environmental crimes and, 269
    McCone and, 66, 75
    Lee's espionage case and, 252, 253
    Pollard's arrest by, 14, 181–82, 346n181
    possible bribery of South Korean officials
        and, 349n190
Federal Emergency Management Agency
        (FEMA), 164, 246, 248
Federal Financing Bank, 296
Federal Trade Commission (FTC), 116, 119,
        122, 336n122
Feinstein, Dianne, 292
Feith, Peter, 306–07
fertilizer plant construction projects, 58,
        95, 101
Financial Times, 176, 198, 232
Fluor Corporation, 122, 336n122
Flynn, Raymond, 207
Flynn, Tom, 198
Fonda, Jane, 149
Forbes (magazine), 8, 135, 213, 214, 219, 220
Ford, Gerald, 89, 111, 113, 116, 125, 126,
        130, 132, 146, 153, 163, 167, 281
Ford, Henry, 25, 86
Ford Motor Company, 25–26
Foreign Affairs (magazine), 98
Foreign Corrupt Practices Act (1977), 190,
        349n190
Foreign Intelligence Advisory Board,
        132
foreign policy. *See* US foreign policy
Foreign Policy (magazine), 210, 307
Foreign Relations Committee, Senate, 139,
        145
Formerly Utilized Sites Remedial Action
        Program (FUSRAP), 152
Forrestal, James, 66, 67
Fortune (magazine), 6, 29, 32, 47, 52, 53,
        86

"four horsemen of the apocalypse," 277–78, 282, 318

"Four Horsemen of the Non-Apocalypse," 153–54, 282, 283–84

Frank, Barney, 207

Franks, Tommy, 235

Freedom of Information Act, 290, 318, 363–64n290

Freeh, Louis, 253

"Free Jonathan Pollard" movement, 14–15, 300

Fremont Group, 219–20

Fremont Properties, 220

Friedman, Alan, 172, 176

Friedman, Milton, 113, 167, 245–46

Friends in High Places (McCartney), 310–11

Gabon, 304

Galbraith, Francis J., 96

Galbraith, John Kenneth, 249

Garbuzov, Vasiliy, 110

Garner, Jay, 235, 240

Gatwick Airport, London, 9

Gejdenson, Sam, 200

General Accounting Office (GAO), 52, 162, 240

General Construction Co., 30

Generals Highway, Sequoia National Park, 25

Georgetown University Center for Strategic and International Studies, 309

Getty, J. Paul, 85

Getty Oil Company, 85

Giuffrida, Louis Onorato, 164

Glaspie, April, 193, 201

Glickman, Daniel R., 261

globalization, 203, 236

Goethals, George Washington, 31

Gofman, John, 268

Goldwater, Barry, 89

Gonzalez, Henry, 198–99

Gorbachev, Mikhail, 258

Gore, Al, 254

Gottlieb, Robert, 33, 42, 89, 136, 145

Government Accountability Project, 293

government owned and contractor operated (GOCO) model, 157, 258

Grand Canyon, 28

Great Depression, 11, 12, 30, 34, 38

Greece, 121, 208

Greeley, Horace, 21

Greider, William, 148, 153, 199, 308

Guardian, 168, 173, 307

Gulf War, 200, 212, 241, 269

Gusterson, Hugh, 251, 252, 265

Gwertzman, Bernard, 111

Gwilliam, J. Gary, 264, 285–90
  background of, 285–87
  earlier successful cases brought by, 287–88

Habib, Philip C., 142, 147, 148, 165, 168

Habiger, Eugene A., 253

Haifa, Israel, project proposal, 124

Haig, Alexander M. Jr., 140–41, 142, 143, 144, 147, 155, 165

Haldeman, Robert, 110

Halliburton, 82, 239, 244

Hamad International Airport, Doha, Qatar, 9

Hamilton, Lee, 300

Hammer, Armand, 94, 101–02, 215

Hanauer, Stephen, 120–21

Hanford Site, Washington (nuclear reactor and radioactive-waste treatment plant), 10, 68, 256, 292–93

Harriman, Ed, 240

Hart, Parker T. ("Pete"), 122–23, 170

Hartung, William D., 281

Harvard University, 40, 118, 164, 268

Hecker, Siegfried, 254–55

Helms, Richard
  Allende coup in Chile and, 97, 98–99
  as Bechtel consultant, 99, 127, 128, 162
  as CIA director, 80, 97–98, 162
  Kennedy's assassination and, 80

Henry J. Kaiser Co., 30

Herbert, Bob, 230

Hercules Powder Company, 50

Heritage Foundation, 163, 229, 309

Hersh, Seymour, 128, 235, 301, 329n80,
    344n174, 346n178

Hezbollah, 187

Hiltzik, Michael, 28, 38

Hiroshima bombing, Japan, 10, 68–69

Hobson, David, 11, 263

Hoffman, Gil, 182

Hoffman, Ian, 254, 255

Hogan and Hartson, 129

Holder, Eric, 298

Holocaust, 177

Hong Kong, 9, 208, 211

Hoover, Herbert, 26, 31, 55, 88, 89, 118

Hoover Dam, 28–42
    background to development of, 30–31
    Bechtel's reputation after, 59, 296
    Boulder City community built for, 39,
        40, 41, 318
    completion of, 37, 44
    Crowe as chief engineer during
        construction of, 34–36, 38, 39, 40
    Dad Bechtel's work on, 26–27, 38, 40, 41,
        42
    deaths during construction of, 40, 42
    diverting Colorado River for, 36–37
    as engineering epic, 29
    government contract in, 12, 32–33,
        38–39
    heat conditions during construction of,
        39–40
    joint venture for construction of, 29
    modern machinery used for, 36
    safety violations and labor unrest at, 38,
        40–42, 62
    as signature project for Bechtel, 6, 29,
        44
    Six Companies' construction of, 29, 36,
        47
    Steve Jr.'s childhood visits to, 86
    Steve Sr.'s work on, 6, 38, 48
    utility company connection from
        construction of, 71

western development powered by, 30, 31,
    33
    workers on, 35, 42, 317
    working conditions on, 39–40

Hoover Institution, 163, 318

Hore-Lacy, Ian, 261

Hoskinson, Samuel, 132

hospital construction projects, 5, 122, 235,
    241–42, 243

Hoyle, Russ, 228

Hull, Cordell, 219

Humphrey, Hubert, 90

Hurricane Katrina, 244, 245–48, 262

Hussein, Qusay, 2, 238n356

Hussein, Saddam
    Aqaba pipeline proposal and, 169,
        170–71, 172, 188–89, 192, 200
    Bechtel's business relationships with,
        15, 87, 124, 168, 171, 230, 233, 234,
        237
    chemical weapons used by, 168, 169–70,
        173, 200, 230
    CIA operations and, 80
    Iran-Iraq war and, 169–70, 172
    Osirak nuclear reactor attack and, 141
    PC2 petrochemicals complex and,
        180–81
    Pollard's intelligence information on,
        180–81
    Reagan administration and, 141
    Rumsfeld's visit to, 168–69
    seizure of Republican Palace
        headquarters of, 1–2
    terrorists supported by, 170

Hussein, Uday, 1, 2, 235

hydroelectric plant construction projects,
    9, 43, 71, 233

hydrogen bombs (H-bombs), 69–70, 149,
    251

Ickes, Harold L., 41–42, 51

Illich, Jim, 236

Imperial Chemical Industries, 85

Imperial Valley, California, farms, 30,
    37

Independent (London), 99, 237
India, 87, 94, 120–21, 123, 226, 274, 305
Indonesia, 95–96, 123, 205, 209, 225
Industrial Workers of the World, 40–41
infrastructure projects, 5–6, 9, 30, 62, 63,
    82, 95, 134, 135, 162, 208, 209, 216,
    233–34, 235, 306–07, 304
Institute for Policy Studies (IPS), 169, 229
Intelligence Committee, Senate, 141, 181,
    292, 301
Interagency Contingency Operations Plan,
    177–78
Inter-American Development Bank, 112
intercontinental ballistic MX missiles
    (ICBMs), 162
InterGen, 218, 220, 225–26
International Herald Tribune, 172
International Monetary Fund, 112, 308
International Bechtel Inc., 59, 76, 306
International Telephone and Telegraph
    (ITT), 97, 318
International Water, 222
Investigative Reporting Program,
    University of California at Berkeley
    Graduate School of Journalism,
    307–08
Iran
    Bechtel's projects in, 63, 64–65, 78, 127,
        168
    Bechtel's ties with the Shah and, 87, 121,
        124
    hostage crisis in, 133, 138–39
    intelligence gathering in, 65
    Khomeini and Islamic revolution in,
        168
    Mossadegh's overthrow in, 65, 76
    oil industry in, 65, 96, 168
    Shah's proposed restoration in, 65
    US clandestine sale by weapons to,
        347–48n185
Iran-Contra affair, 187–92, 240
    background to, 187–88
    Bechtel and, 213
    Colley's murder in, 77, 192
    investigation of, 187, 190

Meese's resignation and, 191–92
    Pollard affair and, 184–85, 347n185
    Rappaport's involvement in, 189–91
    Rumsfield's visit with Saddam about
        pipeline and, 188–89
    Weinberger's role in, 185–86, 188, 191,
        213–14, 302
Iran-Iraq war, 167–68, 169, 172, 176, 187
Iraq
    Bechtel employees as hostages in, after
        US invasion, 201–02
    Bechtel's arrival in, 5
    Bechtel's business relationships with, 15,
        124, 168, 192–94, 197
    Bechtel's headquarters in Republican
        Palace in Green Zone in, 3–4, 242
    Bechtel's projects in, 5–6, 63
    Bush's reconstruction plans for, 5, 202,
        235
    chemical weapons production facilities
        in, 174, 176, 180–81, 198–99, 230,
        237
    CIA operations in, 80, 175
    Coalition Provisional Authority (CPA)
        in, 238, 239–40
    depth of feeling about Israel held by,
        188–89
    ISIS in, 3
    Israel's bombing of reactor in, 141, 142,
        175
    lobbying for projects in, 141, 166, 173,
        189–90, 194
    PC2 petrochemicals plant in, 175–76,
        180, 184, 197, 199–200, 201,
        202–03
    Reagan administration and, 141–42
    Rumsfield's visit with Saddam in, 166,
        167, 168–71, 172–73
    Saddam's use of chemical weapons in,
        168, 169–70, 173, 200, 230
    Shultz's support for Bechtel's projects in,
        166, 167, 168–73
    US financing of projects in, 198–99,
        200–01
    US invasion of, 3, 201

Iraq (cont.)
  weapons of mass destruction of, 3, 172, 199, 228, 229
  Weinberger and weapons transfer to, 188, 198
Iraq Petroleum Company, 62
Iraq War, 3
iron-ore slurry pipelines, 146
irrigation construction projects, 235
ISIS, 3
Israel
  Arab boycott of trade with, 124, 125–26, 129, 146
  Bechtel's pipeline project in Iraq and guarantee from, 188–90, 191, 192
  Bechtel's business approach and, 148
  Bechtel's refusal to build in, 61, 124, 125
  bombing of Iraqi reactor by, 141, 142, 175
  Connally's proposal on borders of, 131
  depth of Iraqi feeling about, 188–89
  distrust of Bechtel by, 124–25, 189
  espionage operations against American targets by, 15
  "Free Jonathan Pollard" crusade and, 14–15
  Iran-Contra affair and, 188
  Kerry's proposal of prisoner swap for Pollard with, 301
  nuclear test ban treaty and, 274
  Pollard's concern about threats to existence of, 174–76, 177–78, 180, 184–85
  Pollard's documents returned by, 182
  Pollard's release requested by, 13, 298, 299
  Pollard's spying for, 15, 178–82, 300
  Qaddafi in Libya and, 306
  Reagan administration and, 140–41, 142, 165, 166
  Six-Day War (1967) of, 168
  US spying on prime ministers of, 14

  US support for, 61, 168
  Weinberger's hostility toward, 139–41, 142, 174–75, 303

J. F. Shea Co. Inc., 30
J. Henry Schroder Banking Corporation, 56–57
J.P. Morgan & Company, 57, 112
J.P. Morgan Bank, 109
Jackson, Henry ("Scoop"), 102, 110
Jacobson, Todd, 258
Jamail, Dahr, 238
Japan
  Bechtel projects in, 121, 211
  Hiroshima and Nagasaki bombings in, 10, 68–69
  US foreign policy and, 83–84, 89
Jerusalem Post, 174, 182, 301
Jewish workers
  Justice Department charges of discrimination against, 126–27
  Saudi Arabian projects and exclusion of, 61, 124–25
Jews
  American spy cases involving, 13, 182, 183
  Pollard affair opinions of, 13, 14, 183
  Steve Sr.'s opinions on, 124, 204
  Weinberger's ancestry and, 117, 118, 174–75
Johnson, Lyndon (LBJ), 80, 81, 82, 95
Johnstone, Clint, 204
Johnstone, Shana Bechtel, 204
Jubail project, Saudi Arabia, 9, 122–23, 127
Juhasz, Antonia, 201

Kaiser, Edgar, Jr., 88
Kaiser, Henry J., 26, 30, 41–42, 54
Kamil, Husayn, 193
Kapleau, Philip, 269
Kazakhstan, 211
Kearns, Henry, 101, 102–03
Kearns International, 103
Kellogg Brown & Root (KBR), 233

Kennecott Copper Corporation, 122
Kennedy, John F. (JFK), 112
    assassination of, 80–81, 82, 131, 318
    Bay of Pigs invasion and, 78
    McCone's disagreements with, 82
    normalization of relations with Cuba
        and, 81
    plots against Cuba and, 78, 80
    as president, 87, 119
    proposed CIA reform by, 78
Kennedy, Joseph P. Sr., 78
Kennedy, Robert
    brother's assassination and, 80–81
    plots against Cuba and, 78
Kerry, John, 301
Keystone Pipeline System, 9
Khomeini, Ayatollah Ruholla, 168
Kim Jong-il, 281
King, Ralph, 226, 309
Kirkpatrick, Jeane, 140
Kissinger, Henry, 238
    Allende coup in Chile and, 97, 98–99
    as Bechtel consultant, 99, 121, 126–27,
        184, 209
    Bechtel's participation in Arab boycott
        of trade with Israel and, 126–27
    biotech company Theranos and, 305
    on George Shultz, 109
    Iran-Iraq war and, 172
    Nixon administration and, 110, 132
    nuclear nonproliferation and, 276,
        283–84
    nuclear technology export and, 146
    Pollard affair and, 300
Klamath River Highway, California, 25
Klein, Aaron, 302
Klein, Naomi, 230, 245, 246
Klotz, Frank G., 294
Knolls Atomic Power Laboratory,
    Niskayuna, New York, 294–95
Koch brothers (Charles and David), 11,
    309
Koch, Ed, 165–66
Koch Industries, 7
Komes, Jerome, 85

Kondrake, Morton, 140
Kopf, Rick, 219–20
Koppel, Ted, 175, 233, 234
Korb, Lawrence, 139
Korea, 89
Kosovo, 306–08
Kostikov, Valeriy, 81
Kurtz, Howard, 150
Kuwait
    Bechtel projects in, 62–63, 202–03, 206,
        212
    Iraqi invasion of, 200, 201, 202
    oil industry in, 62, 85, 202, 242
Kuwait Oil Company, 62
Kwitny, Jonathan, 104
Kyl, Jon, 281–82

Labaton, Stephen, 311
Labor-Management Advisory Committee,
    US Treasury Department, 95
Laird, Melvin, 133
Lando, Barry, 193
LANS LLC, 258, 263, 270, 271, 282
Lardner, George, 190
La Rocque, Gene, 137
Latin America, 64, 96, 146, 225
Lauer, Eliot, 302
Laughlin, Robert B., 296
Lawrence, Ernest, 251
Lawrence Livermore National Laboratory,
    Livermore, California, 154
    background of, 10–11
    founding of, 251
    layoffs at, 263–64
    LLNS, LLC, formed by Bechtel to
        manage, 258, 263–64, 265–66, 283,
        289, 290, 294
    National Ignition Facility at, 265–66
    national laboratory system with, 157
    University of California management of,
        252, 253
Lebanon, 168
    American hostages held in, 185, 187
    Bechtel projects in, 63, 139
    warfare in, 142, 147, 177

Lee, Wen Ho, 252–53
Levi, Edward, 125–26
Libya, 178
  Bechtel's projects in, 63, 94, 96, 124,
    139
  CIA's covert operations in, 78, 96
  oil industry in, 94, 96
  Qaddafi in, 87, 96, 124, 306
Lidgerwood Manufacturing, 36
Liedle, Steven B., 264
Life (magazine), 67
liquefied natural gas (LNG) industry, 9,
  95–96, 101, 158, 205, 304
Livermore. *See* Lawrence Livermore
  National Laboratory
LLNS, LLC, 258, 263–64, 265–66, 283,
  289, 290, 294
lobbying
  Bechtel's use of, 27, 41–42, 76, 104, 113,
    121, 128, 130, 141, 146, 148, 149, 150,
    162, 173, 189–90, 202, 207, 211, 218,
    224, 257, 261, 282, 291, 307
  for Boston's Big Dig project, 207
  Business Roundtable for, 112–13, 130
  Dad Bechtel and, 27, 41–42
  former government officials as, 211, 246,
    261, 307
  Hoover Dam labor problems and,
    41–42
  Kearns International for, 103
  for Iran nuclear reactors, 121
  for Kuwait reconstruction, 202
  for MX missiles, 162
  nuclear industry and, 149, 150, 257, 261,
    282
  Rappaport and, 189–90
  for sale of AWACS planes to Saudi
    Arabia, 131, 146
  for projects in Iraq, 141, 166, 173,
    189–90, 194
  Rumsfeld and, 173
  Saudi Arabia's use of, 128
  Snodgrass's firm for, 76
  against Soviet expansionism, 131,
    163

Lohbeck, Kurt, 181
Los Alamos National Laboratory, Los
  Alamos, New Mexico
  Bechtel-led partnership to manage,
    10–11
  Bechtel's construction of, 68, 262
  Bechtel's contracts at, 157
  end of Cold War and, 263
  LANS LLC, formed by Bechtel to
    manage, 258, 263, 270, 271, 282
  Lee's espionage case and, 252–55
  Manhattan Project and, 68–69
  national laboratory system with, 157
  as "a separate state," 156
  University of California management of,
    251
Los Alamos National Security, 258
Los Alamos Study Group (LASG), 254,
  269–70
Los Angeles Herald Examiner, 139
Los Angeles Times, 91, 190, 202, 234, 236,
  242, 260, 297
LSG Associates, 76
Luce, Henry, 67
Ludwig, Daniel, 86
Lugar, Richard, 215

M-1 tanks, 165
MacArthur, Douglas, 118
MacDonald & Kahn Co., Inc., 30
Mack Companies, 36
Malaysia, 209
Manhattan Project, 68, 104, 149, 150, 157,
  161, 276
Manila, Philippines, 223, 225
Marchetti, Victor, 97
Marks, Herbert S., 156
Marks, John D., 97
Marshall Islands, 262, 295
Marshall Plan, 5
Mars Observer probe, 206
Masco, Joseph, 270
Mayer, Jane, 219
Mayman, Raynal, 134
McCain, John, 300

McCarran International Airport, Las
    Vegas, 9
McCartney, Laton, 24, 38, 46, 61, 75, 88,
    94, 125, 158, 310–11
McCone, John Alex, 48–52, 78–82
    Allende coup in Chile and, 97
    anti-Communist and anti-Soviet views
        of, 66–67, 75, 130–31, 163
    background of, 48
    Bechtel culture and, 74
    Bechtel-McCone Corporation formed
        by, 49–50
    Bohemian Grove membership of, 88,
        184
    as CIA director, 74, 78–82
    conflicts-of-interest accusations against,
        72
    cost-plus model of business contract
        invented by, 49, 262
    Cuba and, 81–82
    departure from Bechtel by, 54, 72
    government connections of, 54, 66, 68,
        72, 74–75, 78, 79, 82, 83, 97, 162
    Hoover Dam construction and, 48
    intelligence community and, 75–76,
        78
    Kennedy's assassination and, 80–81,
        82
    legacy of, 82
    move to Bechtel by, 48–50
    nuclear industry and, 68, 70–71, 72–73,
        154
    oil industry connections of, 48–49
    personality of, 50, 67, 79
    shipbuilding contracts and, 50–51, 52
    Steve Sr.'s bond with, 48, 49–50, 68,
        82
    stock investments of, 53–54, 59, 72
    turnkey contract used by, 49
McCoy, Charlie, 226
McFarlane, Robert C. ("Bud"), 300, 303
McGrory, Mary, 214
McKay, James C., 190, 191
Meese, Edwin III, 163, 178, 189–90,
    191–92, 201

Mello, Greg, 254, 255, 257–58, 266,
    267–71, 272–73, 282, 283
    background of, 267
Metzenbaum, Howard, 147
Mexico, 31, 81, 87, 157, 207, 218, 225
Michael, Michelle, 307
Middle East
    Bechtel's role in, 53, 58, 59–65, 131,
        146
    nationalization of resources in, 96–97
    Steve Jr.'s projects in, 87
    Steve Sr.'s intelligence reporting on, 76
    US-Iraq relations and, 3
Middle East Free Trade Area (MEFTA),
    244
Mies, Richard, 292
military base construction projects, 10, 51,
    53, 58, 82, 122, 236
military-industrial complex, 83, 88, 275
Miller, George, 265–66
Miller, T. Christopher, 235
mining and minerals, Bechtel projects in,
    9, 80, 87, 104, 111, 152, 157, 304
Mississippi, 246–47
Mobutu, Joseph, 80
Mohammad Bin Fahd, Prince, 127
Mojave Desert, California, Ivanpah Solar
    Power Facility in, 7, 206, 296–97
Moore, John L., 157
Moral Majority, 136
Morgan Guaranty Trust Company, 112
Mormans, 23, 29, 285–86
Morris, Edmund, 114–15
Morris, Roger, 37, 65, 167
Morrison and Knudsen, 30
Mossad, 178
Mossadegh, Mohammad, 65
Motorola facility, Tianjin, China, 208
Moyers, Bill, 81
Mumm, Cliff, 239, 242, 243
MX missile system, 162

Nagasaki bombing, Japan, 10, 68–69
Nation (magazine), 309
National Academy of Sciences, 70, 259

National Aeronautics and Space
    Administration (NASA), 206
National Business Advisory Council, 74
National Committee for a Free Asia, 75
National Environmental Policy Act, 270
National Ignition Facility (NIF), 265–66
National Industrial Conference Board,
    87
nationalization policies, 65, 95, 96–97,
    209
National Laboratory System, 256 *see also*
    Lawrence Livermore National
    Laboratory; Los Alamos National
    Laboratory
    function of, 157
    government owned and contractor
        operated (GOCO) model of, 157, 258
    privatization of management of, 10, 11,
        251, 255, 256–60, 261, 263, 265–66,
        270, 272, 290, 292
    University of California management of,
        10–11
National Nuclear Security Administration
    (NNSA), 253, 256, 257, 260, 263, 265,
    266, 271, 282, 292, 294, 295
National Reactor Testing Station, Arco,
    Idaho, 10
National Research Council, 259
National Resources Defense Council,
    265
National Security Act (1947), 64, 67
National Security Agency, 14, 79, 276
National Security Archive, 200, 302
National Security Council (NSC), 76, 132,
    171, 190, 198
Natsios, Andrew, 233, 234, 238
natural gas industry, Bechtel's projects in,
    7, 86, 87, 205
natural gas pipeline projects, 101–02,
    110–11, 240
Naval Intelligence Anti-Terrorism Unit,
    184
Naval Ocean Surveillance Information
    Center (NOSIC), 177, 181
Netanyahu, Benjamin, 13, 299, 300

Nevada Test Site, Las Vegas, 256
new cities projects, 9, 122–23, 127
New Deal, 30, 118, 214
Newmont Mining Company, 122
New Right, 136
New START (Strategic Arms Reduction
    Treaty), 274–75, 280, 281–82, 283
Newsweek (magazine), 6, 11, 88, 143
New Yorker (magazine), 219–20, 235,
    272
New York Times, 5, 20, 36, 43, 46, 75,
    110, 111, 128, 140, 166, 173, 189,
    191, 192, 195, 201, 225, 230, 233,
    238, 239, 246, 251, 252, 265, 276,
    279, 283, 300, 311
Nicaragua, 185, 187–88
Nidal, Abu, 170
Nies, Judith, 30, 122, 151, 207
Nixon, Richard
    arms control efforts of, 163
    Bechtel contracts and, 90, 95, 100, 104,
        105
    China's nationalization of ITT and, 97
    CIA covert operations and, 95, 96, 97
    energy policy of, 103
    McCone's relationship with, 78
    Pacific Rim strategy of, 88, 89, 100
    presidential run of, 89–90, 119
    Shultz's Cabinet posts with, 105, 109–11,
        123, 143
    Soviet policy of, 101–02, 110–11
    Steve Jr. and, 87–88, 89, 90
    Steve Sr. and, 75, 95, 101
    Weinberger and, 119
Nixon Doctrine, 100
Nobel Peace Prize (2000), for Obama, 280,
    281, 282
Norquist, Grover, 11
Norris, Stan, 163
North, Oliver, 139, 347n185
North Atlantic Treaty Organization
    (NATO), 68, 167, 229, 306
North Korea, 178, 274, 281
Northwestern Pacific Railroad, 23, 24
Nuclear Energy Institute (NEI), 261

Nuclear Nonproliferation Treaty, 158
nuclear power plants
    AEC's policy on, 70–71
    Bechtel's construction of, 10, 68, 70–71, 79, 104
    in China, 158
    cleanup after accidents in, 10, 149–50, 152, 216
    construction of first nuclear plant, 10
    Davis as champion of, 153–55
    decline in contracts for, 151, 153
    DOE's program for, 156–57
    Nixon's push for, 103
    potential for catastrophe in, 120, 121
    public opposition to, 71
    Reagan's s policy on, 153–54, 157–58
    in South Korea, 10
    Steve Jr.'s focus on safety of, 149–50
    switch to coal from, 121–22
nuclear test ban treaty proposals, 70, 158, 274
nuclear weapons development and testing
    Bechtel's involvement in, 70–71
    Cold War arms race on, 69–70
    DOE's program for, 156–57
    Eisenhower's "Atoms for Peace" speech (1953) on, 69
    nuclear test ban proposals on, 70, 158, 274
    opposition to, 72
nuclear weapons laboratories. See National Laboratory System
nuclear weapons production facilities
    Bechtel as global leader in, 10
    Oak Ridge, Tennessee, 67
    Rocky Flats Plant, Colorado, 269
"Nuclear Winter, The" (Sagan), 164–65
Nunn, Sam, 215, 276, 284, 318

Oak Ridge, Tennessee, nuclear weapons plant, 67
Obama, Barack
    New START treaty proposal of, 281–82, 283
    Nobel Peace Prize (2000) for, 280, 281, 282
    nuclear facilities modernization and, 272, 279, 281–82
    nuclear-free world doctrine of, 274–76, 279, 283
    nuclear material safeguards promoted by, 280–81
    Pollard affair and, 13, 298–300, 301, 303
    Prague speech (2009) on disarmament by, 274–75, 279, 280
    Shultz on disarmament policies of, 278–79
Occidental Petroleum, 94, 101, 155
Office of Management and Budget (OMB), 109, 114, 116, 119, 247, 264
Office of Strategic Services (OSS), 8, 55, 56, 59, 64, 132
Office of the Special Inspector General for Iraq Reconstruction (SIGIR), 240–41, 243
oil industry
    Bechtel's Middle Eastern projects and, 58, 59, 60, 62
    Dad Bechtel's move into, 26
    in Iran, 65, 96, 168
    in Libya, 94, 96
    Mideast crisis (1970s) in, 103
    Reagan's policy in Iraq and, 172
    in Saudi Arabia, 60–61, 62, 85, 96
    Steve Sr. and, 48–49, 58, 59, 60, 62, 63, 124
    US financial inducements to, 59
oil refinery construction projects, 26, 48–49, 50, 53, 58, 62, 96, 122, 134, 191, 201, 202, 225, 305
O'Konski, Alvin, 72
O'Leary, Hazel, 260
Olmert, Ehud, 299
Olympics (1992), 208
Oppenheimer, J. Robert, 68, 69, 70, 251
Operation Ajax, 65
Operation Desert Storm, 202
Operation Eagle Claw, 133

Operation Iraqi Freedom, 3
Organization of Petroleum Exporting
     Countries (OPEC), 58, 96, 100
Orrick, Herrington, 290 law firm
Osirak nuclear reactor, Iraq, 141, 142,
     178
Oswald, Lee Harvey, 81
Overseas Private Investment Corporation
     (OPIC), 171, 215–16, 226, 229

Pacific Bridge Co., 30
Pacific Builder (magazine), 12
Pacific Gas and Electric Company (PG&E),
     26, 71, 155, 218, 297
Pacific Legal Foundation, 309
Pacific Rim strategy
   Nixon and, 88, 89, 100
   SRI's development of, 84, 100
   Steve Sr. and, 84
Page, Larry, 295
Pahlavi, Shah Mohammad Reza, 65, 87,
     121, 124, 168
Pakistan, 121, 179, 274
palace construction projects, 58, 61
Palestine, 61, 63, 124, 140, 141, 170,
     298
Palestine Liberation Organization (PLO),
     184–85
Pantex Plant, Amarillo, Texas, 256
Papua New Guinea, 96
Parade (magazine), 164
Paretsky, Nick, 113, 130
Parker, James, 254
Parsons, Ralph M., 49
Parsons Brinckerhoff, 206
Paxon, Bill, 261
PC2 petrochemicals complex, Iraq,
     175–76, 180, 184, 197, 199–200, 201,
     202–03
Peabody Coal Company, 122, 123
Peabody Holding Company, 122
Pearson, Drew, 72, 79, 80, 148, 318
Pelosi, Nancy, 247
Peres, Shimon, 182, 189–90, 192,
     298–99

Peretz, Martin, 301
Perkins, John, 268
Perkovich, Charles, 270
Perle, Richard, 281
Perry, William, 276, 284, 318
Pershing II nuclear missiles, 161
Pertamina, Indonesia, LNG plant,
     205
petrochemical plant projects, 87, 94, 193,
     304. *See also* PC2 petrochemicals
     complex, Iraq
Philippines
   Bechtel projects in, 51, 53, 101, 209, 218,
     223, 225
   Bechtel workers transported from,
     123
Pinochet, Augusto, 97
pipeline construction projects, 9, 26, 47, 48,
     49, 50, 51–52, 58, 60, 61, 62, 65, 85, 87,
     93, 94, 95, 96, 101, 103, 110–11, 120,
     121–22, 124–25, 142, 146, 262,
     304–05. *See also* Aqaba pipeline
     proposal
Pollard, Jonathan ("Jay"), 13–15, 174–86
   background of, 176–77
   Bechtel and, 15
   as a committed Zionist, 345n174
   concern about threats to existence of
     Israel and, 174–76, 177–78, 180,
     184–85
   Eitan as handler of, 174, 178–79, 180,
     181–82
   FBI's arrest of, 14, 181–82
   "Free Jonathan Pollard" crusade and,
     14–15, 300
   guilty plea and sentencing of, 182–84,
     185
   Iran-Contra affair and, 184–85
   Israeli petitions to US presidents for
     release of, 13
   promise to commute sentence of, 14
   questions about lifetime sentence given
     to, 13–14
   Shultz and, 15
   spying for Israel by, 15, 178–82, 300

Weinberger's hostility to Israel and, 174–75
Weinberger's involvement in sentencing of, 15, 183–84, 302–03
Pollard, Morris and Mildred Klein, 176, 182
port facilities, 53, 123, 304
Portland, Oregon, light-rail system, 220–21
Powell, Colin, 115
Pressler, Larry, 145, 146, 147, 148
privatization
  Asian companies and, 225
  Bechtel projects and, 213, 296
  Bush administration and, 256–57, 261, 290
  global shift to, 203, 209
  Iraq reconstruction and, 235–36, 238–39, 244
  management of national laboratories and, 10–11, 251, 255, 256–60, 261, 263, 265–66, 270, 272, 290, 292
  revenues from, 225
  Riley's approach to partnerships in, 216, 218–19
  water services and, 222, 223, 225, 239
Project MKULTRA, 98
Project on Government Oversight (POGO), 233–34, 258, 290
Pueblo Chemical Agent-Destruction Pilot Plant, Pueblo, Colorado, 305

Qaddafi, Mu'ammar, 87, 96, 124, 306
Qatar, 9, 205, 304

Rabin, Yitzhak, 13
railroad projects, 9, 208
  Dad Bechtel's work on, 19, 20–23, 24, 26, 47, 217
  in Saudi Arabia, 53, 58, 60–61, 125
Ramsay, Nonie Bechtel, 93, 205
Ramsay, Sheldon, 205
Rand, Christopher T., 94
rapid transit systems and subway, 9, 87, 103, 208, 220–21, 304

Rappaport, Baruch ("Bruce"), 189–91, 192, 197
Reagan, Ronald, 15
  Aqaba pipeline proposal and, 171, 192
  Bechtel's contracts under, 152, 153–54, 157–58
  Bechtel's relationship with, 145, 149, 192, 197
  Connally's campaign against, 130–32
  defense policy of, 160–63
  DOE operations and, 150–51
  as "an evil empire," 67, 275
  Iran-Contra affair and, 186, 187–88
  Iraq policy of, 15, 172–73, 184, 198, 200
  Iran hostage crisis and, 138–39
  Middle East policy of, 184
  Nixon's presidential run and, 89
  nonproliferation policy of, 153
  nuclear plant licensing under, 150, 155, 157–58
  Obama's opinion about Soviet policy of, 275
  Pollard affair and, 15, 184, 299, 303
  presidency of, 136
  Shultz and, 131, 135, 276–77
  Shultz-Weinberger conflict and, 143–44
  Soviet policy of, 162, 164–65, 275
  Weinberger's enthusiasm for, at Bechtel, 130–31
  Weinberger's policy on Israel and, 139–41, 142
  Weinberger's arms sales to Saudi Arabia and, 165–66
"Real Story, The" (Bechtel), 311
Reinsch, Jim, 294
Reisner, Marc, 28, 30, 39
Republican Party, 5, 11, 240
Reykjavik Summit (1986), 278
Ribicoff, Abraham, 72
Rice, Condoleezza, 241, 244
Rice, Sister Megan, 272
Richardson, Bill, 252, 253, 254

Richmond Belt Railroad, 21
Riyadh projects, Saudi Arabia, 127, 304
Riyadh Metro, Saudi Arabia, 304
road construction projects, 5, 6, 9, 22, 25, 26, 36, 47, 61, 77, 82, 235
Rocca, Al M., 35
Rockefeller, Avery, 57
Rockefeller, John D., 86
Rockefeller, Nelson, 89
Rocky Flats nuclear weapons production facility, Colorado, 269
Rodman, John, 268
Rodriguez, Acacia, 248
Romania, 304
Romney, Mitt, 207–08
Roosevelt, Franklin D. ("FDR"), 41, 42, 68, 118
Rosenberg, Ethel, 182
Rosenberg, Julius, 182, 252
Ross, Thomas B., 78
Royal Air Force (UK), 85
Rumsfeld, Donald H., 167–73
   background of, 167
   Defense Policy Board with, 229
   Iraqi reconstruction and, 235
   as Shultz's envoy to Saddam in Iraq, 166, 167, 168–71, 172–73, 188, 201
Russia, 9, 42–43
   Bechtel's projects in, 110
   US foreign policy and, 83
Russo, Frank, 264, 293

Sagan, Carl, 164–65
St. Clair, Jeffrey, 188, 343n170
Sandia National Laboratories, New Mexico, 157
San Francisco Chronicle, 235, 243
San Francisco Examiner, 41, 113
San Francisco–Oakland Bay Bridge, 9
Santa Fe New Mexican, 271
Santa Fe Railroad, 21, 25
ibn Saud, Abdul Aziz, King of Saudi Arabia, 58, 61, 62, 85

Saudi Arabia
   Bechtel projects in, 58, 59–62, 63, 75, 76, 124, 127, 139
   Bechtel workers in, 61–62
   description of, 60
   Jewish workers excluded from Bechtel projects in, 61, 124–25
   Justice Department charges of discrimination against Jewish employees and, 126–27
   oil industry in, 60–61, 62, 85, 96
   Riyadh projects in, 127, 304
   sale of F-15 warplanes to, 127–28
   US foreign policy on, 63
   Weinberger's arms sales to, 165–66
   Weinberger's support for, 139–40
Saudi Arabian Bechtel Company, 127
Savannah (atomic-powered merchant ship), 72
Savannah River National Laboratory, South Carolina, 256
Scheer, Robert, 163
Schlesinger, Arthur M., 80, 81
Schlesinger, James, 172, 189, 281
Schlosser, Eric, 271, 272
Schmidt, Eric, 295
school construction projects, 5, 235
Schroder Banking Corporation, 56–57
Schumer, Charles Jr., 300
Scowcroft, Brent, 132, 283–84
Sears, Roebuck, 112
Seattle Weekly, 293
Securities and Exchange Commission (SEC), 8, 132, 211, 237
Sella, Aviem ("Avi"), 178
Semmelman, Jacques, 302
September 11, 2001, terrorist attacks, 3, 228, 229, 256, 231, 272
Sequoia National Park, California, 25
Sequoia Ventures, 135, 220
Serious Texans Against Nuclear Dumping (STAND), 270
Service, Robert W., 51

sewage system projects, 4, 5, 29, 61, 225, 241, 247

SF Weekly, 236, 308, 309

Shamir, Yitzhak, 179

Sheehan, John J. ("Jack"), 229

Shepard, Paul, 268

Sheridan, Walter, 81

Sherman Antitrust Act, 126, 129

Sherwin, Martin J., 70

shipbuilding, 47–48, 50–51, 78

Shultz, George P.
  background of, 111
  Bechtel position of, 105, 111–14, 115, 116, 117, 119, 120, 121–22, 126–27, 129, 134–35, 138, 145–46, 147, 148, 199
  biotech company Theranos and, 305
  Casey's friendship with, 132
  changes at Bechtel under, 134–35
  Iraq projects and, 199
  Iran-Contra affair and, 352n214
  Levi's clashes with, 125–26
  lobbying by, 112, 113, 130, 166, 167
  Nixon Cabinet posts held by, 105, 109–11, 123, 136
  nuclear nonproliferation and, 153–54
  Pollard's affair and, 15, 182
  proposed sanctions against Iraq and, 193–94
  Reagan's election and, 133, 135–36, 137–38
  as Reagan's secretary of state, 105, 109, 112, 133, 135, 136, 137–38, 142–43, 144, 145, 154, 155, 157, 166, 167
  Rumsfield's visit with Saddam in Iraq and, 166, 167, 168–71, 172–73
  Senate hearings on secretary of state nomination of, 145–47
  Soviet Union and, 110, 163
  Weinberger's conflicts with, 114–15, 116, 130, 133, 136, 137–38, 143–44

Shultz, Helena ("Obie") O'Brien, 111

Shultz, Margaret, 207

Simon, William, 126, 127

Simon & Schuster, 310–11

Simpson, Alan, 300

Simpson, John Lowery ("Uncle John"), 318
  background of, 55–56
  as chief financial officer of Bechtel, 57
  government ties of, 55, 57
  intelligence community and, 56–57
  Steve Jr.'s advice from, 86
  Steve Sr.'s partnership with, 55, 57

Singapore, 209

Six Companies
  completion of Hoover Dam and, 44
  eight member companies of, 29–30
  formation of, 29
  Hoover Dam construction by, 29, 36, 47
  Hoover Dam contract and, 12, 32, 34, 38–39
  lobbying against Ickes's investigation of, 41–42
  profit made by, 38–39
  Steve Sr. as chief administrator of, 47
  transition to defense contracts by, 47
  workers hired by, 35
  working conditions and, 40–41

Six-Day War (1967), 168

60 Minutes (TV program), 193, 235

Slusser, Nancy, 117

Slusser, Willis, 116, 117

Smith, Gerard C., 163

Smith, Hedrick, 114

Smith, Philip M., 309

Snodgrass, Cornelius Stribling, 76

Snowden, Edward, 14, 15, 276

Society of Professional Scientists and Engineers, 288

solar energy plants, 295
  Bechtel's investment in California for, 297
  Ivanpah Valley, Mojave Desert, California, 7, 206, 296–97
  US energy policy on, 155, 296, 297

Sonatrach, 101, 103

Sontag, Fred, 286

Solnit, Rebecca, 59

South Africa, 87, 95, 158

South America, 50, 87, 222

Southern California Edison, 297

Southern Pacific Railroad, 20, 21

South Korea, 10, 122, 123, 211, 225,
    349n190

Soviet Union
    Bechtel contracts with, 101–02
    CIA and, 79, 82
    Cold War arms race with, 69
    Dad Bechtel's visit to, 42–44
    fall of, 203, 209
    Iran and, 64–65
    Kennedy and, 82
    Libya and, 96
    McCone's views on, 66–67, 75, 79,
        130–31, 163
    Mexico and, 87
    Middle East expansion of, 64
    Nixon's policy on, 101–02, 110–11
    nuclear weapons testing by, 69
    Reagan's policy on, 164–65
    Reykjavik Summit (1986) with, 278
    Shultz's approach to, 110, 163
    US aid to Afghan rebels troops from,
        349n189
    US defense policy and, 66–67, 75
    US foreign policy on, 63, 64, 84, 85,
        131
    Weinberger's policies and, 160, 163,
        164

Spain, 87, 95

Sputnik satellite, 85

Stalin, Joseph, 42

Standard Oil Company, 26, 76

Standard Oil Company of California
    (SOCAL), 48, 50, 54, 59, 124, 155

Standard Oil Company of Venezuela,
    50

Stanford Research Institute (SRI), 84–85,
    100, 101, 104

Stanford University, 54, 84, 111

Starr, Kevin, 29, 291

Steele, James B., 244

Stevenson, Adlai, 70

Stevens, Joseph E., 23, 41

Stober, Dan, 254, 255

Stockton, Peter, 258–59

Stone, I. F., 50

Strategic Air Command (SAC), 66

Strategic Arms Reduction Treaty (New
    START), 274–75, 280, 281–82,
    283

Streitfeld, David, 260

subway and rapid transit systems, 9, 43, 87,
    103, 208, 220–21, 304

Suez Canal, 60, 123

Suharto, 95

Sukarno, 95–96

Suleiman, Abdul, 76

Summit Bechtel Family National Scout
    Reserve, Mount Hope, West Virginia,
    309

Sunday Herald (Glasgow, UK), 240

Survival in the Air Age (President's Air
    Policy Commission), 66

Syria, 62, 63, 64, 139, 142, 168, 306

Taiwan, 123, 157, 220, 276

Tamosaitis, Walter, 293

Tapline (Trans-Arabian Pipeline),
    60–61

Tarapur, India, atomic power station, 94,
    120–21

Teicher, Howard, 198

telecommunication projects, 4, 96, 217,
    233, 304

Teller, Edward, 70, 149, 251

Tenet, George, 300

terrorist attacks, September 11, 2001, 3,
    228, 229, 256, 231, 272

Thailand, 209, 225, 304

Thelen, Marrin, Johnson & Bridges,
    205

theme parks, 305

Theranos, 305

Tholan, Stuart, 215–16

Thornburgh, Richard L., 102
Three Days of the Condor (film), 182
Three Mile Island Nuclear Generating
    Station, Pennsylvania, 10, 149–50,
    152
Thurmond, Strom, 79
Time (magazine), 46, 53, 85, 123, 277, 278,
    284
Trans-Alaska Pipeline System (TAPS), 9
Trans-Arabian Pipeline ("Tapline"),
    60–61
transit and subway systems, 9, 87, 103, 208,
    220–21, 304
Trans-Turkish Motorway, 211
Treaty on the Non-Proliferation of Nuclear
    Weapons (Nuclear Nonproliferation
    Treaty), 158
Trial Lawyers for Public Justice (TLPJ),
    288
Trident submarines, 161
Trilateral Commission, 113, 224
Truman, Harry S., 51, 54, 64, 66, 67, 68, 69,
    71
Tuchman, Barbara, 78, 79
Turkey, 123, 211, 306
turnkey contracts, 49

Ukraine, 10, 216
Union Carbide Corporation, 104
Union of Soviet Socialist Republics (USSR).
    See Soviet Union
United Nations, 5, 69, 140, 234
US Agency for International Development
    (USAID), 232–33, 238–39, 241
US Air Force, 66, 85, 160, 162, 165,
    253
US Arms Control and Disarmament
    Agency, 163
US Army, 10, 51, 56, 160, 165, 237
US Army Corps of Engineers, 152,
    295
US Bureau of Public Roads, 25
US Bureau of Reclamation, 12, 32
United States Committee for Energy
    Awareness, 150

US Department of Commerce, 77, 175, 176,
    197, 198
US Department of Defense (DOD)
    Bechtel's contacts at, 77, 161
    Bechtel officers' moving to, 7
    Bechtel projects for, 9
    Carter's energy policy and, 150
    Council on Foreign Relations and,
        113
    criticism of management by, 162
    SRI's close alliance with, 84
    Weinberger as Reagan's secretary of
        defense in, 137, 139, 144, 160–63
US Department of Energy (DOE)
    Bechtel projects under, 9, 10, 150,
        151–52, 153, 155, 157–58, 255, 296,
        318
    Cold War and, 156
    Davis's appointment to, 154–55
    Livermore workforce restructuring and
    national laboratories and, 157, 251, 253,
        256, 257, 364n290
    nuclear weapons program of, 156–57
    Reagan's approach to, 150–51
US Department of Health, Education, and
    Welfare (HEW), 105, 116, 119
US Department of Homeland Security,
    266
US Department of Justice, 125–27, 129,
    191
US Department of State, 126
    Bechtel officers' moving to, 7
    Bechtel's contacts at, 77, 123
    Bechtel's participation in Arab boycott
        of trade with Israel and, 126–27
    Bush's reconstruction plans for Iraq
        and, 5
    Cooperative Threat Reduction (CTR)
        program of, 215
    Council on Foreign Relations and,
        113
    nuclear weapons dispersion and, 72
    Shultz as Reagan's secretary of state at,
        133, 135, 136, 137–38, 142–43, 144,
        145, 154, 155, 157, 166, 167

US Department of State (*cont.*)
    Shultz's Iraq policy and, 168–71, 173
US Department of the Treasury, 119
    Labor-Management Advisory Committee of, 95
    Shultz as Reagan's secretary of state at, 105, 109, 112, 133, 135, 136, 137–38, 142–43, 144, 145, 154, 155, 157, 166, 167
    Steve Jr.'s position with, 95
US Energy Policy Act (1992), 218
US Federal Aviation Administration (FAA), 305
US Food and Drug Administration (FDA), 305
US foreign policy
    anti-Communist approach of, 64
    Bechtel's foreign policy at odds with, 7, 146–47
    Bechtel's influence on, 148
    Bechtel's possible involvement in Syrian coup and, 64
    Carter's administration and, 160
    CIA creation and, 64
    defense industry and, 83
    domino theory and, 75, 87, 98, 100
    Indonesian coup and, 95–96
    internationalist viewpoint and, 67
    investment in Middle East as part of, 63
    Israel and, 131, 165
    Justice Department charges of discrimination against Jewish employees and impact on, 126–27
    Nixon and, 100–02
    nuclear weapons and, 69
    oil industry and, 64–65
    Pacific Rim strategy in, 84, 89, 100
    Syrian coup and, 64
    Weinberger's defense budget and, 162–63
US General Accounting Office (GAO), 52, 162, 240
US Generating Company (USGen), 218

US Interior Department, 31, 264
US Maritime Commission, 51
US Missile Defense Agency, 295
US National Aeronautics and Space Administration (NASA), 206
US National Security Agency, 14, 79, 276
US Navy, 10, 51, 160, 174, 206, 295
US Nuclear Regulatory Commission (NRC), 154, 157–58
US Parole Commission, 303
US Reclamation Service, 32
US Supreme Court, 129
U.S. Steel, 87
US War Department, 51
University of California, and management Los Alamos, 251–52, 255, 265
University of California at Berkeley Graduate School of Journalism, Investigative Reporting Program, 307–08
University of California Radiation Laboratory, 251
University of Chicago, 125–26
Unruh, Vincent Paul, 220, 221, 226, 227
Uranium Enrichment Associates (UEA), 104
uranium enrichment facilities, 67–68, 104, 109, 113, 121, 152, 154, 156–57, 162, 258, 271, 272, 295
uranium mining projects, 23, 30, 87, 152, 156, 157
USA Today, 91, 236, 242
USSR. *See* Soviet Union
Utah Construction Company, 23, 30
Utah Corporation, 23

Vallette, Jim, 169
van der Zee, John, 85
Venezuela, 50, 96
venture capital, 95, 135
Vietnam, 84, 209, 236
Vietnam War
    Bechtel and, 84, 236
    Johnson's policy on, 82

Kennedy's policy on, 82
Nixon's policy on, 95, 100
protests against, 84, 126, 267
Village Voice, 170
Viorst, Milton, 300

W. A. Bechtel Co., 22, 30, 45, 50
Walker, Charls, 130, 133
Walker, John, 347n184
Wall Street Journal, 14, 70, 181, 234, 277,
    296, 310
Walsh, Lawrence E., 187, 190, 191,
    214
Warren Commission, 82
Washington, DC, Metro subway system,
    103
Washington Group International (WGI),
    258
Washingtonian (magazine), 14
Washington Post, 103, 126, 128, 142, 147,
    150, 173, 188, 190, 230, 246
Washington Star, 120
Washington Times, 306
Waste Isolation Pilot Plant (WIPP),
    Carlsbad, New Mexico, 152,
    294
water supply and treatment projects, 4, 5, 7,
    30–31, 33, 209, 217, 222–23, 225, 235,
    239, 241, 247, 304
Watson, Tom, 88
Wattis, E. O., 22–23, 30, 44
Wattis, W. H., 22–23, 30, 41, 44
Waxman, Henry A., 247
We Almost Lost Detroit (Fuller), 71
weapons of mass destruction
    destruction of, at Pueblo, Colorado,
        pilot plant, 305
    Iraq's program for, 3, 172, 199, 228,
        229
Weaver, Craig, 152
Weeks, Sinclair, 75
Weinberger, Caspar ("Cap")
    Arab boycott of trade with Israel and,
        127, 128–29
    background of, 117–18

Bechtel position of, 105, 115, 116–17,
    119–20, 123, 126, 127, 128–29,
    133–34, 139, 160, 176
defense policy of, 160–63
Haig's feud with, 141, 142, 143, 144
hostility toward Israel by, 139–41, 142,
    174–75, 303
Iran-Contra affair and, 185–86, 188, 191,
    213–14, 302
Jewish ancestry of, 117, 118, 140,
    174–75
Nixon administration and, 119
political career of, 119
Pollard's sentencing of, 15, 183–84,
    302–03
as possible secretary of state under
    Reagan, 133, 136, 137
Reagan's election and, 133, 136
as Reagan's secretary of defense, 137,
    139, 144, 160–63
Saudi arms sales and, 165–66
Schultz's conflicts with, 114–15, 116,
    130, 133, 136, 137–38, 143–44
weapons transfer to Iraq and, 188,
    198
Weinberger, Herman and Cerise Carpenter
    Hampson, 117–18
Weinberger, Jane, 116, 119
Welch, C. David, 305–06
Weld, William, 207
Western Pacific Railroad, 22, 29
Western States Legal Foundation, 263
Wheeless, Charlene, 307
Wiesel, Elie, 300
Wiley, Peter, 33, 42, 89, 136, 145
Wiley, Richard, 315
Williams-Mello, Trish, 270
Wise, David, 78
Woolsey, R. James, 300, 301
World Bank, 112, 222, 226, 308
World Energy Conference, Detroit (1974),
    113
"World Free of Nuclear Weapons, A" (*Wall
    Street Journal* editorial), 277
World Nuclear Association, 261

World Trade Center, New York City, September 11, 2001, terrorist attacks on, 3, 228, 229, 256, 231, 272

World War I, 46, 47, 55, 61, 113, 117

World War II, 5, 47–48, 50–52, 53, 56, 68, 92, 111, 132, 163, 164, 174

Y-12 National Security Complex, Oak Ridge, Tennessee, 256, 271, 272, 295

Yakutsk natural gas pipeline, Soviet Union, 110–11

Yanbu project, Saudi Arabia, 127

Yates, Perry, 93

Yemen, 63

Yosemite National Park, California, 25

Zaccaria, Adrian, 228

Zucatur, count, 43–44

Zwicker, Heather, 24